SPATIAL ECONOMETRICS: QUALITATIVE AND LIMITED DEPENDENT VARIABLES

ADVANCES IN ECONOMETRICS

Series Editors: Thomas B. Fomby,
R. Carter Hill, Ivan Jeliazkov,
Juan Carlos Escanciano,
Eric Hillebrand, Daniel L. Millimet,
Rodney Strachan

Recent Volumes:

Volume 28: DSGE Models in Macroeconomics: Estimation, Evaluation and New Developments – Edited by Nathan Balke, Fabio Canova, Fabio Milani and Mark Wynne

Volume 29: Essays in Honor of Jerry Hausman – Edited by Badi H. Baltagi, Whitney Newey, Hal White and R. Carter Hill

Volume 30: 30th Anniversary Edition – Edited by Dek Terrell and Daniel Millmet

Volume 31: Structural Econometric Models – Edited by Eugene Choo and Matthew Shum

Volume 32: VAR Models in Macroeconomics – New Developments and Applications: Essays in Honor of Christopher A. Sims – Edited by Thomas B. Fomby, Lutz Kilian and Anthony Murphy

Volume 33: Essays in Honor of Peter C. B. Phillips – Edited by Thomas B. Fomby, Yoosoon Chang and Joon Y. Park

Volume 34: Bayesian Model Comparison – Edited by Ivan Jeliazkov and Dale J. Poirier

Volume 35: Dynamic Factor Models – Edited by Eric Hillebrand and Siem Jan Koopman

Volume36: Essays in Honor of Aman Ullah – Edited by Gloria González-Rivera, R. Carter Hill and Tae-Hwy Lee

ADVANCES IN ECONOMETRICS VOLUME 37

SPATIAL ECONOMETRICS: QUALITATIVE AND LIMITED DEPENDENT VARIABLES

EDITED BY

BADI H. BALTAGI

Syracuse University, Syracuse, NY, USA

JAMES P. LESAGE

Texas State University, San Marcos, TX, USA

R. KELLEY PACE

Louisiana State University, Baton Rouge, LA, USA

Emerald

United Kingdom – North America – Japan
India – Malaysia – China

Emerald Group Publishing Limited
Howard House, Wagon Lane, Bingley BD16 1WA, UK

First edition 2017

British Library Cataloguing in Publication Data
A catalogue record for this book is available from the British Library

ISBN: 978-1-78560-986-2
ISSN: 0731-9053 (Series)

Printed and bound by CPI Group (UK) Ltd, Croydon, CR0 4YY

ISOQAR
REGISTERED
Certificate Number 1985
ISO 14001

ISOQAR certified Management System, awarded to Emerald for adherence to Environmental standard ISO 14001:2004.

FSC
www.fsc.org
MIX
Paper from responsible sources
FSC® C013604

INVESTOR IN PEOPLE

CONTENTS

LIST OF CONTRIBUTORS

Badi H. Baltagi	Department of Economics and Center for Policy Research, Syracuse University, Syracuse, NY, USA
Peter Burridge	Department of Economics and Related Studies, University of York, York, UK
Raffaella Calabrese	Business School, University of Edinburgh, Edinburgh, UK
Mihaela Craioveanu	Department of Economics and Finance, University of Central Missouri, Warrensburg, MO, USA
Paul Damien	Department of Information Risk and Operations Management, The University of Texas at Austin, TX, USA
Jacob Dearmon	Meinders School of Business, Oklahoma City University, USA
Peter H. Egger	ETH Zurich, Zurich, Switzerland, CEPR, CESifo
J. Paul Elhorst	Faculty of Economics and Business, University of Groningen, Groningen, The Netherlands
Johan A. Elkink	School of Politics and International Relations, University College Dublin, Dublin
Jaepil Han	Korea Development Institute, Sejong, South Korea
Michaela Kesina	ETH Zurich, Zurich, Switzerland
Kara M. Kockelman	Department of Civil, Architectural, and Environmental Engineering, The University of Texas at Austin, TX, USA

James P. LeSage	Department of Finance und Economics, Texas State University, San Marcos, TX, USA
Roman Liesenfeld	Institut für Ökonometrie und Statistik, Universität Köln, Cologne, Germany
R. Kelley Pace	Department of Finance, Louisiana State University, Baton Rouge, LA, USA
Jean-François Richard	Department of Economics, University of Pittsburgh, Pittsburgh, PA, USA
Deockhyun Ryu	School of Economics, Chung-Ang University, Seoul, South Korea
Robin Sickles	Department of Economics, Rice University, Houston, TX, USA
Yuxue Sheng	China-ASEAN Research Institute, Guangxi University, Nanning, China
Tony E. Smith	Department of Electrical and Systems Engineering, University of Pennsylvania, USA
Dek Terrell	Department of Economics, Louisiana State University, Baton Rouge, LA, USA
Jan Vogler	Institut für Ökonometrie und Statistik, Universität Köln, Cologne, Germany
Yiyi Wang	Civil Engineering Department, Montana State University, Bozeman, MT, USA
Xiaokun Wang	Department of Civil and Environmental Engineering, Rensselaer Polytechnic Institute, Troy, NY, USA
Katarina Zigova	Department of Economics, University of Konstanz, Konstanz, Germany
Wei Zou	Rensselaer Polytechnic Institute, Troy, NY, USA

PART I
INTRODUCTION

PROGRESS IN SPATIAL MODELING OF DISCRETE AND CONTINUOUS DEPENDENT VARIABLES

The first *Advances in Econometrics* devoted to spatial econometrics appeared in 2004. Since 2004, spatial econometrics has made great progress. In particular, some of the issues of estimation and interpretation of regressions involving continuous dependent variables have been explored and now the frontier has shifted to ways of handling spatial dependence for discrete or limited dependent variables. Consequently, *Spatial Econometrics: Qualitative and Limited Dependent Variables* addresses this research topic with seven papers that estimate binary- and count-dependent variables using both maximum likelihood and Bayesian methods in addition to four papers that examine issues involving continuous-dependent variables.

Specifically, Part II contains two papers that examine discrete-dependent variables with spatial dependence estimated using maximum likelihood. R. Kelley Pace and James P. LeSage in "Fast Simulated Maximum Likelihood Estimation of the Spatial Probit Model Capable of Handling Large Samples" address the computational issues posed by spatial probit. The likelihood in this case requires n-dimensional integration which ordinarily would not be possible for a large number of observations. However, the authors show how to take advantage of sparsity in standard algorithms to overcome this problem. The next paper by Roman Liesenfeld, Jean-François Richard, and Jan Vogler, entitled "Likelihood Evaluation of High-Dimensional Spatial Latent Gaussian Models with Non-Gaussian Response Variables" also takes advantage of sparsity to handle large numbers of observations and uses importance sampling to improve the numerical performance of estimation. In addition, this paper also provides means to handle count data. A number of links exist between these two papers and they should be read together.

Part III consists of five papers that use Bayesian methods to estimate binary- and count-dependent variables. The first paper by Mihaela

Craioveanu and Dek Terrell, entitled "The Impact of Storms on Firm Survival: A Bayesian Spatial Econometric Model for Firm Survival," uses unique data on firm-level employment before and after hurricane Katrina. It handles the computational challenges by using spatially structured effects based on a smaller number of nodes. Interestingly, the computational simplifications relied on a paper from the 2004 *Advances in Econometrics* by James LeSage and Tony Smith, authors in both volumes. The second paper by Badi H. Baltagi, Peter H. Egger, and Michaela Kesina, entitled "Bayesian Spatial Bivariate Panel Probit Estimation," provides an elegant solution that encompasses four important features – longitudinal nature of the data, spatial dependence, binary-dependent variable, and simultaneity. The third paper by Raffaella Calabrese and Johan A. Elkink, entitled "Estimating Binary Spatial Autoregressive Models for Rare Events," examines the issue when a great imbalance exists among the zeros and ones in binary-dependent variables. In such cases, even data sets with large numbers of observations can exhibit small *n* artifacts. By using the generalized extreme value distribution, they can give more weight to the rare event which may avoid some of the small *n* problems. The fourth paper by Wei Zou, Xiaokun (Cara) Wang, and Yiyi Wang, entitled "A Multivariate Spatial-Time of Day Analysis of Truck Crash Frequency across Neighborhoods in New York City," employs a multivariate conditional autoregressive count model that recognizes both spatial and temporal dependence. Interestingly, it appears that areas with high traffic volume are safer with fewer crash counts as a result of a lower average driving speed, especially when more buses and taxies are involved. The fifth paper by YiYi Wang, Kara M. Kockelman, and Paul Damien, entitled "A Multivariate Spatial Analysis for Anticipating New Firm Counts," analyzes county-level firm births across the United States using a spatial count model that permits spatial dependence, cross-correlation among different industry types, and over-dispersion commonly found in empirical count data. Again, this serves as another example of allowing for multiple forms of dependence in the context of count models.

Although spatial dependence with qualitative and discrete-dependent variables provides the main focus of this volume of *Advances in Econometrics*, many research issues remain when dealing with continuous-dependent variables and spatial dependence. We begin with two of these papers in Part IV which use maximum likelihood estimation. The first paper by Peter Burridge, Paul Elhorst, and Katarina Zigova, entitled "Group Interaction in Research and the Use of General Nesting Spatial Models," examines a linear spatial econometric model with a full set of interaction effects, namely, among the dependent variable, the exogenous variables, and among the disturbances. They point out that this model is almost never employed in empirical applications. They show that the model is identified in this context, but find evidence in favor of the more parsimonious spatial Durbin model and the spatial Durbin error model. They use both likelihood ratios as well as Bayesian model comparisons in their analysis. Although we placed this in the maximum likelihood category, it shows that both approaches may have utility in applications. The second paper by Jaepil Han, Deockhyun Ryu, and Robin Sickles, entitled "How to Measure Spillover Effects of Public Capital Stock: A Spatial Autoregressive Stochastic Frontier Model," applies spatial econometrics to stochastic frontier models. The application of spatial econometrics to stochastic frontier models is relatively recent and has great potential. The results show that indirect effects comprise around 30% of the total elasticities.

Part V contains two Bayesian spatial papers using continuous-dependent variables. The first paper by Jacob Dearmon and Tony E. Smith, "Local Marginal Analysis of Spatial Data: A Gaussian Process Regression Approach with Bayesian Model and Kernel Averaging," handles an impressive set of issues. Specifically, they allow dependence to vary not only with distance but also with direction (anisotropy), calculate local marginal effects, and provide individual location inference in a coherent way. The second paper by Yuxue Sheng and James LeSage, "City and Industry Network Impacts on Innovation by Chinese Manufacturing Firms: A Hierarchical Spatial-Interindustry Model," examines spatial and interindustry dependence on firm-level innovation of Chinese firms. They construct a Bayesian hierarchical model that allows for both city- and industry-level interaction (global spillovers) and subsumes other innovation scenarios such as heterogeneity that implies level differences (fixed effects), and contextual effects that imply local spillovers as special cases.

Comparing the current volume and the 2004 volume, the new set of papers show greater sophistication in handling discrete-dependent variables and the ability to jointly handle multiple econometric issues while providing coherent inference for both parameters as well as marginal effects (direct and indirect). As with the first *Advances in Econometrics* volume, this volume displays the interdisciplinary aspect of spatial econometrics with authors from departments of economics, finance, real estate, operations management, civil, architectural, electrical, environmental, and transportation engineering, as well as political science. Since the quantity of spatial data continues to increase and many econometric problems do not yet have spatially adapted solutions, we look forward to future spatial volumes of *Advances in Econometrics* that will show progress on a number of topics useful for a variety of academic fields.

Badi H. Baltagi
James P. LeSage
R. Kelley Pace
Editors

PART II
DISCRETE DEPENDENT VARIABLES – MAXIMUM LIKELIHOOD

FAST SIMULATED MAXIMUM LIKELIHOOD ESTIMATION OF THE SPATIAL PROBIT MODEL CAPABLE OF HANDLING LARGE SAMPLES

R. Kelley Pace[a] and James P. LeSage[b]

[a]*Department of Finance, E.J. Ourso Colege of Business Administration, Louisiana State University, Baton Rouge, LA, USA*
[b]*Texas State University, Department of Finance and Economics, San Marcos, TX, USA*

ABSTRACT

We show how to quickly estimate spatial probit models for large data sets using maximum likelihood. Like Beron and Vijverberg (2004), we use the GHK (Geweke-Hajivassiliou-Keane) algorithm to perform maximum simulated likelihood estimation. However, using the GHK for large sample sizes has been viewed as extremely difficult (Wang, Iglesias, & Wooldridge, 2013). Nonetheless, for sparse covariance and precision matrices often encountered in spatial settings, the GHK can be applied to

Spatial Econometrics: Qualitative and Limited Dependent Variables
Advances in Econometrics, Volume 37, 3–34

ISSN: 0731-9053/doi:10.1108/S0731-905320160000037008

very large sample sizes as its operation counts and memory requirements increase almost linearly with n *when using sparse matrix techniques.*

Keywords: GHK; truncated multivariate normal; spatial probit; sparse matrix; maximum simulated likelihood; CAR

JEL classifications: C21; C53; C55; R30; R10

1. INTRODUCTION

Many economic explanatory variables display substantial amounts of spatial dependence and so omission of these variables (to the extent that they are not correlated with included variables) can lead to spatial dependence in the disturbances. If the observed regressand at each of n locations is binary, but the underlying latent variable is multivariate normal, evaluating the likelihood function involves the integral of a truncated n-dimensional normal distribution. For large n, this is known to be a difficult computational problem (Phinikettos & Gandy, 2011).

Techniques for computing these integrals have been a subject of research for many years (Deák, 2011; Genz, 1992; Genz & Bretz, 1999, 2002). One of the most effective techniques, known as the GHK (Geweke-Hajivassiliou-Keane) simulator, has itself spawned a large literature.[1] The GHK method reduces the problem of n-dimensional integration over a multivariate normal joint density with bounds in each dimension to the product of n univariate integrals of estimated conditional densities.

From a computational perspective, the GHK technique involves a Cholesky decomposition which ordinarily requires $O(n^3)$ operations. This produces a Cholesky triangular matrix with up to $n(n+1)/2$ non-zero elements. The GHK uses these non-zero elements in its computations. Therefore, in most cases, the GHK requires $O(n^2)$ operations to compute the integral, and $O(n^2)$ memory locations.[2] This works well in situations with small n, but operation counts and memory requirements become challenging for large n. Therefore, spatial probit estimators based on the GHK and its variants such as the RIS require at least $O(n^2)$ computations.[3]

As Wang, Iglesias, and Wooldridge (2013) state:

> Estimating a probit spatial autocorrelation model by full MLE is a prodigious task, although several approaches have been applied. The EM algorithm can be used (McMillen, 1992), the RIS simulator (Beron & Vijverberg, 2003), and the Bayesian Gibbs sampler

(LeSage, 2000). But each of these approaches is still computationally burdensome. To combine such approaches with simulation studies, or to be able to quickly estimate a range of models, is outside the abilities of even current computation capabilities for even moderate sample sizes.

Fortunately, each observation located in space may only depend upon a small number of nearby neighbors. This implies that either the variance-covariance matrix is sparse or the inverse variance-covariance (precision) matrix is sparse. Spatial moving average (MA) processes naturally lead to sparse variance-covariance matrices and conditional spatial autoregressive (CAR) processes naturally lead to sparse precision matrices (Cressie, 1993). Sparse variance-covariance or precision matrices can yield sparse Cholesky triangles (LeSage & Pace, 2009; Pace & Barry, 1997). This sparsity can be exploited to produce a variant of the GHK simulator that is almost linear in n for both operation counts and memory locations. This overcomes the computational barrier for spatial probit.

We demonstrate that implementing these changes to the GHK procedure allows estimation of a spatial probit regression with 100,000 observations on a desktop machine in 2–4 minutes and that the time required to compute these regressions rises almost linearly with n. To place this in context, Beron and Vijverberg (2004, p. 181) found that doubling the sample size increased computing time by a factor of 3.75, which is close to order n^2. LeSage and Pace (2009, pp. 289–293) provided a Bayesian MCMC spatial probit example with 3,107 observations and reported that 1,200 draws took 45 minutes computing time.

In Section 2, we introduce various spatial probit specifications for situations involving spatial dependence in observed choice outcomes. We provide sparse GHK procedures to produce maximum likelihood estimates for these models. Section 3 details the advantages of sparsity in a spatial context. Specifically, we set forth the usual GHK procedure, appropriate for spatial probit with spatial MA disturbances, and a version of GHK adapted to work with a sparse precision matrix, appropriate for spatial probit with CAR disturbances. In addition, we discuss how sparsity of the spatial weight matrix W can greatly aid in estimating spatial MA or CAR probit models. Section 4 reports results from several Monte Carlo experiments to document that maximization of the spatial probit likelihood using the GHK procedure yields accurate parameter estimates and greatly speeds computations needed for dealing with large sample sizes. Section 5 provides two brief empirical illustrations of spatial probit in the context of residential development and mortgage default. Section 6 discusses ways of further accelerating computations as well as issues related to large n. Section 7 summarizes our findings and discusses extensions.

2. SPATIAL PROBIT MODELS

For the case of spatial dependence in the disturbance structure, the model in Eq. (1) represents a general data-generating process (DGP), with various specific spatial dependence structures for the disturbances enumerated for the spatial error model in Eq. (2), conditional autoregression in Eq. (3), and MA in Eq. (4). The $n \times 1$ vector $\tilde{y}$ represents unobserved utility/profits, and y is an associated 0,1 vector reflecting the observed decisions. The $n \times k$ full-rank matrix X contains n observations on k explanatory variables, and W represents a symmetric $n \times n$ spatial weight matrix. The $n \times 1$ vector ε follows a multivariate normal distribution. Like the typical binary probit model, the parameter σ^2 is set to 1 to achieve identification as shown in Eq. (5).

$$\tilde{y} = X\beta + \varepsilon, \tag{1}$$

$$\text{SEM}: \quad \varepsilon \sim \mathcal{N}\left(0, \sigma^2 (I_n - \rho W)^{-2}\right), \tag{2}$$

$$\text{CAR}: \quad \varepsilon \sim \mathcal{N}\left(0, \sigma^2 (I_n - \rho W)^{-1}\right), \tag{3}$$

$$\text{MA}: \quad \varepsilon \sim \mathcal{N}\left(0, \sigma^2 (I_n - \rho W)\right), \tag{4}$$

$$\sigma^2 = 1, \tag{5}$$

$$y = 0, 1,$$

$$\tilde{y}_i > 0 \rightarrow y_i = 1 \quad \text{otherwise } y_i = 0 \quad \text{for} \quad i = 1, \ldots, n.$$

The spatial weight matrix W plays a key role in these models. The element W_{ij} equals some positive exogenous constant when observation or region j is a neighbor to observation i and 0 otherwise. By convention, an observation is not a neighbor to itself ($W_{ii} = 0$). For simplicity, we assume that W is symmetric which implies that W has n real and distinct eigenvalues. Assume that through scaling or construction that W has a principal eigenvalue $\lambda_{\max}$ of 1. Since $\mathrm{tr}(W) = 0$ and the trace equals the sum of the eigenvalues, this implies that some eigenvalues are negative. As a sufficient condition, $\rho \in (-1, 1)$ will ensure that $(I_n - \rho W)^{-1}$ exists and furthermore that the infinite expansion $(I_n - \rho W)^{-1} = I_n + \rho W + \rho^2 W^2 + \cdots$ exists (LeSage & Pace, 2009). A non-zero $\left(W^2\right)_{ij}$ indicates that observation j is the neighbor of the neighbor to observation i. Similarly, the non-zeros in W^3 specify the neighbors to the neighbors of the neighbors.

As an example of where such a DGP might arise, consider observed voting decisions for two candidates. Such voting decisions could exhibit this type of dependence in the disturbances arising from unmeasurable election influences such as social interactions among neighboring residents, campaign signs in yards, or grass root electoral efforts of various efficacy. Since these unmeasurable factors are not included in or spanned by the set of model explanatory variables, the unmeasurable factors enter the model disturbances.

Suitable specification of the explanatory variables, however, as shown in Eqs. (6)–(9) can generalize this model involving spatial dependence among the disturbances,

$$X = \begin{bmatrix} \iota_n & Z \end{bmatrix}, \tag{6}$$

$$X = \begin{bmatrix} \iota_n & Z & WZ \end{bmatrix}, \tag{7}$$

$$X = \begin{bmatrix} \iota_n & (I - \varphi W)^{-1} Z \end{bmatrix}, \tag{8}$$

$$X = \begin{bmatrix} \iota_n & Z & W(I - \varphi W)^{-1} Z \end{bmatrix}, \tag{9}$$

where Z is an $n \times p$ matrix containing n observations on p non-constant explanatory variables, ι_n is an $n \times 1$ vector of ones, and φ is a real scalar parameter in $(1, -1)$. The specification in Eq. (7) augments the basic non-constant random variables Z from Eq. (6) with a *local* average of these variables (WZ). For example, characteristics of other houses on the block could affect a borrower's decision to pay or default on a mortgage. If the other houses in the block were in poor physical condition, this would reduce expectations of future appreciation and might provide fewer incentives for the borrower to pay. In contrast, Eq. (8) makes decisions a function of not only immediate neighbors (as specified by W), but also neighbors of neighbors (W^2), neighbors of neighbors of neighbors (W^3), and even higher order neighboring relations since $(I - \varphi W)^{-1}Z$ can be expressed as an infinite series involving $Z + \varphi WZ + \varphi^2 W^2 Z + \cdots$. Note that the restriction $\varphi = \rho$ yields the well-known SAR probit model (Beron & Vijverberg, 2004; LeSage, Pace, Lam, Campanella, & Liu, 2011). One can devise more elaborate specifications such as Eq. (9) which involve both local and global influences from other observations on the observation itself (spillovers). The important point is that having a feasible way of estimating a spatial probit model with multivariate normal disturbances such as in Eq. (1) also facilitates estimation of more advanced models that involve spillovers.

No matter which specification of the explanatory variables that a researcher adopts, in the presence of spatial dependence in the disturbances, it is necessary to calculate the integral of a truncated multivariate normal distribution to fit a spatial probit model. This can be accomplished using a sparse matrix variant of the GHK procedure that we detail in the next section.

3. GHK MECHANICS

In Section 3.1, we review the GHK procedure when applied to the variance-covariance matrix. We subsequently discuss the issue of sparsity in the variance-covariance matrix in Section 3.2, and how this has the potential to greatly accelerate computational speed of the GHK. In many cases, the inverse of the variance-covariance matrix (precision matrix) reflects sparsity, so Section 3.3 adapts the GHK to work with the precision matrix.

3.1. GHK Applied to the Variance-Covariance Matrix

In this section, we examine the GHK applied to the covariance matrix, the standard setting for the GHK. Let Ω represent an $n \times n$ variance-covariance matrix which has the Cholesky decomposition involving a lower triangular matrix L and an upper triangular matrix U (where $U = L'$ due to the symmetry of Ω), as shown in Eq. (10). Multiplication of an $n \times 1$ vector of *iid* normal random variates u by L yields an $n \times 1$ vector v of correlated random deviates whose variance-covariance matrix is Ω as shown in Eqs. (11) and (12).

$$\Omega = LL' = LU \quad \text{where } U = L', \tag{10}$$

$$v = Lu, \tag{11}$$

$$E(vv') = E(Luu'U) = \Omega. \tag{12}$$

Therefore, taking an independent random normal variable vector and imposing a covariance structure on it is not very difficult. However, truncated multivariate normal random variates should also obey the restrictions shown in Eq. (13).

$$\begin{bmatrix} v_1 \\ v_2 \\ \vdots \\ v_n \end{bmatrix} = \begin{bmatrix} L_{11} & & & \\ L_{21} & L_{22} & & \\ \vdots & & \ddots & \\ L_{n1} & L_{n2} & \dots & L_{nn} \end{bmatrix} \begin{bmatrix} u_1 \\ u_2 \\ \vdots \\ u_n \end{bmatrix} \quad \text{s.t.} \quad \begin{bmatrix} v_1 \\ v_2 \\ \vdots \\ v_n \end{bmatrix} < \begin{bmatrix} b_1 \\ b_2 \\ \vdots \\ b_n \end{bmatrix}. \tag{13}$$

The triangular system in Eq. (13) leads to v_i, for $i = 1, \ldots, n$ as a function of u_i and prior $(t < i)$ u_t. However, substitution of the inequality relation on v_i allows expressing u_i as functions of prior u_t and the restrictions, b_i.

Although these restrictions may make the problem of integration slightly more feasible, the problem is still intractable as it requires up to n-order numerical integration (if approached in a direct way).

To make this operational, the GHK begins for $i = 1$ with the following calculation:

$$a_1 = \frac{b_1}{L_{11}}, \tag{14}$$

$$\tilde{P}_1 = \Phi[u_1 < a_1], \tag{15}$$

$$u_1^* \sim \mathcal{TN}(a_1), \tag{16}$$

where a_1 is the limit of integration, $\tilde{P}_1$ is the initial probability in the sequence, and u_1^* is a unit normal deviate truncated from above at the limit a_1.

One means of generating a unit normal deviate u_1^* truncated from above at a_1 is to take a uniform random variable or a quasi-random variable over (0, 1), shown as r_1^*, multiply it by $\tilde{P}_1$, and use the inverse of the normal cdf to find the corresponding truncated normal deviate as in Eq. (17):

$$u_1^* = \Phi^{-1}\left[r_1^* \tilde{P}_1\right]. \tag{17}$$

A key implementation detail in the GHK is how to select the best set of r^* (pseudo or quasi-random numbers) and to use the same set for all computations. Using the same set is sometimes labeled as a common random number or correlated sampling variance reduction technique.

For $i = 2$, the GHK builds upon the specific realization of u_1^* in the previous step as a way of handling dependence.

$$a_2^* = \frac{b_2 - L_{21} u_1^*}{L_{22}}, \tag{18}$$

$$\tilde{P}_2 = \Phi\left[u_2 < a_2^*\right], \tag{19}$$

$$u_2^* \sim \mathcal{TN}\left(a_2^*\right). \tag{20}$$

Note that unlike the first step which involved a non-random limit of integration, this second step relied on the realization of the random variable u_1^* from the first step to determine the limit of integration a_2^*. Using specific realizations of the random variates u^* to specify dependence is the simplification of the intractable integration problem that the GHK employs to make each step feasible.

The GHK for $i = 2, \ldots, n$ computes

$$a_i^* = \frac{b_i - \sum_{t=1}^{i-1} L_{it} u_t^*}{L_{ii}}, \tag{21}$$

$$\tilde{P}_i = \Phi\left[u_i < a_i^*\right], \tag{22}$$

$$u_i^* \sim \mathcal{TN}\left(a_i^*\right), \tag{23}$$

where a_i^* is the limit of integration for the *i*th integral based on previously computed $(t < i)$ univariate truncated normal random variates u_t^*, and $\tilde{P}_i$ is an estimate of the *i*th conditional probability. As the GHK proceeds, it computes the current limit of integration a_i^* as given by Eq. (21), the *i*th conditional probability in Eq. (22), and augments the previously computed u_t^* with a univariate truncated normal random variate u_i^* in Eq. (23). At the end of the process, the GHK provides estimates of $\tilde{P}_i$ for $i = 1, \ldots, n$, a vector of estimated limits of integration a^*, and the u^* vector.

This is the GHK algorithm associated with a particular u^* vector or draw. One could repeat this for different possible draws to gain more accuracy. Let the u^* vector associated with the *d*th draw be denoted as $u^*(d_r)$ for $r = 1, \ldots, R$ with associated vector $a^*(d_r)$. Expression (24) provides an estimate of the joint probability as a product of individual conditional probabilities based on draw *d*. Averaging over the *R* independent draws as in Eq. (25) results in an improved estimate $\tilde{P}$.

$$\tilde{P}(d_r) = \prod_{i=1}^{n} \tilde{P}_i(d_r), \tag{24}$$

$$\tilde{P} = \frac{1}{R} \sum_{r=1}^{R} \tilde{P}(d_r). \tag{25}$$

To reduce notational clutter, we only specified the inequalities in a single direction $v_i < b_i$, but one can obtain similar results for inequalities of differing directions.

3.2. *Sparsity and the GHK*

Often in a spatial setting, an observation or region depends only on nearby observations or regions and may have no dependence on distant observations or regions. In this case, the variance-covariance matrix may contain a large proportion of zeros, the definition of a sparse matrix. For example, geostatistical models of the variance-covariance such as the spherical specification only have positive elements for observations located within some finite distance range (Barry & Pace, 1997; Rue & Held, 2005). Also, MA models such as $\Omega = (I_n + \rho W)$ that rely on sparse weight matrices have sparse variance-covariance matrices.

In the common case of W based on contiguous regions on a plane, there will be approximately six neighbors for each observation. In other words, the number of non-zero elements will approximately equal $6n$ and the proportion of non-zeros in W will approximately equal $6/n$, so W becomes very sparse for large n.

The relevance of sparsity to the GHK is through the Cholesky decomposition as the number of operations required is a function of the number of non-zeros in the Cholesky lower triangular matrix L. The Cholesky decomposition of a dense covariance matrix has, in general, $n(n+1)/2$ non-zero elements.

However, for sparse variance-covariance matrices (or inverse variance-covariance matrices), a number of methods have been used to maximize the sparsity of the resulting Cholesky decomposition. These typically work by reordering the rows and columns of a sparse matrix. For example, the reverse Cuthill-McKee algorithm (Alan & Liu, 1981) tries to make a sparse matrix into a band matrix, while minimum degree algorithms try to reduce the number of additional non-zero elements or *fill in* that occurs in the process of forming the Cholesky triangular matrix. Pace and Barry (1997) as well as LeSage and Pace (2009) discuss these orderings in conjunction with spatial weight matrices in some detail.

To see the effect of reordering the rows and columns of a matrix, Table 1 shows the proportion of non-zeros in the Cholesky triangle of the sparse contiguity weight matrix relative to the conventional Cholesky triangle which has $n(n+1)/2$ non-zeros. Even a random ordering of the rows and columns of $\Omega = I_n - \rho W$ results in fewer non-zeros in the Cholesky triangle relative to a dense Cholesky triangle. This proportion ranges from 0.295 to 0.236 and declines slowly with n. Ordering by the magnitude of a function of the locational coordinates performs much better. For example,

Table 1. Proportion of Non-Zeros Relative to Dense Cholesky across n for Different Orderings of Rows and Columns.

n	1,000	5,000	10,000	25,000
Random order	0.2945	0.2382	0.2400	0.2362
Reverse Cuthill-McKee	0.1122	0.0478	0.0371	0.0300
E-W coordinates	0.0766	0.0325	0.0229	0.0141
N-S coordinates	0.0762	0.0322	0.0227	0.0142
NE-SW coordinates	0.0726	0.0302	0.0217	0.0133
Minimum degree	0.0253	0.0064	0.0037	0.0017

ordering the observations from east to west (EW), north to south (NS), or northeast to southwest (NE-SW) reduces the number of non-zero elements relative to the random ordering. Specifically, the northeast to southwest (NE-SW) ordering resulted in the proportion of non-zeros (relative to the dense Cholesky) ranging between 0.0726 and 0.0133.[4] The band-like reverse Cuthill-McKee ordering performs worse than ordering by any of the locational coordinates. However, the approximate minimum degree ordering (Amestoy, Davis, & Duff, 1996) outperforms all the other methods with only 0.0253–0.0017 proportion of non-zeros relative to the dense Cholesky triangle. As shown in Table 1, the reduction in work for sparse methods increases greatly with n.

There are many other orderings and ways of organizing Cholesky computations to maximize the use of parallel computing and to handle very large systems. For example, graph partitioning and nested dissection can divide the area into subareas that can be computed independently of each other and border areas separating the individual subareas (Duff, Ersiman, & Reid, 1989; George & Liu, 1981).

3.3. GHK Applied to the Precision Matrix

In many cases, the inverse variance-covariance matrix ($\Omega^{-1} = \Psi$), also known as the precision matrix, has greater sparsity than the covariance matrix. For example, a CAR specification for the model disturbances would lead to the variance-covariance matrix $\Omega = (I_n - \rho W)^{-1}$ and a spatial autoregressive disturbance specification with symmetric W would produce

$\Omega = (I_n - \rho W)^{-2}$. In these cases, Ω is dense while the precision matrix Ψ is sparse.[5] Accordingly, to handle these important spatial specifications, the GHK algorithm requires modification to work with the precision matrix.

We begin by examining how the *iid* random deviates in u need to be transformed to exhibit the desired variance-covariance matrix as shown in Eqs. (26)–(29):

$$\Psi = LU = \Omega^{-1} \quad \text{and} \quad U = L', \tag{26}$$

$$\Omega = (LU)^{-1} = U^{-1}L^{-1}, \tag{27}$$

$$v = U^{-1}u, \tag{28}$$

$$E(vv') = E\left(U^{-1}uu'L^{-1}\right) = \Omega. \tag{29}$$

This leads to the system in Eq. (30).

$$Uv = u \quad \text{s.t. } v_i < b_i \quad \text{for } i = 1, \ldots, n. \tag{30}$$

Expanding out the system in Eq. (30) produces an equation in terms of an upper triangular matrix U. Note that unlike the lower triangular matrix L for the case of the covariance matrix, working with U for the case of the precision matrix means that the GHK procedure begins with the last observation, n, and works toward the first observation.

$$\begin{bmatrix} U_{11} & U_{12} & \cdots & U_{1n} \\ & & & \vdots \\ & & U_{(n-1)(n-1)} & U_{(n-1)n} \\ & & & U_{nn} \end{bmatrix} \begin{bmatrix} v_1 \\ \vdots \\ v_{n-1} \\ v_n \end{bmatrix} = \begin{bmatrix} u_1 \\ \vdots \\ u_{n-1} \\ u_n \end{bmatrix} \quad \text{s.t.} \quad \begin{bmatrix} v_1 \\ \vdots \\ v_{n-1} \\ v_n \end{bmatrix} < \begin{bmatrix} b_1 \\ \vdots \\ b_{n-1} \\ b_n \end{bmatrix}.$$

Use of the inequality relations eliminate some of the variables, as in the previous case of the covariance matrix. Specifically, the inequality restrictions eliminate v_i which leaves the system as a function of b_i, u_i, and u_t for $t > i$ as given by Eqs. (31)–(33).

$$b_n > \frac{u_n}{U_{nn}}, \tag{31}$$

$$b_{n-1} > \frac{u_{n-1} - U_{(n-1)n}v_n}{U_{(n-1)(n-1)}}, \tag{32}$$

$$\vdots$$

$$b_1 > \frac{u_1 - \sum_{t=2}^{n} U_{1t}v_t}{U_{11}}. \tag{33}$$

We begin the actual GHK calculations with the last observation (n) which does not depend on any other observation. In this case, the nth probability is a simple univariate problem as shown in Eq. (35) based on the exogenous limit of integration a_n given in Eq. (34). Generating u_n^* and calculating v_n^* are also simple as shown in Eqs. (36) and (37):

$$a_n = b_n U_{nn}, \tag{34}$$

$$\tilde{P}_n = \Phi[u_n < a_n], \tag{35}$$

$$u_n^* \sim T\mathcal{N}(a_n), \tag{36}$$

$$v_n^* = \frac{u_n^*}{U_{nn}}. \tag{37}$$

Given v_n^* (based on the random u_n^*), we compute the limit of integration a_{n-1}^* as shown in Eq. (38), form an estimate of P_{n-1} in Eq. (39), generate u_{n-1}^* in Eq. (40), and calculate the associated v_{n-1}^* in Eq. (41).

$$a_{n-1}^* = b_{n-1} U_{(n-1)(n-1)} + U_{(n-1)n} v_n^*, \tag{38}$$

$$\tilde{P}_{n-1} = \Phi\left[u_{n-1} < a^*_{n-1}\right], \tag{39}$$

$$u^*_{n-1} \sim \mathcal{TN}\left(a^*_{n-1}\right), \tag{40}$$

$$v^*_{n-1} = \frac{u^*_{n-1} - U_{(n-1)n} v^*_n}{U_{(n-1)(n-1)}}. \tag{41}$$

For any observation i, we follow a similar process as shown in Eqs. (42)–(45).

$$a^*_i = b_i U_{ii} + \sum_{t=i+1}^{n} U_{it} v^*_t, \tag{42}$$

$$\tilde{P}_i = \Phi\left[u_i < a^*_i\right], \tag{43}$$

$$u^*_i \sim \mathcal{TN}\left(a^*_i\right), \tag{44}$$

$$v^*_i = \frac{u^*_i - \sum_{t=i+1}^{n} U_{it} v^*_t}{U_{ii}}. \tag{45}$$

Finally, for the first observation (last in the process), we compute the limit of integration in Eq. (46) and the associated estimated conditional probability in Eq. (47):

$$a^*_1 = b_1 U_{11} + \sum_{t=2}^{n} U_{1t} v^*_t, \tag{46}$$

$$\tilde{P}_1 = \Phi\left[u_1 < a^*_1\right]. \tag{47}$$

The estimate of the joint probability in Eq. (48) is a product of individual conditional probabilities based on $u^*_1, u^*_2, \ldots, u^*_n$. Repetition of the process for different u^* vector would result in different estimates. In other words, each repetition or draw d_r for $r = 1, \ldots, R$ yields different $u^*(d_r)$. Averaging over different draws provides a better estimate of the joint probability as shown in Eq. (49):

$$\tilde{P}(d_r) = \prod_{i=1}^{n} \tilde{P}_i(d_r), \tag{48}$$

$$\tilde{P} = \frac{1}{R}\sum_{r=1}^{R} \tilde{P}(d_r). \tag{49}$$

4. GHK PERFORMANCE

In this section, we document the almost linear with n-computational performance of the GHK with sparse precision matrices that underlie the CAR spatial probit estimator. In addition, we conduct some Monte Carlo experiments of the CAR-based spatial probit estimator to investigate its statistical performance.

In terms of spatial modeling, the setup in Section 3.1 works better for MA models, while the GHK setup in Section 3.3 works better for CAR models. However, as the development of the GHK for MA models is well known, we will explore how the GHK functions for the CAR model in the experiments described below.

All of the experiments use the spatial binary DGP in Eqs. (50)–(52),

$$\tilde{y} = X\beta + \varepsilon, \tag{50}$$

$$\varepsilon \sim \mathcal{N}\left(0, (I_n - \rho W)^{-1}\right), \tag{51}$$

$$\tilde{y}_i > 0 \rightarrow y_i = 1 \quad \text{otherwise } y_i = 0 \quad \text{for} \quad i = 1, \ldots, n, \tag{52}$$

where $\tilde{y}_i$ is a latent continuous variable and y_i is the observed binary variable. The $n \times 1$ binary vector y and $n \times k$ matrix X of exogenous regressors represent the sample data. As before, W is a symmetric $n \times n$ spatial weight matrix composed of non-negative exogenous constants and has real eigenvalues. Essentially, the latent variable $\tilde{y}_i$ comes from a CAR disturbance specification with covariance matrix $\Omega = (I_n - \rho W)^{-1}$.

As in Beron and Vijverberg (2004), we used numerical differentiation of the conditional probabilities resulting from the GHK for each observation for each parameter. Specifically, we used the central difference method for β and ρ (difference used was $h = 0.0001$). We employed these numerical gradients in the outer-product-of-the-gradient method to calculate the variance-covariance matrix. Given the numerical gradients and the estimate of the variance-covariance matrix, we conducted iterative maximization of the likelihood using the BHHH method (Berndt, Hall, Hall, & Hausman, 1974).

Although the normal GHK simulator is without bias in terms of the simulated probabilities, this does not hold true for the derivatives of the simulated log-likelihood. As Lee (2005) showed, simulation error can lead to bias in the results. This bias is reduced by increasing R relative to n. Lee (2005) found that the bias was not as severe for correlated data relative to independent data. For his time series panel probit simulations, where the time-dependence parameter $\rho = 0.4, 0.9$, the bias was small and negative. Lee (2005) also proposed a bias correction term. Despite this bias, many studies use numerical derivatives and we will examine in the Monte Carlo results below the bias and its sensitivity to R.

We begin by examining the relation between the computation time of the GHK-based spatial probit estimator for a base case of $\rho = 0.75$, pseudo-$R^2 = 0.5$, and $R = 25$. We estimated regressions using $n = 1$K, 5K, 10K, 50K, 100K, 500K, and 1M and recorded the computational duration of the GHK computations. We subsequently fit the model $\ln(\text{time}) = \beta_1 + \beta_2 \ln(n) + \varepsilon$. As shown in Table 2, the fit among the seven sample sizes was quite good with an $R^2 = 0.995$. The estimated value of 1.089 for $\hat{\beta}_2$ indicates that increasing the sample size by 1 percent

Table 2. Double Log Regression of Spatial Probit Time versus n.

	$\hat{\beta}$	t
Intercept	−7.3298	−23.8022
ln(n)	1.0894	38.2358
R^2	0.9952	

increases the computational time of the spatial probit estimator by less than 1.1 percent. Although this rate is superlinear, it is much better than the quadratic relation found in earlier research (Beron & Vijverberg, 2004, p. 181).

We now provide some Monte Carlo results to examine the sensitivity of spatial probit based on the GHK to (a) the number of draws R used in the GHK ($R = 25, 100, 400$), (b) sample size n ($n = 1{,}000, 100{,}000$) (c) extent of spatial dependence ρ ($\rho = 0.4, 0.75, 0.9$), goodness-of-fit pseudo-R^2 (0.25, 0.5, 0.75), proportion of 1s and 0s (as affected by the intercept $\beta_1 = 0, 1, 2$), and the spatial weight matrix W. For the Monte Carlo study implementations, we employed four forms of W. Specifically, we used W based on contiguity (as derived from Delaunay triangles) as well as 6, 12, and 18 nearest neighbors. We scaled W to have row and, through symmetry, column sums of 1 (doubly stochastic). This form of W has all real eigenvalues with the maximum eigenvalue equal to 1 and a minimum eigenvalue between −1 and 0. As a sufficient condition, $(I_n - \rho W)^{-1}$ exists for $\rho \in (-1, 1)$.

We initially examine the effect of using different numbers of draws R in computing the GHK. Specifically, we examine the three scenarios $R = 25, 100, 400$ for each likelihood evaluation as shown in Table 3. In these scenarios, we use 250 trials of estimating a probit model given the DGP above using $n = 1{,}000$ observations where we vary the number of draws R. For each of the three scenarios, W was based on contiguity (the locational coordinates followed a unit random uniform distribution). Both y and u_{d_r} for $r = 1, \ldots, R$ were generated anew for each of the 250 trials. We set the length of $X\beta$ to generate a pseudo-R^2 of 0.5. The overall estimate of ρ changed from 0.7439 when using $R = 25$ to 0.7554 when using $R = 400$ (true value of $\rho = 0.75$). The standard deviation of the ρ estimates decreased from 0.0823 for $R = 25$ to 0.0795 for $R = 400$. For 250 trials, the observed bias of 0.0054 was not significantly different from the true value of ρ of 0.75 given the standard error of $(250^{-0.5})0.0795$. The same applies to the estimates of β for the spatial estimator in contrast to the non-spatial estimator that showed substantial attenuation bias.

We now examine large sample sizes. For all the remaining scenarios, $n = 100{,}000$ and we use 50 trials. In Table 4, the first two scenarios corroborate the earlier findings when using $n = 1{,}000$. Namely, that going from $R = 25$ to $R = 100$ raises the estimate of ρ by around 0.009. However, for these two scenarios, the standard deviation of the estimates of ρ only decreased by 0.001. For large sample sizes, R mainly affects the bias and

Table 3. Monte Carlo Results for Spatial and Independence Probit for $n = 1{,}000$.

	β	$\tilde{\beta}_s$	σ	$\tilde{\beta}_{iid}$	σ
$R = 25$					
1	0.0000	0.0062	0.0717	0.0054	0.0664
2	1.0000	1.0140	0.0999	0.9304	0.0961
3	1.0000	1.0014	0.1055	0.9182	0.1022
4	−1.0000	−1.0024	0.1058	−0.9217	0.1018
5	−1.0000	−0.9990	0.1053	−0.9154	0.0984
$\tilde{\rho}$	0.7500	0.7439	0.0823		
$R = 100$					
1	0.0000	0.0060	0.0717	0.0054	0.0664
2	1.0000	1.0152	0.1001	0.9304	0.0961
3	1.0000	1.0025	0.1055	0.9182	0.1022
4	−1.0000	−1.0034	0.1054	−0.9217	0.1018
5	−1.0000	−1.0000	0.1053	−0.9154	0.0984
$\tilde{\rho}$	0.7500	0.7529	0.0813		
$R = 400$					
1	0.0000	0.0062	0.0717	0.0054	0.0664
2	1.0000	1.0155	0.1001	0.9304	0.0961
3	1.0000	1.0027	0.1056	0.9182	0.1022
4	−1.0000	−1.0035	0.1055	−0.9217	0.1018
5	−1.0000	−1.0001	0.1054	−0.9154	0.0984
$\tilde{\rho}$	0.7500	0.7554	0.0795		

not the variability of estimates of ρ. For both $R = 25$ and $R = 100$, the estimates of ρ were statistically significantly different from 0.75. Insofar as ρ is often viewed as a nuisance parameter, the actual bias may not be important in the context of an application (especially when the alternative is to assume independence). In the next two scenarios, we examine the effects of differing values of ρ. In the case of $\rho = 0.4$, the estimated $\tilde{\rho}$ of 0.3968 was very close to the true value of 0.4 (and not statistically different from the true value). In the case of $\rho = 0.9$, the estimate was 0.9136 and significantly different from the true value of 0.9.

Table 5 shows four scenarios where the signal-to-noise changes and the proportion of 1s and 0s changes (different intercepts). In the first scenario,

Table 4. Monte Carlo Results for Different R and ρ.

	β	$\tilde{\beta}_s$	σ	$\tilde{\beta}_{iid}$	σ
$R = 25$					
1	0.0000	−0.0002	0.0063	−0.0005	0.0063
2	1.0000	0.9965	0.0099	0.9124	0.0101
3	1.0000	0.9963	0.0088	0.9130	0.0088
4	−1.0000	−0.9969	0.0110	−0.9130	0.0114
5	−1.0000	−0.9995	0.0113	−0.9159	0.0116
$\tilde{\rho}$	0.7500	0.7613	0.0066		
$R = 100$					
1	0.0000	−0.0004	0.0063	−0.0005	0.0063
2	1.0000	0.9977	0.0100	0.9124	0.0101
3	1.0000	0.9976	0.0089	0.9130	0.0088
4	−1.0000	−0.9981	0.0113	−0.9130	0.0114
5	−1.0000	−1.0008	0.0115	−0.9159	0.0116
$\tilde{\rho}$	0.7500	0.7708	0.0067		
$R = 25, \rho = 0.4$					
1	0.0000	−0.0004	0.0047	−0.0005	0.0052
2	1.0000	0.9986	0.0093	0.9807	0.0102
3	1.0000	0.9986	0.0085	0.9811	0.0093
4	−1.0000	−0.9979	0.0106	−0.9801	0.0115
5	−1.0000	−1.0010	0.0113	−0.9835	0.0122
$\tilde{\rho}$	0.4000	0.3968	0.0139		
$R = 25, \rho = 0.9$					
1	0.0000	0.0000	0.0097	−0.0006	0.0085
2	1.0000	0.9904	0.0117	0.8352	0.0114
3	1.0000	0.9909	0.0094	0.8368	0.0089
4	−1.0000	−0.9913	0.0109	−0.8363	0.0105
5	−1.0000	−0.9942	0.0119	−0.8393	0.0108
$\tilde{\rho}$	0.9000	0.9136	0.0037		

the pseudo-R^2 goes from 0.5 (base case) to 0.75. In the second scenario, the signal-to-noise drops to a pseudo-R^2 of 0.25. The bias and standard error rise slightly for lower levels of signal-to-noise. In contrast, the last two scenarios deal with different intercepts which changes the proportion of zeros

Table 5. Monte Carlo Results for Different Intercepts and Signal-Noise.

	β	$\tilde{\beta}_s$	σ	$\tilde{\beta}_{iid}$	σ
$R = 25, R^2 = 0.75$					
1	0.0000	−0.0001	0.0064	−0.0003	0.0067
2	1.0000	0.9987	0.0071	0.9151	0.0076
3	1.0000	0.9969	0.0054	0.9137	0.0058
4	−1.0000	−0.9974	0.0081	−0.9140	0.0085
5	−1.0000	−0.9981	0.0080	−0.9149	0.0081
$\tilde{\rho}$	0.7500	0.7569	0.0076		
$R = 25, R^2 = 0.25$					
1	0.0000	−0.0006	0.0059	−0.0007	0.0058
2	1.0000	0.9961	0.0170	0.9116	0.0167
3	1.0000	0.9974	0.0149	0.9144	0.0147
4	−1.0000	−0.9963	0.0180	−0.9126	0.0176
5	−1.0000	−1.0016	0.0166	−0.9178	0.0168
$\tilde{\rho}$	0.7500	0.7627	0.0078		
$R = 25, R^2 = 0.5, \beta_1 = 1$					
1	1.0000	0.9982	0.0074	0.9139	0.0073
2	1.0000	0.9969	0.0133	0.9137	0.0132
3	1.0000	0.9977	0.0100	0.9141	0.0099
4	−1.0000	−0.9967	0.0119	−0.9132	0.0122
5	−1.0000	−0.9991	0.0111	−0.9160	0.0117
$\tilde{\rho}$	0.7500	0.7602	0.0094		
$R = 25, R^2 = 0.5, \beta_1 = 2$					
1	2.0000	1.9934	0.0105	1.8263	0.0107
2	1.0000	0.9954	0.0137	0.9130	0.0143
3	1.0000	0.9963	0.0117	0.9136	0.0123
4	−1.0000	−0.9939	0.0120	−0.9105	0.0120
5	−1.0000	−0.9966	0.0148	−0.9142	0.0153
$\tilde{\rho}$	0.7500	0.7480	0.0079		

and ones in y. In these scenarios, raising the intercept reduces the bias and standard deviation of the estimates. In the last scenario, the average estimate of ρ does not differ significantly from 0.75.

Finally, Table 6 contains three scenarios that differ by the number of nearest neighbors in the matrix W. In this table, we see that the bias rises

Table 6. Monte Carlo Results for Differing Numbers of Neighbors.

	β	$\tilde{\beta}_s$	σ	$\tilde{\beta}_{iid}$	σ
$m = 6$					
1	0.0000	0.0003	0.0069	0.0004	0.0069
2	1.0000	0.9969	0.0098	0.9166	0.0099
3	1.0000	0.9983	0.0085	0.9182	0.0086
4	−1.0000	−0.9967	0.0107	−0.9170	0.0102
5	−1.0000	−0.9987	0.0094	−0.9188	0.0100
$\tilde{\rho}$	0.7500	0.7640	0.0066		
$m = 12$					
1	0.0000	−0.0005	0.0063	−0.0005	0.0066
2	1.0000	0.9974	0.0096	0.9535	0.0098
3	1.0000	0.9987	0.0095	0.9549	0.0102
4	−1.0000	−0.9978	0.0101	−0.9540	0.0106
5	−1.0000	−1.0008	0.0104	−0.9568	0.0107
$\tilde{\rho}$	0.7500	0.7692	0.0100		
$m = 18$					
1	0.0000	0.0012	0.0089	0.0021	0.0093
2	1.0000	0.9980	0.0108	0.9677	0.0119
3	1.0000	1.0000	0.0096	0.9696	0.0106
4	−1.0000	−0.9989	0.0127	−0.9683	0.0132
5	−1.0000	−1.0011	0.0117	−0.9707	0.0120
$\tilde{\rho}$	0.7500	0.7724	0.0141		

as the number of nearest neighbors rises from $m = 6$ to $m = 18$, as does the standard deviation of $\tilde{\rho}$.

Although we have used the CAR specification, nothing in this development precludes using other specifications for spatial dependence in the disturbances such as MA models. The only requirement is to have a sparse Cholesky triangle of the variance-covariance or precision matrix.

In addition, nothing in this development precludes modeling spillovers in the specification of the explanatory variables (using specifications (8) or (9)). In fact, Pace and Zhu (2012) argue there are many advantages to separately specifying spatial spillovers and spatial dependence in the disturbances. They show that many situations lead to different forms of specifications for the spillovers and spatial dependence in the disturbances, and argue that it is more robust to provide separate parameters to govern spatial spillovers and spatial dependence in the disturbances. Using the same parameter for both the spillovers and the disturbances allows misspecification in the mean to affect the error dependence model and *vice versa*.

5. EMPIRICAL EXAMPLES

In this section, we use spatial probit to shed light on two applications based upon real estate data. The first example in Section 5.1 examines above and below average intensity of building activity as a function of elevation and other control variables. The second example in Section 5.2 examines mortgage default as a function of financial leverage and credit scores as well as their spatial lags.

5.1. A Development Application

Coastal areas often give rise to employment opportunities because many firms locate on the water to reduce transportation costs of their products or inputs. In addition, individuals may wish to live near the coast for recreational and other reasons. However, building in coastal areas carries risk of flooding. Moreover, subsidence and sea level rise may decrease existing elevations in the future as well as move the coast further inland. The question is how sensitive residential development is to elevation and distance to the coast. In particular, at which elevation does building become more or less probable.

We examined this by collecting building permit data from mypermitnow.com which manages building permit information technology for a number of local governments. We restricted this to Saint Tammany Parish Louisiana for areas west of 90° and south of 30.45°. In addition, we limited observations to those between 6 and 150 feet of elevation. The variable Height equals the elevation. The variable Distance measures distance to the coast for each house. We also obtain the individual house latitude and longitude. In summary, the variables Height, Distance, latitude, and longitude are measured at the level of the individual house. The block-level Population, Houses (number of houses), and Land area variables come from the 2010 Census data. We aggregate the individual house level data to the block group level. This leaves 744 blocks. Each block therefore has a discrete number of permits with values that go between 1 and 195. Although one

Table 7. Spatial and Independence Probit Parameter Estimates.

	Estimates			
	iid	*t*	Spatial	*t*
Intercept	−5.0219	−9.5807	−5.5615	−7.6630
log(Height)	0.4420	3.4840	0.4665	2.8651
log(Land area)	0.1009	2.1623	0.1274	2.3538
log(Distance)	0.1777	1.0156	0.1892	0.9889
log(Houses)	0.6841	8.7551	0.7289	9.2836
ρ			0.8544	8.3492
Log-Lik	−283.9234		−271.4353	
n	744			
Time (seconds)	43.8			

could model the data using some other distribution such as a Poisson, to illustrate spatial probit we set the dependent variable to 1 if the census block has above average building activity (greater number of permits than the average across all blocks which equals 5.36) and 0 otherwise.

We based W on contiguity and gave W a doubly stochastic scaling (the elements are non-stochastic in the statistical sense, but the matrix is doubly stochastic in the linear algebra sense). We estimated a CAR spatial probit model and the results appear in Table 7 along with conventional *iid* probit estimates.

The results show that above average development activity becomes more probable as elevation increases. The spatial dependence parameter ρ had the second largest t value (8.35) of any variable in the model and showed a relatively large magnitude of 0.85. Not surprisingly, unexplained factors that raise building activity tend to cluster geographically.

In terms of the spatial probit computational performance, despite having only 744 observations, it took about 44 seconds to compute the estimates. This came about due to slow convergence to the estimates rather than the time spent in any one iteration. The next application will show that a larger sample size may not require much more time to compute since large sample sizes can lead to a more defined mode in the log-likelihood.

5.2. A Mortgage Application

As an illustrative example, we examine mortgage default ($y = 1$ for default) in the Las Vegas area during 2008 for 79,652 locations as a function of the borrower's credit score and of their loan-to-value (LTV) ratio. Lower credit score borrowers tend to default more, all else equal. Individuals have incentive to default whenever they owe more than the house value (LTV >1). These two factors are the most important variables in conventional mortgage models. In this section, we examine the consequences of allowing spatial dependence among the disturbances and of allowing for spillovers. In particular, we examine the spillovers coming from neighbor credit scores and leverage (LTV).

The data come from Zhu and Pace (2014) and that paper contains a fuller description of the data as well as more elaborate mortgage modeling. The data contain locations of the houses with mortgages and this allows us to create a spatial weight matrix. Specifically, we use a contiguity-based weight matrix which yields a symmetric W. We rescale W to have both rows and columns that sum to 1 (doubly stochastic scaling).

Table 8 shows a number of interesting results. First, like the Monte Carlo experiments, most of the *iid* estimates are attenuated relative to the spatial probit estimates (barring the parameter on $W \cdot$ LTV) and the *iid* estimates have lower standard errors than their spatial counterparts. Second, spatial dependence (ρ) has the highest t statistic of any of the variables, including the important credit score and LTV variables. Third, modeling spatial dependence can make a difference in inference as neglecting it would lead a researcher to conclude that $W \cdot LTV$ was statistically significant (*iid* estimates), while a researcher using spatial probit would reach the opposite conclusion. Finally, even when modeling the spatial disturbances, the

Table 8. Spatial and Independence Probit Parameter Estimates.

	Estimates			
	iid	t	Spatial	t
Intercept	−0.4504	−96.0211	−0.4734	−74.7133
Score	−0.2573	−53.2515	−0.2717	−53.1068
$W \cdot$ Score	−0.0785	−8.5737	−0.0870	−8.3524
LTV	0.0938	18.8459	0.1015	20.2555
$W \cdot$ LTV	0.0206	2.1802	0.0160	1.5093
ρ			0.6716	64.4536
Log-Lik	−48,657.8951		−47,500.2170	
n	79,652			
Time (seconds)	80.5			

spillover related to neighbors' credit scores ($W \cdot \text{Score}$) still has both statistical and economic significance. Individuals tend to pay their mortgage when they are surrounded by neighbors who have historically timely paid their bills (even after modeling spatial disturbances). Economically, it may prove useful to default earlier than your neighbors due to possible negative externalities from foreclosures (houses sitting vacant, attracting vagrants, and decaying). If your neighbors do not seem prone to default, this lessens the advantage of early default. Alternatively, credit scores predict a number of behaviors. For example, insurance companies use this in setting rates as credit scores predict accident behavior. Dokko, Li, and Hayes (2015) found that credit scores of a couple help explain the length of the relationship and that credit scores seem to pick up "trustworthiness." Accordingly, having "trustworthy" neighbors may increase the borrower's utility from keeping the property and thus reduce default.

6. IMPLEMENTATION ISSUES AND OPPORTUNITIES

We discuss specific details in coding that make a material difference to performance in Section 6.1, opportunities to improve computational performance in Section 6.2, and issues that arise in estimating the log-likelihood in Section 6.3.

6.1. Implementation

A straightforward implementation in Matlab (and possibly other languages) will run many times slower, possibly 100 times slower than the approach used herein. The GHK requires observation-level programming (row by row of U) and this leads to a large overhead cost. Rather than loop, perform a task, loop, and perform another task, it reduces overhead cost to loop once, and perform many observation-level tasks together. Specifically, for the $k + 1$ parameters (β, ρ), a numerical gradient based on central differences would require $2(k + 1)$ log-likelihood evaluations and performing these together under one loop improves speed dramatically over computing a gradient for each parameter at a time for $2(k + 1)$ parameters.

Although Matlab has native sparse routines, these have too much overhead when working with vectors such as required by the GHK. To avoid this problem requires rolling your own sparsity by keeping track of indices of non-zero elements. As a simple example, suppose we have $n \times 1$ vectors a, b and wish to compute $a'b$. If rows u, v, w of b contain the non-zero elements and the others contain zeros, we could form $a_* = \begin{bmatrix} a(u) & a(v) & a(w) \end{bmatrix}'$, $b_* = \begin{bmatrix} b(u) & b(v) & b(w) \end{bmatrix}'$, and $a'b = a_*'b_*$. Given the indices, forming quantities such as a_* and b_* requires almost no time as indexing is one of fastest operations. The non-zero elements can be identified and stored for indexing outside of the loop. Even though ρ changes, the non-zeros always remain in the same locations for a given W.

Somewhat counterintuitively, the GHK probit procedure in some cases performs faster with larger n (e.g., $n > 1{,}000$) relative to smaller n (e.g., $n < 100$). This happens because small samples increase the difficulty of optimization which may lead to using many iterations or even a failure to converge. In contrast, GHK probit with large n and good starting values will converge quickly. Much depends upon the quality as well as quantity of the regressors and the imbalance between 0s and 1s in y.

6.2. Opportunities

Although estimation of the spatial probit is quite fast (at least relative to the past), there are many other opportunities for possible speed or speed relative to accuracy improvements, which we enumerate below. First, using an incomplete Cholesky decomposition that discards very low values in the Cholesky triangle could reduce the number of non-zeros and therefore increase the speed of computations at the cost of some reduction in numerical accuracy. For example, setting the threshold in the incomplete Cholesky routine to 0.001 as the minimum magnitude non-zero element in the triangle reduced the number of non-zeros by over 60 percent for W based on first-order contiguity.

Second, variants of the GHK that use other means of importance sampling, such as those proposed by Vijverberg (1996), Richard and Zhang (2007), as well as Phinikettos and Gandy (2011), might improve the precision of the estimates relative to running time. Indeed, Liesenfeld, Richard, and Vogler (2015) have already used some of the results of this study to aid in computing an EIS (efficient important sampling) version of the spatial probit model with excellent results.

Third, the current code was executed in Matlab and compiled code would run faster. Fourth, there may be decompositions in the spirit of

Stern (1992) or Phinikettos and Gandy (2011) that remove a more easily estimated part of the problem which could improve accuracy.

Fourth, using the analytical derivatives from Bolduc (1999) would improve speed and accuracy. The analytic derivatives actually require computations similar to the GHK (with some additional function calls involving densities) and so should cost more than k evaluations of the likelihood, whereas numerical derivatives for the β parameters currently require $2k$ likelihood evaluations. However, the analytic derivatives of the elements in the Cholesky decomposition would require more time to compute than the two likelihood function evaluations needed to find the numerical derivative of the likelihood with respect to the parameter ρ.

Lastly, the GHK is highly suited to parallel computing. All $2k+2$ likelihood evaluations required to compute numerical derivatives at each step in the optimization process could be done in parallel. In addition, each likelihood evaluation consists of R iterations, which are amenable to parallel processing. Although the number of general purpose CPU cores will continue to rise on desktop machines, some of the highest potential improvements on existing hardware involve use of graphical processor units (GPUs). Matlab (as well as other languages) can take advantage of GPUs to increase computational throughput. Currently, relatively inexpensive graphics cards for desktop computers have over 6,000 CUDA (Compute Unified Device Architecture) cores. If each core could handle one or part of the R iterations, this would help greatly in computing the GHK. Since the GPU approach has a high proportion of processors relative to memory, this interacts with sparsity because sparse calculations use fewer memory locations relative to the conventional GHK. Also, parallel techniques used in computing the Cholesky such as nested dissection would allow for much larger problem sizes.

6.3. Evaluation of Likelihood

Equations (48) and (49) reflect the conventional way of calculating the probabilities. However, these methods do not work well for large n.

To illustrate this, we examined a spatial probit regression from the Monte Carlo experiment with 100,000 observations based on the DGP in Eq. (50) with $\rho = 0.8$ where the first element of β equaled 0, two elements equaled 1.0 and the other two elements equaled -1.0. Subsequently, we computed the product of the 100,000 conditional probabilities for each of the 20 draws to yield 20 joint probabilities. Scaling the 20 estimated joint probabilities by the maximum of the 20 joint probabilities meant that the maximum scaled estimated joint probability equaled 1. The following sequence of scaled estimated joint probabilities by magnitude shows the problem: 1, 1.9×10^{-12}, 5.4×10^{-13}, 1.2×10^{-14}, ..., 3.9×10^{-81}. This extremely skewed sequence suggests that the arithmetic mean is not very efficient given this distribution of estimated probabilities. The result more or less equals the draw with the largest probability divided by R. Note that this problem becomes more acute for larger ρ and larger n.

In the development of GHK probit, we initially tried grid optimization using the conventional approach of multiplying the estimated conditional probabilities to form a joint probability estimate for each draw, and averaging over the joint probability estimates as shown in Eqs. (24) and (25) or (48) and (49). We found that this did not work in practice for large n (it behaved well for small n). Specifically, even though we knew the true parameters following the conventional approach did not result in a peak of the likelihood near the true parameters. As a work around, we did find that direct optimization of Eq. (53) performed well.

$$\sum_{i=1}^{n} \ln\left(R^{-1}\sum_{r=1}^{R}\tilde{P}_i(d_r)\right). \tag{53}$$

The individual estimated conditional probabilities are conditional upon a_i^* which in turn depends upon other random variables, so the individual $\tilde{P}_i(d_r)$ condition on different random quantities. The intuition is that averaging over the individual estimated conditional probabilities reduces the simulation noise or yields expected conditional probabilities. To give some idea of the dispersion of the estimated probabilities, we ran a simulation with $n = 1{,}000$, a pseudo-R^2 of 0.5 with a $\rho = 0.8$ with R, the number of draws, set to $1,000$. Overall, the standard deviation of the estimated probabilities associated with a particular observation was on average 0.067 which translates to a standard error of 0.0021. If one scales the standard error by observation with the mean of the estimated probabilities for that observation, this averages 0.0042 with a maximum of 0.0241. We do not pursue this alternative means of estimating the log-likelihood further here because we did not use Eq. (53) in computing the estimates. We used the gradient approach which differences the log-likelihood at each observation with respect to a small difference of parameter values and then aggregates across the observations. This appears to avoid some of the underflow issues which come from direct maximization of the log-likelihood. However, we point out the issue of the difficulty with the conventional method in Eqs. (24), (25) or (48), (49) and suggest further research into alternative methods of estimating the likelihood.

7. CONCLUSION

One of the common tools used in simulating the spatial probit likelihood is the GHK algorithm which uses a Cholesky decomposition. For general specifications of the variance-covariance matrix, the Cholesky triangle is dense and simulating the likelihood requires at least $O(n^2)$ operations and memory locations. This makes estimation of spatial probit and other similar models a *prodigious task* (Wang, Iglesias, & Wooldridge 2013). However, for spatial data, the variance-covariance matrix or precision matrix is often sparse, having a large proportion of zeros. Moreover, there are tools that maximize the sparsity of the Cholesky triangle of the variance-covariance matrix. Since the operation count of the GHK is directly related to the number of non-zeros in the Cholesky triangle, these tools can greatly accelerate the GHK and associated likelihood calculations.

Often, spatial precision matrices are sparser than the associated variance-covariance matrices. For example, for spatial autoregressive processes, the variance-covariance matrix is dense while the precision matrix is sparse. We show how to compute a variant of the GHK for the precision matrix that preserves sparsity.

The culmination of these modifications to the GHK allows computation of probabilities for virtually any sample size. For example, it takes two to four minutes to estimate a spatial probit model with 100,000 observations. We examine the ensemble of proposed techniques by conducting some illustrative Monte Carlo experiments that produced accurate estimates using a moderate number of iterations or draws for a variety of parameter values. In addition, we provide an empirical example with 79,652 observations on Las Vegas mortgages in 2008 where the spatial dependence parameter has a higher significance than the most important mortgage variables and modeling spatial dependence leads to one parameter changing from significant (using *iid* estimates) to not significant using spatial probit.

Having a fast GHK procedure that can handle large sample sizes facilitates development of fast spatial probit and spatial multinomial probit routines. Also, spatiotemporal data, after ordering by time, lead to a naturally sparse triangular system that should be well-suited for sparse GHK calculations. This applies to both panel data and data where observations occur at different locations over time as in Pace, Barry, Gilley, and Sirmans (2000). In addition, some of the techniques may help accelerate estimation of other spatial discrete choice models.

NOTES

1. Some of the earliest references are Geweke (1991), Hajivassiliou and McFadden (1990), or Keane (1994). As evidence of the impact of the GHK, Geweke (1991), has received over 640 Google Scholar citations.

2. In addition, the GHK also requires $O(n^3)$ operations for the Cholesky decomposition. However, this constitutes only part of the overall GHK computations. For small and moderate n, the other calculations needed for the GHK dominate the cost. However, for a sufficiently large n, the Cholesky decomposition operations would dominate the GHK calculations.

3. The GHK also has other labels and variants such as smooth recursive conditioning (SRC) or recursive importance sampling (RIS).

4. The reason for the slightly better performance of NE-SW is that it lies on the diagonal of the square area defined by the random uniform NS and EW coordinates. This is longer or more band like than the NS or EW orderings.

5. To see this, note that $(I_n - \rho W)^{-1} = I_n + \rho W + \rho^2 W^2 + \cdots$, so fill-in of zero elements in the inverse arises due to the matrix powers W^2, W^3, etc. A non-zero $(W^2)_{ij}$ indicates that observation j is the neighbor of the neighbor to observation i. Similarly, the non-zeros in W^3 give the neighbors to the neighbors of the neighbors. If W^j is dense for a large enough j, the inverse will be dense. This is just expressing the idea that every observation is a high-order relation to each other observation.

ACKNOWLEDGMENTS

The authors would like to acknowledge support for this research provided by the National Science Foundation (BCS-0136193, SES-0554937, SES-0729264, and award number 1212112). Additional funding was from the SEA Grant (Texas SEA Grant n NA06OAR41770076 and the Louisiana SEA Grant GOM/RP-02 programs). The statements, findings, conclusions, and recommendations are those of the authors and do not necessarily reflect the views of the National Science Foundation or the National Oceanic and Atmospheric Administration. We thank Aaron Lin for the building data. In addition, we would like to thank Shuang Zhu for her insightful comments and for the empirical mortgage data. Finally, we would like to thank seminar participants at Wuhan University for their helpful remarks.

REFERENCES

Amestoy, P., Davis, T. A., & Duff, I. S. (1996). An approximate minimum degree ordering algorithm. *SIAM Journal on Matrix Analysis and Applications*, *17*, 886–905.

Barry, R., & Pace, R. K. (1997). Kriging with large data sets using sparse matrix techniques. *Communications in Statistics: Computation and Simulation*, *26*, 619–629.

Beron, K. J., & Vijverberg, W. P. (2003). Probit in a spatial context: A Monte Carlo approach. *Advances in spatial econometrics* (pp. 169–196). Berlin: Springer-Verlag.

Beron, K. J., & Vijverberg, W. P. M. (2004). Probit in a spatial context: A Monte Carlo analysis. In L. Anselin, R. J. G. M. Florax, & S. J. Rey (Eds.). *Advances in spatial econometrics: Methodology, tools and applications* (pp. 169–195). Berlin: Springer-Verlag.

Berndt, E., Hall, B., Hall, R., & Hausman, J. (1974). Estimation and inference in nonlinear structural models. *Annals of Economic and Social Measurement*, *3*, 653–665.

Bolduc, D. (1999). A practical technique to estimate multinomial probit models in transportation. *Transportation Research B*, *33*, 63–79.

Cressie, N. (1993). *Statistics for spatial data*. (Revised ed.). New York, NY: Wiley.

Deák, I. (2011). Efficiency of Monte Carlo computations in very high dimensional spaces. *Central European Journal of Operations Research*, *19*(2), 177–189.

Dokko, J., Geng, L., & Hayes, J. (2015). Credit scores and committed relationships. *Finance and Economics Discussion Series 2015-081*. Board of Governors of the Federal Reserve System, Washington, DC.

Duff, I. S., Ersiman, A. M., & Reid, J. K. (1989). *Direct methods for sparse matrices*. Oxford University Press.

Genz, A. (1992). Numerical computation of multivariate normal probabilities. *Journal of Computational and Graphical Statistics*, *1*, 141–149.

Genz, A., & Bretz, F. (1999). Numerical computation of multivariate *t* probabilities with application to power calculation of multiple contrasts. *Journal of Statistical Computation and Simulation*, *63*, 361–378.

Genz, A., & Bretz, F. (2002). Comparison of methods for the computation of multivariate *t* probabilities. *Journal of Computational and Graphical Statistics*, *11*, 950–971.

George, A., & Liu, J. (1981). *Computer solution of large sparse positive definite systems*. Englewood Cliffs, NJ: Prentice-Hall.

Geweke, J. (1991). Efficient simulation from the multivariate normal and student-*t* distributions subject to linear constraints. *Computer science and statistics: Proceedings of the twenty-third symposium on the interface* (pp. 571–578). Alexandria, VA: American Statistical Association.

Hajivassiliou, V., & McFadden, D. (1990). *The method of simulated scores for the estimation of LDV models with an application to external debt crises*. Cowles Foundation Discussion Paper No. 967, Yale University.

Keane, M. (1994). A computationally practical simulation estimator for panel data. *Econometrica*, *62*, 95–116.

Lee, L.-F. (1995). Asymptotic bias in simulated maximum likelihood estimation of discrete choice models. *Econometric Theory*, *11*, 437–483.

LeSage, J. P. (2000). Bayesian estimation of limited dependent variable spatial autoregressive models. *Geographical Analysis*, *32*, 19–35.

LeSage, J., & Pace, R. K. (2009). *Introduction to spatial econometrics*. Boca Raton, FL: Taylor and Francis/CRC.

LeSage, J., Pace, R. K., Lam, N., Campanella, R., & Liu, X. (2011). New Orleans business recovery in the aftermath of Hurricane Katrina. *Journal of the Royal Statistical Society, Series A*, *174*(4), 1007–1027.

Liesenfeld, R., Richard, J.-F., & Jan, V. (2015). Likelihood evaluation of high-dimensional spatial latent Gaussian models with non-Gaussian response variables. LSU advances in econometrics conference.

McMillen, D. (1992). Probit with spatial autocorrelation. *Journal of Regional Science*, *32*, 335–348.

Pace, R. K., Barry, R., Gilley, O. W., & Sirmans, C. F. (2000). A method for spatial-temporal forecasting with an application to real estate prices. *International Journal of Forecasting*, *16*, 229–246.

Pace, R. K., & Barry, R. (1997). Quick computation of regressions with a spatially autoregressive dependent variable. *Geographical Analysis*, *29*, 232–247.

Pace, R. K., & Zhu, S. (2012). Separable spatial modeling of spillovers and disturbances. *Journal of Geographical Systems*, *14*(1), 75–90.

Phinikettos, I., & Gandy, A. (2011). Fast computation of high-dimensional multivariate normal probabilities. *Computational Statistics and Data Analysis*, *55*, 1521–1529.

Richard, J.-F., & Zhang, W. (2007). Efficient high-dimensional importance sampling. *Journal of Econometrics*, *141*(2), 1385–1411.

Rue, H., & Held, L. (2005). *Gaussian Markov random fields: Theory and applications*. Boca Raton, FL: CRC Press.

Stern, S. (1992). A method for smoothing simulated moments of discrete probabilities in multinomial probit models. *Econometrica*, *60*, 943–952.

Vijverberg, W. P. M. (1996). Monte Carlo evaluation of multivariate Student's *t* probabilities. *Economics Letters*, *52*, 1–6.

Wang, H., Iglesias, E. M., & Wooldridge, J. M. (2013). Partial maximum likelihood estimation of a spatial probit model. *Journal of Econometrics*, *172*(1), 77–89.

Zhu, S., & Pace, R. K. (2014). Modeling spatially interdependent mortgage decisions. *Journal of Real Estate Finance and Economics*, *49*(4), 598–620.

LIKELIHOOD EVALUATION OF HIGH-DIMENSIONAL SPATIAL LATENT GAUSSIAN MODELS WITH NON-GAUSSIAN RESPONSE VARIABLES

Roman Liesenfeld[a], Jean-François Richard[b] and Jan Vogler[a]

[a]*Institut für Ökonometrie und Statistik, Universität Köln, Cologne, Germany*
[b]*Department of Economics, University of Pittsburgh, PA, USA*

ABSTRACT

We propose a generic algorithm for numerically accurate likelihood evaluation of a broad class of spatial models characterized by a high-dimensional latent Gaussian process and non-Gaussian response variables. The class of models under consideration includes specifications for discrete choices, event counts and limited-dependent variables (truncation, censoring, and sample selection) among others. Our algorithm relies upon a novel implementation of efficient importance sampling (EIS) specifically designed to exploit typical sparsity of high-dimensional

Spatial Econometrics: Qualitative and Limited Dependent Variables
Advances in Econometrics, Volume 37, 35–77

ISSN: 0731-9053/doi:10.1108/S0731-905320160000037009

spatial precision (or covariance) matrices. It is numerically very accurate and computationally feasible even for very high-dimensional latent processes. Thus, maximum likelihood (ML) estimation of high-dimensional non-Gaussian spatial models, hitherto considered to be computationally prohibitive, becomes feasible. We illustrate our approach with ML estimation of a spatial probit for US presidential voting decisions and spatial count data models (Poisson and Negbin) for firm location choices.

Keywords: Count data models; discrete choice models; firm location choice; importance sampling; Monte Carlo integration; spatial econometrics

JEL classifications: C15; C21; C25; D22; R12

1. INTRODUCTION

Models that incorporate spatial dependence have received much attention over the last two decades. Foremost, there has been an explosive growth in the size of spatial databases across fields (including economics, social sciences, ecology, epidemiology and transportation, among others). Recent overviews including extensive lists of references can be found in the monographs of Arbia (2006) and LeSage and Pace (2009), as well as in the handbooks edited by Anselin, Florax, and Rey (2010) and Fischer and Nijkamp (2014).

In this paper, we propose a generic efficient importance sampling (EIS) procedure for accurate numerical evaluation of likelihood functions for a broad class of high-dimensional spatial "latent Gaussian models," in the terminology of Rue, Martino, and Chopin (2009). These are models in which the observable response variables are linked to a latent (state) Gaussian process that is spatially correlated. It follows that likelihood evaluation requires integration of a potentially high-dimensional interdependent state vector. When the response variables are themselves normally distributed with means that depend linearly on the state variables (and variances independent of the latter) integration of the state vector is carried out analytically.

However, response variables are frequently non-Gaussian as they represent discrete choices, event counts, censored and truncated data in which case likelihood evaluation requires numerical integration that becomes "prohibitively difficult" (Wang, Iglesias, & Wooldridge, 2013), poses "challenging problems" (Pace, 2014), and/or "sometimes impossible computational burdens" (Wang, 2014) for high-dimensional state processes. As discussed further in Section 2, a variety of alternative inference techniques have been applied to specific sub-classes of spatial models such as probit models. See also Wang (2014) for a recent survey of methods that can be applied to spatial models for limited- and censored-dependent variables.

In this paper, we propose a novel, generic, and flexible procedure to compute likelihoods for a wide range of spatial-dependent variable models for non-Gaussian responses. Our procedure is computationally feasible and numerically accurate even for very high-dimensional spatial applications. It consists of an original and powerful combination of two existing techniques. One is the EIS procedure of Richard and Zhang (2007) which belongs to the class of importance sampling (IS) procedures, where analytically intractable integrals are approximated by weighted averages of Monte Carlo (MC) random draws from an auxiliary IS density (Geweke, 1989; Robert & Casella, 2004). EIS provides a generic approach for constructing IS densities based on simple LS approximations designed to maximize the accuracy of MC approximations for target integrals like likelihood functions in the presence of latent variables. It has been successfully applied to numerous time-series applications, including high-dimensional ones. See Liesenfeld and Richard (2003, 2006, 2008), Bauwens and Galli (2009), Pastorello and Rossi (2010), Liesenfeld, Moura, and Richard (2010), Jung, Liesenfeld, and Richard (2011), Hafner and Manner (2012), or Kleppe and Skaug (2012). The other technique regroups tools that allow for fast computations on large sparse matrices, such as the reverse Cuthill-McKee algorithm (Alan & Liu, 1981) or the approximate minimum degree ordering (Amestoy, Davis, & Duff, 1996; LeSage & Pace, 2009; Pace & Barry, 1997; Pace & LeSage, 2016).

While combining EIS and sparse matrix algebra is conceptually fairly simple, it does require a novel implementation of EIS for spatial applications. EIS relies upon full sequential factorizations of the likelihood integral. It was developed specifically for time-series models with low-order Markovian (time-sequential) specifications for the latent state process, which directly translate into a likelihood factorization consisting of parsimoniously parameterized conditional densities. In this case, EIS relies upon recursive sequence of operations on low-dimensional (covariance) matrices.

However, spatial models share a critical characteristic, which prevent using standard EIS. They do not have a sequential Markovian structure, so that any likelihood factorization inherently consist of a sequence of conditional densities that depend on large (auxiliary) parameter vectors in high-dimensional applications. In such cases, standard EIS becomes rapidly computationally prohibitive as sample size (n) increases. However, spatial units typically have small numbers of direct neighbors so that spatial precision matrices are generally sparse with large proportions of zero entries. Thus, the key to computationally feasible high-dimensional spatial EIS lies in sequential factorizations that operate on precision matrices (instead of covariance matrices) and, foremost, preserve sparsity through the entire sequence. In particular, it requires an appropriate and automated (re)ordering of the data.

The likelihood factorization we propose resembles that used by Pace and LeSage (2016) to construct a fast GHK (Geweke, 1991; Hajivassiliou, 1990; Keane, 1994) IS procedure for high-dimensional spatial probit models. Their approach relies upon a sparse Cholesky factorization of the precision matrix as needed to apply GHK. Our approach is different in that it is based upon a sparse sequential factorization of the likelihood function based on a sequential partitioning of the precision matrix.[1] Nor is our approach restricted to probit applications. Last but not least, it is well known that the numerical accuracy of GHK rapidly deteriorates as the sample size n increases (Lee, 1997). In Section 4.1, we illustrate the fact that our ML-EIS estimates are numerically significantly more accurate than their GHK counterparts.

The only EIS application to a model without a Markovian structure we are aware of is that by Liesenfeld and Richard (2010), where the authors analyze a low-dimensional ($n=20$) probit model with a dense covariance matrix for the latent process. They do so by "brute-force" Cholesky factorization of the covariance matrix resulting in an EIS implementation whose extension to high-dimensional spatial applications would be computationally prohibitive, requiring $O(n^3)$ operations. In sharp contrast, the combination of EIS and sparse matrix algebra we propose requires computing times that are $O(n^\delta)$ with $\delta \ll 3$, keeping it computationally feasible even for high dimensions ($n = 5,000^+$). Foremost, it is generic in that it allows for considerable flexibility in the specification of the response process since adjustments for different response processes leave the core algorithm unchanged. As highlighted by an MC study for spatial probit and Poisson models in Section 4, our spatial EIS algorithm is very fast and remains numerically accurate even for very large n.

The remainder of this paper is organized as follows. The class of spatial models we consider is introduced in Section 2, with specific sub-classes and brief surveys of existing estimation methods. Our sparse spatial EIS algorithm is presented in Section 3, where we also analyze its performance by an MC study. Section 4 presents two empirical applications: a spatial probit model for US presidential voting decisions and spatial count data models for firm location decisions. Section 5 concludes.

2. SPATIAL-DEPENDENT VARIABLE MODELS

2.1. Baseline Model

Let $y = (y_1, \ldots, y_n)' \in \times_{i=1}^{n} S_i$ denote a vector of (non-Gaussian) observable response variables with support S_i, that are assumed to be mutually independent conditional on a spatial Gaussian latent vector $\lambda = (\lambda_1, \ldots, \lambda_n)'$. Let X denote an $(n \times \ell)$ matrix of observable exogenous variables. The class of models we consider here is characterized by the following two assumptions:

$$\text{A1}: \quad f(y|\lambda, X) \equiv \prod_{i=1}^{n} f(y_i|\lambda_i), \tag{1}$$

$$\text{A2}: \quad \lambda|X \sim \mathrm{N}_n\left(m, H^{-1}\right), \tag{2}$$

where m denotes the conditional mean of λ given X and H its sparse precision matrix. $\mathrm{N}_n(\cdot, \cdot)$ is used to denote an n-dimensional Gaussian distribution.

The spatial EIS algorithm we propose in Section 3 allows for considerable flexibility in the specification of $f(y_i|\lambda_i)$, m, and H (subject to sparsity of H). Nevertheless, for illustration purposes, we shall pay special attention to some of the specifications commonly discussed in the spatial literature, whereby[2]

$$\text{A3}: \quad H = \left(1/\sigma^2\right)(I_n - \rho W)'(I_n - \rho W), \quad \text{and} \tag{3}$$

$$\begin{aligned} &\text{A4.1}: \quad m = (I_n - \rho W)^{-1} X\beta, \quad \text{or} \\ &\text{A4.2}: \quad m = X\beta, \end{aligned} \tag{4}$$

where $\sigma > 0$ denotes a scale factor and I_n the n-dimensional identity matrix. The $(n \times n)$ matrix W represents distance or contiguity relations across units, and the scalar ρ measures the overall intensity of spatial correlation.

By convention, the diagonal elements of W are set equal to zero. In typical spatial settings, $w_{ij}>0$ only for direct neighbors and $w_{ij}=0$, otherwise. It follows that W and H are sparse matrices with increasingly large proportions of zeros as n increases. Conditions for the invertibility of $(I-\rho W)$ are discussed in LeSage and Pace (2009, Section 4.3). For matrices with real eigenvalues, a sufficient condition is that $\rho \in (1/\zeta_{\max}, 1/\zeta_{\min})$, where $\zeta_{\min}$ and $\zeta_{\max}$ denote the extreme eigenvalues of W. We note that the matrix W itself could be a (parametric) function of X. Since, however, this would not impact our EIS procedure, we ignore such extensions in our notation for H. Next, we briefly survey commonly used specifications for the conditional response density $f(y_i|\lambda_i)$ in Eq. (1).

2.2. *Spatial Probit Models*

If $y_i \in \{0,1\}$ denotes a binary choice outcome, such that $y_i=1$ if $\lambda_i \geq 0$ and $y_i=0$ otherwise, then y_i is binomial with a conditional probability density function (pdf)

$$f(y_i|\lambda_i) = \mathbb{1}(z_i\lambda_i < 0), \quad \text{with} \quad z_i = 1-2y_i, \tag{5}$$

where $\mathbb{1}(\cdot)$ denotes an indicator function. The latent variable λ_i is typically interpreted as a utility difference and the scale factor σ is set equal to one for identification. Eqs. (1)–(5) characterize spatial probit models.

Spatial probit models and multinomial extensions thereof have received considerable attention in the literature. See Case (1992) or McMillen (1992) for early contributions or LeSage and Pace (2009) for a textbook treatment. A few other references of interest (theory and/or applications) are McMillen (1995), Bolduc, Fortin, and Gordon (1997), Vijverberg (1997), Pinkse and Slade (1998), Beron and Vijverberg (2004), Smith and LeSage (2004), Wang and Kockelman (2009), Franzese, Hays, and Schaeffer (2010), Bhat (2011), and Elhorst, Heijnen, Samarina, and Jacobs (2013). Two recent papers deserve special mention in the context of the present paper. The first one is that by Wang et al. (2013), in which the authors propose a partial ML estimator (PMLE) obtained by regrouping observations into spatially correlated pairs and ignoring correlation across pairs.[3] Though partial, PMLE turns out to be statistically more efficient than generalized method of moments (GMM) counterparts used by Pinkse and Slade (1998). Naturally, we do expect additional efficiency gains by accounting for the complete spatial correlation structure. The second paper is that of Pace and LeSage (2016), in which the authors provide a fast implementation of GHK obtained by application of sparse matrix techniques to a likelihood factorization based on a Cholesky decomposition of the precision matrix H. Reliance upon sparse matrix techniques constitutes a very significant advance for high-dimensional applications. The procedure we propose below also relies upon sparse matrix operations but bypasses Cholesky to produce a direct sparse factorization of the likelihood immediately amenable to EIS (nor is it restricted to probit models).

2.3. Spatial Count Data Models

The Poisson distribution is often used when y_i is a count variable with support $\mathbb{N} = \{0, 1, 2, \ldots\}$. Specifically, let the distribution of y_i given λ_i be a Poisson distribution whose mean $\theta_i > 0$ is a monotone increasing function of λ_i. If, in particular, $\theta_i = \exp(\lambda_i)$ then $\theta_i > 0$ without restrictions on the state parameters (β, ρ, σ^2) in Eqs. (3) and (4), and the conditional pdf for y_i is given by

$$f(y_i|\lambda_i) = \frac{1}{y_i!} \exp\{y_i \lambda_i - \exp(\lambda_i)\}. \tag{6}$$

The Poisson models defined by Eqs. (1)–(4) and (6) represent spatial counterparts to the class of "parameter-driven" time-series models for serially correlated counts introduced by Zeger (1988). They also generalize a model used by Lambert, Brown, and Florax (2010) in which θ_i is a measurable function of spatially lagged θ_i's and X with $\sigma^2 \to 0$ in Eq. (3). Examples of applications of spatial Poisson models are found in LeSage, Fischer, and Scherngell (2007), Gschlößl and Czado (2008), Lambert et al. (2010), and Buczkowska and de Lapparent (2014).

The dispersion index (ratio between the variance and the mean) associated with the conditional Poisson distribution in Eq. (6) equals one. Marginalization with respect to λ_i generates overdispersion but may not suffice to capture the significant overdispersion frequently exhibited by count data. In such cases, the Poisson can usefully be replaced by a distribution allowing for conditional overdispersion, such as the negative binomial (Negbin). With its mean set equal to $\exp(\lambda_i)$ as above, the conditional pdf of a Negbin with dispersion parameter $s>0$ is given by

$$f(y_i|\lambda_i) = \frac{\Gamma(y_i+s)}{\Gamma(s)\Gamma(y_i+1)}\left(\frac{1}{1+\exp\{\lambda_i\}/s}\right)^s\left(\frac{\exp\{\lambda_i\}}{\exp\{\lambda_i\}+s}\right)^{y_i}, \tag{7}$$

where $\Gamma(\cdot)$ denotes the Gamma function. Its dispersion index is given by $1+\exp(\lambda_i)/s$ with a Poisson as limiting distribution when $s \to \infty$.

2.4. Censored Data

Recent years have witnessed an increasing number of applications involving spatially correlated (interval) censored data. Examples are infant mortality in Kneib (2005) and Banerjee, Wall, and Carlin (2003), water quality detection in Toscas (2010) and uranium grade measurements in Militino and Ugarte (1999). A fairly generic and easily generalizable representation of such models is one whereby λ_i is measured as zero if $\lambda_i \leqslant 0$ and is measured with error if $\lambda_i > 0$. The corresponding pdf is given by

$$f(y_i|\lambda_i) = f_m(y_i|\lambda_i)\cdot \mathbb{1}(\lambda_i>0) + \mathbb{1}(y_i=0)\cdot \mathbb{1}(\lambda_i \leqslant 0). \tag{8}$$

A special case is the spatial tobit model which assumes that λ_i is measured without error when $\lambda_i > 0$, in which case $f_m(y_i|\lambda_i)$ is $\mathbb{1}(y_i=\lambda_i)$ (Winkelmann & Boes, 2006). In such a case, the likelihood contribution of the censored observations has the same form as that of the spatial probit in Section 2.2 with a latent distribution that is Gaussian, conditional on the observed (uncensored) λ_i's. See LeSage and Pace (2009, Chap. 10) for an application to interregional origin-destination commuting flows using a data set where 15% of the observations are reported as zeros.

3. SPATIAL EIS

The EIS procedure introduced by Richard and Zhang (2007) has been designed for and successfully applied to likelihood evaluation for a wide range of high-dimensional time-series models for which there exists a natural ordering of the data and, foremost, where latent state processes are specified in the form of parsimonious low-order Markovian conditional densities. EIS takes full advantage of the "natural" likelihood factorization based on those parsimonious conditional densities to construct a forward sequential efficient importance sampler obtained by means of a backward-recursive sequence of low-dimensional auxiliary regressions and matrix operations.

The situation is quite different for the spatial models in Section 2. There is neither a natural ordering of the n observations nor a corresponding likelihood factorization that would consist of a sequence of parsimoniously parameterized conditional densities. Actually, sequential factorizations of the likelihood function (whether based upon H or H^{-1}) imply sequences of conditional densities with increasing numbers of auxiliary parameters. In this case, the EIS auxiliary regressions are not inherently parsimonious and EIS computations will need to operate on a sequence of large-dimensional parameter matrices. Thus, overall computing time of a "brute-force" EIS implementation would be $O(n^3)$, as in Liesenfeld and Richard (2010) where the authors analyze low-dimensional ($n = 20$) correlated probit models. Our key contribution in the present paper is that of proposing a novel implementation of EIS that takes full advantage of the sparsity of H to produce a recursive sequence of EIS regressions with a fixed small number of regression parameters irrespective of the sample size n and overall computing time $O(n^\delta)$ with $\delta \ll 3$ ($\delta \simeq 1$ for Poisson and Negbin models and $\delta \simeq 1.5$ for probits).

The necessary modifications of the original EIS principle while conceptually fairly simple are far from trivial in their identification and implementations. They are presented in the next five subsections: In Section 3.1, we outline the basic principle of EIS and in Section 3.2 its sequential implementation; in Section 3.3 we develop a generic sequential EIS designed for spatial models and apply it in Section 3.4 to spatial probit and in Section 3.5 to Poisson and Negbin models.

3.1. EIS Principle

Consider an analytically intractable integral of the form

$$L = \int_D \varphi(u)\,\mathrm{d}u, \tag{9}$$

where $\varphi(u) > 0$ on $D \subseteq \mathbb{R}^n$. In the context of our application, L represents the likelihood function for a model with a vector of latent variables

$u=(u_1,\ldots,u_n)'$. For ease of notation, fixed arguments (data and parameters) in φ and L are ignored. IS relies upon an auxiliary parametric density kernel $k(u;a)$, $a\in A$ with known integrating factor $\chi(a)$. The corresponding IS density on D is given by

$$g(u;a)=\frac{k(u;a)}{\chi(a)},\quad \text{with } \chi(a)=\int_D k(u;a)\,\mathrm{d}u. \tag{10}$$

The integral in Eq. (9) is then rewritten as

$$L=\chi(a)\int_D w(u;a)g(u;a)\,\mathrm{d}u,\quad \text{with } w(u;a)=\frac{\varphi(u)}{k(u;a)}, \tag{11}$$

and can be approximated by the following IS-MC estimate (Geweke, 1989; Robert & Casella, 2004):

$$\hat{L}_S(a)=\chi(a)\frac{1}{S}\sum_{s=1}^{S}w\left(\tilde{u}^{(s)};a\right), \tag{12}$$

where $\{\tilde{u}^{(s)}\}_{s=1}^{S}$ denotes S simulated i.i.d. draws from $g(u;a)$.

EIS aims at selecting a value of a which provides the best match between φ and k as functions in u in order to minimize the MC sampling variance of the resulting IS weight w. As proposed by Richard and Zhang (2007), a near optimal solution obtains as

$$\breve{a}=\arg\min_{a\in A}\int_D\left\{\ln\varphi(u)-\ln k(u;a)\right\}^2 g(u;a)\,\mathrm{d}u, \tag{13}$$

itself approximated by the least-squares (LS) solution

$$\hat{a}=\arg\min_{a\in A}\sum_{s=1}^{S}\left\{\ln\varphi\left(\tilde{u}^{(s)}\right)-\ln k\left(\tilde{u}^{(s)};a\right)\right\}^2, \tag{14}$$

where $\{\tilde{u}^{(s)}\}_{s=1}^{S}$ denotes S simulated i.i.d. draws from $g(u;\hat{a})$ itself. The fact that these draws depend on the solution $\hat{a}$ is addressed by constructing an iterative sequence of auxiliary LS regressions of the form

$$\hat{a}^{[j+1]} = \arg\min_{a \in A} \sum_{s=1}^{S} \left\{ \ln \varphi\left(\tilde{u}^{(s,j)}\right) - \ln k\left(\tilde{u}^{(s,j)}; a\right) \right\}^2, \tag{15}$$

where $\{\tilde{u}^{(s,j)}\}_{s=1}^{S}$ denotes S simulated i.i.d. draws from $g(u; \hat{a}^{[j]})$ with $j = 0, 1, 2, \ldots$. As illustrated below, an initial value $\hat{a}^{[0]}$ can be obtained by standard analytical approximation techniques such as second-order Taylor Series expansions of $\ln \varphi(u)$ for Gaussian kernels. Convergence of the sequence $\{\hat{a}^{[0]}, \hat{a}^{[1]}, \ldots\}$ to an approximate fixed point solution $\hat{a}$ is typically fast when the draws $\{\tilde{u}^{(s,j)}\}_{s=1}^{S}$ all obtain by transformations of a canonical set $\{\tilde{z}^{(s)}\}_{s=1}^{S}$ of common random numbers (CRNs).

3.2. Sequential EIS

In all but very low-dimensional applications, the EIS LS problem in Eq. (15) needs to be broken into low-dimensional auxiliary regression problems. This also applies to the EIS likelihood evaluation for spatial models with a latent state process λ as introduced in Section 2. For these models, we momentarily consider an arbitrary ordering of the observations (ordering will be discussed in Section 3.3.6). Let $u = \lambda - m$. It follows from Eq. (2) that

$$u \sim \mathrm{N}_n\left(0, H^{-1}\right). \tag{16}$$

For the joint Gaussian density $f(u)$ of u, we introduce the following back-recursive factorization:

$$f(u) = \prod_{i=1}^{n} f\left(u_i | u_{(i+1)}\right), \quad \text{with } u_{(i)} = (u_i, \ldots, u_n)', \ u_{(n+1)} = \varnothing. \tag{17}$$

Accounting for the measurement densities in Eq. (1), the likelihood function is factorized accordingly as

$$L = \int_D \prod_{i=1}^{n} \varphi_i\left(u_{(i)}\right) du, \quad \text{with } \varphi_i\left(u_{(i)}\right) = f(y_i | u_i) f\left(u_i | u_{(i+1)}\right), \tag{18}$$

where $f(y_i|u_i)$ obtains from $f(y_i|\lambda_i)$ through the linear transformation $u_i = \lambda_i - m_i$. The domain of integration is $D = \times_{i=1}^{n} D_i$, where D_i is the domain of $u_i = \lambda_i - m_i$ given y_i,

$$D_i = \{u_i | f(y_i|u_i) > 0\}. \tag{19}$$

The IS density $g(u;a)$ is itself to be factorized conformably into

$$g(u;a) = \prod_{i=1}^{n} g_i(u_i|u_{(i+1)};a_i), \tag{20}$$

with $a_i \in A_i$ and $a = (a_1, \ldots, a_n) \in A = \times_{i=1}^{n} A_i$. The conditional density g_i, which depends on $u_{(i)} = (u_i, u_{(i+1)})$, is defined as the normalized version of a parametric density kernel $k_i(u_{(i)};a_i)$, so that

$$g_i(u_i|u_{(i+1)};a_i) = \frac{k_i(u_{(i)};a_i)}{\chi_i(u_{(i+1)};a_i)}, \quad \text{with } \chi_i(u_{(i+1)};a_i) = \int_{D_i} k_i(u_{(i)};a_i)\, \mathrm{d}u_i, \tag{21}$$

where $\chi_n(u_{(n+1)};a_n) \equiv \chi_n(a_n)$. The forward-recursively factorized version of Eq. (11) follows from Eqs. (18)–(21) and can be written as

$$L = \chi_n(a_n) \int_D \left[\prod_{i=1}^{n} w_i(u_{(i)};a_{i-1},a_i)\right] \left[\prod_{i=1}^{n} g_i(u_i|u_{(i+1)};a_i)\right] \mathrm{d}u, \tag{22}$$

where

$$w_i(u_{(i)};a_{i-1},a_i) = \frac{\varphi_i(u_{(i)}) \cdot \chi_{i-1}(u_{(i)};a_{i-1})}{k_i(u_{(i)};a_i)}, \tag{23}$$

with $\chi_0(\cdot) \equiv 1$. Note that the integrating factor χ_{i-1} depends on $u_{(i)}$, not on $u_{(i-1)}$, which is why it is not assigned to the IS weight w_{i-1} but forward transferred into w_i. For any given $a \in A$, the corresponding IS-MC likelihood estimate obtains as

$$\hat{L}_S(a) = \chi_n(a_n) \cdot \frac{1}{S} \sum_{s=1}^{S} w(\tilde{u}^{(s)};a), \quad \text{with } w(\tilde{u}^{(s)};a) = \prod_{i=1}^{n} w_i\left(\tilde{u}_{(i)}^{(s)};a_{i-1},a_i\right), \tag{24}$$

where $\{\tilde{u}^{(s)}\}_{s=1}^{S}$ denotes S i.i.d. trajectories drawn from the sequential IS density $g(u;a)$ in Eq. (20). The corresponding sequential and forward recursive version of the EIS LS optimization problem in Eq. (15) is given by

$$\hat{a}_i = \arg\min_{a_i \in A_i} \sum_{s=1}^{S} \left\{ \ln\left[\varphi_i\left(\tilde{u}_{(i)}^{(s)}\right) \cdot \chi_{i-1}\left(\tilde{u}_{(i)}^{(s)}; \hat{a}_{i-1}\right)\right] - \ln k_i\left(\tilde{u}_{(i)}^{(s)}; a_i\right)\right\}^2, \quad i = 1, \ldots, n, \tag{25}$$

where $\{\tilde{u}^{(s)}\}_{s=1}^{S}$ denotes S independent trajectories drawn from $g(u;\hat{a})$ (and where the index $j = 0, \ldots, J$ for the fixed point iterations on $\hat{a}$ are deleted for ease of notation). As illustrated below, convergence to an (approximate) fixed-point solution is typically very fast under CRNs with J preset from 3 to 5. Note that $\hat{a} = (\hat{a}_1, \ldots, \hat{a}_n)$ is an implicit function of the model parameters, which we denote by ψ. Thus, the sequence of EIS-LS optimizations in Eq. (25) have to be rerun for each new value of ψ. The use of CRNs offers the additional advantage that the EIS-MC likelihood estimates $\hat{L}_S(\hat{a})$ are continuous in ψ and generally amenable to numerical differentiation.

It should be noted that, as discussed in Koopman, Lucas, and Scharth (2015), using the same set of CRNs for EIS optimization in Eq. (25) and likelihood estimation in Eq. (24) biases the latter. Note, however, that the subsequent log transformation to obtain the log-likelihood also generates a bias that is an increasing function of the MC variance of the likelihood estimate (Gourieroux & Monfort, 1996). As illustrated in DeJong, Liesenfeld, Moura, Richard, and Dharmarajan (2013), this "log bias" can be significantly larger than the "CRN bias," so that MC-variance reduction is by far the most critical component of EIS. Moreover, the CRN bias can trivially be eliminated at little costs by using a new set of random draws in Eq. (24).

A critical difference between spatial and Markovian time-series implementations of EIS lies in the fact that the dimension of $u_{(i)}$ in the likelihood factor φ_i is $n - i + 1$ (as opposed to a low order and fixed dimension for time series). Thus, for a Gaussian kernel k_i in $u_{(i)}$, for example, the EIS parameter a_i to be obtained from the EIS regressions (25) could potentially include $O([n - i + 1]^2)$ parameters for $i = 1, \ldots, n$, implying a prohibitive $O(n^3)$ dimension for the auxiliary parameter space A. Moreover, the construction of the resulting sequence of EIS densities in Eq. (21) will require operations on a sequence of $O([n - i + 1]^2)$ auxiliary parameter matrices. However, as we shall discuss in the next sections, a likelihood factorization based on a sequential partitioning of the sparse spatial precision matrix H together with a careful selection of the EIS kernels $k_i(u_{(i)}; a_i)$ enables us to take full advantage of the fact that the latent process in Eq. (2) is Gaussian and, accordingly, to reduce the set of parameters in regression (25) to a small and fixed number, irrespectively of i and n. It also allows us to use fast matrix functions for all high-dimensional matrix operations needed to construct the corresponding EIS densities. Such matrix operations for sparse matrices generally require significantly fewer operation counts and reduced memory requirements than the corresponding operations on dense matrices (Pace & LeSage, 2016), and are available in software packages like GAUSS and MATLAB.

Finally, we note that in the context of the probit model as discussed in Section 3.4, the back-recursive factorization of $f(u)$ we use yields an EIS implementation which is directly comparable to the spatial GHK implementation of Beron and Vijverberg (2004) and Pace and LeSage (2016), allowing for a direct comparison of relative numerical efficiency.

3.3. Sequential EIS for Spatial Models

In this section, we propose a generic spatial EIS implementation which applies to the broad class of (high-dimensional) spatial models introduced in Section 2.1. It only requires that, as function of u_i given y_i, $f(y_i|u_i)$ be of the form[4]

$$f(y_i|u_i) \equiv \mathbb{1}(u_i \in D_i) \cdot t_i(u_i), \tag{26}$$

where D_i is defined in Eq. (19). It follows from Eqs. (18), (25), and (26) that the log of the EIS density kernel $k_i(u_{(i)}; \hat{a}_i)$ has to LS approximate the log of the product

$$\varphi_i\big(u_{(i)}\big)\chi_{i-1}\big(u_{(i)}; \hat{a}_{i-1}\big) = \mathbb{1}(u_i \in D_i)\, t_i(u_i) f\big(u_i|u_{(i+1)}\big)\, \chi_{i-1}\big(u_{(i)}; \hat{a}_{i-1}\big). \tag{27}$$

As we shall see, the component $f(u_i|u_{(i+1)})$ in this EIS target function can be reformulated as a Gaussian kernel in $u_{(i)}$ and the factor $\chi_{i-1}(u_{(i)}; \hat{a}_{i-1})$ will include an additional Gaussian kernel in $u_{(i)}$. As the family of Gaussian kernels is closed under multiplications, it is natural to select for k_i a (truncated) Gaussian kernel in $u_{(i)}$ (notwithstanding the issue of dimensionality which restricts the choice of operational kernels), say[5]

$$k_i\big(u_{(i)}; a_i\big) = \mathbb{1}(u_i \in D_i)\exp\left\{-\frac{1}{2}\Big(u'_{(i)}P_i u_{(i)} - 2u'_{(i)}q_i + r_i + \ln(2\pi)\Big)\right\}, \tag{28}$$

with EIS auxiliary parameters $a_i = (P_i, q_i, r_i)$. We note that the dimension of a_i is $(n-i+1)^2/2 + (n-i+1) + 1$. It follows that a brute-force approach to the EIS regressions in Eq. (25) aiming at directly producing the optimal EIS parameters $\hat{a}_i$ would require $O(n^3)$ operations, which would be computationally prohibitive for large n's.

Our approach combines two critical components in order to reduce the computational burden to a manageable $O(n^\delta)$ with $\delta \ll 3$. One, to be discussed in Section 3.3.6, is the use of sparse matrix operations exploiting the sparsity of the spatial precision matrix. The other, which we discuss next, is a careful construction of the EIS density kernel k_i in Eq. (28) in order to dramatically reduce the number of parameters in the auxiliary EIS regressions to a small fixed number irrespectively of i and n. Such a construction of k_i proceeds in three successive steps: (i) the derivation of the integrating factor χ_i for the truncated Gaussian kernel k_i, as defined in Eq. (28); (ii) the reformulation of the Gaussian density $f(u_i|u_{(i+1)})$ as a Gaussian kernel in $u_{(i)}$; and (iii) the construction of k_i as a (truncated) product of Gaussian kernels that will result in the elimination of all high-dimensional factors in the auxiliary EIS regressions (25).

3.3.1. The Integrating Factors $\chi_i(u_{(i+1)}; a_i)$
In order to integrate the EIS density kernel $k_i(u_{(i)}; a_i)$ in u_i, we need first to partition its parameters P_i and q_i conformably with $u'_{(i)} = (u_i, u'_{(i+1)})$, say

$$P_i = \begin{pmatrix} p^i_{11} & P^i_{12} \\ p^i_{21} & P^i_{22} \end{pmatrix}, \quad q_i = \begin{pmatrix} q^i_1 \\ q^i_2 \end{pmatrix}. \tag{29}$$

Lemma 1. The integrating factor χ_i of the truncated Gaussian kernel k_i in Eq. (28) takes the form of a product of two kernels in $u_{(i+1)}$:

$$\chi_i\left(u_{(i+1)}; a_i\right) = \chi^1_i\left(u_{(i+1)}; a_i\right) \cdot \chi^2_i(v_{i+1}; a_i), \tag{30}$$

where χ^1_i is a Gaussian kernel in $u_{(i+1)}$ of the form:

$$\chi^1_i\left(u_{(i+1)}; a_i\right) = \exp\left\{-\frac{1}{2}\left(u'_{(i+1)}P^*_i u_{(i+1)} - 2u'_{(i+1)}q^*_i + r^*_i\right)\right\}, \tag{31}$$

with

$$P^*_i = P^i_{22} - \frac{p^i_{21}P^i_{12}}{p^i_{11}}, \quad q^*_i = q^i_2 - \frac{p^i_{21}q^i_1}{p^i_{11}}, \quad r^*_i = r_i - \frac{\left(q^i_1\right)^2}{p^i_{11}} + \ln p^i_{11}, \tag{32}$$

and χ^2_i is a non-Gaussian kernel that depends only on a_i and a scalar linear combination of $u_{(i+1)}$ given by

$$\nu_{i+1} = \alpha_i + \beta_i' u_{(i+1)}, \quad \text{where } \alpha_i = \frac{q_1^i}{p_{11}^i}, \quad \beta_i' = -\frac{p_{12}^i}{p_{11}^i}. \tag{33}$$

Proof. We rely upon the partitioning introduced in Eq. (29) in order to factorize k_i in Eq. (28) into a product of a truncated Gaussian density in u_i given ν_{i+1} and a Gaussian kernel in $u_{(i+1)}$. Standard Gaussian algebra produces the factorization of k_i

$$k_i\left(u_{(i)}; a_i\right) = \left[\chi_i^1\left(u_{(i+1)}; a_i\right)\right] \left[\mathbb{1}(u_i \in D_i) f_N\left(u_i | \nu_{i+1}, 1/p_{11}^i\right)\right], \tag{34}$$

where $f_N(\cdot | \nu_{i+1}, 1/p_{11}^i))$ denotes the density of a Gaussian random variable with mean ν_{i+1} and variance $1/p_{11}^i$. It immediately follows that:

$$\chi_i^2(\nu_{i+1}; a_i) = \int \mathbb{1}(u_i \in D_i) f_N\left(u_i | \nu_{i+1}, 1/p_{11}^i\right) du_i, \tag{35}$$

which, as a function of $u_{(i+1)}$, only depends on ν_{i+1}. ■

3.3.2. Kernel Representation of $f(u_i | u_{(i+1)})$

The following lemma regroups standard results for the forward-recursive factorization of the Gaussian density $f(u)$ in Eq. (17) based on a sequential partitioning of its precision matrix H as well as for a Gaussian kernel representation of the resulting conditional densities $f(u_i | u_{(i+1)})$.

Lemma 2. Let $u_{(i)} \sim \mathrm{N}_{n-i+1}(0, H_i^{-1})$ for $i = 1, \ldots, n$, with $H_1 = H$ for $u_{(1)} = u$. Let partition H_i conformably with $u_{(i)} = (u_i, u'_{(i+1)})'$ into

$$H_i = \begin{pmatrix} h_{11}^i & h_{12}^i \\ h_{21}^i & H_{22}^i \end{pmatrix}. \tag{36}$$

Then $u_{(i+1)} \sim \mathrm{N}_{n-i}(0, H_{i+1}^{-1})$ with

$$H_{i+1} = H_{22}^i - h_{21}^i h_{12}^i / h_{11}^i, \tag{37}$$

and $u_i | u_{(i+1)} \sim \mathrm{N}_1\left(-[h_{12}^i / h_{11}^i] u_{(i+1)}, 1/h_{11}^i\right)$, whose density can be represented by the following Gaussian density kernel for $u_{(i)}$:

$$f\left(u_i | u_{(i+1)}\right) = \frac{1}{\sqrt{2\pi}} \sqrt{h_{11}^i} \exp\left\{-\frac{1}{2} u'_{(i)} H_i^* u_{(i)}\right\}, \tag{38}$$

$$\text{where} \quad H_i^* = \begin{pmatrix} h_{11}^i & h_{12}^i \\ h_{21}^i & h_{21}^i h_{12}^i / h_{11}^i \end{pmatrix}. \tag{39}$$

3.3.3. *Construction of the EIS Kernel $k_i(u_{(i)}; a_i)$*

Using the specific forms of the integrating factor χ_i and the conditional density $f(u_i|u_{(i+1)})$ as provided in Lemmas 1 and 2, we can now construct the EIS kernel k_i in Eq. (28) such that it will result in an elimination of all high-dimensional factors in the EIS regressions (25). Following Eq. (27) and Lemma 1, the EIS target $\varphi_i\chi_{i-1}$ to be LS approximated by k_i is given by

$$\varphi_i\left(u_{(i)}\right)\chi_{i-1}\left(u_{(i)};a_{i-1}\right)=\mathbb{1}(u_i\in D_i)\left[f\left(u_i|u_{(i+1)}\right)\chi_{i-1}^1\left(u_{(i)};a_{i-1}\right)\right]\left[t_i(u_i)\chi_{i-1}^2(\nu_i;a_{i-1})\right], \tag{40}$$

where the product $t_i\chi_{i-1}^2$ is the sole non-Gaussian kernel. Thus, in order to reduce the dimensionality of the EIS LS regressions (25), we define k_i as the (truncated) product of the two Gaussian kernels already included in $\varphi_i\chi_{i-1}$ and of an additional EIS Gaussian kernel approximation to the non-Gaussian product $t_i\chi_{i-1}^2$ (or just t_1 for $i = 1$, since $\chi_0 \equiv 1$).

Thus, for $i > 1$, the kernel k_i in Eq. (28) is constructed through the following product of three Gaussian kernels:

$$k_i\left(u_{(i)};a_i\right) = \mathbb{1}(u_i \in D_i)\left[f\left(u_i|u_{(i+1)}\right)\chi_{i-1}^1\left(u_{(i)};a_{i-1}\right)\right]k_i^2\left(u_i,\nu_i;a_i^*\right), \tag{41}$$

where k_i^2 denotes a bivariate EIS Gaussian kernel approximation of the product $t_i\chi_{i-1}^2$ in Eq. (40), which can be written as

$$k_i^2\left(u_i,\nu_i;a_i^*\right) = k_i^2\left(\omega_i;a_i^*\right) = \exp\left\{-\frac{1}{2}\left(\omega_i'B_i\omega_i - 2\omega_i'c_i + d_i\right)\right\}, \tag{42}$$

with

$$\omega_i = \begin{pmatrix} u_i \\ \nu_i \end{pmatrix} = \gamma_i + \Delta_i u_{(i)}, \quad \gamma_i = \begin{pmatrix} 0 \\ \alpha_{i-1} \end{pmatrix}, \quad \Delta_i = \begin{pmatrix} e_i' \\ \beta_{i-1}' \end{pmatrix}, \quad e_i' = (1,0,\ldots,0), \tag{43}$$

and the EIS regression parameters $a_i^* = (B_i, c_i, d_i)$.

For $i=1$, we have $\chi_0 \equiv 1$, in which case k_1^2 only needs to approximate $t_1(u_1)$ and can be written as

$$k_1^2(u_1, \nu_1; a_1^*) = k_1^2(u_1; a_1^*) = \exp\left\{-\frac{1}{2}(b_1 u_1^2 - 2c_1 u_1 + d_1)\right\}, \tag{44}$$

with EIS regression parameter $a_1^* = (b_1, c_1, d_1)$. As we shall see below, similar univariate simplifications apply to the spatial probit model, for which $t_i(u_i) \equiv 1$, and to spatial count data models for which $D_i \equiv \mathbb{R}$ so that $\chi_i^2 = 1$.

With these definitions in place, it is now a simple matter to derive the recursion providing the parameters $a = (a_1, \ldots, a_n)$ of the EIS kernels k_i in Eq. (28) as a function of the EIS regression parameters $a^* = (a_1^*, \ldots, a_n^*)$ indexing the Gaussian kernel approximations k_i^2 in Eqs. (42) and (44). It amounts to combining the three Gaussian kernels in Eq. (41). For the ease of later reference, we regroup these recursion formulas in the following lemma.

Lemma 3. With k_i as defined in Eq. (41), the EIS auxiliary parameters $\{a_i\}_{i=1}^n$ in Eq. (28) with $a_i = (P_i, q_i, r_i)$ obtain through the following recursion:

For $i=1$ (k_i with only two Gaussian kernels),

$$P_1 = H_1^* + b_1 e_1 e_1', \qquad q_1 = e_1 c_1, \qquad r_1 = d_1 - \ln h_{11}^1. \tag{45}$$

For $i>1$ (k_i with three Gaussian kernels),

$$P_i = H_i^* + P_{i-1}^* + \Delta_i' B_i \Delta_i, \tag{46}$$

$$q_i = q_{i-1}^* + \Delta_i'(c_i - B_i \gamma_i), \tag{47}$$

$$r_i = r_{i-1}^* + d_i + \gamma_i' B_i \gamma_i - 2\gamma_i' c_i - \ln h_{11}^i, \tag{48}$$

where $(P_{i-1}^*, q_{i-1}^*, r_{i-1}^*)$ and (γ_i, Δ_i), as defined respectively in Eqs. (32) and (43) are all functions of $a_{i-1} = (P_{i-1}, q_{i-1}, r_{i-1})$.

3.3.4. Spatial EIS Implementation

With Lemmas 1–3, we now have in hands all the components we need to present our simplified spatial EIS implementation (auxiliary EIS regression, EIS sampling densities and corresponding IS weights). Foremost, we note that after elimination of the high-dimensional common factors in $\varphi_i\chi_{i-1}$ and k_i, as given, respectively, by Eqs. (40) and (41), the EIS regressions (25) simplify into

$$\hat{a}_i^* = \arg\min_{a_i^*} \sum_{s=1}^{S} \left\{ \ln\left[t_i\left(\tilde{u}_i^{(s)}\right)\cdot\chi_{i-1}^2\left(\tilde{\nu}_i^{(s)};\hat{a}_{i-1}\right)\right] - \ln k_i^2\left(\tilde{u}_i^{(s)},\tilde{\nu}_i(s);a_i^*\right)\right\}^2, \quad i = 1,\ldots,n, \tag{49}$$

where $\{\tilde{u}^{(s)}\}_{s=1}^S$ denotes S i.i.d. trajectories drawn from $g(u;\hat{a})$ (here again, the index $j = 0,\ldots,J$ for the fixed point iterations on $\hat{a}^*$ are deleted for ease of notation). It follows from Eqs. (49) together with Eqs. (42) and (44) that the EIS regressions are simple linear LS regressions of $\{\ln[t_i(\tilde{u}_i^{(s)})\chi_{i-1}^2(\tilde{\nu}_i^{(s)};\hat{a}_{i-1})]\}$ on a constant and $\{\tilde{u}_i^{(s)},\tilde{\nu}_i^{(s)},[\tilde{u}_i^{(s)}]^2,[\tilde{\nu}_i^{(s)}]^2,[\tilde{u}_i^{(s)}\tilde{\nu}_i^{(s)}]\}$ for $i>1$, and of $\{\ln[t_1(\tilde{u}_1^{(s)})]\}$ on a constant and $\{\tilde{u}_1^{(s)},[\tilde{u}_1^{(s)}]^2\}$ for $i=1$. Hence, the dimension of the regression is 6 for the more general case and 3 in the special cases ($i=1$, $t_i(u_i)\equiv 1$ or $D_i\equiv\mathbb{R}$) irrespectively of n and i.

The EIS density for u factorizes into a sequence of the following conditional densities for u_i given $u_{(i+1)}$:

$$g_i\left(u_i|u_{(i+1)},a_i\right) = \frac{\mathbb{1}(u_i\in D_i)\cdot f_N\left(u_i|\nu_{i+1},1/p_{11}^i\right)}{\chi_i^2(\nu_{i+1};a_i)}, \tag{50}$$

which results from dividing the kernel k_i as represented by Eq. (34) by the normalizing factor χ_i as given in Eq. (30). Thus, the EIS densities g_i are truncated Gaussian densities. Accounting for observation $i=1$ for which $\chi_0^2 = 1$, the corresponding IS weights as required for the MC-IS likelihood estimate in Eq. (24) are given by

$$w\left(\tilde{u}^{(s)};\hat{a}\right) = \frac{t_1\left(\tilde{u}_1^{(s)}\right)}{k_1^2\left(\tilde{u}_1^{(s)};\hat{a}_1^*\right)}\prod_{i=2}^{n}\frac{t_i\left(\tilde{u}_i^{(s)}\right)\chi_{i-1}^2\left(\tilde{\nu}_i^{(s)};\hat{a}_{i-1}\right)}{k_i^2\left(\tilde{\omega}_i^{(s)};\hat{a}_i^*\right)}, \tag{51}$$

which follows from Eqs. (23) and (24) together with Eqs. (40) and (41).

As already discussed in Section 3.2, the forward-recursive sequence of auxiliary regressions in Eq. (49) are to be rerun until a near fixed-point solution $\hat{a}$ is achieved. Specifically, at step $j=0$, an initial $\hat{a}^{[0]}$ can be constructed from initial values for $\hat{a}_i^*$ obtained by an analytical local approximation (such as Laplace) of the log products $\ln(t_i\chi_{i-1}^2)$ or by setting $\hat{a}_i^* = 0$. For iteration step $j = 1, \ldots, J$, the auxiliary regressions are run under CRNs i.i.d. trajectories simulated from $g(u|\hat{a}^{[j-1]})$. For all the applications presented below, we have found that convergence is very fast to the effect that $J = 3 - 5$ iterations suffice to produce a numerically highly efficient solution. This is hardly surprising in view of the fact that the two high-dimensional kernel components of k_i taken from the EIS target are already Gaussian.

3.3.5. *Pseudo-Code*

In conclusion of our generic presentation (and pending discussion of sparse operations in the next section), we now provide a pseudo-code summary of the spatial EIS algorithm. Full MATLAB codes are available at http://www.wisostat.uni-koeln.de/index.php?id=27287.

Spatial EIS Algorithm

For $j \geqslant 1$:

(i) *Use CRNs to generate S i.i.d. trajectories* $\{\tilde{u}^{(s)}\}$ *from* $g(u;\hat{a}^{[j-1]})$, *where* $\hat{a}^{[j-1]} = (\hat{a}_1^{[j-1]}, \ldots, \hat{a}_n^{[j-1]})$.

(ii) *For i = 1*

– *run the linear LS regression as defined by Eqs.* (44) *and* (49)

$$\ln t_1\left(\tilde{u}_1^{(s)}\right) = -\frac{1}{2}\left(b_1\left[\tilde{u}_1^{(s)}\right]^2 - 2c_1\left[\tilde{u}_1^{(s)}\right] + d_1\right) + \xi_1^{(s)}, \tag{52}$$

where $\xi_1^{(s)}$ denotes the implicit regression error term;

– *use the LS estimate* $\hat{a}_1^* = (\hat{b}_1, \hat{c}_1, \hat{d}_1)$ *and* H_1^* *in Eq.* (39) *to compute* $\hat{a}_1^{[j]} = (P_1, q_1, r_1)$ *according to Eq.* (45);

– *use Eqs.* (32) *and* (33) *to compute* $(P_1^*, q_1^*, r_1^*, \alpha_1, \beta_1)$.

For $i : 2 \to n$:

– *use* $(\alpha_{i-1}, \beta_{i-1})$ *to obtain the simulated values* $\tilde{\omega}_i^{(s)} = \left(\tilde{u}_i^{(s)}, \tilde{\upsilon}_i^{(s)}\right)'$ *according to Eq.* (43), *and* $\chi_{i-1}^2\left(\tilde{\upsilon}_i^{(s)}; \hat{a}_{i-1}^{[j]}\right)$ *from Eq.* (35), *and run the linear LS regression as defined by Eqs.* (42) *and* (49)

$$\ln\left[t_i\left(\tilde{u}_i^{(s)}\right)\cdot\chi_{i-1}^2\left(\tilde{\nu}_i^{(s)};\hat{a}_{i-1}^{[j]}\right)\right]=-\frac{1}{2}\left(\left[\tilde{\omega}_i^{(s)}\right]'B_i\left[\tilde{\omega}_i^{(s)}\right]-2\left[\tilde{\omega}_i^{(s)}\right]'c_i+d_i\right)+\xi_i^{(s)};\tag{53}$$

- *use the LS estimate* $\hat{a}_i^* = (\hat{B}_i, \hat{c}_i, \hat{d}_i)$ *together with* $(P_{i-1}^*, q_{i-1}^*, r_{i-1}^*)$ *and* H_i^* *in Eq.* (39) *to compute* $\hat{a}_i^{[j]} = (P_i, q_i, r_i)$ *according to Eqs.* (46)–(48);
- *use Eqs.* (32) *and* (33) *to compute* $(P_i^*, q_i^*, r_i^*, \alpha_i, \beta_i)$ *and pass them to step* $i + 1$.

(iii) *Construct the EIS density* $g(u; \hat{a}^{[j]}) = \prod_{i=1}^n g_i(u_i|u_{(i+1)}; \hat{a}_i^{[j]})$ *according to Eq.* (50).

If $j<J$, *then* $j\to j+1$ *and rerun steps* (i)–(iii), *else set* $\hat{a} = \hat{a}^{[J]}$ *and generate S i.i.d. trajectories* $\{\tilde{u}^{(s)}\}$ *from* $g(u;\hat{a})$ *and compute the EIS likelihood estimate from Eqs.* (24) *and* (51).

For $j=0$ (initialization of the fixed point iterations), the steps (ii) and (iii) can be run without the EIS regression in Eqs. (52) and (53) and with initial values for $\hat{a}_i^*$ obtained by second-order Taylor series approximations in u_1 to $\ln t_1$ $(i=1)$ and in (u_i, ν_i) to $\ln[t_i\chi_{i-1}^2]$ $(i>1)$, or even by setting $\hat{a}_i^* = 0$.

3.3.6. Sparse EIS Operations

While the EIS implementation presented in Section 3.3.4 already considerably simplifies the auxiliary regressions, the fact remains that the implementation operates on a sequence of potentially high-dimensional precision matrices (H_i) and related auxiliary parameters $(H_i^*, P_i^*, q_i^*, \beta_i, P_i, q_i)$ (Section 3.3.5). Thus, for an implementation that remains computationally feasible for high-dimensional applications with very large n's it is critical to preserve the initial sparsity of the spatial precision matrix H such that the entire sequence of those high-dimensional parameters obtain as sparse matrices. In that case, the reliance on sparse matrix functions can produce dramatic reduction in computing time, as highlighted by the pioneering contribution of Pace and LeSage (2016) for high-dimensional GHK implementations for spatial probit models.

Lemma 2 where the joint density $f(u)$ is factorized based on a sequential partitioning of H provides the key for sparse EIS operations. We start the recursive sequence with $H_1 = H$, which obviously needs to be sparse by assumption. Next, we note from Eqs. (37) and (39) that H_{i+1} and H_i^* essentially operate on the first row (and column) of the $(n-i+1)\times(n-i+1)$

matrix H_i. Thus, as long as we can maximize the sparsity of first row h_{12}^i of the H_i matrices when they are large (corresponding to low values of i), the number of floating point operations to compute the entire sequences $\{H_{i+1}\}$ and $\{H_i^*\}$ will be greatly reduced by the use of fast sparse matrix functions. In order to achieve this and before factorizing $f(u)$ according to Lemma 2 and running the EIS algorithm, we reorder the n spatial units relying upon a symmetric approximate minimum degree (SAMD) permutation that concentrates the non-zero elements of H in its lower right corner (Amestoy et al., 1996).[6] The effect of such a permutation is illustrated in Fig. 1 (right panel) where we plot the non-zero elements of a typical H matrix as shown before permutation in the left panel. The specific matrix we use contains 99.7% zero elements and is constructed in the same way as those we use for our MC study (Section 4) and spatial applications (Section 5). In turn, the sequential computation of the high-dimensional auxiliary parameters $(P_i, P_i^*, q_i, q_i^*, \beta_i)$ according to Lemmas 1 and 3 all depend upon the first row of H_i^* and, therefore, remain sparse under the initial SAMD permutation. Thus, the recursive computation of all the high-dimensional auxiliary parameter vectors required for the spatial EIS can be computed using computationally fast sparse matrix functions. This together with the low-dimensional auxiliary regressions (49) are the two key components of our sparse spatial EIS implementation which produce computing times that are $O(n^\delta)$ with $\delta \ll 3$, instead of $O(n^3)$ that would obtain under brute force EIS.

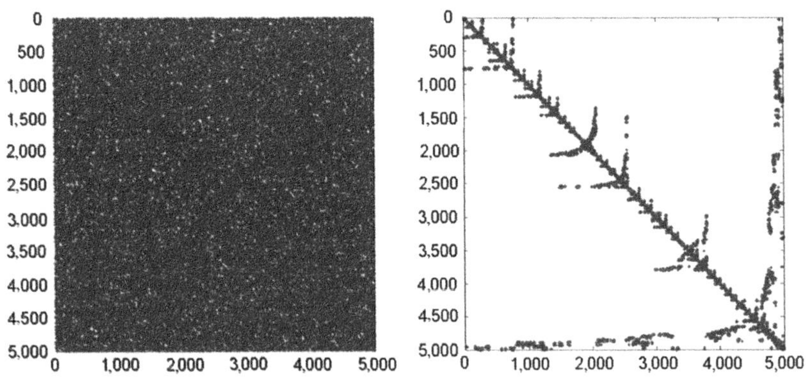

Fig. 1. Left panel: $(5,000 \times 5,000)$ spatial precision matrix H as defined in Eq. (3) and using a spatial weight matrix W assigning six neighbors to each spatial unit i; black dots indicate the non-zero elements; Right panel: H after reordering the spatial units using the symmetric minimum degree permutation (Amestoy, et al., 1996).

3.4. Spatial Probit Model

Under the spatial probit models in Eqs. (1)–(5), the two factors in the measurement density in Eq. (26) are given by

$$\mathbb{1}(u_i \in D_i) = \mathbb{1}(z_i u_i \leqslant -z_i m_i), \qquad t_i(u_i) \equiv 1. \tag{54}$$

It follows that the integrating factor χ_i^2 in Eqs. (30) and (35) is given by

$$\chi_i^2(\nu_{i+1}; a_i) = \Phi\left(-z_i\sqrt{p_{11}^i}[m_i + \nu_{i+1}]\right), \tag{55}$$

where Φ denotes the cdf of a standard normal. For ease of comparison with GHK, it proves convenient to redefine accordingly α_i and β_i in Eq. (33) as

$$\alpha_i = -z_i\sqrt{p_{11}^i}\left(m_i + \frac{q_1^i}{p_{11}^i}\right), \qquad \beta_i' = z_i\frac{p_{12}^i}{\sqrt{p_{11}^i}}, \tag{56}$$

so that $\chi_i^2(\nu_{i+1}, a_i) = \Phi(\nu_{i+1})$. Moreover, since in Eq. (40) $t_i(u_i) \equiv 1$, $\ln k_i^2$ in Eq. (42) only needs to approximate $\ln \Phi(\nu_i)$. This implies the following simplifications of the spatial EIS algorithm.

For $i = 1$ with $\chi_0 \equiv 1$ and $t_1 \equiv 1$, the factor in the EIS target (40) to be LS approximated by k_1^2 in Eq. (44) is $t_1\chi_0^2 = 1$. Hence, we immediately have $\hat{a}_1^* = (\hat{b}_1, \hat{c}_1, \hat{d}_1) = 0$ and according to Eq. (41) $k_1(u_{(1)}; a_1) = \mathbb{1}(u_1 \in D_1)$ $f(u_1|u_{(2)})$ (yielding a perfect fit).

For $i > 1$, the auxiliary kernel k_i^2 in Eq. (42) only depends on ν_i and Eqs. (42), (43), and (45)–(48) simplify accordingly into

$$k_i^2(u_i, \nu_i; a_i^*) = k_i^2(\nu_i; a_i^*) = \exp\left\{-\frac{1}{2}(b_i\nu_i^2 - 2c_i\nu_i + d_i)\right\}, \tag{57}$$

$$\gamma_i = \begin{pmatrix} 0 \\ \alpha_{i-1} \end{pmatrix}, \qquad \Delta_i = \begin{pmatrix} 0 \\ \beta_{i-1}' \end{pmatrix}, \tag{58}$$

$$P_i = H_i^* + P_{i-1}^* + b_i\beta_{i-1}\beta_{i-1}', \qquad P_1 = H_1^*, \tag{59}$$

$$q_i = q_{i-1}^* + (c_i - b_i\alpha_{i-1})\beta_{i-1}, \qquad q_1 = 0, \tag{60}$$

$$r_i = r^*_{i-1} + d_i + b_i\alpha^2_{i-1} - 2\alpha_{i-1}c_i - \ln h^i_{11}, \qquad r_1 = -\ln h^1_{11}, \tag{61}$$

and the EIS regressions for $i = 2, \ldots, n$ have the form

$$\ln \Phi\left(\tilde{\nu}_i^{(s)}\right) = -\frac{1}{2}\left(b_i\left[\tilde{\nu}_i^{(s)}\right]^2 - 2c_i\left[\tilde{\nu}_i^{(s)}\right] + d_i\right) + \xi_i^{(s)}. \tag{62}$$

The EIS weights in Eq. (51) are then given by

$$w\left(\tilde{u}^{(s)}; \hat{a}\right) = \prod_{i=2}^{n} \frac{\Phi\left(\tilde{\nu}_i^{(s)}\right)}{\exp\left\{-\frac{1}{2}\left(\hat{b}_i\left[\tilde{\nu}_i^{(s)}\right]^2 - 2\hat{c}_i\tilde{\nu}_i^{(s)} + \hat{d}_i\right)\right\}}. \tag{63}$$

As mentioned above, our EIS procedure covers GHK as a special case. Specifically, the IS density kernels under GHK are defined as

$$k_i\left(u_{(i)}; \cdot\right) = \varphi_i\left(u_{(i)}\right) = \mathbb{1}(z_i u_i \leqslant -z_i m_i) \cdot f\left(u_i | u_{(i+1)}\right), \tag{64}$$

with integrating factor $\chi_i(\nu_{i+1}; \cdot) = \Phi(\nu_{i+1})$. This is equivalent to setting $k_i^2 \equiv 1$ with $a_i^* = (b_i, c_i, d_i) = 0$ in Eqs. (57)–(63). The resulting IS weights in Eq. (63) simplify into

$$w\left(\tilde{u}^{(s)}; \cdot\right) = \prod_{i=2}^{n} \Phi\left(\tilde{\nu}_i^{(s)}\right), \tag{65}$$

where $\left\{\tilde{\nu}_i^{(s)}\right\}$ are drawn from the sequential GHK-IS truncated Gaussian densities associated with the kernels in Eq. (64). Since $a_i^* = 0$ is generally EIS-suboptimal, it immediately follows that GHK is numerically less efficient than EIS. See Liesenfeld and Richard (2010) for a low-dimensional application (for which sparse matrix operations are not required). In Section 4.1, we provide a high-dimensional comparison of the relative numerical efficiencies of GHK and EIS, which is trivial since we initialize EIS with the GHK sampler by setting $\hat{a}_i^* = 0$ to obtain the initial EIS auxiliary parameters $\hat{a}^{[0]}$. We note that our GHK implementation is directly comparable to those of Beron and Vijverberg (2004) and Pace and LeSage (2016).

3.5. Spatial Poisson Model

Under the Poisson models in Eqs. (1)–(4) and (6), the measurement density as given by Eq. (26) consists of

$$\mathbb{1}(u_i \in D_i) \equiv 1, \quad t_i(u_i) = f(y_i|u_i) = \frac{1}{y_i!}\exp\{y_i(m_i + u_i) - \exp(m_i + u_i)\}. \quad (66)$$

Therefore, $\chi_i^2 \equiv 1$ in Eqs. (30) and (35). It follows from Eq. (49) that for $i = 1, \ldots, n$, we only have to EIS approximate $\ln f(y_i|u_i)$ by a univariate (log)kernel $\ln k_i^2(u_i; a_i^*)$. Thus, Eqs. (42), (43), and (46)–(48) simplify accordingly into

$$k_i^2(u_i, \nu_i; a_i^*) = k_i^2(u_i; a_i^*) = \exp\left\{-\frac{1}{2}(b_i u_i^2 - 2c_i u_i + d_i)\right\}, \quad (67)$$

$$\gamma_i = 0, \qquad \Delta_i = \begin{pmatrix} e_i' \\ 0 \end{pmatrix}, \quad (68)$$

$$P_i = H_i^* + P_{i-1}^* + b_i e_i e_i', \quad q_i = q_{i-1}^* + c_i e_i, \quad r_i = r_{i-1}^* + d_i - \ln h_{11}^i. \quad (69)$$

The corresponding EIS regression $i = 1, \ldots, n$ is then given by

$$\ln f\left(y_i|\tilde{u}_i^{(s)}\right) = -\frac{1}{2}\left(b_i\left[\tilde{u}_i^{(s)}\right]^2 - 2c_i\left[\tilde{u}_i^{(s)}\right] + d_i\right) + \xi_i^{(s)}, \quad (70)$$

and the EIS weights in Eq. (51) by

$$w\left(\tilde{u}^{(s)}; \hat{a}\right) = \prod_{i=1}^{n} \frac{\exp\left\{y_i\left(m_i + \tilde{u}_i^{(s)}\right) - \exp\left(m_i + \tilde{u}_i^{(s)}\right)\right\}/y_i!}{\exp\left\{-\frac{1}{2}\left(\hat{b}_i\left[\tilde{u}_i^{(s)}\right]^2 - 2\hat{c}_i\tilde{u}_i^{(s)} + \hat{d}_i\right)\right\}}. \quad (71)$$

Since the EIS regressions only require approximating $\ln f(y_i|u_i)$ by $\ln k_i^2(u_i; a_i^*)$, it immediately follows that we can directly construct the joint EIS density from Eqs. (20), (21), (41), and (67) as

$$g(u; a) = \frac{f(u)\prod_{i=1}^{n} k_i^2(u_i; a_i^*)}{\chi_n(a_n)}, \quad (72)$$

where

$$\chi_n(a_n) = \int_{\mathbb{R}^n} f(u) \prod_{i=1}^{n} k_i^2 \left(u_i; a_i^*\right) \mathrm{d}u \tag{73}$$

obtains directly using standard Gaussian algebra since the integrand in Eq. (73) represents an untruncated Gaussian kernel in u. This construction of the joint EIS density in a single step eliminates sequential combination of large matrices and reduces accordingly the computing times (by a factor of 45 in the application presented in Section 4).

Replacing the conditional Poisson density in Eq. (6) by the conditional Negbin density in Eq. (7) only requires modifying accordingly the dependent variable $\ln f(y_i|u_i)$ in the EIS auxiliary regressions.

3.6. Censored Data

Under censoring as defined by Eq. (8), the pdf for censored data is of the generic form given by Eq. (26), where D_i can represent an arbitrary censoring interval for observation i. It follows that k_i^2 in Eq. (42) effectively depends on both u_i and ν_i so that the auxiliary EIS parameter a_i^* is now six-dimensional. Thus, our generic EIS algorithm as described in Section 3.3 immediately applies to a wide range of spatial models for censored data.

4. MONTE CARLO STUDY

In this section, we conduct an MC analysis of the statistical and numerical properties of ML-EIS estimates for spatial probit and Poisson models. We consider both the SAL (A4.1) and the SAE (A4.2) specifications introduced in Eq. (4), where the regression function $X\beta$ for unit i is specified as

$$x_i'\beta = \beta_0 + \beta_1 x_i. \tag{74}$$

The regressors x_i are assumed to be i.i.d. uniform random variables on the interval $(-3,4)$ for the probit models, and on the interval $(0,1)$ for the Poisson models. Following LeSage and Pace (2009, Chapter 4.11), we construct the spatial weight matrix W by simulating a pair of coordinates from a uniform-$(0,1)^2$ distribution for each spatial unit i. The points associated with those coordinates are then transformed into a spatial weight matrix W assigning six neighbors to each unit by using a Delaunay triangulation carried out with the function *fasymneighbors2.m* in Kelley Pace's spatial statistics toolbox for MATLAB 2.0 (http://www.spatial-statistics.com). Finally, the spatial weight matrix is row-standardized.

The parameter values for the four model specifications are selected as follows: For the probit models we set the regression parameters at $(\beta_0, \beta_1) = (-1.5, 3)$ and for the Poisson models at $(\beta_0, \beta_1, \sigma) = (-0.25, 0.8, 0.3)$, where σ is the scale parameter in Eq. (3) (for the probit models it is set equal to one to ensure identification). For all four specifications we vary the degree of spatial correlation by taking $\rho = 0.75$ or $\rho = 0.85$. We consider different sample sizes ranging from a moderate $n = 100$ to a fairly large $n = 5,000$. We only report the results for $n = 5,000$, which represents a compromise between our interest in large data sets and the need to conduct an extended MC analysis. We also ran a few tries with $n = 50,000$ in order to confirm the feasibility of our approach for very large sample sizes and to verify that computing times are indeed $O(n^\delta)$ with $\delta \ll 3$.

Using the Data-Generating Processes (DGPs) we just described we construct two different MC sampling distributions for the ML-EIS estimators. One is the conventional (finite-sample) *statistical* distribution (used for likelihood-based inference) and the other is the *numerical* distribution used to assess numerical accuracy (Richard & Zhang, 2007). The statistical distribution of the ML-EIS estimator is obtained by repeating the ML-EIS estimation for 50 different data sets using a single set of CRNs for EIS. In contrast, the numerical properties of the ML-EIS estimates as MC approximations to the true but infeasible ML estimates are analyzed by repeating the ML-EIS estimation for a given data set using 50 different sets of CRNs. Clearly, reliable statistical inference requires that numerical biases and standard deviations be negligible relative to statistical standard deviations.

As explained in Section 3.4, we use GHK to initialize our EIS procedure for spatial probit models. This enables us to trivially compare the statistical and numerical properties of ML-GHK and ML-EIS estimates for these models. Unfortunately, no such direct ML competitor is readily available for spatial count models.

ML-EIS estimates are computed using simulation sample size $S = 20$ and $J = 3$ EIS iterations. For the probit models with $n = 5,000$, a single likelihood EIS evaluation using a MATLAB code takes of the order of 45 s on an Intel i7 Core computer with 2.67 GHz. The corresponding computing time for the Poisson models is only 1 s, as we rely upon the joint EIS implementation described in Eq. (72). For the probit models GHK is much faster than EIS (by an approximate factor of 25), since it does not require (iterated) auxiliary regressions, but is also significantly less accurate. Thus, we compare EIS based on $S=20$ with GHK using $S=500$ in order to approximately equate computing times. For all ML estimations, we use the BFGS optimizer.

4.1. Spatial Probit Models

The main results of our four MC experiments for the spatial probit model are reported in Table 1. The DGP parameter values are listed in column 1. Statistical means, standard deviations, and root mean-squared errors (RMSEs) for ML-GHK and ML-EIS are reported in columns 2 and 3, respectively. "True" ML estimates, defined as ML-EIS estimates with $S = 1{,}000$, are listed in column 5. Numerical means, standard deviations, and RMSEs for ML-GHK and ML-EIS are listed in column 6 and 7, respectively.

Our main finding is that the ML-EIS estimates are statistically virtually unbiased and numerically highly accurate. The ratios between statistical and numerical standard errors range roughly from 20 to 100. Thus, statistical inference based on ML-EIS is largely unaffected by numerical errors and fully reliable.

In sharp contrast, ML-GHK estimates are statistically significantly biased with RMSEs 2–23 times larger than those of ML-EIS. Foremost, ML-GHK estimates are numerically considerably less accurate than their ML-EIS counterparts with RMSEs ratios ranging from 90 to 384. Clearly, statistical results obtained by ML-GHK are subject to large numerical errors and are essentially unreliable. In order to match ML-EIS numerical accuracy, GHK would require a prohibitively large simulation sample size S.

The explanation for such poor numerical performance is that the GHK-IS density $g(u;.)$ obtained from the kernels in Eq. (64) represents a very poor *global* approximation to the high-dimensional target $\prod_i \varphi_i(u_{(i)})$. In order to verify this conjecture, we present in Figure 2 histograms of the normalized IS weights $\overline{w}^{(s)} = w(\tilde{u}^{(s)};\cdot)/\sum_{s=1}^{S} w(\tilde{u}^{(s)};\cdot)$ for both EIS and GHK, as defined in Eqs. (63) and (65), respectively. A perfect IS fit would imply that $\overline{\omega}^{(s)} = 1/S, \forall s$. The histogram of the normalized GHK-IS weights exhibits extreme skewness with only 2 out of 500 weights that are effectively larger than zero (0.39 and 0.61). The corresponding histogram for the 500 EIS weights is clearly much better behaved. Our results are

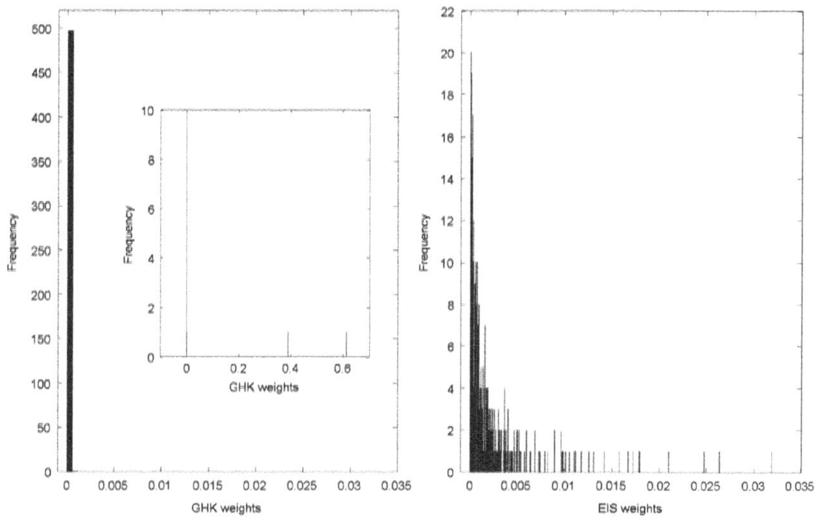

Fig. 2. Histogram of the normalized IS weights $w(u^{(s)};\cdot)/\sum_{s=1}^{S}w(u^{(s)};\cdot)$ of the GHK (plotted for different scales) and EIS procedure with $S=500$ for the likelihood of the SAE probit model with $\rho=0.85$. The model parameters ψ are set to their true values.

consistent with the findings of Pace and LeSage (2016), who also report an extremely skewed distribution of the GHK-IS weights for $n=100,000$ and $S=20$. As a remedy, they propose to replace the GHK likelihood estimate $\hat{L}_S=\chi_n\cdot\frac{1}{S}\sum_{s=1}^{S}\prod_{i=2}^{n}\Phi(\tilde{\nu}_i^{(s)})$, as defined by Eqs. (24) and (65), by the alternative estimate $\check{L}_S=\chi_n\cdot\prod_{i=2}^{n}\left[\frac{1}{S}\sum_{s=1}^{S}\Phi(\tilde{\nu}_i^{(s)})\right]$ which would remain unbiased if the terms of the sequence $\{\Phi(\tilde{\nu}_i^{(s)})\}_{i=2}^{n}$ were mutually uncorrelated. This condition, however, would need to be checked empirically for each application.

The results of the four MC experiments obtained by using Pace and LeSage's modified MC likelihood estimate $\check{L}_S$ using $S=500$ (GHK^{PL}) are reported in columns 4 and 8 of Table 1. They reveal that ML-GHK^{PL} performs significantly better than the standard ML-GHK in terms of statistical and numerical properties but remains dominated by ML-EIS with statistical RMSEs ratios ranging from 1 to 1.5 and numerical RMSEs ratios between 4 and 53.

Table 1. ML-EIS, ML-GHK, and ML-GHK^{PL} for the SAL and SAE Probit Model.

Parameter	True	Statistical Properties			True ML	Numerical Properties		
		GHK	EIS	GHK^{PL}		GHK	EIS	GHK^{PL}
SAL-probit model								
ρ	.750	.740	.750	.750	.748	.739	.748	.748
		(.006)	(.005)	(.005)		(.003)	(.0001)	(.0002)
		[.012]	[.005]	[.005]		[.009]	[.0001]	[.0006]
β_1	−1.500	−1.354	−1.498	−1.482	−1.502	−1.371	−1.502	−1.496
		(.061)	(.050)	(.055)		(.025)	(.0006)	(.002)
		[.158]	[.050]	[.057]		[.134]	[.0007]	[.007]
β_2	3.000	2.726	3.007	2.975	3.039	2.770	3.038	3.020
		(.121)	(.108)	(.114)		(.049)	(.001)	(.004)
		[.300]	[.108]	[.117]		[.273]	[.001]	[.019]
ρ	.850	.839	.850	.851	0.851	.840	.851	.853
		(.005)	(.003)	(.004)		(.003)	(.0001)	(.0002)
		[.012]	[.003]	[.004]		[.011]	[.0001]	[.002]
β_1	−1.500	−1.243	−1.516	−1.475	−1.489	−1.220	−1.488	−1.454
		(.076)	(.070)	(.072)		(.034)	(.002)	(.004)
		[.268]	[.072]	[.076]		[.272]	[.002]	[.036]
β_2	3.000	2.488	3.037	2.954	2.989	2.444	2.986	2.909
		(.145)	(.138)	(.140)		(.067)	(.003)	(.008)
		[.532]	[.142]	[.147]		[.549]	[.004]	[.080]

SAE-probit model								
ρ	.750	.380	.748	.771	.747	.364	.748	.800
		(.033)	(.028)	(.037)		(.024)	(.001)	(.005)
		[.372]	[.028]	[.042]		[.384]	[.001]	[.053]
β_1	−1.500	−1.108	−1.480	−1.520	−1.381	−1.027	−1.381	−1.504
		(.068)	(.111)	(.129)		(.011)	(.003)	(.020)
		[.398]	[.113]	[.130]		[.354]	[.003]	[.125]
β_2	3.000	2.246	2.987	3.078	2.879	2.133	2.880	3.107
		(.096)	(.158)	(.216)		(.015)	(.006)	(.038)
		[.760]	[.159]	[.229]		[.746]	[.006]	[.231]
ρ	.850	.482	0.848	.849	.843	.513	.843	.854
		(.033)	(.016)	(.019)		(.021)	(.0009)	(.002)
		[.369]	[.016]	[.019]		[.331]	[.0009]	[.012]
β_1	−1.500	−.894	−1.483	−1.434	−1.444	−.898	−1.443	−1.476
		(.076)	(.140)	(.148)		(.018)	(.004)	(.012)
		[.610]	[.141]	[.162]		[.546]	[.004]	[.034]
β_2	3.000	1.829	3.013	2.937	2.845	1.759	2.844	2.821
		(.067)	(.176)	(.180)		(.019)	(.007)	(.019)
		[1.173]	[.177]	[.191]		[1.086]	[.008]	[.031]

Notes: The reported numbers for ML-EIS, ML-GHK, and ML-GHK^{PL} are mean, standard deviation (in parentheses), and RMSE (in brackets). The simulation sample size for EIS is $S = 20$ and for GHK and GHK^{PL} $S = 500$. The true ML values are the ML-EIS estimates based on $S = 1,000$.

4.2. Spatial Poisson Models

The MC results for the Spatial SAL and SAE Poisson model are reported in Table 2. They show that for all four DGPs and for all parameters, the ML-EIS estimators are virtually unbiased with S as low as 20. Numerical accuracy is high with means that are close to the "true" ML values and standard deviations that are significantly smaller than their statistical counterparts.

We conclude that likelihood-based inference results obtained by spatial EIS for probit and Poisson models with $n = 5,000$ are numerically very accurate even with MC sample sizes as low as 20. As for the dependence on n, we have run experiments with larger n's (up to 50,000) and have found computing times of the order of $O(n^{1.5})$ for the probit models and virtually

Table 2. ML-EIS for the SAL and SAE Poisson Model.

Parameter	True	Statistical Properties	True ML	Numerical Properties
SAL-Poisson model				
ρ	.750	.750	.756	.756
		(.019)		(.0007)
		[.019]		[.0008]
β_1	−.250	−.249	−.254	−.254
		(.017)		(.0001)
		[.017]		[.0001]
β_2	.800	.800	.801	.800
		(.032)		(.0006)
		[.032]		[.0007]
σ	.300	.294	.286	.285
		(.015)		(.0009)
		[.016]		[.0015]
ρ	.850	.854	.841	.842
		(.018)		(.002)
		[.018]		[.002]
β_1	−.250	−.241	−.188	−.186
		(.022)		(.003)
		[.024]		[.004]
β_2	.800	.786	.737	.735
		(.034)		(.003)
		[.036]		[.004]
σ	.300	.291	.285	.284
		(.014)		(.003)
		[.016]		[.003]

Table 2. *(Continued)*

Parameter	True	Statistical Properties	True ML	Numerical Properties
SAE-Poisson model				
ρ	.750	.747	.741	.741
		(.031)		(.002)
		[.031]		[.002]
β_1	−.250	−.244	−.237	−.236
		(.038)		(.0006)
		[.038]		[.0007]
β_2	.800	.794	.760	.760
		(.048)		(.0002)
		[.048]		[.0002]
σ	.300	.301	.304	.303
		(.026)		(.002)
		[.026]		[.002]
ρ	.850	.855	.849	.849
		(.024)		(.002)
		[.025]		[.002]
β_1	−.250	−.223	−.276	−0.272
		(.065)		(.006)
		[.070]		[.008]
β_2	.800	.794	.830	.830
		(.043)		(.0005)
		[.043]		[.0005]
σ	.300	.289	.304	.302
		(.033)		(.003)
		[.035]		[.004]

Notes: The reported numbers for ML-EIS are mean, standard deviation (in parentheses), and RMSE (in brackets). The simulation sample size for EIS is $S = 20$. The true ML values are the ML-EIS estimates based on $S = 1,000$.

$O(n)$ for the Poisson models under the simplified implementation according to Eq. (72).

5. EMPIRICAL APPLICATIONS

In this section, we present two empirical applications relying upon ML-EIS. One uses a spatial probit model for voting decisions at the county level in the 1996 US presidential election, and the other a spatial count model (Poisson and Negbin) for firm location decisions in US manufacturing. Both models rely upon the SAL specification A4.1 in Eq. (4).

5.1. Spatial Probit for the 1996 US Presidential Election

We use an SAL probit to model the voting decisions of the $n = 3,110$ US counties in the 1996 US presidential election. The dependent variable y_i equals one if the Democratic Candidate Bill Clinton won the majority in county i and zero if the Republican candidate Bob Dole won. The SAL specification is the same as that used for the MC study in Section 4, expect that x_i in Eq. (74) is now a vector which includes the log urban population and the following four educational level variables (expressed as a proportion of the county population): some years at college, associate degrees, college degrees and graduate or professional degrees. The data are taken from LeSage's spatial econometric toolbox (http://www.spatial-econometrics.com).

Spatial dependence reflects the fact that voters from neighboring counties tend to exhibit similar voting patterns. As was the case for our MC study, we construct W using the geographical coordinates (latitude and longitude) of the counties and transforming them by a Delaunay triangulation in order to assign to each county its six "closest" neighbors. As in Section 4.1, the ML-EIS parameter estimates rely upon simulation sample size $S=20$ and $J=3$ EIS iterations, while ML-GHK uses $S=500$.

Following, for example, Beron and Vijverberg (2004), we also compute average marginal effects defined as:

$$\frac{1}{n}\sum_{i=1}^{n}\frac{\partial \text{prob}(y_i = 1|X, W)}{\partial x_i} = \frac{1}{n}\sum_{i=1}^{n}\phi\left(h_i^{\frac{1}{2}}\left[v_{i1}x_1'\beta + \cdots + v_{in}x_n'\beta\right]\right)\cdot h_i^{\frac{1}{2}}v_{ii}\beta, \quad (75)$$

where $\phi(\cdot)$ denotes the standardized normal density function, v_{ij} is the element (i,j) of the matrix $V = (I - \rho W)^{-1}$, and h_i is the precision of the marginal distribution of the error u_i. These marginal effects account for both the direct impact on λ_i of a change in $x_i'\beta$ and its indirect impact through the spatial interdependence reflected by the matrix V.

The results are reported in Table 3. Asymptotic (statistical) standard deviations are derived from a numerical approximation of the Hessian. Numerical standard deviations are based upon 50 ML-EIS estimations using different CRNs. They confirm our earlier finding that ML-EIS is numerically far more accurate than ML-GHK. Our ML-EIS estimate of ρ

Table 3. ML-EIS and ML-GHK results for the SAL Probit Model for the 1996 US Presidential Election

Variable	Parameters		Marg. Eff.	
	GHK	EIS	GHK	EIS
Constant	.634*	.597*		
	(.120)	(.122)		
	[.033]	[.0001]		
Urban population	8.445	4.894	3.131	1.745
	(5.494)	(5.635)	(2.058)	(2.030)
	[1.386]	[.0003]	[.512]	[.0002]
Some college	−3.192*	−2.792*	−1.183*	−.996*
	(.470)	(.479)	(.167)	(.165)
	[.122]	[.0005]	[.044]	[.0002]
Associate degree	1.118	.901	.414	.321
	(.893)	(.909)	(.331)	(.323)
	[.241]	[.0005]	[.089]	[.0002]
College degree	−2.056*	−1.885	−.762*	−.672
	(.783)	(.805)	(.299)	(.295)
	[.171]	[.0006]	[.063]	[.0002]
Graduate/professional degree	5.185*	4.610*	1.922*	1.644*
	(1.371)	(1.405)	(.507)	(.450)
	[.317]	[.0009]	[.115]	[.0004]
Spatial lag (ρ)	.508*	.633*		
	(.024)	(.025)		
	[.009]	[.0001]		
Log-likelihood	−1947.3	−1910.2		

Note: The reported numbers are mean ML-EIS and ML-GHK estimates for the parameters and the marginal effects, the asymptotic (statistical) standard deviation (in parentheses) and the numerical standard deviation (in brackets). The asymptotic standard deviation for the ML parameter estimates are obtained from a numerical approximation to the Hessian and those for the marginal effects are obtained as MC approximation using 2,000 draws from the asymptotic distribution of the ML estimators. The simulation sample size for EIS is $S = 20$ and for GHK $S = 500$; *statistically significant at the 1% level.

is highly significant and implies strong spatial dependence across neighboring counties, in line with the Bayesian MCMC results obtained by LeSage and Pace (2009, Table 10.3) for the 2000 US presidential election. Our results also confirm the downward bias of the ML-GHK estimates of ρ, as already observed in our MC study. The ML-EIS estimates of the β parameters and the corresponding marginal effects are systematically lower in absolute value than their ML-GHK counterparts. Under ML-EIS only two variables have a significant impact: negative for *some college* and positive for *graduate/professional degree*. Thus, higher education levels play in favor of Clinton. Finally, ML-EIS produces a significantly higher value than ML-GHK for the maximized log likelihood. This confirms a negative bias we had previously observed when comparing GHK with "brute force" EIS for $n=20$ in Liesenfeld and Richard (2010).

5.2. Spatial Count Model for US Firms Location Choices

In this section, we apply the spatial count models (Poisson and Negbin) introduced in Section 2.3 to US firm births (start-ups) at the county level ($n = 3,078$) during the period 2000–2004. We rely upon a data set from Lambert et al. (2010, Section 6), hereafter LBF, who applied a two-step limited-information ML (LIML) procedure to estimate an "observation-driven" version of the SAL-Poisson model introduced in Section 2.3, with $\sigma \rightarrow 0$ in Eq. (3). Instead we apply Full-Information ML (FIML) to the "parameter-driven" version ($\sigma > 0$) of that model. Spatial correlation is expected to reflect such factors as industry clustering and regional economic development policies. We refer the reader to LBF for an insightful discussion of the covariates used in the SAL regression.

The dependent variable y_i is defined as the cumulative number of new single-unit start-ups from 2000 to 2004. Following LBF, we construct the weight matrix W using the Delaunay triangulation algorithm to assign eight neighbors to each county. The set of explanatory variables consists of location factors of the counties related to agglomeration economies, market structure, labor market, infrastructure, and the fiscal policy regime. The agglomeration variables are the manufacturing share of employment (*Msemp*), total establishment density (*Tfdens*), percentage of manufacturing establishments with less than 10 (*Pelt10*), and more than 100 employees (*Pemt100*). The market structure variables are median household income (*Mhhi*), population (*Pop*), and the share of workers in creative occupations (*Cclass*). Properties of the regional labor markets are measured by the average wage per job (*Awage*), net flows of wages per commuter (*Netflow*), Unemployment rate (*Uer*), percentage of adults with associate degree (*Pedas*). The variables characterizing the regional infrastructure are the public road density (*Proad*), interstate highway miles (*Interst*), public expenditures on highways per capita (*Hwypc*), the percentage of farmland to total county area (*Avland*). The fiscal policy variables are a tax business climate index (*Bci*), per capita government expenditures on education (*Educpc*). Also included in the set of regressors are dummy variables identifying counties as belonging to metropolitan (*Metro*) or micropolitan (*Micro*) areas.

Our SAL-Poisson ML-EIS estimates obtained with an MC sample size $S=20$ and $J=3$ EIS iterations are reported in the left panel of Table 4. They are mostly in line with those reported in LBF's Table 6, though generally with significantly smaller statistical standard deviations, as expected from using FIML instead of LIML. We observe significant sign changes for only three covariates *Pelt10*, *Awage*, and *Netflow*. Three other parameters have the same sign but are, nevertheless, significantly different

Table 4. ML-EIS results for the SAL Poisson and Negbin Model for Firm Location Choice

Variable		Poisson			Negbin	
Constant	−1.113*	(.130)	[.044]	−.855*	(0.139)	[.0002]
Msemp	.032*	(.002)	[.0005]	.042*	(0.002)	[.00003]
Pelt10	.006*	(.0009)	[.0002]	.005*	(0.001)	[.00001]
Pemt100	−.014*	(.002)	[.0004]	−.015*	(0.002)	[.00002]
Tfdens	−.003	(.011)	[.004]	−.056*	(0.018)	[.0001]
Mhhi	−.250	(.278)	[.134]	.517	(0.369)	[.005]
Pop	.006*	(.0002)	[.0001]	.013*	(0.001)	[.00002]
Cclass	.059*	(.003)	[.001]	.084*	(0.004)	[.00001]
Uer	.030*	(.006)	[.003]	.047*	(0.010)	[.0001]
Pedas	.030*	(.006)	[.002]	.035*	(0.007)	[.00002]
Awage	−.025*	(.003)	[.001]	−.035*	(0.005)	[.00003]
Netflow	−.004*	(.0005)	[.0002]	−.016*	(0.001)	[.00001]
Proad	.020	(.010)	[.004]	.053*	(0.012)	[.00003]
Interst	.003*	(.0004)	[.0002]	.004*	(0.0006)	[.000003]
Avland	−.003*	(.0005)	[.0002]	−.004*	(0.0006)	[.00001]
Bci	.095*	(.009)	[.004]	.028	(0.011)	[.00002]
Educpc	.006*	(.001)	[.0005]	.004*	(0.001)	[.00001]
Hwypc	−.044*	(.007)	[.003]	−.032*	(0.008)	[.00006]
Metro	1.025*	(.037)	[.009]	.823*	(0.040)	[.0002]
Micro	.683*	(.038)	[.006]	.541*	(0.036)	[.00003]
Spatial lag (ρ)	.514*	(.018)	[.008]	.321*	(0.024)	[.0006]
σ	.697*	(.013)	[.002]	.261*	(0.042)	[.002]
s				2.902*	(0.204)	[.008]
Log likelihood		−10,720			−10,325	

Notes: The reported numbers are mean ML-EIS estimates for the parameters, the asymptotic (statistical) standard deviation (in parentheses) and the numerical standard deviation (in brackets). The asymptotic standard deviation for the ML parameter estimates are obtained from a numerical approximation to the Hessian. The simulation sample size for EIS is $S=20$; *statistically significant at the 1% level.

(based on the FIML standard deviations): *Pemt100*, *Pop* and *Pedas*. Overall our results confirm LBF's conclusion that counties with agglomeration economies, labor availability, low costs for labor, availability of skilled labor, a business-friendly infrastructure and fiscal policy were more likely to attract new start-ups. However, there are two key differences with LBF's results. One is that we find a significantly higher estimate of the spatial correlation parameter ρ: 0.514 (0.018) instead of 0.181 (0.062). The other is that our estimate of σ is 0.697 (0.013) and implies a strong rejection of LBF's specification where σ is set equal to zero.

Since counts frequently exhibit over-dispersion, we also estimated a SAL-Negbin model version that, as explained above, only requires minor modifications of the baseline spatial-EIS algorithm. The ML-EIS Negbin results are reported in the right panel of Table 4. The estimates of the regression coefficients are largely in agreement with those obtained under the Poisson specification, with only one statistically significant sign difference for *Mhhi*. The dispersion parameter estimate of s equals 2.902 (0.204) and is statistically significantly smaller than infinity, implying rejection of the Poisson model, as further confirmed by a large log-likelihood difference of 395. The Negbin estimate of σ is significantly lower (0.261 instead of 0.697), but this was to be expected from the substitution of an over-dispersed Negbin for the Poisson. Last but not least, we also find a significantly lower estimate of ρ (0.321 instead of 0.514). These differences suggest that a significant part of the variation in the firm-birth events across counties, which was attributed to shocks with global spatial feedback and feed-forward transmission between locations under the Poisson model, is interpreted as conditional over-dispersion together with lesser spatial transmission under the Negbin model. Numerical accuracy is good for the Poisson model and excellent for the Negbin specification. While we could easily improve the numerical accuracy of the Poisson estimates by increasing S, we decided there was little reason for doing so, since the Poisson model is strongly rejected against the Negbin model.

6. CONCLUSIONS

We have proposed a generic EIS-based procedure for numerically accurate likelihood evaluation of a broad class of high-dimensional spatial latent Gaussian models with non-Gaussian response variables (discrete choices, counts, truncation, censoring, and sample selection). Our algorithm consists of an original and powerful combination of sparse-matrix techniques and EIS. Its two key features are: (i) a novel forward-recursive implementation of EIS that is specifically constructed in such a way that it preserves the sparsity of large (auxiliary) precision matrices throughout the entire recursive sequence so that all high-dimensional EIS matrix operations can be performed using computationally fast sparse matrix functions; and (ii) a selection of auxiliary IS kernels that produces low-dimensional auxiliary EIS regressions, irrespectively of the data size n. The combination of these two features produces an algorithm that remains computationally feasible for large sample sizes n, with computing times of $O(n^{\delta})$ with $\delta \ll 3$ ($\delta \simeq 1.5$ for probit applications and $\delta \simeq 1$ for Poisson and Negbin models with n as large as 5,000, or even 50,000 in test trials).

Two empirical applications with sample sizes of the order of 3,000 have illustrated further the full potential of our spatial EIS procedure for accurate likelihood-based inference. While in the paper, we restricted our attention to probit, Poisson and Negbin models, the generic structure of our algorithm, as presented in Section 3, indicates that it can easily be applied to a much broader class of spatial models including but not limited to spatial ordered or multinomial probits, spatial tobit models, spatial truncated, and sample selection models. Most importantly, applications to such models would only require minor adjustments of the baseline spatial EIS implementation presented in Section 3 (essentially adapting the dependent variable in the auxiliary EIS regressions and the corresponding (E)IS weights). All in all, our procedure allows for numerically accurate likelihood-based inference in a broad class of high-dimensional spatial latent Gaussian models, a task hitherto considered to be computationally prohibitive.

While we have focussed in this paper on spatial models for cross-sectional applications, the efficiency of the spatial EIS motivates ongoing research where we extend EIS to panel models for non-Gaussian spatial response variables. In a current project, we have generalized the cross-sectional spatial EIS for a fairly extensive empirical study of urban crime using a spatio-temporal panel count model accounting for complex combination of latent spatial heterogeneity and spatial as well as temporal dependence (Liesenfeld, Richard, & Vogler, 2016). We also propose to investigate how one might improve further the performance of EIS in very high-dimensional spatial applications by taking advantage of the massively parallel desktop computing capabilities offered by Graphic Processing Units (GPUs) (Durham & Geweke, 2014).

NOTES

1. We initially attempted to implement EIS within the Cholesky framework used by Pace and LeSage (2016) but an EIS sequential updating of Cholesky factors appears to be computationally significantly more demanding than the sequential sparse matrix updating described in Section 3.2.
2. The terminology in the spatial literature is somewhat ambiguous. Under A3 and A4.1, the model is referred to as "spatial autoregressive" (SAR) or "spatial autoregressive lagged dependent" (SAL). Under A3 and A4.2 it is referred to as "Spatial Autoregressive Error" (SAE) or "Spatial Error Model" (SEM). See Anselin (1999) or LeSage and Pace (2009, Chapter 2), where alternative specifications for m and H are also discussed.
3. A closely related PMLE approach based on pairwise likelihood contribution is found in Heagerty and Lele (1998).
4. Our approach trivially covers the more general case where $f(y_i|u_i) = \sum_j \mathbb{1}(u_i \in D_{ij}) \cdot t_{ij}(u_i)$ as, for example, in Eq. (8).
5. The inclusion of r_i and $\ln(2\pi)$ in Eq. (28) simplifies tracking normalizing constants across recursive operations.
6. An SAMD permutation is also used by Pace and LeSage (2016) for their fast GHK implementation. However, there it is used in order to maximize the sparsity of the Cholesky factor of H.

ACKNOWLEDGMENTS

The authors thank the anonymous referee for its helpful and constructive comments. They also thank Jason Brown for providing the firm location choice data set used in this paper and Albrecht Mengel for providing access to the grid computing facilities of the Institute of Statistics and Econometrics at University of Kiel. R. Liesenfeld and J. Vogler acknowledge support by the Deutsche Forschungsgemeinschaft (grant LI 901/3-1). For the helpful comments and suggestions they provided on earlier versions of the paper, we thank seminar and conference participants at the University of Kiel, University of Cologne, University of Université catholique de Louvain (CORE), Erasmus University of Rotterdam, 2013 Spatial Statistics conference (Ohio), the 2013 Econometric Society European Meeting (Gothenburg), the 2013 International Conference on Computational and Financial Econometrics (London), the 2014 World Conference of the Spatial Econometrics Association (Zürich), the 2014 International Conference on Computational Statistics (Geneva), the 2014 ERSA Congress (Saint Petersburg), the Statistische Woche 2014 (Hannover) and the 2015 Advances in Econometrics Conference (Louisiana State University). A former version of this paper circulated under the title "Analysis of discrete-dependent variable models with spatial correlation."

REFERENCES

Alan, G., & Liu, J. W. H. (1981). *Computer solution of large sparse positive definite systems*. Englewood Cliffs, NJ: Prentice-Hall.

Amestoy, P. R., Davis, T. A., & Duff, I. S. (1996). An approximate minimum degree ordering algorithm. *SIAM Journal on Matrix Analysis and Applications*, *17*, 886–905.

Anselin, L. (1999). *Spatial econometrics*. University of Texas at Dallas School of Social Sciences, Bruton Center.

Anselin, L., Florax, R. J. G. M., & Rey, S. J. (2010). *Advances in spatial econometrics: Methodology, tools and applications*. Berlin: Springer.

Arbia, G. (2006). *Spatial econometrics*. Berlin: Springer.

Banerjee, S., Wall, M. M., & Carlin, B. P. (2003). Frailty modeling for spatially correlated survival data, with applications to infant mortality in Minnesota. *Biostatistics*, *4*, 123–142.

Bauwens, L., & Galli, F. (2009). Efficient importance sampling for ML estimation of SCD models. *Computational Statistics and Data Analysis*, *53*, 1974–1992.

Beron, K. J., & Vijverberg, W. P. M. (2004). Probit in a spatial context: A Monte-Carlo analysis. In Anselin, L., Florax, R., & Rey, S. J. (Eds.). *Advances in spatial econometrics: Methodology, tools and applications* (pp. 169–195). Berlin: Springer-Verlag.

Bhat, C. R. (2011). The maximum approximated composite marginal likelihood (MACML) estimation of multinomial probit-based unordered response choice models. *Transportation Research Part B: Methodological*, *45*, 923–939.

Bolduc, D., Fortin, B., & Gordon, S. (1997). Multinomial probit estimation of spatially interdependent choices: An empirical comparison of two new techniques. *International Regional Science Review*, *20*, 77–101.

Buczkowska, S., & de Lapparent, M. (2014). Location choices of newly created establishments: Spatial patterns at the aggregate level. *Regional Science and Urban Economics*, *48*, 68–81.

Case, A. C. (1992). Neighborhood influence and technological change. *Regional Science and Urban Economics*, *22*, 491–508.

DeJong, D. N., Liesenfeld, R., Moura, G. V., Richard, J.-F., & Dharmarajan, H. (2013). Efficient likelihood evaluation of state-space representations. *Reviews of Economic Studies*, *80*, 538–567.

Durham, G., & Geweke, J. (2014). Adaptive sequential posterior simulators for massively parallel computing environments. *Advances in Econometrics*, *34*, 1–44.

Elhorst, P., Heijnen, P., Samarina, A., & Jacobs, J. (2013). *State transfers at different moments in time: A spatial probit approach*. Working Paper No. 13006-EEF, University of Groningen.

Fischer, M. M., & Nijkamp, P. (2014). *Handbook of regional science*. Berlin: Springer-Verlag.

Franzese, R. J., Hays, J. C., & Schaeffer, L. M. (2010). *Spatial, temporal, and spatiotemporal autoregressive probit models of binary outcomes: Estimation, interpretation, and presentation*. Working Paper, University of Michigan, Ann Arbor.

Geweke, J. (1989). Bayesian inference in econometric models using Monte Carlo integration. *Econometrica*, *57*, 1317–1339.

Geweke, J. (1991). *Efficient simulation from the multivariate normal and student-t distributions subject to linear constraints and the evaluation of constraint probabilities* (pp. 571–578). University of Minnesota Department of Economics; Published in: Computer Science and Statistics: Proceedings of the Twenty-Third Symposium on the Interface.

Gourieroux, C., & Monfort, A. (1996). *Simulation-based econometric methods*. Oxford: Oxford University Press.

Gschlößl, S., & Czado, C. (2008). Does a Gibbs sampler approach to spatial Poisson regression models outperform a single site MH sampler? *Computational Statistics and Data Analysis*, *52*, 4184–4202.

Hafner, C. M., & Manner, H. (2012). Dynamic stochastic copula models: estimation, inference and applications. *Journal of Applied Econometrics*, *27*, 269–295.

Hajivassiliou, V. (1990). *Smooth simulation estimation of panel data LDV models*. Mimeo Yale University.

Heagerty, P. J., & Lele, S. R. (1998). A composite likelihood approach to binary spatial data. *Journal of the American Statistical Association*, *93*, 1099–1111.

Jung, R. C., Liesenfeld, R., & Richard, J.-F. (2011). Dynamic factor models for multivariate count data: An application to stock-market trading activity. *Journal of Business and Economic Statistics*, *29*, 73–85.

Keane, M. (1994). A computationally practical simulation estimator for panel data. *Econometrica*, *62*, 95–116.

Kleppe, T. S., & Skaug, H. J. (2012). Fitting general stochastic volatility models using Laplace accelerated sequential importance sampling. *Computational Statistics and Data Analysis*, *56*, 3105–3119.

Kneib, T. (2005). *Geoadditive hazard regression for interval censored survival times*. Working Paper No. 447, Sonderforschungsbereich 386, Ludwig-Maximilians-Universität München.

Koopman, S. J., Lucas, A., & Scharth, M. (2015). Numerically accelerated importance sampling for nonlinear non-Gaussian state space models. *Journal of Business and Economic Statistic*, *33*, 114–127.

Lambert, D. M., Brown, J. P., & Florax, R. J. G. M. (2010). A two-step estimator for spatial lag model of counts: Theory, small sample performance and application. *Regional Science and Urban Economics*, *40*, 241–252.

Lee, L.-F. (1997). Simulated maximum likelihood estimation of dynamic discrete choice statistical models – Some Monte Carlo results. *Journal of Econometrics*, *82*, 1–35.

LeSage, J. P., Fischer, M. M., & Scherngell, T. (2007). Knowledge spillovers across Europe: Evidence from a Poisson spatial interaction model with spatial effects. *Papers in Regional Science*, *86*, 393–422.

LeSage, J. P., & Pace, R. K. (2009). *Introduction to Spatial Econometrics*. Boca Raton: CRC Press, Taylor and Francis Group.

Liesenfeld, R., Moura, G. V., & Richard, J.-F. (2010). Determinants and dynamics of current account reversals: An empirical analysis. *Oxford Bulletin of Economics and Statistics*, *72*, 486–517.

Liesenfeld, R., & Richard, J.-F. (2003). Univariate and multivariate stochastic volatility models: Estimation and diagnostics. *Journal of Empirical Finance*, *10*, 505–531.

Liesenfeld, R., & Richard, J.-F. (2006). Classical and Bayesian analysis of univariate and multivariate stochastic volatility models. *Econometric Reviews*, *25*, 335–360.

Liesenfeld, R., & Richard, J.-F. (2008). Improving MCMC using efficient importance sampling. *Computational Statistics and Data Analysis*, *53*, 272–288.

Liesenfeld, R., & Richard, J.-F. (2010). Efficient estimation of probit models with correlated errors. *Journal of Econometrics*, *156*, 367–376.

Liesenfeld, R., Richard, J.-F., & Vogler, J. (2016). Likelihood based inference and prediction in spatio-temporal panel count models for urban crimes. *Journal of Applied Econometrics*, (forthcoming).

McMillen, D. P. (1992). Probit with spatial autocorrelation. *Journal of Regional Science, 32*, 335–348.

McMillen, D. P. (1995). Spatial effects in probit models: A Monte Carlo investigation. In L. Anselin & R. Florax (Eds.). *New directions in spatial econometrics* (pp. 169–195). Berlin: Springer-Verlag.

Militino, A. F., & Ugarte, M. D. (1999). Analyzing censored spatial data. *Mathematical Geology, 31*, 551–561.

Pace, R. K. (2014). Maximum likelihood estimation. In M. M. Fischer & P. Nijkamp (Eds.). *Handbook of Regional Science* (pp. 1553–1569). Berlin: Springer-Verlag.

Pace, R. K., & Barry, R. (1997). Quick computation of regressions with a spatially autoregressive-dependent variable. *Geographical Analysis, 29*, 232–247.

Pace, R. K., & LeSage, J. P. (2016). Fast simulated maximum likelihood estimation of the spatial probit model capable of handling large samples. *Advances in Econometrics, 37*, 3–34.

Pastorello, S., & Rossi, E. (2010). Efficient importance sampling maximum likelihood estimation of stochastic differential equations. *Computational Statistics and Data Analysis, 54*, 2753–2762.

Pinkse, J., & Slade, M. E. (1998). Contracting in space: An application of spatial statistics to discrete choice models. *Journal of Econometrics, 85*, 125–154.

Richard, J.-F., & Zhang, W. (2007). Efficient high-dimensional importance sampling. *Journal of Econometrics, 141*, 1385–1411.

Robert, C. P., Casella, G. (2004). *Monte Carlo statistical methods*. New York: Springer.

Rue, H., Martino, S., & Chopin, N. (2009). Approximate Bayesian inference for latent Gaussian models by using integrated nested Laplace approximations. *Journal of the Royal Statistical Society, Series B, 71*, 319–392.

Smith, T. E., & LeSage, J. P. (2004). A Bayesian probit model with spatial dependencies. In J. P. LeSage & R. K. Pace (Eds.). *Advances in econometrics, vol. 18, spatial and spatiotemporal econometrics* (pp. 127–160). Amsterdam: Elsevier.

Toscas, P. J. (2010). Spatial modelling of left censored water quality data. *Environmetrics, 21*, 632–644.

Vijverberg, W. P. M. (1997). Monte Carlo evaluation of multivariate normal probabilities. *Journal of Econometrics, 76*, 281–307.

Wang, H., Iglesias, E. M., & Wooldridge, J. M. (2013). Partial maximum likelihood estimation of spatial probit models. *Journal of Econometrics, 172*, 77–89.

Wang, X. (2014). Limited and censored-dependent variable models. In M. M. Fischer & P. Nijkamp (Eds.). *Handbook of regional science* (pp. 1619–1635). Berlin: Springer-Verlag.

Wang, X., & Kockelman, K. (2009). Bayesian inference for ordered response data with a dynamic spatial-ordered probit model. *Journal of Regional Science, 49*, 877–913.

Winkelmann, R., & Boes, S. (2006). *Analysis of microdata*. Berlin: Springer.

Zeger, S. L. (1988). A regression model for time series of counts. *Biometrika, 75*, 621–629.

PART III
DISCRETE DEPENDENT VARIABLES – BAYESIAN

THE IMPACT OF STORMS ON FIRM SURVIVAL: A BAYESIAN SPATIAL ECONOMETRIC MODEL FOR FIRM SURVIVAL

Mihaela Craioveanu[a] and Dek Terrell[b]

[a]*Department of Economics and Finance, University of Central Missouri, Warrensburg, MO, USA*
[b]*Department of Economics, Louisiana State University, Baton Rouge, LA, USA*

ABSTRACT

This paper investigates the impact of the storms Katrina and Rita on firm survival in the Orleans Parish. In particular, a Bayesian spatial probit model is used to assess the impact of a number of firm characteristics on firm survival. The results reveal that larger firms and those with less flooding are more likely to survive. Larger chain stores were less likely to return to the city than sole proprietorships. Spatial results also reveal a very strong spatial component to firm survival just after the storm which diminishes as time passed.

Spatial Econometrics: Qualitative and Limited Dependent Variables
Advances in Econometrics, Volume 37, 81–118

ISSN: 0731-9053/doi:10.1108/S0731-905320160000037010

Keywords: Spatial probit; firm survival; hurricane seem appropriate

JEL classifications: L25; C11

1. INTRODUCTION

In the form of hurricanes Katrina and Rita, New Orleans and the gulf coast faced perhaps the most devastating natural disasters in the history of the United States. The disasters left policy makers with difficult questions not addressed in the academic literature. Fortunately, the disaster also left researchers with empirical data from a natural experiment of epic proportions.

This study addresses one key policy question, the determinant of business survival and recovery in the aftermath of a large-scale natural disaster. According to the White House,[1] the Federal Government has provided over $114 billion in resources ($127 billion including tax relief) to the Gulf States to assist in rebuilding. State and Federal government officials faced the challenge of quickly implementing programs to minimize business failures and aide in the recovery process.

A lot of research has been developed to model business survival. Much of the academic literature focuses on business survival under normal operating conditions. One body of literature is based on the theoretical model developed by Jovanovic (1982), which predicts a positive relationship between firm survival and firm age. The implications predicted by this model have been tested empirically by several authors. Dunne, Roberts, and Samuleson (1989) study survival rates for plants in the manufacturing industry and find that survival increases with age and size. Audretsch (1991) finds the same relationship between firm survival, firm size, and age by analyzing survival rates for firms across different manufacturing industries. The study also finds that differences in survival rates are due to differences in technological regimes and industry-specific characteristics such as scale economies and capital intensity. The aggregation to the industry level is motivated by data limitations. Audretsch and Mahmood (1995) address this problem and extend the analysis by allowing firm-specific characteristics to influence survival rates. The authors estimate a hazard duration model for firms in the manufacturing sector and find that survival rates depend not only on industry-specific characteristics such as technological conditions and scale economies, but also on establishment-specific characteristics. The establishment-specific characteristics identified are ownership structure and size. The study also confirms the positive relationship between firm survival and firm size and age. Caves (1998), Sutton (1997), and Geroski (1995) present ample surveys of the relevant literature and offer a summary of the main stylized facts. For other countries, similar findings are found for: Canada (Baldwin, 1995; Baldwin & Gorecki, 1991; Baldwin & Rafiquzzaman, 1995), Portugal (Mata & Portugal, 1994; Mata Portugal & Guimaraes, 1995), and Germany (Wagner, 1994).

The second body of literature has evolved in the direction of analyzing firm survival at the product market level. A novelty of these studies is that firm survival is analyzed in the context of an evolutionary product market. The idea was first introduced by Gort and Klepper (1982), who identify five stages of product life cycle based on net entry in the market. The authors conclude that firm survival is determined by technological changes as the market evolves over the life cycle of the products. Agarwal (1996) and Agarwal and Gort (1996) analyze firm survival in the product life cycle framework. Agarwal (1997) follows the same framework and considers the influence on firm survival of both firm-specific characteristics and market product characteristics. The common finding across these studies is that the probability of survival changes across different stages of product life cycle development. Agarwal and Audretsch (2001) analyze the relationship between firm survival and size in the context of the product life cycle framework. The study finds that while there is a positive relationship between size and survival in the early stages of development of the market, this relationship is no longer true for later stages of development. Agarwal and Gort (2002) conduct an analysis on firm survival by grouping data according to the different stages of the product life cycle. The authors separate the different impacts on firm survival in industry-specific life cycle factors and firm-specific life cycle ones and take into account the effect of the two on each other. Their findings confirm the importance of both product and firm life cycle in determining firm survival.

Both of these strains of literature provide general guidance for our study, but do not specifically address the issue of business survival in a large-scale disaster. One exception is Dahlhamer and Tierney (1996), who investigate the impact of the Northridge earthquake on 1,110 Los Angeles firms. Dahlhamer and Tierney find that the key factors predicting business performance are business size, disruption of operations, earthquake shaking intensity, and utilization of post-disaster aid. Much of the other literature on economic consequences of disasters focuses on community level effects (Friesma, Caporaso, Goldstein, Lineberry, & McClearly, 1979; Rossi, Wright, Weber-Burdin, & Pereira, 1983; Wright, Rossi, Wright, & Weber-Burdin, 1979). Another approach is case study or qualitative analysis. For example, Runyan's (2006) qualitative analysis of Katrina is based on face-to-face interviews of 17 small business owners affected by the storm. Another related study is the street survey of businesses after hurricane Katrina conducted by Campanella (2007). On a dataset containing 651 businesses established before the storm hit and 56 new businesses over a period of 15 months, the author conducts weekly street surveys to assess the status of New Orleans businesses recovery. The author finds that locally owned businesses opened faster than large chain stores and businesses offering luxury items opened faster than businesses offering necessity goods. Finally, businesses located in less flooded areas opened faster when compared to ones located in more heavily flooded areas. The most closely related study to this one is LeSage, Pace, Lam, Campanella, and Liu (2011). This paper uses the same dataset of 673 establishments collected by Campanella (2007) in order to investigate business survival following hurricane Katrina. The authors employ a spatial probit model and argue the importance of the spatial component in business recovery. Other factors that influence survival are ownership type and flood levels.

Following LeSage et al. (2011), we employ a spatial probit model to explore the recovery of businesses in the wake of Hurricane Katrina. The primary difference between this study and LeSage et al. (2011) is the dataset. We use a dataset based on all employers filing unemployment reports (over 8,000 employers) rather than the Campanella database of 673 employers that he monitored in three corridors following the storm. Our dataset offers a more complete characterization of firms in the wake of the storm though with the limitation that we rely on the reports of firms concerning payrolls rather than eyewitness accounts at a particular geographic location.

We find that the spatial component is important in explaining business survival in the quarters immediately following the storm, but diminishes in importance in the long run. We also find that several firm characteristics influence firm survival. First, we find that larger firms are more likely to survive compared to smaller firms. Second, sole proprietorships are more likely to reopen compared to large chain stores. Finally, we find that establishments with less flooding are more likely to reopen.

The remainder of this paper is organized as follows. In the next section, we describe the dataset used. Sections 3 and 4 describe the spatial probit model specification and the methodology used. The results are presented in Section 5. Section 6 concludes.

2. DATA

This paper examines the impact of Hurricanes Katrina and Rita on firm survival in Orleans Parish, Louisiana. In particular, we focus on explaining firm survival for the whole parish and by industry. Hurricane Katrina was characterized as one of the deadliest hurricanes to make landfall in the United States. The most affected area was New Orleans, Louisiana, both in terms of loss of life and property destruction. The cause was the failure of the levee system resulting in flooding for most of the city and surrounding areas.

As previously stated, the key difference in this study and earlier work by LeSage et al. (2011) is the dataset employed. The dataset used in this study offers maximal breadth, covering the population of all firms filing unemployment insurance reports in Orleans Parish. The key advantage over other work is the use of this data for firms—a group estimated to cover 94–96% of all employees.

The primary disadvantage of the data used in this study is the reliance on reports by employers. Some employers chose to pay workers during the period immediately after the storm and others may have continued operations at a different location. In some sense, both issues implicitly involve defining open status of establishments in a manner other than a return to engaging in operations at the original location. Luckily, a close inspection of results and a comparison of our results reveals significant similarities to those of LeSage et al. (2011).

The dataset used for this study spans the period of 2004Q3–2007Q3. The most basic unit of observation in our dataset is an establishment. An establishment is a particular firm situated at a single geographical location. Some establishments are independent, while other ones are linked to a parent firm.[2] Because Hurricane Katrina hit on August 29, 2005, we estimate our model for each quarter following the 2005Q2 quarter when the hurricanes hit: 2005Q3, 2005Q4, 2006Q1, 2006Q2, 2006Q3, 2006Q4, 2007Q1, 2007Q2, and 2007Q3. For presentation purposes we present detailed results for 2005Q4, 2006Q2, and 2007Q2.

Just prior to the storm, a total of 9,592 firms reported employment or wages to the LDOL in Orleans Parish in 2005Q2.[3] Following Terrell and Bilbo (2007), this study considers firms as open if they reported either employment or wages in any month of a quarter to the LDOL for unemployment insurance purposes. Out of the 9,592 employers open in 2005Q2, 8,171 had valid latitudes and longitudes that could be used to determine location and append elevation data. This results in a sample of 8,171 employers with detailed quarterly data from 2004 to 2007, including employment, wages, and location. Using GIS maps, we are able to append flood depths to this data. Table 1 reports the total number of firms open in our sample in each quarter by industry type in Orleans Parish. The loss in terms of employers for the three chosen quarters are: 3,208 employers

(39.26%) for 2005Q4, 3,055 (37.39%) for 2006Q2, and 3,146 (38.50%) for 2007Q2.

The primary dependent variable for our study is a binary variable assuming values of 1 or 0, depending on whether the firm is open or not in a particular quarter. In assigning this value for each firm, we follow the methodology proposed in Terrell and Bilbo (2007).[4] Louisiana firms are required by law to report employment and wage data to the Louisiana Department of Labor (LDOL). This data is reported on a quarterly basis and is the basis for the Quarterly Census of Employment and Wages (QCEW). Several issues must be addressed to assess whether businesses are open or closed. First, the LDOL removes a firm from the data only after that particular firm fails to file a report for seven consecutive quarters or requests removal from the database. The standard BLS measure of number of employers is based on a count of the number of employers in the QCEW database. Typically, this provides a reasonable measure of the number of firms, and offers a potential advantage by not removing seasonal firms or those simply failing to report in a given quarter.

A second important issue is that some businesses report zero employment and wages, but are still considered open by the LDOL. For the purpose of our study, these firms will not be considered as operating. Third, in some cases LDOL estimates the employment and wages for some firms that fail to report. These three issues might be unimportant for most purposes. However, in the wake of an event such as Hurricane Katrina, particularly when the goal is to determine the patterns of entry and exit, these issues are crucial. This study follows Terrell and Bilbo's method of using a very conservative measure to determine whether an employer is open. The methodology uses the fact that the QCEW data includes a variable describing the way in which the data was obtained (whether it was estimated or reported by the employer). Based on this variable, we define employers as open only if they report positive values for employment or wages in at least one month in a particular quarter.

The next task consists of defining explanatory variables. One obvious factor that may affect the probability of being open is the flood depth. To focus on areas where flooding is relatively easy to measure, this study is limited to the city limits of New Orleans or equivalently Orleans Parish, Louisiana. Within the city, there are two distinct geographic areas, the East Bank and West Bank. The West Bank levees held and thus the area experienced minimal flooding. The levees failed in the East Bank where the majority of businesses existed. As a result, this area filled with water much like a bowl. Elevation of these employers is thus a reasonable predictor of flood damage. Based on this logic, a flood value of zero is assigned to all West Bank employers, while latitude and longitude is used to assign flood elevations of East Bank employers.

More specifically, a second dataset of Orleans Parish elevations was obtained from the Louisiana CADGIS Laboratory. This dataset consists of LIDAR Edited Points – a massive dataset of three-dimensional points: latitude, longitude, and elevation. These points are considered to be "edited" points which means that ground obstructions such as vegetation foliage, and manmade structures have been removed. The dataset is intended only to contain land elevations. The LIDAR and QCEW datasets were combined using a GIS software and each employer was assigned the elevation of the point nearest to it from the LIDAR edited points data. This provides elevation to 8,171 firms in Orleans Parish. The elevation is measured in feet relative to the sea level. The elevation variable was then used to calculate flood depth for all firms in our sample. As previously stated, West Bank employers were assigned a flooding variable of zero, while East Bank employer's flooding can be measured based on the elevation of the firm. The average flooding in New Orleans was roughly 2 feet above sea level. Therefore, the flood depth was calculated as two minus the elevation variable. A survey of establishments was used to evaluate the accuracy of these measures of flood depth based on elevation is in determining whether businesses were flooded or not. A phone survey of 1,833 Orleans Parish businesses asked whether they were flooded or not. The results based on the phone survey correspond to the results based on the elevation measure and confirm that we have a good measure for flood depth.

We expect heavily flooded establishments to reopen more slowly than the less flooded ones. In order to test this hypothesis, we construct a categorical variable capturing the feet of water as following: no flood, between 0 and 2 feet of water, between 2 and 4 feet of water, between 4 and 6 feet of water, between 6 and 8 feet of water, and finally above 8 feet of water.

One of the main contributions of this paper is the analysis of the spatial interactions between firms. We allow for dependence between firm decisions by introducing a latent/unobservable vector of effects that are spatially structured. The structure is such that the unobserved factors influencing firm i's decision exert influences of similar magnitude on neighboring firms j. Intuitively, unobservable influences arising from location of firm i should be similar to those of influences impacting firms j located nearby.

The latitude and longitude data was used to identify the nearest neighbors for each firm in our sample. Based on this, we construct a $8{,}171 \times 8{,}171$ spatial weight matrix (W) for every combination of firms in our dataset. We rely on a spatial contiguity relationship between firms in constructing the matrix W. Therefore, the weight matrix reflects the spatial relationship between firms and is constructed such that each element w_{ij} of the matrix is assigned a value of 1 if firm j and firm i have a contiguity relationship and 0 in the absence of such a relationship. When we use the term contiguity relationship, we follow the spatial literature and refer to the fact that firms i and j have a common border and therefore are considered neighbors. The diagonal elements were all set to zero. Next we row standardize the matrix by dividing each element w_{ij} in the matrix by the row sum such that all rows sum to one. The row standardization does not change the relative spatial dependency among observations. By dividing each element of the matrix by the row sum, we implicitly assume that the decision of reopening for each firm is a weighted average of the same decision of nearby firms and that all nearby firms are assigned the same weight. Other more complicated weighting schemes are possible, depending on how one wishes to quantify the degree of contiguity between firms. For the purpose of this paper, we simply want to account for spatial effects in the reopening decision, therefore any type of spatial dependency is acceptable.

Before proceeding any further we want to provide the reader with some intuition regarding the importance of the spatial weight matrix. A related concept in spatial econometrics is the spatial lag concept. While the first-order contiguity matrix W provides information about each firm's neighbors, the spatial lag matrix provides information about the neighbors of neighbors. For the purpose of this study, this concept is very important since by using spatial lags the initial impact of neighbors on the decision to reopen propagates through space and has an impact on the decision of reopening of neighbors of neighbors.

The size of each establishment is another factor affecting the probability of reopening. We construct four categories based on the average employment across the three months of that quarter: size1 includes firms with average employment between 1 and 4 employees; size2 between 5 and 49 employees; size3 between 50 and 249 employees, and size4 includes firms with more than 250 employees.

The relative size of the establishment is also a factor that could affect the reopening decision. The variable relative size is calculated to make a distinction between locally owned businesses and chain stores. This hypothesis was also tested by Campanella (2007), who finds that locally owned businesses are reopening sooner than large chain stores. We calculate the variable relative size for each quarter by dividing the average employment across the three months of that quarter for each establishment by the sum of average employment across all Louisiana establishments with the same reporting unit. Therefore, a value close to one implies that we are looking at a locally owned business, while a value close to zero indicates a chain store. We also construct interactions between this variable and flooding variables (rel size&flood).

The type of industry is also expected to affect the firm reopening decision. We expect establishments in certain industries to open faster than in other ones. For this purpose, we construct dummy variables for each of the 20 business categories presented in Table 1.

Summary statistics for all these variables are presented in Table 2.

3. SPATIAL PROBIT MODEL SPECIFICATION

This section focuses on the statistical model for whether an establishment is open conditional on that establishment's characteristics. As previously stated, an "establishment" denotes a single location for an employer. We use a modified version of the spatial probit model introduced by Smith and LeSage (2004). We model the establishment's decision to stay in business or not as a function of temporally and spatially varying observable and unobservable factors. The goal is to characterize the probability that an establishment is open in a given time period.

We start by introducing the main assumptions in the model and the notation that will be used for the remainder of this paper. Let m be the number of individual establishments. Each establishment is confronted in each period with choosing among two alternatives, labeled as 0 for closed and 1 for open. For each establishment, we observe whether the firm is open or closed and model it as the realization of a random variable y_i. The decision to open after the storm ranges from consideration of profits of one store in a large chain by a manager of a fortune 500 company to a sole proprietorship's decision to reopen. Economic theory suggests that the decision to reopen is primarily made to maximize the discounted value of future profits.[5] However, the decision to open may be the same as the decision to return to the city for some proprietors who rely on business income as their primary source of funds. For ease of exposition, assume that the choice of whether to be open or closed is the result of an entrepreneur's decision to maximize their utility. An event will occur with a certain probability p if the utility derived from choosing that alternative is greater than the utility from the other alternative. Let z_i be the

Table 1. Firms by Industry and Quarter.

	04Q3	04Q4	05Q1	05Q2	05Q3	05Q4	06Q1	06Q2	06Q3	06Q4	07Q1	07Q2	07Q3
1. Agriculture, Forestry, Fishing and Hunting	9	10	10	10	10	9	9	8	9	9	8	9	9
2. Mining	36	35	39	40	33	33	31	32	28	29	29	27	26
3. Utilities	5	5	8	19	3	4	2	6	10	8	7	7	2
4. Construction	269	275	277	298	199	194	207	216	212	226	222	220	214
5. Manufacturing	172	173	188	196	146	126	131	132	134	140	135	134	135
6. Wholesale Trade	328	336	342	356	292	275	261	257	243	253	240	239	238
7. Retail Trade	1,186	1,201	1,275	1,336	932	609	630	680	682	694	711	716	687
8. Transportation & Warehousing	195	207	212	222	178	167	164	168	171	162	153	154	146
9. Information	107	111	115	128	97	82	80	74	77	71	68	68	58
10. Finance & Insurance	396	414	425	466	356	305	304	317	284	312	298	291	282
11. Real Estate, Rental & Leasing	360	362	379	402	295	249	237	231	232	232	229	226	211
12. Professional, Scientific & Technical Services	1,125	1,161	1,195	1,264	970	943	932	959	940	968	921	919	905
13. Management of Companies & Enterprises	29	30	32	37	23	25	21	21	19	20	19	21	16
14. Administrative, Support, Waste Management & Remediation	344	352	371	389	307	260	262	274	267	272	259	251	245
15. Educational Services	78	81	84	91	72	59	66	60	61	64	65	65	65
16. Health Care & Social Assistance	753	786	800	838	576	487	445	462	454	461	456	465	444
17. Arts, Entertainment & Recreation	134	139	138	149	113	100	99	96	95	96	93	97	92
18. Accommodation & Food Services	848	880	926	981	726	559	566	583	571	586	595	585	557
19. Other Services	708	732	748	784	526	392	426	450	437	452	443	453	440
20. Public Administration	139	141	155	165	108	85	86	90	83	83	81	78	79
Total	7,221	7,431	7,719	8,171	5,962	4,963	4,959	5,116	5,009	5,138	5,032	5,025	4,851

Notes: The first column displays the industry. Columns 1–13 report the number of firms open for each quarter.

Table 2. Descriptive Statistics.

	Obs	Mean	Std. Dev.	Min	Max
open 2005Q4	8,171	0.607	0.488	0	1
open 2006Q2	8,171	0.626	0.484	0	1
open 2007Q2	8,171	0.615	0.487	0	1
rel size	8,171	0.890	0.298	0.0001	1
rel size&flood	8,171	0.409	0.487	0.0000	1
size1	8,171	0.486	0.500	0	1
size2	8,171	0.435	0.496	0	1
size3	8,171	0.065	0.247	0	1
size4	8,171	0.011	0.106	0	1
Agriculture, Forestry, Fishing & Hunting	8,171	0.001	0.035	0	1
Mining	8,171	0.005	0.070	0	1
Utilities	8,171	0.002	0.048	0	1
Construction	8,171	0.036	0.187	0	1
Manufacturing	8,171	0.024	0.153	0	1
Wholesale Trade	8,171	0.044	0.204	0	1
Retail Trade	8,171	0.164	0.370	0	1
Transportation & Warehousing	8,171	0.027	0.163	0	1
Information	8,171	0.016	0.124	0	1
Finance & Insurance	8,171	0.057	0.232	0	1
Real Estate, Rental & Leasing	8,171	0.049	0.216	0	1
Professional, Scientific & Technical Services	8,171	0.155	0.362	0	1
Management of Companies & Enterprises	8,171	0.005	0.067	0	1
Administrative, Support, Waste Management & Remediation	8,171	0.048	0.213	0	1
Educational Services	8,171	0.011	0.105	0	1
Health Care & Social Assistance	8,171	0.103	0.303	0	1
Arts, Entertainment & Recreation	8,171	0.018	0.134	0	1
Accommodation & Food Services	8,171	0.120	0.325	0	1
Other Services	8,171	0.096	0.295	0	1
Public Administration	8,171	0.020	0.140	0	1

Table 2. *(Continued)*

	Obs	Mean	Std. Dev.	Min	Max
flood 0–2	8,171	0.152	0.359	0	1
flood 2–4	8,171	0.109	0.311	0	1
flood 4–6	8,171	0.101	0.302	0	1
flood 6–8	8,171	0.044	0.204	0	1
flood 8	8,171	0.067	0.251	0	1

Notes: The first column displays the variable symbol. Column 2 reports the number of observations. Columns 3 and 4 report the mean and standard deviation. The last two columns present the min and max values.

difference in utility from alternatives 1 and 0. The difference in utility is modeled as:

$$z_i = x_i\beta + \theta_i + \varepsilon_i, \tag{1}$$

where $i = 1 \ldots m$, x_i is a vector of observed establishment-specific attributes, β is a vector of unobserved parameters to be estimated, θ_i is an unobserved random effect component, and ε_i is the stochastic error term with $\varepsilon_i \sim N(0,1)$. We do not observe z_i, but only observe the sign of z_i. We observe the establishment choice y_i being equal to 1 or 0, depending on whether z_i has a positive sign indicating the higher utility from this alternative or a negative sign associated with the lower utility associated with this alternative. Therefore, we observe

$$y_i = \begin{cases} 1 & \text{if } z_i > 0; \\ 0 & \text{if } z_i \leqslant 0. \end{cases} \tag{2}$$

The probability of choosing alternative 1 is given by:

$$P_i = P(y_i = 1) = P(z_i > 0). \tag{3}$$

The distinction between this model and the standard probit model is the term θ_i. The unobserved component θ_i is constructed such that it allows for spatial correlation across establishments. In other words, we assume that differences in utilities are similar for neighboring establishments. This is obtained by specifying θ_i according to a spatial autoregressive structure:

$$\theta_i = \rho \sum_{j=1}^{m} w_{ij}\theta_j + u_i \tag{4}$$

with $u_i \sim N(0, \sigma^2)$, $W = (w_{ij} : i,j = 1 \ldots m)$ is a row standardized spatial weight matrix such that $\sum_{j=1}^{m} w_{ij} = 1$. ρ can be interpreted as the degree of spatial dependence across establishments. The spatial autocorrelation is thus determined by both ρ and W. We can write Eq. (4) in matrix notation:

$$\theta = \rho W \theta + u, \tag{5}$$

where $u \sim N(0, \sigma^2 I_m)$ and I_m is the identity matrix.

Let $B_\rho = I_m - \rho W$. We can obtain a solution for θ using Eq. (5):

$$\theta = B_\rho^{-1} u. \tag{6}$$

Note that the matrix B_ρ^{-1} plays a role similar to a lag polynomial in time series econometrics. This matrix captures the fact that spatial shocks (u) affect neighbors in space in much the same way that time series shocks affect observations close in time. Given our weight matrix, a shock to one firm has a first-order impact of ρ on contiguous establishments, ρ^2 on establishments contiguous to those establishments, and so forth.

From Eq. (6), we see that the distribution for θ is given by:

$$\theta | (\rho, \sigma^2) \sim N\left(0, \sigma^2 \left(B'_\rho B_\rho\right)^{-1}\right). \tag{7}$$

The error term ε is assumed to be conditionally independent of the spatial unobserved component such that $\varepsilon | \theta \sim N(0, \sigma_\varepsilon^2)$ and we assume $\sigma_\varepsilon^2 = 1$.

The full model in matrix notation is given by:

$$Z = X\beta + \theta + \varepsilon. \tag{8}$$

4. BAYESIAN INFERENCE IN THE SPATIAL PROBIT MODEL SPECIFICATION

Our statistical approach is a simplification of the Smith and LeSage (2004) model assuming a homoscedastic ε_i. Bayesian inference is preferred in this setting primarily because it is easier to implement than the EM algorithm suggested by McMillen (1992) for the analogous frequentist model. In addition, the Bayesian approach provides exact small sample inferences.

Prior distributions for the unknown parameters complete the statistical model. Following LeSage and Smith, we assume

$$\beta \sim N(c, T), \tag{9}$$

$$H_p = 1/\sigma^2 \sim \Gamma(\alpha, v), \tag{10}$$

$$\rho \sim U\left[\left(\lambda_{\min}^{-1}, \lambda_{\max}^{-1}\right)\right]. \tag{11}$$

Given the statistical model summarized in Section 3, Smith and LeSage (2004) provide the full conditionals required to estimate the model by Markov Chain Monte Carlo (MCMC) methods. The MCMC method arrives at the target distribution of the unknown parameters by sequentially sampling from a set of conditional distributions of the parameters. This is very useful since usually it is difficult to find an analytical result for the posterior densities. The MCMC method provides a sample from the posterior density and we can use this sample to draw inferences about the parameters of interest. Under mild regularity conditions satisfied in this application, these samples converge to sample from the posterior distribution.

The MCMC algorithm follows that of Smith and LeSage (2004) and primarily a Gibbs sampling approach. For clarity, the notation used in this paper is identical to that introduced by Smith and LeSage (2004). The problem consists of constructing a sampling algorithm for the set of unknown parameters given by (β, ρ, σ^2). Implementing the MCMC method also requires data augmentation to sample θ and z.

Intuitively, one can see that conditional on θ and the latent variable z, the equation

$$z_i - \theta_i = x_i\beta + \varepsilon_i \tag{12}$$

is simply a linear regression model.

Thus, the conditional posterior distribution of β is proportional to the multinormal density:

$$\beta|(\theta, \rho, \sigma^2, z, y) \sim N(A^{-1}b, A^{-1}), \tag{13}$$

where $A = X'X + T^{-1}$ and $b = X'(z - \theta) + T^{-1}c$.

The conditional distribution of θ also follows a normal distribution:

$$\theta|(\beta, \rho, \sigma^2, z, y) \sim N(A_0^{-1}b_0, A_0^{-1}), \tag{14}$$

where $A_0 = \sigma^{-2}B_\rho' B_\rho$ and $b_0 = z - X\beta$.

The conditional posterior distribution of σ^2 (or the related precision H_p) is related to a chi-squared distribution in the following way:

$$H_p = \frac{1}{\sigma^2}|(\beta, \theta, \rho, z, y) \sim \frac{\chi^2(m + 2\alpha)}{\theta' B_\rho' B_\rho \theta + 2v}. \tag{15}$$

The conditional posterior distribution of ρ is given by:

$$\rho|(\beta, \theta, \sigma^2, z, y) \propto |B_\rho| \exp\left(-\frac{1}{2\sigma^2}\theta' B_\rho' B_\rho \theta\right), \tag{16}$$

where $\rho \in [\lambda_{\min}^{-1}, \lambda_{\max}^{-1}]$ and $\lambda_{\min}$ and $\lambda_{\max}$ are the minimum and maximum eigenvalues of W.

The distribution in Eq. (16) is non-standard and therefore we cannot sample from it directly. One solution to this problem is to use a Metropolis-Hastings algorithm. Smith and LeSage (2004) suggest using univariate numerical integration rather than a Metropolis-Hastings algorithm in this setting. In particular, we use the properties of the inverted gamma distribution to integrate out the nuisance parameter σ^2. Then Eq. (16) can be written as:

$$\rho|(\beta, \theta, z, y) \propto |B_\rho| \left[m^{-1}\theta' B_\rho' B_\rho \theta\right]^{-m/2} \pi(\rho). \tag{17}$$

Before sampling from this posterior distribution for ρ, we need to calculate the normalizing constant that transforms Eq. (17) in a proper density function that integrates to one. The normalizing constant can be found by integrating Eq. (17) over a grid of ρ values chosen from the interval $[\lambda_{\min}^{-1}, \lambda_{\max}^{-1}]$. The conditional posterior distribution for the grid of ρ values can be obtained by integrating the normalized density. The updated value for the unknown parameter ρ can be obtained by drawing from this distribution using the inversion method. In the estimation part of the paper, we will use this method for updating the values of ρ. For a comparison between this method and the M-H method, see Smith and LeSage (2004).

Finally, we need a conditional posterior distribution for the latent variable z. This distribution is a truncated normal distribution where the truncation depends on the observed choice for each firm:

$$z_i|\left(\beta, \theta, \rho, \sigma^2, V, -z_i, y\right) \sim \begin{cases} TN_{(0,\infty)}\left(x_i'\beta + \theta_i, 1\right) & \text{if } y_i = 1; \\ TN_{(-\infty,0)}\left(x_i'\beta + \theta_i, 1\right) & \text{if } y_i = 0. \end{cases} \tag{18}$$

The Gibbs sampler is given by the following iterative process:

1. Set starting values for the parameters $\beta_0, \theta_0, \rho_0, \sigma_0^2$ and the latent variable z_0.
2. Sample $\beta_1|(\theta_0, \rho_0, \sigma_0^2, z_0)$ from the multinormal distribution given by Eq. (13).
3. Sample $\theta_1|(\beta_1, \rho_0, \sigma_0^2, z_0)$ from the multinormal distribution given by Eq. (14).
4. Sample $\sigma_1^2|(\beta_1, \theta_1, \rho_0, z_0)$ using Eq. (15).
5. Sample $\rho_1|(\beta_1, \theta_1, \sigma_1^2, z_0)$ using numerical integration to obtain the conditional distribution for ρ using Eq. (17).
6. Sample $z_1|(\beta_1, \theta_1, \rho_1, \sigma_1^2)$ from the truncated normal distribution given by Eq. (18).
7. Return to the first step and iterate to generate the posterior sample. Discard the burn-in period of the sampler to avoid dependence on the starting values.

Before proceeding, it is useful to note that the full conditionals may differ substantially from the marginal densities for each of these parameters. For example, the fact that the conditional density of θ_i is mean zero does not imply that the posterior mean of θ_i is zero. In fact, we expect the posterior mean for parameter θ_i to differ substantially across firms to capture the impact of other open or closed businesses on the probability that firm i is open.

5. RESULTS

This section discusses results from the spatial probit model specification developed in Section 3. Detailed results are presented for all three quarters of interest: 2005Q4, 2006Q2, and 2007Q2. Table 3 contains results for all three quarters. While the coefficients are informative in indicating the direction of change in probabilities, their magnitudes are not very informative. Therefore, we also report marginal effects in Table 4. Additional reports for particular firms can be found in the appendix.

Perhaps the most surprising finding is the relationship between the relative size variable and the probability of reopening. Campanella (2007) and LeSage et al. (2011) report results from data gathered during bicycle tours over a 15-month period on three main commercial arteries in the city of New Orleans. One interesting result from these studies is that locally owned businesses are more likely to reopen than large chain businesses. The relative size variable used in our study has a positive sign in all three quarters. To interpret the relative size variable, it is useful to think of a simple example where a firm may have multiple locations with an identical number of employees. In this case, the relative size variable is simply 1 divided by the number of locations. For a sole proprietorship relative size is one, with 2 locations it takes a value one-half, with 20 locations 0.05 and so forth. Thus, the change of 1 is roughly moving from a very large chain to sole proprietorship and implies an increase in probability by 8.6% in 2005Q4, by a factor of 26.5% in 2006Q2, and by a factor of 22.4% in 2007Q2 holding other things constant. Going from 2 locations to 1 location would imply an increase in probability by a factor of 4.3% for 2005Q4, while going from 20 locations to 1 implies an increase in probability of 8.2% for that same quarter.

Though an exact comparison of magnitudes is difficult due to differences in model specification, our results are broadly in line with the findings of Campanella (2007) and LeSage et al. (2011). It is interesting to note that the timing of the storm impact in our data differs substantially from LeSage et al. (2011). Our results show that the impact of flood depth on reopening rises over time from the initial period one quarter after the storm. This illustrates a fundamental difference in the pattern of reopening across the two studies.

The most likely explanation for this difference lies in the definition of "open." In our dataset, an employer is considered "open" if it continued to pay wages and thus taxes on those wages. Our results are consistent with the observation that many employers, particularly those with a single

Table 3. Estimation Results.

	2005Q4				2006Q2				2007Q2			
	p.mean	p.Std dev	2.5%	97.5%	p.mean	p.Std dev	2.5%	97.5%	p.mean	p.Std dev	2.5%	97.5%
Intercept	0.826	0.238	0.353	1.286	0.592	0.254	0.090	1.095	0.023	0.248	−0.440	0.507
rel size	0.238	0.115	0.007	0.463	0.762	0.115	0.538	0.990	0.626	0.114	0.409	0.853
rel size&flood	−0.247	0.146	−0.526	0.048	0.363	0.147	0.076	0.644	0.778	0.150	0.489	1.078
size1	−1.040	0.187	−1.411	−0.693	−1.037	0.197	−1.438	−0.664	−0.464	0.185	−0.847	−0.110
size2	−0.186	0.187	−0.553	0.166	−0.142	0.191	−0.529	0.227	0.383	0.186	0.006	0.732
size3	0.551	0.203	0.145	0.938	0.348	0.211	−0.064	0.752	0.470	0.203	0.075	0.880
Agriculture, Forestry, Fishing & Hunting	2.073	0.846	0.561	3.866	0.886	0.684	−0.376	2.257	1.579	0.794	0.143	3.227
Mining	1.212	0.366	0.505	1.942	0.928	0.365	0.221	1.656	0.515	0.347	−0.151	1.181
Utilities	−1.289	0.515	−2.337	−0.312	−0.498	0.494	−1.478	0.428	0.138	0.455	−0.735	1.026
Construction	0.709	0.187	0.338	1.071	0.632	0.194	0.260	1.030	0.756	0.193	0.377	1.131
Manufacturing	0.467	0.202	0.058	0.864	0.174	0.200	−0.212	0.566	0.321	0.199	−0.062	0.720
Wholesale Trade	1.210	0.186	0.840	1.570	0.596	0.186	0.237	0.957	0.415	0.182	0.059	0.775
Retail Trade	−0.185	0.156	−0.488	0.121	−0.220	0.158	−0.533	0.094	−0.032	0.159	−0.341	0.276
Transportation & Warehousing	0.884	0.201	0.492	1.282	0.700	0.206	0.304	1.103	0.503	0.200	0.109	0.890
Information	0.523	0.219	0.101	0.955	0.114	0.221	−0.304	0.553	0.062	0.219	−0.374	0.478
Finance & Insurance	0.680	0.170	0.349	1.007	0.697	0.179	0.351	1.051	0.590	0.174	0.255	0.937
Real Estate, Rental & Leasing	0.554	0.177	0.207	0.910	0.175	0.181	−0.176	0.541	0.213	0.181	−0.132	0.580
Professional, Scientific & Technical Services	0.997	0.155	0.700	1.296	0.704	0.166	0.385	1.037	0.651	0.163	0.340	0.965

Management of Companies & Enterprises	0.395	0.343	−0.266	1.078	−0.092	0.338	−0.786	0.571	0.084	0.340	−0.619	0.717
Administrative, Support, Waste Management & Remediation	0.525	0.175	0.186	0.866	0.361	0.183	0.009	0.732	0.203	0.180	0.156	0.559
Educational Services	0.482	0.246	−0.002	0.961	0.242	0.263	−0.264	0.765	0.444	0.261	−0.054	0.961
Health Care & Social Assistance	0.434	0.163	0.118	0.754	0.038	0.166	−0.285	0.361	0.100	0.164	−0.223	0.420
Arts, Entertainment & Recreation	0.500	0.214	0.080	0.922	0.088	0.212	−0.327	0.493	0.268	0.214	−0.158	0.677
Accommodation & Food Services	−0.153	0.157	−0.459	0.154	−0.339	0.163	−0.650	−0.011	−0.183	0.162	−0.499	0.129
Other Services	0.047	0.159	−0.270	0.357	−0.024	0.165	−0.350	0.297	0.077	0.163	−0.243	0.398
flood 0–2	−0.325	0.146	−0.622	−0.038	−0.747	0.144	−1.028	−0.458	−1.109	0.149	−1.407	−0.817
flood 2–4	−0.675	0.152	−0.968	−0.379	−1.079	0.151	−1.374	−0.785	−1.210	0.150	−1.513	−0.925
flood 4–6	−0.580	0.153	−0.876	−0.280	−1.174	0.156	−1.482	−0.866	−1.325	0.160	−1.630	−1.011
flood 6–8	−0.646	0.173	−0.997	−0.320	−1.359	0.180	−1.725	−1.009	−1.589	0.191	−1.970	−1.224
flood 8	−0.965	0.158	−1.286	−0.658	−1.645	0.167	−1.962	−1.316	−1.956	0.178	−2.310	−1.619
σ^2	1.031	0.069	0.896	1.169	1.033	0.133	0.750	1.245	1.090	0.140	0.757	1.302
ρ	0.454	0.109	0.202	0.633	0.318	0.185	0.001	0.616	0.288	0.176	−0.025	0.566

Notes: The first column displays the variable symbol. For each quarter, columns 1, 2, 3, and 4 report posterior means, posterior standard deviations, 2.5%, and 97.5% percentile.

Table 4. Marginal Effects.

	2005Q4				2006Q2				2007Q2			
	Marg.eff	p.Std dev	2.5%	97.5%	Marg.eff	p.Std dev	2.5%	97.5%	Marg.eff	p.Std dev	2.5%	97.5%
rel size	0.086	0.041	0.003	0.166	0.265	0.039	0.189	0.342	0.224	0.040	0.147	0.303
rel size&flood	−0.089	0.053	−0.190	0.017	0.126	0.051	0.027	0.223	0.279	0.053	0.176	0.384
size1	−0.382	0.070	−0.514	−0.246	−0.375	0.074	−0.517	−0.233	−0.149	0.067	−0.292	−0.032
size2	−0.070	0.070	−0.204	0.065	−0.054	0.073	−0.197	0.089	0.143	0.067	0.003	0.267
size3	0.183	0.073	0.045	0.330	0.126	0.078	−0.021	0.279	0.178	0.074	0.029	0.323
Agriculture, Forestry, Fishing & Hunting	0.351	0.099	0.159	0.546	0.232	0.163	−0.141	0.499	0.476	0.180	0.053	0.743
Mining	0.305	0.085	0.144	0.481	0.270	0.096	0.074	0.456	0.194	0.129	−0.053	0.435
Utilities	−0.425	0.137	−0.651	−0.119	−0.183	0.174	−0.500	0.156	0.057	0.161	−0.233	0.386
Construction	0.221	0.065	0.099	0.353	0.210	0.068	0.083	0.353	0.286	0.070	0.146	0.421
Manufacturing	0.156	0.069	0.020	0.295	0.064	0.074	−0.079	0.210	0.120	0.074	−0.023	0.267
Wholesale Trade	0.313	0.072	0.181	0.460	0.201	0.067	0.076	0.337	0.156	0.067	0.023	0.288
Retail Trade	−0.070	0.059	−0.186	0.046	−0.084	0.061	−0.202	0.037	−0.013	0.057	−0.125	0.094
Transportation & Warehousing	0.259	0.068	0.134	0.404	0.228	0.071	0.095	0.374	0.190	0.074	0.043	0.333
Information	0.171	0.072	0.036	0.316	0.042	0.082	−0.116	0.204	0.023	0.079	−0.132	0.175
Finance & Insurance	0.215	0.061	0.103	0.339	0.228	0.065	0.105	0.363	0.224	0.064	0.099	0.349
Real Estate, Rental & Leasing	0.182	0.062	0.066	0.309	0.065	0.067	−0.065	0.199	0.078	0.067	−0.051	0.212
Professional, Scientific & Technical Services	0.282	0.065	0.162	0.413	0.231	0.063	0.113	0.361	0.247	0.059	0.133	0.358
Management of Companies & Enterprises	0.127	0.110	−0.100	0.328	−0.037	0.126	−0.297	0.204	0.035	0.121	−0.197	0.269

Administrative, Support, Waste Management & Remediation	0.174	0.062	0.060	0.299	0.129	0.067	0.003	0.265	0.074	0.065	−0.058	0.199
Educational Services	0.159	0.081	−0.001	0.317	0.087	0.094	−0.098	0.275	0.167	0.098	−0.020	0.358
Health Care & Social Assistance	0.148	0.059	0.038	0.271	0.015	0.063	−0.106	0.139	0.035	0.059	−0.085	0.149
Arts, Entertainment & Recreation	0.165	0.071	0.027	0.305	0.033	0.079	−0.124	0.183	0.099	0.080	−0.060	0.252
Accommodation & Food Services	−0.058	0.060	−0.174	0.058	−0.131	0.062	−0.249	−0.004	−0.064	0.057	−0.180	0.042
Other Services	0.018	0.059	−0.099	0.134	−0.009	0.063	−0.132	0.114	0.027	0.059	−0.092	0.138
flood 0–2	−0.099	0.048	−0.198	−0.012	−0.175	0.051	−0.281	−0.086	−0.390	0.056	−0.496	−0.281
flood 2–4	−0.225	0.057	−0.340	−0.118	−0.289	0.066	−0.417	−0.168	−0.428	0.055	−0.533	−0.319
flood 4–6	−0.189	0.056	−0.301	−0.084	−0.325	0.068	−0.456	−0.198	−0.470	0.056	−0.572	−0.358
flood 6–8	−0.214	0.065	−0.350	−0.098	−0.396	0.077	−0.545	−0.244	−0.557	0.059	−0.665	−0.435
flood 8	−0.337	0.062	−0.458	−0.216	−0.506	0.071	−0.633	−0.359	−0.656	0.046	−0.740	−0.558

Notes: The first column displays the variable symbol. For each quarter, columns 1, 2, 3, and 4 report the posterior means, posterior standard deviations, 2.5%, and 97.5% percentile.

location, continued to pay wages for a few months after the storm. Terrell and Bilbo (2007) provide detailed analysis which shows that the maximum reduction in number of employers occurred in early 2006 before the recovery began in terms of total number of businesses.

It should be noted that the second increase in the size of the flood impact variables for 2007Q2 likely stems from a different source. This comes at a time at which the overall number of businesses in the parishes was rising. This likely captures the uneven pattern of recovery in the wake of Hurricane Katrina. Employers in the French Quarter or Central Business district were very likely to reopen. Other areas like the Lower Ninth or New Orleans East getting more floodwater experienced a much greater failure rate for employers.

This has important implications for an economies ability to weather a natural disaster or resiliency to any disruption. Our results suggest that employers are able to continue functioning in some respects (continue paying employees) for a period of a few months. However, the resiliency is not strong enough to get through a longer period of disruption like that experienced in New Orleans.

The interaction term between the relative size of the firm and the flood variable has a negative sign in the first quarter. The sign flips for the following two quarters considered. Two years later after Katrina hit, locally owned businesses that were flooded are more likely to reopen.

With respect to the size of the firm, Tables 3 and 4 contain three dummy variables with over 250 employees as the omitted group. Recall that the literature predicts higher survival rates for larger firms. With regard to very small employers, our results conform to this prediction. Table 4 predicts that firms with less than five employees (size1 = 1) were 38% less likely to be open in 2005Q4 or 2006Q2 and 15% less likely in 2007Q2. The pattern varies across time periods for firms with 5–49 employees (size2 = 1). Firms with 50 to 249 were more likely to be open in all three quarters than the largest firms (18% more likely in 2005Q4 and 2007Q2 and 13% more likely in 2006Q2).

When we examine the relationship between the industry category and the reopening decision, we find the following. All industry types except utilities and accommodation and food services were more likely to reopen immediately after the storm when compared to public administration businesses. Firms in construction had a higher probability of reopening by a factor of 0.2 in all three quarters considered when compared to public administration businesses.

Not surprisingly, the coefficients attached to all flood variables have a negative sign and are generally quite large for all three quarters considered. For example, having been flooded with less than 2 feet of water compared with no flooding decreases the reopening probability by 9.9% in 2005Q4. The magnitude increases for the next two quarters considered, in 2007Q2 the probability of reopening decreases by a factor of 39%. All the flood variables increase in magnitude over time. The largest magnitudes occur for employers with eight or more feet of flooding. Holding other things constant, this level of flooding reduces the probability of opening by 34% in 2005Q4, 51% in 2006Q4, and 66% in 2007Q2 relative to firms with no flooding. The growing impact of flooding on firm survival is somewhat surprising and may indicate that some firms tried to reopen in areas with heavy damage, only to fail after a short period.

The error term attached to the spatial component θ is just over one in all three quarters. The spatial autocorrelation term ρ diminishes in magnitude as time passes. This finding suggests that spatial interactions between establishments were very important in the quarters immediately after the storm, but that the spatial component loses importance as time passes.

6. CONCLUSION

In this paper a Bayesian framework is used in order to investigate the post-storm survival of firms in the Orleans Parish. A novelty of our approach is the spatial component in the model specification. In particular, we allow for dependence between firm decisions by introducing a latent/unobservable vector of effects that are spatially structured. We estimate a spatial probit model on a dataset containing quarterly data on 8,171 firms from the Orleans Parish and find evidence indicating the presence of spatial components, especially in the quarters immediately following the storms. Other findings are: larger firms are more likely to survive; also, less flooded firms are more likely to survive; finally, sole proprietorships are more likely to reopen than large chain stores.

This paper also has important implications regarding an economy's resiliency in the wake of a large-scale disaster. Our results suggest that many employers will continue paying wages in the face of a disruption lasting a few months. Over longer periods, the sensitivity of employers rises, even when controlling for spatial impacts.

NOTES

1. www.whitehouse.gov/infocus/katrina
2. For example, each Walmart is considered as a separate establishment though there are multiple units in New Orleans.
3. Terrell and Bilbo, A Report on the Impact of Hurricanes Katrina and Rita on Louisiana Businesses: 2005Q2–2006Q4, found at www.bus.lsu.edu/ded
4. www.bus.lsu.edu/ded
5. We address differences in behavior across the ownership class variable relative size (see discussion in the section "Data") measuring employment at this establishment as a ratio of total employment at this location to that of all establishments under the same ownership in Louisiana.

ACKNOWLEDGMENTS

The authors are thankful to the Louisiana Recovery Authority, Louisiana Workforce Commission, and Louisiana Department of Economic Development for supporting this research. The views expressed are those of the authors and do not necessarily reflect the positions of these state agencies.

REFERENCES

Agarwal, R. (1996). Technological activity and survival of firms. *Economic Letters*, *52*(1), 101–108.

Agarwal, R. (1997). Survival of firms over the product life cycle. *Southern Economic Journal*, *63*(3), 571–584.

Agarwal, R., & Audretsch, D. B. (2001). Does entry size matter? The impact of the life cycle and technology on firm survival. *The Journal of Industrial Economics*, *49*(1), 21–43.

Agarwal, R., & Gort, M. (1996). The evolution of markets and entry, exit and survival of firms. *The Review of Economics and Statistics*, *78*(3), 489–498.

Agarwal, R., & Gort, M. (2002). Firm and product life cycles and firm survival. *The American Economic Review, Papers and Proceedings of the One Hundred Fourteenth Annual Meeting of the American Economic Association*, *92*(2), 184–190.

Albert, J., & Chib, S. (1993). Bayesian analysis of binary and polychotomous response data. *Journal of the American Statistical Association*, *88*, 669–679.

Audretsch, D. B. (1991). New-firm survival and the technological regime. *The Review of Economics and Statistics*, *73*(3), 441–450.

Audretsch, D. B., & Mahmood, T. (1995). New firm survival: New results using a hazard function. *The Review of Economics and Statistics*, *77*(1), 97–103.

Baldwin, J. R. (1995). *The dynamics of industrial competition*. Cambridge: Cambridge University Press.

Baldwin, J. R., & Gorecki, P. K. (1991). Firm entry and exit in the Canadian manufacturing sector, 1970–1982. *The Canadian Journal of Economics/Revue canadienne d'Economique*, *24*(2), 300–323.

Baldwin, J. R., & Rafiquzzaman, M. (1995). Selection versus evolutionary adaptation: Learning and post-entry performance. *International Journal of Industrial Organization*, *13*, 501–522.

Campanella, R. (2007). *Street survey of business reopenings in post-Katrina New Orleans*. CBR Whitepaper funded by National Science Foundation Award 0554937. Retrieved from www.kerrn.org/pdf/campanella2.pdf

Caves, R. E. (1998). Industrial organization and new findings on the turnover and mobility of firms. *Journal of Economic Literature*, *36*(4), 1947–1982.

Dahlhamer, J. M., & Tierney, K. J. (1996). *Winners and losers: Predicting business disaster recovery outcomes following the Northridge Earthquake*. University of Delaware Disaster Research Center.

Dunne, T., Roberts, M. J., & Samuelson, L. (1988). Patterns of firm entry and exit in U.S. manufacturing industries. *The Rand Journal of Economics*, *19*(4), 495–515.

Friesma, P., Caporaso, J., Goldstein, G., Lineberry, R., & McClearly, R. (1979). *Aftermath: Communities and natural disasters*. Beverly Hills, CA: Sage.

Geroski, P. A. (1995). What do we know about entry. *International Journal of Industrial Organization*, *13*, 450–456.

Gort, M., & Klepper, S. (1982). Time paths in the diffusion of product innovations. *The Economic Journal*, *92*(367), 630–653.

Jovanovic, B. (1982). Selection and the evolution of industry. *Econometrica*, *50*(3), 649–670.

LeSage, J. P., Pace, K., Lam, N., Campanella, R., & Liu, X. (2011). New Orleans business recovery in the aftermath of Hurricane Katrina. *Journal of the Royal Statistical Society Series A Royal Statistical Society: Series A*, *174*(4), 1007–1027.

Mata, J., & Portugal, P. (1994). Life duration of new firms. *Journal of Industrial Economics*, *27*, 227–246.

Mata, J., Portugal, P., & Guimaraes, P. (1995). The survival of new plants: Start-up conditions and post-entry evolution. *International Journal of Industrial Organization*, *13*, 459–481.

McMillen, D. P. (1992). Probit with spatial autocorrelation. *Journal of Regional Science*, *32*(3), 335–348.

Rossi, P. H., Wright, J. D., Weber-Burdin, E., & Pereira, J. (1983). *Victims of the environment loss from natural hazards in the United States, 1970–1980*. New York, NY: Plenum.

Runyan, R. C. (2006). Small business in the face of crisis: Identifying barriers to recovery from a natural disaster. *Journal of Contingencies and Crisis Management*, *14*(1), 12–26.

Smith, T. E., & LeSage, J. P. (2004). A Bayesian probit model with spatial dependencies. In J. P. LeSage & R. K. Pace (Eds.), *Advances in Econometrics* (Vol. 18, pp. 127–160). Advances in econometrics Spatial and Spatiotemporal Econometrics. Amsterdam: Elsevier.

Sutton, J. (1997). Gibrat's legacy. *Journal of Economic Literature*, *35*(1), 40–59.

Terrell, M. D., & Bilbo, R. (2007). *A report on the impact of Hurricanes Katrina and Rita on Louisiana Businesses. 2005Q2-2006Q4*. Retrieved from www.bus.lsu.edu/ded

Wagner, J. (1994). The post-entry performance of new small firms in German manufacturing industries. *Journal of Industrial Economics*, *62*, 141–154.

Wright, J. D., Rossi, P. H., Wright, S. R., & Weber-Burdin, E. (1979). *After the clean-up: Long range effects of natural disasters*. Beverly Hills, CA: Sage.

APPENDIX

Table A1. Marginal effects for firm with probability of opening in the 25% percentile and no open neighbors.

	2005Q4				2006Q2				2007Q2			
	Marg.eff	p.Std dev	2.5%	97.5%	Marg.eff	p.Std dev	2.5%	97.5%	Marg.eff	p.Std dev	2.5%	97.5%
type	0.070	0.045	0.001	0.162	0.233	0.082	0.046	0.366	0.191	0.071	0.039	0.312
typeflood	−0.073	0.053	−0.188	0.011	0.111	0.058	0.012	0.230	0.237	0.089	0.049	0.391
size1	−0.291	0.052	−0.399	−0.197	−0.049	0.018	−0.092	−0.021	−0.116	0.044	−0.206	−0.033
size2	−0.072	0.072	−0.215	0.061	−0.021	0.029	−0.092	0.021	0.098	0.046	0.002	0.185
size3	0.180	0.060	0.054	0.289	0.026	0.017	−0.007	0.061	0.117	0.047	0.023	0.210
Agriculture, Forestry, Fishing & Hunting	0.358	0.085	0.173	0.506	0.036	0.037	−0.049	0.093	0.211	0.075	0.038	0.344
Mining	0.311	0.076	0.157	0.459	0.046	0.020	0.012	0.093	0.121	0.079	−0.046	0.265
Utilities	−0.425	0.132	−0.637	−0.122	−0.099	0.110	−0.374	0.040	0.024	0.128	−0.269	0.232
Construction	0.227	0.063	0.105	0.353	0.041	0.019	0.013	0.086	0.170	0.052	0.076	0.279
Manufacturing	0.160	0.070	0.020	0.296	0.017	0.020	−0.019	0.060	0.088	0.056	−0.017	0.203
Wholesale Trade	0.320	0.062	0.203	0.446	0.040	0.019	0.011	0.084	0.110	0.052	0.014	0.217
Retail Trade	−0.071	0.059	−0.184	0.047	−0.026	0.019	−0.062	0.013	−0.008	0.050	−0.101	0.093
Transportation & Warehousing	0.265	0.064	0.145	0.393	0.043	0.019	0.015	0.088	0.128	0.054	0.027	0.236
Information	0.176	0.073	0.035	0.318	0.011	0.023	−0.031	0.058	0.018	0.067	−0.116	0.145
Finance & Insurance	0.220	0.060	0.106	0.340	0.043	0.019	0.014	0.088	0.145	0.051	0.055	0.250
Real Estate, Rental & Leasing	0.187	0.063	0.066	0.316	0.017	0.019	−0.014	0.062	0.063	0.054	−0.037	0.176
Professional, Scientific & Technical Services	0.288	0.059	0.178	0.406	0.044	0.019	0.015	0.089	0.156	0.050	0.069	0.258

Table A1. *(Continued)*

	2005Q4				2006Q2				2007Q2			
	Marg.eff	p.Std dev	2.5%	97.5%	Marg.eff	p.Std dev	2.5%	97.5%	Marg.eff	p.Std dev	2.5%	97.5%
Management of Companies & Enterprises	0.131	0.112	−0.102	0.336	−0.017	0.045	−0.126	0.053	0.018	0.102	−0.208	0.190
Administrative, Support, Waste Management & Remediation	0.178	0.062	0.059	0.301	0.030	0.019	0.001	0.073	0.060	0.054	−0.042	0.169
Educational Services	0.162	0.081	−0.001	0.318	0.020	0.023	−0.026	0.069	0.113	0.065	−0.015	0.242
Health Care & Social Assistance	0.152	0.060	0.040	0.271	0.005	0.018	−0.025	0.046	0.032	0.050	−0.063	0.134
Arts, Entertainment & Recreation	0.169	0.072	0.027	0.313	0.009	0.022	−0.035	0.053	0.075	0.060	−0.046	0.194
Accommodation & Food Services	−0.058	0.060	−0.173	0.061	−0.045	0.022	−0.089	−0.002	−0.059	0.052	−0.159	0.044
Other Services	0.019	0.060	−0.098	0.137	−0.001	0.018	−0.034	0.039	0.025	0.050	−0.071	0.129
flood 0–2	−0.126	0.056	−0.241	−0.015	−0.136	0.038	−0.218	−0.072	−0.411	0.052	−0.510	−0.307
flood 2–4	−0.260	0.057	−0.368	−0.148	−0.238	0.054	−0.353	−0.142	−0.446	0.051	−0.544	−0.347
flood 4–6	−0.225	0.058	−0.335	−0.111	−0.271	0.059	−0.392	−0.165	−0.485	0.052	−0.580	−0.381
flood 6–8	−0.249	0.064	−0.377	−0.125	−0.339	0.073	−0.486	−0.206	−0.561	0.054	−0.666	−0.451
flood 8	−0.358	0.055	−0.467	−0.250	−0.449	0.073	−0.589	−0.313	−0.644	0.045	−0.727	−0.552

Notes: The first column displays the variable symbol. For each quarter, columns 2, 3, 4, and 5 report the estimates, posterior standard deviations, 2.5% and 97.5% percentile.

Table A2. Marginal effects for firm with probability of opening in the 25% percentile and all neighbors open.

	2005Q4				2006Q2				2007Q2			
	Marg.eff	p.Std dev	2.5%	97.5%	Marg.eff	p.Std dev	2.5%	97.5%	Marg.eff	p.Std dev	2.5%	97.5%
type	0.062	0.043	0.000	0.155	0.204	0.096	0.016	0.362	0.180	0.076	0.021	0.312
typeflood	−0.065	0.051	−0.176	0.010	0.097	0.060	0.004	0.223	0.223	0.096	0.025	0.391
size1	−0.168	0.022	−0.210	−0.126	−0.117	0.017	−0.152	−0.087	−0.032	0.010	−0.052	−0.010
size2	−0.060	0.060	−0.188	0.042	−0.038	0.049	−0.150	0.043	0.028	0.012	0.001	0.048
size3	0.114	0.034	0.038	0.172	0.057	0.032	−0.014	0.110	0.032	0.011	0.007	0.053
Agriculture, Forestry, Fishing & Hunting	0.189	0.032	0.118	0.239	0.086	0.068	−0.098	0.154	0.047	0.014	0.013	0.067
Mining	0.174	0.029	0.110	0.224	0.107	0.027	0.041	0.150	0.031	0.019	−0.018	0.056
Utilities	−0.453	0.169	−0.732	−0.096	−0.158	0.156	−0.507	0.074	−0.002	0.050	−0.136	0.052
Construction	0.136	0.026	0.081	0.183	0.091	0.020	0.047	0.129	0.043	0.008	0.027	0.060
Manufacturing	0.100	0.036	0.016	0.162	0.030	0.036	−0.053	0.089	0.024	0.014	−0.007	0.046
Wholesale Trade	0.179	0.020	0.139	0.219	0.088	0.021	0.043	0.125	0.030	0.011	0.006	0.050
Retail Trade	−0.058	0.050	−0.163	0.032	−0.056	0.043	−0.150	0.019	−0.006	0.019	−0.048	0.024
Transportation & Warehousing	0.155	0.024	0.105	0.200	0.096	0.020	0.054	0.134	0.034	0.011	0.010	0.053
Information	0.109	0.037	0.027	0.172	0.018	0.043	−0.076	0.089	0.002	0.023	−0.053	0.036
Finance & Insurance	0.134	0.025	0.082	0.179	0.097	0.018	0.059	0.133	0.038	0.009	0.021	0.055
Real Estate, Rental & Leasing	0.115	0.029	0.052	0.168	0.031	0.033	−0.042	0.087	0.017	0.014	−0.016	0.040
Professional, Scientific & Technical Services	0.166	0.020	0.127	0.206	0.098	0.018	0.063	0.133	0.040	0.008	0.025	0.056
Management of Companies & Enterprises	0.079	0.068	−0.083	0.179	−0.034	0.083	−0.240	0.090	−0.001	0.039	−0.104	0.046
Administrative, Support, Waste Management & Remediation	0.111	0.030	0.047	0.164	0.060	0.026	0.002	0.106	0.016	0.015	−0.019	0.040

Table A2. *(Continued)*

	2005Q4				2006Q2				2007Q2			
	Marg.eff	p.Std dev	2.5%	97.5%	Marg.eff	p.Std dev	2.5%	97.5%	Marg.eff	p.Std dev	2.5%	97.5%
Educational Services	0.101	0.044	−0.001	0.170	0.038	0.044	−0.065	0.108	0.030	0.015	−0.006	0.054
Health Care & Social Assistance	0.096	0.030	0.030	0.151	0.005	0.035	−0.071	0.065	0.008	0.016	−0.027	0.033
Arts, Entertainment & Recreation	0.105	0.037	0.022	0.167	0.013	0.043	−0.083	0.080	0.020	0.016	−0.019	0.045
Accommodation & Food Services	−0.038	0.040	−0.111	0.044	−0.059	0.026	−0.106	−0.002	−0.016	0.014	−0.041	0.014
Other Services	0.010	0.043	−0.082	0.085	−0.008	0.037	−0.091	0.055	0.006	0.016	−0.032	0.032
flood 0–2	−0.104	0.051	−0.214	−0.011	−0.227	0.055	−0.339	−0.123	−0.253	0.056	−0.367	−0.151
flood 2–4	−0.234	0.060	−0.355	−0.120	−0.354	0.062	−0.475	−0.233	−0.288	0.059	−0.411	−0.181
flood 4–6	−0.198	0.059	−0.318	−0.086	−0.392	0.063	−0.514	−0.264	−0.331	0.065	−0.459	−0.209
flood 6–8	−0.223	0.067	−0.361	−0.101	−0.463	0.070	−0.599	−0.324	−0.433	0.079	−0.591	−0.282
flood 8	−0.348	0.062	−0.471	−0.226	−0.567	0.059	−0.670	−0.444	−0.574	0.071	−0.704	−0.428

Notes: The first column displays the variable symbol. For each quarter, column 2, 3, 4, and 5 report the estimates, posterior standard deviations, 2.5% and 97.5% percentile.

Table A3. Marginal effects for firm with probability of opening in the 50% percentile and no open neighbors.

	2005Q4				2006Q2				2007Q2			
	Marg.eff	p.Std dev	2.5%	97.5%	Marg.eff	p.Std dev	2.5%	97.5%	Marg.eff	p.Std dev	2.5%	97.5%
type	0.057	0.043	0.000	0.153	0.171	0.102	0.005	0.350	0.141	0.086	0.003	0.301
typeflood	−0.060	0.051	−0.175	0.008	0.083	0.061	0.001	0.218	0.176	0.108	0.004	0.376
size1	−0.015	0.008	−0.034	−0.004	−0.111	0.037	−0.190	−0.049	−0.067	0.029	−0.132	−0.018
size2	−0.011	0.013	−0.046	0.005	−0.036	0.048	−0.151	0.041	0.057	0.029	0.001	0.116
size3	0.012	0.006	0.003	0.027	0.053	0.032	−0.014	0.117	0.067	0.030	0.012	0.130
Agriculture, Forestry, Fishing & Hunting	0.015	0.008	0.004	0.036	0.081	0.070	−0.089	0.188	0.108	0.047	0.023	0.206
Mining	0.015	0.008	0.004	0.035	0.101	0.040	0.032	0.183	0.066	0.046	−0.033	0.152
Utilities	−0.198	0.146	−0.569	−0.014	−0.152	0.152	−0.496	0.070	0.004	0.086	−0.215	0.126
Construction	0.013	0.007	0.004	0.030	0.085	0.030	0.034	0.151	0.092	0.032	0.040	0.164
Manufacturing	0.011	0.006	0.002	0.026	0.028	0.036	−0.050	0.096	0.049	0.032	−0.012	0.116
Wholesale Trade	0.015	0.008	0.005	0.035	0.082	0.030	0.032	0.148	0.061	0.029	0.010	0.122
Retail Trade	−0.010	0.011	−0.036	0.004	−0.054	0.043	−0.152	0.017	−0.010	0.034	−0.089	0.049
Transportation & Warehousing	0.014	0.007	0.004	0.033	0.090	0.032	0.038	0.159	0.070	0.030	0.018	0.138
Information	0.011	0.007	0.002	0.027	0.016	0.042	−0.078	0.094	0.007	0.044	−0.094	0.084
Finance & Insurance	0.013	0.007	0.004	0.030	0.091	0.030	0.039	0.157	0.079	0.029	0.032	0.144
Real Estate, Rental & Leasing	0.012	0.006	0.003	0.028	0.028	0.032	−0.042	0.090	0.034	0.031	−0.030	0.094
Professional, Scientific & Technical Services	0.015	0.008	0.004	0.034	0.092	0.030	0.042	0.159	0.085	0.029	0.038	0.150
Management of Companies & Enterprises	0.008	0.010	−0.014	0.026	−0.033	0.080	−0.235	0.086	0.004	0.069	−0.166	0.107
Administrative, Support, Waste Management & Remediation	0.011	0.006	0.003	0.027	0.056	0.029	0.002	0.120	0.032	0.031	−0.034	0.092

Table A3. *(Continued)*

	2005Q4				2006Q2				2007Q2			
	Marg.eff	p.Std dev	2.5%	97.5%	Marg.eff	p.Std dev	2.5%	97.5%	Marg.eff	p.Std dev	2.5%	97.5%
Educational Services	0.029	0.016	0.000	0.063	0.054	0.059	−0.065	0.168	0.109	0.062	−0.015	0.229
Health Care & Social Assistance	0.010	0.006	0.002	0.025	0.004	0.034	−0.073	0.065	0.015	0.031	−0.053	0.072
Arts, Entertainment & Recreation	0.011	0.007	0.002	0.026	0.012	0.042	−0.081	0.087	0.041	0.035	−0.036	0.107
Accommodation & Food Services	−0.008	0.010	−0.034	0.005	−0.086	0.050	−0.197	−0.002	−0.043	0.041	−0.136	0.025
Other Services	0.001	0.007	−0.015	0.013	−0.008	0.036	−0.091	0.054	0.012	0.031	−0.058	0.070
flood 0–2	−0.019	0.014	−0.056	−0.001	−0.216	0.061	−0.340	−0.103	−0.347	0.069	−0.478	−0.214
flood 2–4	−0.055	0.029	−0.124	−0.015	−0.340	0.071	−0.473	−0.201	−0.386	0.071	−0.519	−0.244
flood 4–6	−0.043	0.024	−0.101	−0.010	−0.376	0.071	−0.512	−0.234	−0.430	0.071	−0.561	−0.284
flood 6–8	−0.052	0.030	−0.128	−0.012	−0.447	0.076	−0.586	−0.293	−0.528	0.074	−0.661	−0.375
flood 8	−0.101	0.044	−0.203	−0.036	−0.552	0.065	−0.661	−0.410	−0.648	0.056	−0.743	−0.524

Notes: The first column displays the variable symbol. For each quarter, columns 2, 3, 4, and 5 report the estimates, posterior standard deviations, 2.5% and 97.5% percentile.

Table A4. Marginal effects for firm with probability of opening in the 50% percentile and all neighbors open.

	2005Q4				2006Q2				2007Q2			
	Marg.eff	p.Std dev	2.5%	97.5%	Marg.eff	p.Std dev	2.5%	97.5%	Marg.eff	p.Std dev	2.5%	97.5%
type	0.072	0.043	0.002	0.163	0.222	0.088	0.028	0.363	0.187	0.072	0.027	0.311
typeflood	−0.075	0.052	−0.187	0.012	0.106	0.059	0.006	0.229	0.233	0.091	0.033	0.393
size1	−0.163	0.045	−0.262	−0.086	−0.383	0.068	−0.513	−0.246	−0.161	0.071	−0.312	−0.034
size2	−0.057	0.059	−0.182	0.044	−0.043	0.061	−0.163	0.081	0.131	0.068	0.002	0.266
size3	0.182	0.078	0.039	0.343	0.100	0.058	−0.022	0.210	0.112	0.047	0.021	0.207
Agriculture, Forestry, Fishing & Hunting	0.620	0.177	0.173	0.845	0.176	0.128	−0.132	0.375	0.202	0.079	0.038	0.349
Mining	0.426	0.129	0.162	0.655	0.210	0.073	0.066	0.348	0.113	0.075	−0.049	0.249
Utilities	−0.167	0.058	−0.292	−0.064	−0.186	0.174	−0.516	0.126	0.018	0.124	−0.265	0.213
Construction	0.241	0.075	0.097	0.389	0.167	0.051	0.074	0.271	0.160	0.046	0.080	0.255
Manufacturing	0.152	0.075	0.015	0.306	0.052	0.061	−0.077	0.169	0.081	0.050	−0.018	0.181
Wholesale Trade	0.430	0.072	0.279	0.558	0.160	0.050	0.067	0.263	0.102	0.045	0.017	0.192
Retail Trade	−0.044	0.038	−0.117	0.034	−0.080	0.059	−0.200	0.030	−0.012	0.049	−0.118	0.076
Transportation & Warehousing	0.307	0.081	0.152	0.464	0.180	0.053	0.085	0.288	0.119	0.047	0.029	0.216
Information	0.172	0.082	0.028	0.344	0.032	0.070	−0.114	0.165	0.013	0.065	−0.128	0.131
Finance & Insurance	0.230	0.069	0.100	0.364	0.181	0.048	0.091	0.280	0.135	0.042	0.058	0.223
Real Estate, Rental & Leasing	0.183	0.069	0.057	0.326	0.052	0.056	−0.064	0.157	0.055	0.048	−0.043	0.148
Professional, Scientific & Technical Services	0.351	0.065	0.223	0.468	0.182	0.047	0.097	0.278	0.146	0.042	0.073	0.233

Table A4. (Continued)

	2005Q4				2006Q2				2007Q2			
	Marg.eff	p.Std dev	2.5%	97.5%	Marg.eff	p.Std dev	2.5%	97.5%	Marg.eff	p.Std dev	2.5%	97.5%
Management of Companies & Enterprises	0.132	0.117	−0.063	0.387	−0.040	0.115	−0.300	0.158	0.012	0.098	−0.215	0.171
Administrative, Support, Waste Management & Remediation	0.172	0.067	0.050	0.308	0.105	0.051	0.003	0.209	0.053	0.048	−0.050	0.144
Educational Services	0.106	0.060	0.000	0.237	0.085	0.092	−0.099	0.263	0.150	0.086	−0.019	0.316
Health Care & Social Assistance	0.139	0.060	0.032	0.267	0.010	0.055	−0.105	0.112	0.026	0.047	−0.074	0.113
Arts, Entertainment & Recreation	0.164	0.079	0.021	0.330	0.025	0.068	−0.121	0.148	0.067	0.055	−0.050	0.169
Accommodation & Food Services	−0.036	0.039	−0.109	0.046	−0.124	0.062	−0.248	0.004	−0.061	0.055	−0.178	0.038
Other Services	0.016	0.045	−0.064	0.111	−0.010	0.057	−0.130	0.092	0.020	0.047	−0.080	0.108
flood 0–2	−0.073	0.034	−0.145	−0.009	−0.279	0.056	−0.384	−0.164	−0.405	0.056	−0.509	−0.292
flood 2–4	−0.129	0.037	−0.211	−0.068	−0.399	0.053	−0.497	−0.290	−0.440	0.054	−0.541	−0.330
flood 4–6	−0.191	0.058	−0.309	−0.081	−0.249	0.059	−0.361	−0.135	−0.213	0.057	−0.328	−0.109
flood 6–8	−0.125	0.039	−0.213	−0.062	−0.486	0.055	−0.594	−0.374	−0.558	0.055	−0.663	−0.445
flood 8	−0.159	0.044	−0.258	−0.085	−0.558	0.050	−0.653	−0.458	0.644	0.047	−0.730	−0.547

Notes: The first column displays the variable symbol. For each quarter, columns 2, 3, 4, and 5 report the estimates, posterior standard deviations, 2.5% and 97.5% percentile.

Table A5. Marginal effects for firm with probability of opening in the 75% percentile and no open neighbors.

	2005Q4				2006Q2				2007Q2			
	Marg.eff	p.Std dev	2.5%	97.5%	Marg.eff	p.Std dev	2.5%	97.5%	Marg.eff	p.Std dev	2.5%	97.5%
type	0.044	0.041	0.000	0.142	0.144	0.103	0.003	0.339	0.194	0.070	0.040	0.316
typeflood	−0.046	0.046	−0.162	0.006	0.069	0.059	0.001	0.205	0.240	0.087	0.051	0.396
size1	−0.378	0.054	−0.476	−0.269	−0.382	0.059	−0.489	−0.260	−0.111	0.054	−0.235	−0.020
size2	−0.067	0.067	−0.192	0.066	−0.050	0.068	−0.179	0.089	0.088	0.050	0.001	0.195
size3	0.214	0.076	0.056	0.353	0.136	0.082	−0.025	0.290	0.113	0.059	0.015	0.247
Agriculture, Forestry, Fishing & Hunting	0.516	0.105	0.220	0.625	0.301	0.202	−0.133	0.595	0.487	0.245	0.026	0.871
Mining	0.414	0.093	0.198	0.558	0.339	0.116	0.087	0.527	0.134	0.102	−0.024	0.362
Utilities	−0.317	0.079	−0.422	−0.112	−0.145	0.140	−0.352	0.169	0.049	0.101	−0.079	0.305
Construction	0.272	0.066	0.134	0.393	0.245	0.071	0.101	0.383	0.203	0.068	0.079	0.348
Manufacturing	0.182	0.077	0.023	0.326	0.068	0.077	−0.078	0.223	0.073	0.051	−0.010	0.188
Wholesale Trade	0.424	0.048	0.321	0.508	0.232	0.070	0.091	0.361	0.097	0.051	0.011	0.207
Retail Trade	−0.068	0.056	−0.172	0.047	−0.078	0.055	−0.179	0.036	−0.003	0.027	−0.049	0.057
Transportation & Warehousing	0.330	0.065	0.194	0.446	0.269	0.074	0.119	0.406	0.123	0.060	0.020	0.253
Information	0.203	0.082	0.040	0.357	0.046	0.085	−0.109	0.218	0.017	0.043	−0.051	0.113
Finance & Insurance	0.262	0.061	0.138	0.375	0.269	0.065	0.137	0.388	0.148	0.056	0.050	0.268
Real Estate, Rental & Leasing	0.216	0.066	0.081	0.343	0.069	0.070	−0.064	0.213	0.047	0.042	−0.021	0.141
Professional, Scientific & Technical Services	0.294	0.036	0.222	0.362	0.222	0.045	0.130	0.307	0.072	0.015	0.043	0.101

Table A5. *(Continued)*

	2005Q4				2006Q2				2007Q2			
	Marg.eff	p.Std dev	2.5%	97.5%	Marg.eff	p.Std dev	2.5%	97.5%	Marg.eff	p.Std dev	2.5%	97.5%
Management of Companies & Enterprises	0.153	0.128	−0.100	0.392	−0.027	0.120	−0.246	0.224	0.028	0.068	−0.073	0.188
Administrative, Support, Waste Management & Remediation	0.205	0.066	0.073	0.329	0.142	0.071	0.003	0.285	0.044	0.041	−0.024	0.138
Educational Services	0.187	0.093	−0.001	0.359	0.095	0.101	−0.096	0.295	0.109	0.075	−0.008	0.276
Health Care & Social Assistance	0.170	0.063	0.045	0.291	0.016	0.063	−0.102	0.142	0.022	0.033	−0.034	0.095
Arts, Entertainment & Recreation	0.195	0.081	0.031	0.346	0.036	0.081	−0.116	0.195	0.061	0.052	−0.025	0.176
Accommodation & Food Services	−0.056	0.058	−0.164	0.061	−0.118	0.053	−0.212	−0.004	−0.026	0.023	−0.064	0.024
Other Services	0.019	0.061	−0.100	0.141	−0.007	0.062	−0.125	0.116	0.017	0.032	−0.036	0.089
flood 0–2	−0.116	0.049	−0.208	−0.015	−0.232	0.035	−0.297	−0.157	−0.091	0.011	−0.114	−0.071
flood 2–4	−0.222	0.041	−0.294	−0.137	−0.296	0.029	−0.350	−0.238	−0.093	0.011	−0.116	−0.073
flood 4–6	−0.196	0.044	−0.275	−0.103	−0.310	0.028	−0.364	−0.253	−0.095	0.012	−0.119	−0.074
flood 6–8	−0.213	0.047	−0.299	−0.117	−0.332	0.029	−0.388	−0.274	−0.098	0.012	−0.122	−0.076
flood 8	−0.287	0.034	−0.351	−0.219	−0.356	0.026	−0.404	−0.305	−0.100	0.012	−0.124	−0.078

Notes: The first column displays the variable symbol. For each quarter, columns 2, 3, 4, and 5 report the estimates, posterior standard deviations, 2.5% and 97.5% percentile.

Table A6. Marginal effects for firm with probability of opening in the 75% percentile and all neighbors open.

	2005Q4				2006Q2				2007Q2			
	Marg.eff	p.Std dev	2.5%	97.5%	Marg.eff	p.Std dev	2.5%	97.5%	Marg.eff	p.Std dev	2.5%	97.5%
type	0.035	0.037	0.000	0.133	0.121	0.100	0.001	0.329	0.119	0.087	0.001	0.292
typeflood	−0.036	0.042	−0.148	0.004	0.058	0.056	0.000	0.195	0.148	0.108	0.002	0.359
size1	−0.109	0.014	−0.138	−0.083	−0.124	0.015	−0.155	−0.096	−0.113	0.037	−0.178	−0.032
size2	−0.047	0.048	−0.152	0.031	−0.039	0.050	−0.151	0.045	0.096	0.042	0.002	0.165
size3	0.077	0.022	0.028	0.115	0.060	0.033	−0.014	0.113	0.113	0.041	0.022	0.183
Agriculture, Forestry, Fishing & Hunting	0.119	0.020	0.078	0.151	0.091	0.071	−0.100	0.162	0.201	0.057	0.040	0.266
Mining	0.112	0.018	0.073	0.143	0.113	0.028	0.043	0.155	0.113	0.069	−0.048	0.210
Utilities	−0.422	0.182	−0.756	−0.077	−0.162	0.158	−0.512	0.077	0.018	0.124	−0.271	0.197
Construction	0.091	0.017	0.055	0.122	0.095	0.020	0.050	0.133	0.161	0.028	0.099	0.211
Manufacturing	0.068	0.024	0.011	0.108	0.031	0.038	−0.054	0.092	0.082	0.046	−0.019	0.162
Wholesale Trade	0.115	0.013	0.090	0.142	0.092	0.021	0.047	0.129	0.103	0.039	0.018	0.171
Retail Trade	−0.045	0.039	−0.127	0.023	−0.059	0.044	−0.154	0.020	−0.013	0.050	−0.117	0.076
Transportation & Warehousing	0.102	0.015	0.070	0.131	0.101	0.020	0.057	0.138	0.120	0.039	0.032	0.185
Information	0.074	0.024	0.020	0.114	0.018	0.045	−0.080	0.091	0.013	0.064	−0.129	0.121
Finance & Insurance	0.089	0.016	0.056	0.120	0.102	0.018	0.064	0.134	0.136	0.030	0.070	0.190
Real Estate, Rental & Leasing	0.078	0.019	0.037	0.112	0.032	0.034	−0.044	0.090	0.056	0.047	−0.042	0.139
Professional, Scientific & Technical Services	0.314	0.058	0.205	0.426	0.217	0.059	0.110	0.335	0.236	0.062	0.118	0.356

Table A6. *(Continued)*

	2005Q4				2006Q2				2007Q2			
	Marg.eff	p.Std dev	2.5%	97.5%	Marg.eff	p.Std dev	2.5%	97.5%	Marg.eff	p.Std dev	2.5%	97.5%
Management of Companies & Enterprises	0.053	0.047	−0.063	0.116	−0.035	0.086	−0.244	0.092	0.013	0.099	−0.222	0.162
Administrative, Support, Waste Management & Remediation	0.076	0.019	0.033	0.110	0.063	0.027	0.002	0.110	0.053	0.047	−0.050	0.135
Educational Services	0.069	0.029	0.000	0.114	0.040	0.046	−0.068	0.110	0.105	0.054	−0.017	0.190
Health Care & Social Assistance	0.066	0.020	0.022	0.102	0.005	0.036	−0.075	0.066	0.026	0.047	−0.073	0.108
Arts, Entertainment & Recreation	0.072	0.025	0.015	0.113	0.014	0.045	−0.089	0.084	0.068	0.053	−0.052	0.153
Accommodation & Food Services	−0.037	0.039	−0.119	0.029	−0.093	0.050	−0.200	−0.003	−0.062	0.055	−0.176	0.037
Other Services	0.007	0.031	−0.064	0.059	−0.009	0.039	−0.096	0.057	0.020	0.047	−0.081	0.103
flood 0–2	−0.082	0.042	−0.175	−0.008	−0.232	0.055	−0.342	−0.127	−0.413	0.054	−0.517	−0.301
flood 2–4	−0.194	0.055	−0.306	−0.093	−0.361	0.060	−0.478	−0.245	−0.449	0.053	−0.550	−0.345
flood 4–6	−0.161	0.052	−0.269	−0.066	−0.399	0.061	−0.519	−0.276	−0.488	0.053	−0.582	−0.380
flood 6–8	−0.184	0.061	−0.316	−0.076	−0.469	0.067	−0.599	−0.336	−0.567	0.052	−0.662	−0.456
flood 8	−0.302	0.062	−0.431	−0.183	−0.572	0.055	−0.671	−0.457	−0.653	0.036	−0.715	−0.577

Notes: The first column displays the variable symbol. For each quarter, column 2, 3, 4, and 5 report the estimates, posterior standard deviations, 2.5% and 97.5% percentile.

BAYESIAN SPATIAL BIVARIATE PANEL PROBIT ESTIMATION

Badi H. Baltagi[a], Peter H. Egger[b] and Michaela Kesina[c]

[a]*Department of Economics and Center for Policy Research, Syracuse University, Syracuse, NY, USA*
[b]*ETH Zurich, Zurich, Switzerland, CEPR, CESifo*
[c]*ETH Zurich, Zurich, Switzerland*

ABSTRACT

This paper formulates and analyzes Bayesian model variants for the analysis of systems of spatial panel data with binary-dependent variables. The paper focuses on cases where latent variables of cross-sectional units in an equation of the system contemporaneously depend on the values of the same and, eventually, other latent variables of other cross-sectional units. Moreover, the paper discusses cases where time-invariant effects are exogenous versus endogenous. Such models may have numerous applications in industrial economics, public economics, or international economics. The paper illustrates that the performance of Bayesian

Spatial Econometrics: Qualitative and Limited Dependent Variables
Advances in Econometrics, Volume 37, 119–144

ISSN: 0731-9053/doi:10.1108/S0731-905320160000037011

estimation methods for such models is supportive of their use with even relatively small panel data sets.

Keywords: Spatial econometrics; panel probit; multivariate probit

JEL classifications: C11; C31; C35

1. INTRODUCTION

Many fields in applied economics involve multinomial choice problems. Examples are the choice of sending children to public schools and to vote in favor of a school budget (Greene, 1984) in public choice; the choice among various types of labor markets in labor economics (Haque & Haque, 2009); the choice of different health care plans or treatments in health economics (Jones, 2007); the choice of different types of preferential agreements (for trade and investment) in international economics (Egger & Wamser, 2013). In treatment studies with a binary outcome such as graduating or not and a binary endogenous treatment such as private versus public schooling in education economics (Altonji, Elder, & Taber, 2005). Historically, applications of such models use cross-section data, but recent applications include panel data (Börsch-Supan, Hajivassiliou, Kotlikoff, & Morris, 1992; Egger & Wamser, 2013; Johnson & Hensher, 1982; Keane, 1997; Mulkay, 2014, to mention a few). While a case for cross-sectional interdependence could be made – due to the presence of peer-group effects, social interaction, strategic interaction, spillovers, and general equilibrium effects – most applications ignore cross-sectional dependence. This paper proposes bivariate panel probit models which could be used in applied work in order to allow for equicorrelation due to the repeated observation of cross-sectional units over time as well as for cross-sectional dependence among the units within time.

The paper proposes a Bayesian bivariate probit model and analyzes its performance in small samples.[1] Monte Carlo simulation results are encouraging as parameter estimates can be obtained without much bias in small samples, and the root-mean-squared errors decline as the sample size increases, in particular, with the cross-sectional dimension. The paper illustrates how such models could readily be extended to the multivariate case with more than two equations. Also, the paper discusses the case where the explanatory variables are correlated with the time-invariant error components.

The remainder of this paper is organized as follows. The next section outlines a parsimonious model version. Section 3 describes the estimation of the model parameters of interest. Section 4 proposes extensions of the model allowing for a richer setting of cross-sectional dependence across equations. In particular, it outlines a multivariate model with more than two equations, and it discusses the case of a correlated random effects model. Section 5 summarizes the Monte Carlo simulation results for leading types of models addressed in the paper, and the last section concludes.

2. ECONOMETRIC MODEL

Let us denote the binary observable variables regarding the mth decision or equation for unit i at time t by $y_{m,it}$, where $m \in \{1,2\}$ reflects the bivariate case. The total number of individual units and time periods be N and T, respectively. We observe this binary variable as

$$y_{m,it} = 1(y^*_{m,it} > 0), \qquad i = 1,2,\ldots,N \text{ and } t = 1,2,\ldots,T, \tag{1}$$

$$y^*_{m,it} = \lambda_m \bar{y}^*_{m,it} + x_{m,it}\beta_m + \alpha_{m,i} + \nu_{m,it} \qquad \text{with } \bar{y}^*_{m,it} = \sum_{j=1}^{N} w_{ijt} y^*_{m,jt}, \tag{2}$$

where $y^*_{m,it}$ is a latent (i.e., unobserved) variable and denotes the net gains for i from choosing m at time t. $\lambda_m \bar{y}^*_{m,it}$ reflects a (global) *spillover effect* of other units on i.[2] w_{ijt} is a normalized weight describing the strength of the relationship between units i and j at time t. In the spatial panel econometrics literature, w_{ijt} is often assumed time invariant. However, assuming that is not necessary, w_{ijt} is nonnegative if two distinct units i and j are neighbors and zero otherwise at time t; it is always zero for $i=j$.[3] Notice that the notion of neighborliness behind w_{ijt} is generic and can be related to space in a narrow sense or to other concepts (such as input-output relations, worker flows, and information flows). λ_m denotes the spatial autocorrelation, contagion, interdependence, or spillover parameter for latent outcome of type m, and it is important to gauge the relative magnitude of spillovers. The $1 \times K$ vector of covariates $x_{m,it} = (x_{k,m,it})$ is indexed by m for reasons of parameter identification in multivariate probit models (see Keane, 1992; Munkin & Trivedi, 2008).

The time-varying idiosyncratic error is denoted by $\nu_{m,it}$ and the time-invariant random effect is denoted by $\alpha_{m,i}$. For these error components, we adopt the conventional assumptions that $E(\nu_{m,it}\nu_{m,jt}) = 0$ for all $i \neq j$, $E(\alpha_{m,i}\nu_{m,it}) = 0$ for all m,t, $E(\nu_{m,it}\nu_{m,is}) = 0$ for all $t \neq s$. More specifically, regarding the bivariate distributions of $(\alpha_{l,i}, \alpha_{m,i})$ and $(\nu_{l,it}, \nu_{m,it})$, we assume bivariate normality

$$\begin{pmatrix} \alpha_{1,i} \\ \alpha_{2,i} \end{pmatrix} \sim N\left(\begin{pmatrix} \overline{\alpha}_1 \\ \overline{\alpha}_2 \end{pmatrix}, \begin{pmatrix} \sigma_{\alpha,11} & \sigma_{\alpha,12} \\ \sigma_{\alpha,12} & \sigma_{\alpha,22} \end{pmatrix}\right), \quad \begin{pmatrix} \nu_{1,it} \\ \nu_{2,it} \end{pmatrix} \sim N\left(\begin{pmatrix} 0 \\ 0 \end{pmatrix}, \begin{pmatrix} 1 & \tau \\ \tau & 1 \end{pmatrix}\right).$$

The variances of $\nu_{1,it}$ and $\nu_{2,it}$ are normalized to unity (see, for instance, Greene, 2003, for a treatment of the bivariate probit model without accounting for any form of spatial correlation) and τ denotes the tetrachoric correlation.

We shall impose the assumption that all elements of $x_{m,it}$ are *doubly exogenous* in the sense that $E[x_{m,it}\alpha_{m,i}] = 0$ and $E[x_{m,it}\nu_{m,it}] = 0$.[4]

As is common in spatial panel econometrics (see, e.g., Kapoor, Kelejian, & Prucha, 2007), the observations are stacked such that i is the fast index and t the slow index, which yields the following stacked model for equation m of the framework given in Eqs. (1) and (2)

$$y_m = 1\left(y_m^* > 0\right), \tag{3}$$

$$y_m^* = \lambda_m \overline{y}_m^* + x_m\beta_m + \alpha_m + \nu_m \qquad \text{with } \overline{y}_m^* = W_{TN}y_m^*, \tag{4}$$

for $m \in \{1,2\}$ where y_m, y_m^*, and ν_m are of dimension $TN \times 1$. The matrix x_m is of dimension $TN \times k_m$ and its parameter vector β_m is $k_m \times 1$. The spatial weights matrix $W_{TN} = \text{diag}(W_{tN})$ is of dimension $TN \times TN$ and contains zero diagonal elements. Its off-diagonal elements of W_{tN} are nonzero, reflecting the neighborliness between two cross-sectional units. Moreover, we assume the elements of W_{TN} to be normalized so that the admissible parameter space of $\{\lambda_1, \lambda_2\}$ is known and less than unity in absolute value. For instance, a convenient normalization is dividing each element by the corresponding sum across elements in a row (see Anselin, 1988, Kelejian & Prucha, 2010 for alternative normalizations).[5] The vector α_m is of dimension $N \times 1$. Stacking both equations for $m \in \{1,2\}$ below one another yields the following model for the latent dependent variables:

$$y^* = (\Lambda \otimes J_{TN}) \odot Wy^* + X\beta + A\alpha + \nu,$$

where $\otimes$ denotes the Kronecker product and $\odot$ the Hadamard product, ι_T is a vector of ones of dimension T, I_N is an identity matrix of dimension N, and J_{TN} is a matrix of ones of dimension TN, and

$$\Lambda = \begin{pmatrix} \lambda_1 & 0 \\ 0 & \lambda_2 \end{pmatrix}, \quad W = \begin{pmatrix} W_{TN} & 0 \\ 0 & W_{TN} \end{pmatrix}, \quad X = \begin{pmatrix} x_1 & 0 \\ 0 & x_2 \end{pmatrix}, \quad A = \begin{pmatrix} \iota_T \otimes I_N & 0 \\ 0 & \iota_T \otimes I_N \end{pmatrix},$$

$$y^* = \left(y_1^{*\prime}, y_2^{*\prime}\right)', \; \beta = \left(\beta_1', \beta_2'\right)', \; \alpha = \left(\alpha_1', \alpha_2'\right)', \text{ and } \nu = \left(\nu_1', \nu_2'\right)'.$$

The reduced form is given by

$$y^* = S^{-1}(X\beta + A\alpha + \nu),$$

with $S = (I_{2TN} - (\Lambda \otimes J_{TN}) \odot W) = \begin{pmatrix} S_1 & 0 \\ 0 & S_2 \end{pmatrix}$, where $S_m = I_{TN} - \lambda_m W_{TN}$.

Together with the normalization of W_{TN}, the admissible parameter space of Λ ensures invertibility of S.

3. MODEL ESTIMATION

3.1. Bayesian Estimation Procedure

Non-spatial bivariate panel data models can be estimated by maximum likelihood. The presence of the spatial lag $\bar{y}^*_{m,it}$ as a determinant of the latent variable $y^*_{m,it}$ leads to a reduced form of the model which is nonlinear in variables and parameters and to an N-dimensional integral in the likelihood function. However, ignoring relevant spatial lags in the system leads to inconsistent estimates of the parameters.

For implementation and estimation, we follow the generic Markov chain Monte Carlo (MCMC) simulation approach suggested by LeSage (2000) and LeSage and Pace (2009), who focused mainly on single-equation and cross-sectional models.

Bayesian MCMC simulation entails estimating the posterior distribution of all parameters by combining prior information on them with the likelihood for the respective model, and sampling each parameter sequentially from its conditional distribution. This approach involves both Gibbs and Metropolis Hastings sampling. Details on those are provided in the next subsections.

Building on the idea of Albert and Chib (1993) for non-spatial, cross-sectional, univariate probit models and on LeSage (2000) and LeSage and

Pace (2009) for spatial, cross-sectional, univariate, and multivariate probits, we introduce the latent variables as additional parameters. This provides for a considerable facilitation of the estimation procedure, as conditioning on latent variables yields simpler distributions which we can sample from.

For modeling the time-invariant, unobserved heterogeneity across cross-sectional units through $\alpha = (\alpha_1', \alpha_2')'$, we assume a hierarchical structure, whereby all $\alpha_i = (\alpha_{1i}, \alpha_{2i})'$ are based on a distribution, which has some parameters in common, which we refer to as *hyperparameters*. These hyperparameters – namely, mean μ_α and variance V_α – are drawn in a separate step and used when drawing α_i.

All parameters to be estimated we subsume in the parameter vector $\theta = \{\beta, \lambda_1, \lambda_2, \tau, y^*, \alpha, \mu_\alpha, V_\alpha\}$.

Using $y = (y_1', y_2')'$, the joint posterior distribution is given by

$$\begin{aligned} &p(\theta|y, X, W) \\ &\propto p(y|y^*, X, W)p(y^*|\beta, \lambda_1, \lambda_2, \tau, \alpha, \mu_\alpha, V_\alpha, X, W) \\ &\quad p(\beta)p(\lambda_1)p(\lambda_2)p(\tau)p(\alpha|\mu_\alpha, V_\alpha)p(\mu_\alpha)p(V_\alpha), \end{aligned}$$

where the first term in the second line relates the observed dependent variables to their latent counterparts, the second term in the second line denotes the likelihood, and the third line contains the priors. Details on these components will be given in the following paragraphs. Since the expressions above turn out to be intractable, we calculate the conditional distributions for all model parameters given the data and the other parameters, $\theta_\ell|\theta_{-\theta_\ell}$, which are given in detail in Section 3.2.

3.1.1. Likelihood

The likelihood is stated in terms of the latent variables y_m^*. The joint distribution of (y_1^*, y_2^*) is given by

$$\begin{pmatrix} y_1^* \\ y_2^* \end{pmatrix} \sim N\left(S^{-1}(X\beta + A\alpha), \begin{pmatrix} (S_1'S_1)^{-1} & \tau(S_2'S_1)^{-1} \\ \tau(S_1'S_2)^{-1} & (S_2'S_2)^{-1} \end{pmatrix}\right).$$

This yields the likelihood

$$p(y_1^*, y_2^*|\theta, X) = \frac{|S_1||S_2|}{(2\pi)^{TN}|\Sigma|^{TN/2}} \exp\left[-\frac{1}{2}\operatorname{trace}(R\Sigma^{-1})\right],$$

where $\Sigma = \begin{pmatrix} 1 & \tau \\ \tau & 1 \end{pmatrix}$ and $R = \begin{pmatrix} r_{11} & r_{12} \\ r_{21} & r_{22} \end{pmatrix}$ is a 2×2 matrix containing the elements $r_{uv} = \left(S_u y_u^* - (x_u \beta_u + (\iota_T \otimes \alpha_u))\right)'(S_v y_v^* - (x_v \beta_v + (\iota_T \otimes \alpha_v)))$.

3.1.2. Priors

The prior distributions are assumed to be

$$\beta \sim N\left(\underline{\beta}, \underline{V}\right) \quad \text{where } \underline{\beta} = 0_{2k \times 1} \text{ and } \underline{V} = I_{2k} \cdot 1e^{12}, \tag{5}$$

$$\lambda_m \sim U(-1,1), \quad \tau \sim U(-1,1). \tag{6}$$

Notice that λ_m and τ are parameters, which are bounded theoretically in absolute value. For instance, with a row-normalized matrix W_{TN} (and, hence W) and the model proposed in this section, both λ_m and τ need to be smaller than unity in absolute value.

Modeling the unobserved heterogeneity with a hierarchical prior, we draw hyperparameters from distributions using the following priors:

$$\mu_\alpha \sim N\left(\underline{\mu}_{\mu\alpha}, \underline{V}_{\mu\alpha}\right) \quad \text{where } \underline{\mu}_{\mu\alpha} = 0_{2 \times 1} \text{ and } \underline{V}_{\mu\alpha} = I_2, \tag{7}$$

$$V_\alpha^{-1} \sim \mathcal{W}\left(\underline{V}_{V\alpha}^{-1}, \underline{v}_{V\alpha}\right) \quad \text{where } \underline{V}_{V\alpha}^{-1} = I_2 \text{ and } \underline{v}_{V\alpha} = 2, \tag{8}$$

where $\mathcal{W}$ denotes the Wishart distribution. The choice of the prior parameters leads to relatively uninformative priors reflecting a large degree of uncertainty about them. Intuitively, in calculating the posterior distribution, less weight is placed on the priors and more on the data as a consequence.

3.2. Conditional Distributions

We calculate the conditional distribution of each of the parameters given all the other parameters of the model.

3.2.1. Conditional Distribution of y_1^* and y_2^*

The posterior distributions for the latent variables are calculated using the joint distribution of (y_1^*, y_2^*). The conditional distribution of y_1^* given the other parameters is given by

$$y_1^* | \theta_{-y_1^*} \sim N\left(S_1^{-1}\{x_1\beta_1 + \iota_T \otimes \alpha_1 + \tau(S_2 y_2^* - x_2\beta_2 - \iota_T \otimes \alpha_2)\}, (1-\tau^2)(S_1' S_1)^{-1}\right).$$

The conditional distribution of y_2^* given the other parameters is given by

$$y_2^* | \theta_{-y_2^*} \sim N\left(S_2^{-1}\{x_2\beta_2 + \iota_T \otimes \alpha_2 + \tau(S_1 y_1^* - x_1\beta_1 - \iota_T \otimes \alpha_1)\}, (1-\tau^2)(S_2' S_2)^{-1}\right).$$

y_m^* is truncated multivariate normal. Thus, we apply the method by Geweke (1991). When drawing y_m^*, we account for the observed binary y_m, taking draws from a right-truncated normal if y_m is 0 and from a left-truncated normal if y_m is 1.

3.2.2. Conditional Distribution of β

The conditional distribution of $\beta = (\beta_1', \beta_2')'$ given the other parameters is

$$\beta | \theta_{-\beta} \sim N(\overline{\beta}, \overline{V}_\beta), \tag{9}$$

where

$$\overline{\beta} = \overline{V}_\beta\left(X'(\Sigma^{-1} \otimes I_{TN})(Sy^* - A\alpha) + \underline{V}^{-1}\underline{\beta}\right),$$
$$\overline{V}_\beta = \left(X'(\Sigma^{-1} \otimes I_{TN})X + \underline{V}^{-1}\right)^{-1}.$$

We apply Gibbs sampling to draw values for β.

3.2.3. Conditional Distribution of λ_1 and λ_2

The conditional distribution of λ_m for $m \in \{1, 2\}$ is given by

$$\lambda_m | \theta_{-\lambda_m} \propto |S_m| \exp\left[-\frac{1}{2}\operatorname{trace}\left(R\Sigma^{-1}\right)\right]. \tag{10}$$

This conditional distribution is of an unknown form. Thus, we apply Metropolis-Hastings rather than Gibbs sampling for drawing it. We follow LeSage and Pace (2009) and draw a proposal candidate λ_m^c using

$\lambda_m^c = \lambda_m + c_{\lambda_m} \cdot N(0,1)$, where λ_m denotes the previous value and c_{λ_m} a tuning parameter. When taking draws we only use candidates lying in the admissible parameter space between -1 and 1. Using λ_m, λ_m^c, and Eq. (10), we calculate an acceptance probability to decide whether using the new candidate value or keeping the previous one. To ensure an acceptance probability between 40% and 60% we adapt the tuning parameter c_{λ_m}.[6]

3.2.4. Conditional Distribution of τ

The conditional distribution of τ is given by

$$\tau|\theta_{-\tau} \propto \frac{1}{(1-\tau^2)^{NT/2}} \exp\left[-\frac{1}{2}\text{trace}\left(R\Sigma^{-1}\right)\right]. \tag{11}$$

Akin to λ_m, the conditional posterior distribution of τ takes an unknown form and we apply Metropolis-Hastings for drawing it. We apply the same approach as for drawing λ_m and draw new values using $\tau^c = \tau + c_\tau \cdot N(0,1)$. Since τ lies in the interval between -1 and $+1$, we only accept those candidate values τ^c which lie in this interval. Both τ and τ^c are evaluated using Eq. (11) to calculate an acceptance probability and the tuning parameter c_τ is adapted to ensure an acceptance probability between 40% and 60%.

3.2.5. Conditional Distribution of α

The conditional distribution of the $2N \times 1$ vector $\alpha = \left(\alpha_1', \alpha_2'\right)'$ is

$$\alpha|\theta_{-\alpha} \sim N\left(\overline{\alpha}, \overline{V}_\alpha\right),$$

where

$$\overline{\alpha} = \overline{V}_\alpha\left(A'\left(\Sigma^{-1} \otimes I_{TN}\right)(Sy^* - X\beta) + \left(V_\alpha^{-1} \otimes I_N\right)\left(\mu_\alpha \otimes \iota_N\right)\right),$$

$$\overline{V}_\alpha = \left(\left(T\Sigma^{-1} + V_\alpha^{-1}\right) \otimes I_N\right)^{-1},$$

which are based on the hyperparameters μ_α and V_α, which are drawn as

$$\mu_\alpha|\theta_{-\mu\alpha} \sim N\left(\overline{\mu}_{\mu\alpha}, \overline{V}_{\mu\alpha}\right),$$

using

$$\overline{\mu}_{\mu\alpha} = \overline{V}_{\mu\alpha}\left(\left(V_\alpha^{-1} \otimes \iota_N'\right)\alpha + \underline{V}_{\mu\alpha}^{-1}\underline{\mu}_{\mu\alpha}\right),$$

$$\overline{V}_{\mu\alpha} = \left(NV_\alpha^{-1} + \underline{V}_{\mu\alpha}^{-1}\right)^{-1},$$

and

$$V_\alpha^{-1}|\theta_{-V_\alpha^{-1}} \sim \mathcal{W}(\overline{V}_{V\alpha}, \overline{\nu}_{V\alpha}),$$

with

$$\overline{\nu}_{V\alpha} = \underline{\nu} + N, \qquad \overline{V}_{V\alpha} = \left(H + \underline{V}_{V\alpha}\right)^{-1}$$

and the 2×2 matrix $H = \begin{pmatrix} h_{11} & h_{12} \\ h_{21} & h_{22} \end{pmatrix}$ containing the elements $h_{uv} = \left(\alpha_u - \mu_{\alpha u}\iota_N\right)' (\alpha_v - \mu_{\alpha v}\iota_N)$, where ι_N is an $N \times 1$ vector of ones. All of these parameters have known distributions. Specifically, we apply Gibbs sampling, drawing the hyperparameters μ_α and V_α first and then using those in drawing the elements of α.

3.2.6. Interpretation of Results

Clearly, the point estimates of the parameters are a key ingredient for a quantitative assessment of the results. As with standard probit models, marginal effects of changes in explanatory variables cannot be read off the parameters but need to be evaluated at a certain point, typically the sample mean of the data. The computation of marginal effects in standard (non-spatial) probit models is outlined, for example, in Greene (2003). With an index of the probit model whose reduced form is itself nonlinear in parameters, this issue is exacerbated. As with standard spatial models, direct, indirect, and total effects can be distinguished. What is of interest in probit models are the direct and total effects (with the indirect effects being defined as the difference between the latter and the former) on the probability that the outcome of interest is unity. This issue is exhaustively discussed for univariate probit models in LeSage, Pace, Lam, Campanella, and Liu (2011) and in Lacombe and LeSage (2015). The computation of marginal effects in bivariate probit models involves a straightforward combination of the approach outlined in Greene (1996) for non-spatial bivariate probits and in LeSage, Pace, Lam, Campanella, and Liu (2011) and Lacombe and LeSage (2015) for spatial univariate probits.

4. EXTENSIONS

In this section, we consider three extensions. First, we introduce a richer framework of interdependence than the one introduced in Sections 2 and 3.

This may be a useful extension, if the researcher believes that spillovers across individuals are related not only to a specific but also to all latent outcomes. Second, we briefly discuss the case of more than two equations, which may be generally referred to as multinomial spatial probit estimation. Such a case may emerge, for instance, if researchers analyze problems with many discrete decisions (e.g., market entry with multi-product firms; market-entry with multi-national firms; etc.). Third, we discuss the case of estimation with correlated random effects, where some of the explanatory variables may be correlated with the unobserved individual-specific characteristics. The latter is often considered to be more plausible than the case of so-called double-exogeneity as assumed before, where the explanatory variables are uncorrelated with both the time-invariant and the time-variant characteristics of the cross-sectional units.

4.1. A Richer Structural Latent-Variable Framework

4.1.1. Model

In what follows, we use the same notation as before as far as this is possible. In applications, the consideration of within-equation spatial dependence dominates. This might even be the case with systems of equations with binary-dependent variables. However, in the latter case, economic theory or intuition of the researcher might support a more general setup, where cross-sectional spillovers are associated not only with the latent variable pertaining to the same equation as the binary outcome but also with the ones pertaining to other binary outcomes in the system.

The model is given by

$$y_{m,it} = 1(y^*_{m,it} > 0), \tag{12}$$

$$y^*_{m,it} = \sum_{l=1}^{2} \lambda_{ml} \bar{y}^*_{ml,it} + x_{m,it}\beta_m + \alpha_{m,i} + \nu_{m,it} \quad \text{with} \quad \bar{y}^*_{ml,it} = \sum_{j=1}^{N} w_{ml,ijt} y^*_{l,jt}. \tag{13}$$

The observations are stacked such that i is the fast index and t the slow index, which yields the following stacked model for equation m of the model given in Eqs. (12) and (13):

$$y_m = 1\left(y^*_m > 0\right), \tag{14}$$

$$y_m^* = \sum_{l=1}^{2} \lambda_{ml} \bar{y}_{ml}^* + x_m \beta_m + \iota_T \otimes \alpha_m + \nu_m \quad \text{with } \bar{y}_{ml}^* = W_{ml,TN} y_l^*. \tag{15}$$

The only thing that is now needed is a redefinition of Λ, W, and S: $\Lambda = \begin{pmatrix} \lambda_{11} & \lambda_{12} \\ \lambda_{21} & \lambda_{22} \end{pmatrix}$, $W = \begin{pmatrix} W_{11,TN} & W_{12,TN} \\ W_{21,TN} & W_{22,TN} \end{pmatrix}$, and $S = (I_{2TN} - (\Lambda \otimes J_{TN}) \odot W)$ $= \begin{pmatrix} S_{11} & S_{12} \\ S_{21} & S_{22} \end{pmatrix}$. The $2TN \times 2TN$ matrix W consists of four $TN \times TN$ spatial weights matrices $W_{ij,TN}$ for $i,j \in \{1,2\}$. Of course, one can also assume the same $W_{ij,TN}$ for all i and j. Define $\tilde{S} = S^{-1} = \begin{pmatrix} \tilde{S}_{11} & \tilde{S}_{12} \\ \tilde{S}_{21} & \tilde{S}_{22} \end{pmatrix}$. Then stacking Eq. (15) for $m \in \{1,2\}$ yields

$$y^* = (\Lambda \otimes J_{TN}) \odot W y^* + X\beta + A\alpha + \nu, \tag{16}$$

and its reduced form is given by

$$y^* = \tilde{S}(X\beta + A\alpha + \nu). \tag{17}$$

4.1.2. Joint Distribution of (y_1^*, y_2^*) and the Likelihood

Based on Eq. (17), the joint distribution of (y_1^*, y_2^*) is given by

$$\begin{pmatrix} y_1^* \\ y_2^* \end{pmatrix} \sim N\left(\begin{pmatrix} \tilde{S}_{11}(x_1\beta_1 + \iota_T \otimes \alpha_1) + \tilde{S}_{12}(x_2\beta_2 + \iota_T \otimes \alpha_2) \\ \tilde{S}_{21}(x_1\beta_1 + \iota_T \otimes \alpha_1) + \tilde{S}_{22}(x_2\beta_2 + \iota_T \otimes \alpha_2) \end{pmatrix}, \begin{pmatrix} \Omega_{11} & \Omega_{12} \\ \Omega_{21} & \Omega_{22} \end{pmatrix} \right) \tag{18}$$

with $\begin{pmatrix} \Omega_{11} & \Omega_{12} \\ \Omega_{21} & \Omega_{22} \end{pmatrix} = \begin{pmatrix} \tilde{S}_{11} & \tilde{S}_{12} \\ \tilde{S}_{21} & \tilde{S}_{22} \end{pmatrix} (\Sigma \otimes I_{TN}) \begin{pmatrix} \tilde{S}'_{11} & \tilde{S}'_{21} \\ \tilde{S}'_{12} & \tilde{S}'_{22} \end{pmatrix}$.

This yields the likelihood

$$p(y^*|\theta, X) = \frac{1}{2\pi^{TN} |\Sigma|^{TN/2}} |S_{22}| |S_{11} - S_{12} S_{22}^{-1} S_{21}| \exp\left[-\frac{1}{2} \operatorname{trace}\left(R\Sigma^{-1}\right) \right],$$

where $\Sigma = \begin{pmatrix} 1 & \tau \\ \tau & 1 \end{pmatrix}$ and $R = \begin{pmatrix} r_{11} & r_{12} \\ r_{21} & r_{22} \end{pmatrix}$ is a 2×2 matrix containing the elements $r_{uv} = r'_u \cdot r_v$ for $u, v \in \{1, 2\}$ with

$$\begin{pmatrix} r_1 \\ r_2 \end{pmatrix} = \begin{pmatrix} S_{11}y_1^* + S_{12}y_2^* - (x_1\beta_1 + \iota_T \otimes \alpha_1) \\ S_{21}y_1^* + S_{22}y_2^* - (x_2\beta_2 + \iota_T \otimes \alpha_2) \end{pmatrix}.$$

4.1.3. Priors

We use the same uninformative priors given by Eqs. (5)–(8). In line with the previous subsection, we assume a uniform uninformative prior for all λ_{ij} for $i, j \in \{1, 2\}$.

4.1.4. Conditional Distribution of y_1^* and y_2^*

Using the joint distribution of (y_1^*, y_2^*) in Eq. (18), the conditional distribution of y_1^* given the other parameters is given by

$$\begin{aligned} y_1^* | \theta_{-y_1^*} \sim N\big(&\tilde{S}_{11}(x_1\beta_1 + \iota_T \otimes \alpha_1) + \tilde{S}_{12}(x_2\beta_2 + \iota_T \otimes \alpha_2) \\ &+ \Omega_{12}\Omega_{22}^{-1}\left[y_2^* - \tilde{S}_{21}(x_1\beta_1 + \iota_T \otimes \alpha_1) - \tilde{S}_{22}(x_2\beta_2 + \iota_T \otimes \alpha_2)\right], \\ &\Omega_{11} - \Omega_{12}\Omega_{22}^{-1}\Omega_{21}\big). \end{aligned}$$

The conditional distribution of y_2^* given the other parameters is given by

$$\begin{aligned} y_2^* | \theta_{-y_2^*} \sim N\big(&\tilde{S}_{21}(x_1\beta_1 + \iota_T \otimes \alpha_1) + \tilde{S}_{22}(x_2\beta_2 + \iota_T \otimes \alpha_2) \\ &+ \Omega_{21}\Omega_{11}^{-1}\left[y_1^* - \tilde{S}_{11}(x_1\beta_1 + \iota_T \otimes \alpha_1) - \tilde{S}_{12}(x_2\beta_2 + \iota_T \otimes \alpha_2)\right], \Omega_{22} - \Omega_{21}\Omega_{11}^{-1}\Omega_{12}\big). \end{aligned}$$

4.1.5. Conditional Distribution of λ_{gh}

The conditional distribution of λ_{11}, λ_{12}, and λ_{21} is given by

$$\lambda_{uv} | \theta_{-\lambda_{uv}} \propto |S_{uu} - S_{uv}S_{vv}^{-1}S_{vu}| \exp\left[-\frac{1}{2}\mathrm{trace}\left(R\Sigma^{-1}\right)\right], \tag{19}$$

for $uv \in \{11, 12, 21\}$. Since this distribution takes an unknown form, we apply a Metropolis-Hastings procedure where we draw the new candidate values for λ_{11}, λ_{12}, and λ_{21}, and for λ_{22} we use

$$\lambda_{22}|\theta_{-\lambda_{22}} \propto |S_{22}||S_{11} - S_{12}S_{22}^{-1}S_{21}|\exp\left[-\frac{1}{2}\,\text{trace}\left(R\Sigma^{-1}\right)\right]. \tag{20}$$

We apply the Metropolis-Hastings procedure as in Section 3.2. However, due to the more complex equation system, we need to take stability conditions into account. For example, when drawing the new candidate values, we only accept those where $|\lambda_{h1}| \leqslant 1 - |\lambda_{h2}|$ and $|\lambda_{h2}| \leqslant 1 - |\lambda_{h1}|$ for $h \in \{1, 2\}$.

4.1.6. Conditional Distribution of β, α, and τ

For β, α, and τ, the conditional distributions are the same as in Section 3.2. The only difference is that we now use the S defined in Section 4.1.1.

4.2. Multinomial Spatial Probit Estimation with More than Two Equations

The proposed procedure can be extended to more than two decisions. Suppose one has M decisions, which corresponds to M equations. The dimensionality of the observed variable y and its latent counterpart y^* is $MTN \times 1$. The matrix of covariates is then of dimension $MTN \times \sum_{m=1}^{M} k_m$, where k_m denotes the dimensionality of the covariate matrix in the respective equation. The spatial weights matrix W and the matrices S and A are of dimension $MTN \times MTN$. The unobserved heterogeneity α is $MN \times 1$. The matrix of the spatial autocorrelation parameters Λ and the matrices R and Σ are then of dimension $M \times M$.[7] The likelihood and the conditional distributions of β, α, and λ are mathematically equivalent to and only of a different dimensionality than in the bivariate case. Each latent variable, y_m^* for the m-th equation, is to be drawn conditional on the ones in all the other equations. The relatively biggest difference is with respect to the estimation of the off-diagonal elements of Σ which have to be drawn based on a Wishart distribution subject to normalization constraints (see the discussion in Koop, 2003).

4.3. Endogenous Time-Invariant Effects

In Bayesian econometrics, it is common to assume that all covariates and also the unobserved individual-specific effect are purely random variables.

However, this is not the case in many empirical applications, where it is likely that some of the covariates of an individual are correlated with its unobserved individual-specific characteristics: in wage equations, education is correlated with individuals' unmeasurable ability, and affects discrete labor-market choices of individuals; total factor productivity is correlated with unobservable managerial or entrepreneurial talent and organization and affects discrete (market-entry or scope) decisions by firms; regional observable attributes are correlated with unobservable amenities and their hedonic valuation by mobile residents; etc. Ignoring potential correlation between unobserved heterogeneity and covariates might lead to an omitted variables bias in coefficients of interest on observable variables.

One prominent way to account for a potential correlation between unobserved heterogeneity and the covariates is proposed by Mundlak (1978). He proposed to include the averages of time-varying covariates as additional regressors into the regression equation to approximate the unobserved heterogeneity. In a second extension, we follow his suggestion. By and large, this leaves our approach described in Section 3.2 unchanged. The only difference is that the matrix of covariates now consists of $[X, \overline{X}]$, where $\overline{X}$ contains the time averages of the columns of X that pertain to time-variant explanatory variables.

5. MONTE CARLO SIMULATION STUDY

To illustrate the performance of the bivariate panel probit model with triangular data, we perform Monte Carlo experiments for a spatial bivariate model structure along the aforementioned lines.

5.1. Design for the Basic Model

In particular, we assume two variables $x_{1,it} \sim N(0, 1)$ and $x_{2,it} \sim N(0, 1)$ which enter both equations of the system. Their true parameter values are for the first equation $\beta_1 = (\beta_{11}, \beta_{12}) = (-2, 1.25)$ and for the second equation $\beta_2 = (\beta_{21}, \beta_{22}) = (-1, 0.5)$.

We assume a time-invariant, row-normalized, 5-before-5-behind neighborhood structure regarding W_N so that $W_{TN} = \text{diag}_T(W_N)$, and $w_{ii} = 0$ and all non-diagonal elements w_{ij} are either zero (non-neighbors) or 0.1 (neighbors).

Moreover, we specify the bivariate normality about the 2×1 vector α_i as $\alpha_i \sim N\left(\begin{pmatrix} 0.5 \\ 0.25 \end{pmatrix}, \begin{pmatrix} 1 & 0.4 \\ 0.4 & 1.25 \end{pmatrix}\right)$.

We consider four alternative sets of parameters $(\lambda_1, \lambda_2, \tau)$ with

$$(\lambda_1, \lambda_2, \tau) = \begin{cases} (0.4, 0.6, 0.5) \\ (0.2, 0.3, 0.5) \\ (0.4, 0.6, 0.8) \\ (0.4, 0.6, 0) \end{cases}$$

In general, we consider two configurations each for N and T with $N \in \{100; 500\}$ and $T \in \{5; 7\}$.

For each of the four parameter and four panel configurations, we draw 500 $2NT \times 1$ vectors of residuals ν. For each one of these 8,000 experiments, we do an MCMC simulation with a chain of 30,000 elements of which 4,000 are burn-ins and only every 10th of the remaining elements is used (i.e., a thinning ratio of one-10th is applied).

5.2. Simulation Results for the Basic Model

We summarize the corresponding simulation results in Tables 1 and 2. In Table 1, we report on $\hat{\theta} = (\hat{\lambda}_1, \hat{\lambda}_2, \hat{\beta}_{11}, \hat{\beta}_{12}, \hat{\beta}_{21}, \hat{\beta}_{22}, \hat{\tau})$ and moments of the elements of $\hat{\alpha}_1$ and $\hat{\alpha}_2$ for the first parameter configuration and alternative sample-size configurations. In Table 2, we focus on the configuration of $N = 100$ and $T = 5$ for the remaining three considered true parameter configurations.

The results in Table 1 suggest that the parameter biases are relatively small, even in the case of $\{N = 100; T = 5\}$. Obviously, the biases decline as the sample size grows in the T- and, in particular, the N-dimensions. With $\{N = 500; T = 5\}$, the biases of most parameters are down to a range of

Table 1. Results for Various Cases of $\{N, T\}$.

	β_{11}	β_{12}	β_{21}	β_{22}	λ_1	λ_2	τ	α_1	α_2
True	−2	1.25	−1	0.5	0.4	0.6	0.5	0.5	0.25
$N = 100$, $T = 5$									
Mean	−2.168	1.329	−1.082	0.517	0.422	0.559	0.440	0.391	0.262
Bias	−0.168	0.079	−0.082	0.017	0.022	−0.041	−0.060	−0.109	0.012
RMSE	0.342	0.219	0.162	0.111	0.068	0.094	0.140	0.145	0.079
I-statistic	5.096	1.963	1.954	1.095	2.393	1.993	3.143	1.176	1.086
GT *p*-value	0.462	0.467	0.530	0.485	0.502	0.511	0.451	0.479	0.504
$N = 100$, $T = 7$									
Mean	−2.084	1.305	−1.107	0.557	0.409	0.617	0.479	0.380	0.180
Bias	−0.084	0.055	−0.107	0.057	0.009	0.017	−0.021	−0.120	−0.070
RMSE	0.205	0.147	0.161	0.111	0.057	0.054	0.106	0.141	0.087
I-statistic	4.014	1.989	1.796	1.114	2.073	1.845	3.261	1.129	1.046
GT *p*-value	0.427	0.440	0.502	0.519	0.478	0.506	0.480	0.441	0.497
$N = 500$, $T = 5$									
Mean	−2.096	1.292	−1.083	0.527	0.407	0.639	0.496	0.531	0.255
Bias	−0.096	0.042	−0.083	0.027	0.007	0.039	−0.004	0.031	0.005
RMSE	0.158	0.092	0.105	0.057	0.031	0.048	0.057	0.057	0.028
I-statistic	4.140	2.430	1.731	1.139	2.285	1.758	3.376	1.416	1.068
GT *p*-value	0.456	0.460	0.494	0.501	0.484	0.469	0.465	0.474	0.511

The *I*-statistic is calculated following Raftery and Lewis (1992). GT *p*-value denotes the *p*-value of the Geweke (1992) test.

about 5–10% of the true values only, across the board. These biases are about twice as high with $\{N = 100; T = 5\}$. However, when comparing these results with non-spatial models, we would support the use of spatial panel data probits even with small to moderate data sets at hand.

The underlying correlations between the true and the predicted latent variables are: 0.8699 for $(y_1^*, \hat{y}_1^*)$ and 0.7760 $(y_2^*, \hat{y}_2^*)$ for $\{N, T\} = \{100, 5\}$; 0.8812 for $(y_1^*, \hat{y}_1^*)$ and 0.8710 $(y_2^*, \hat{y}_2^*)$ for $\{N, T\} = \{100, 7\}$; and 0.7875 for $(y_1^*, \hat{y}_1^*)$ and 0.7760 $(y_2^*, \hat{y}_2^*)$ for $\{N, T\} = \{500, 5\}$. These numbers indicate that there is enough noise in the data-generating process so that the small

Table 2. Results for Alternative Values of $\{\lambda_1, \lambda_2, \tau\}$ and $N = 100$ and $T = 5$.

	β_{11}	β_{12}	β_{21}	β_{22}	λ_1	λ_2	τ	α_1	α_2
True	−2	1.25	−1	0.5	0.2	0.3	0.5	0.5	0.25
Mean	−2.089	1.296	−1.025	0.497	0.215	0.189	0.439	0.400	0.265
Bias	−0.089	0.046	−0.025	−0.003	−0.085	−0.111	−0.061	−0.100	0.015
RMSE	0.264	0.179	0.117	0.093	0.127	0.172	0.144	0.148	0.097
I-statistic	4.759	1.879	1.605	1.075	2.734	2.292	3.187	1.185	1.120
GT *p*-value	0.439	0.449	0.505	0.519	0.465	0.492	0.466	0.477	0.479
True	−2	1.25	−1	0.5	0.4	0.6	0.8	0.5	0.25
Mean	−2.258	1.398	−1.142	0.558	0.443	0.591	0.671	0.394	0.253
Bias	−0.258	0.148	−0.142	0.058	0.043	−0.009	−0.129	−0.106	0.003
RMSE	0.424	0.275	0.223	0.141	0.078	0.079	0.151	0.150	0.076
I-statistic	7.471	2.446	2.658	1.189	3.189	2.669	4.285	1.232	1.104
GT *p*-value	0.461	0.465	0.500	0.515	0.475	0.499	0.472	0.490	0.478
True	−2	1.25	−1	0.5	0.4	0.6	0	0.5	0.25
Mean	−2.150	1.336	−1.059	0.510	0.423	0.549	0.008	0.389	0.261
Bias	−0.150	0.086	−0.059	0.010	0.023	−0.051	0.008	−0.111	0.011
RMSE	0.324	0.219	0.142	0.106	0.069	0.092	0.159	0.150	0.080
I-statistic	4.752	1.799	1.645	1.075	2.036	1.732	3.149	1.137	1.083
GT *p*-value	0.457	0.464	0.486	0.482	0.479	0.514	0.484	0.463	0.522

The *I*-statistic is calculated following Raftery and Lewis (1992). GT *p*-value denotes the *p*-value of the Geweke (1992) test.

bias figures point to a relatively good performance of the proposed estimation routines.

5.3. Design for a Framework for Within- and Across-Equation Spatial Correlation

For an analysis of the richer model, we assume a framework as outlined in Section 4.1, where y_1^* as well as y_2^* affect both latent outcomes y_1^* and y_2^*. For this, we assume the same spatial weights matrix W_N for all terms. The corresponding spatial autocorrelation parameters are: $\{\lambda_{11}, \lambda_{12}, \lambda_{21}, \lambda_{22}\} = \{0.4, 0.2, 0.1, 0.3\}$.

In this design, we assume two variables $x_{11,it} \sim N(0,1)$ and $x_{12,it} \sim N(0,1)$, which enter the first equation, $x_{21,it} \sim N(0,1)$ and $x_{22,it} \sim N(0,1)$, which enter the second equation. Their true parameter values are, as above, $\beta_1 = (\beta_{11}, \beta_{12}) = (-2, 1.25)$ and $\beta_2 = (\beta_{21}, \beta_{22}) = (-1, 0.5)$ for the first and the second equation, respectively. α, and ν are drawn in the same way as in the benchmark design.

5.4. Simulation Results for the Within- and Across-Equation Spatial-Correlation Model

Table 3 summarizes the Monte Carlo simulation results for this richer design.

The findings in the table suggest that the richer design does not involve systematically larger biases or root-mean-squared errors across the parameters of interest. Hence, the findings are assuring that even more complex designs with spillovers across different latent variables in the system between cross-sectional units can be analyzed even with relatively small samples at hand.

5.5. Design for the Correlated Random Effects Model

In an extension, we let α be correlated with X at different intensities. In this setup, we consider the vectors α_1 and α_2 to be correlated with x_2, maintaining the assumption that x_1 is exogenous. Specifically, we decompose x_2 into its between (bar) and within (tilde) parts (where between and within refer to cross-sectional units i), $x_2 = \bar{x}_2 + \tilde{x}_2$ and assume that $\alpha_m = \alpha_m^* + c_\alpha \cdot \bar{x}_2$ for $m = \{1, 2\}$, considering several alternative degrees of endogeneity with $c_\alpha = \{1; 2; 4\}$. α_m^* is drawn in the same way as α_m in the basic design. In the generated data sets for $N = 100$, this yields an average correlation between x_2 and $\{\alpha_1, \alpha_2\}$ of about $\{0.438; 0.387\}$ with $c_\alpha = 1$, of about $\{0.701; 0.654\}$ with $c_\alpha = 2$, and of about $\{0.892; 0.869\}$ with $c_\alpha = 4$, across all Monte Carlo runs, respectively.

Clearly, with this setting of correlated random effects, the parameters on x_2, $\{\beta_{12}; \beta_{22}\}$, will be biased unless $\bar{x}_2$ is included as a control function as suggested by Mundlak (1978), Chamberlain (1982), and Wooldridge (1995). The corresponding results for specifications where the control function (whose parameters we suppress) is included in X are summarized in Table 4 for the sample-size configuration $\{N = 100; T = 5\}$. The true parameter values are $\beta_1 = (\beta_{11}, \beta_{12}) = (-2, 1.25)$, $\beta_2 = (\beta_{21}, \beta_{22}) = (-1, 0.5)$, and $(\lambda_1, \lambda_2, \tau) = (0.4, 0.6, 0.5)$ in this case.

Table 3. Results for Latent Variable Extension, $N = 100$ and $T = 5$

	β_{11}	β_{12}	β_{21}	β_{22}	λ_{11}	λ_{12}	λ_{21}	λ_{22}	τ	α_1	α_2
True	−2	1.25	−1	0.5	0.4	0.2	0.1	0.3	0.5	0.5	0.25
Mean	−2.095	1.364	−1.050	0.538	0.388	0.270	0.114	0.173	0.408	0.561	0.290
Bias	−0.095	0.114	−0.050	0.038	−0.012	0.070	0.014	−0.127	−0.092	0.061	0.040
RMSE	0.336	0.260	0.137	0.111	0.082	0.170	0.082	0.191	0.174	0.158	0.133
I-statistic	6.369	2.117	1.893	1.104	4.173	3.093	2.745	4.437	3.850	1.910	1.689
GT p-value	0.526	0.539	0.535	0.509	0.509	0.507	0.525	0.493	0.457	0.492	0.501

The *I*-statistic is calculated following Raftery and Lewis (1992). GT *p*-value denotes the *p*-value of the Geweke (1992) test.

Table 4. Results for CRE-Variant in CRE World; Different c_α; $N = 100$ and $T = 5$.

	β_{11}	β_{12}	β_{21}	β_{22}	λ_1	λ_2	τ	α_1	α_2
True	−2	1.25	−1	0.5	0.4	0.6	0.5	0.5	0.25
$c_\alpha = 1$									
Mean	−1.901	1.167	−1.022	0.517	0.404	0.571	0.429	0.369	0.264
Bias	0.099	−0.083	−0.022	0.017	0.004	−0.029	−0.071	−0.131	0.014
RMSE	0.277	0.204	0.141	0.120	0.068	0.081	0.143	0.158	0.077
I-statistic	4.493	1.598	1.892	1.086	2.366	2.084	3.219	1.146	1.090
GT *p*-value	0.459	0.458	0.491	0.508	0.501	0.490	0.470	0.469	0.502
$c_\alpha = 2$									
Mean	−1.814	1.107	−1.061	0.543	0.384	0.575	0.429	0.367	0.275
Bias	0.186	−0.143	−0.061	0.043	−0.016	−0.025	−0.071	−0.133	0.02
RMSE	0.320	0.221	0.172	0.135	0.078	0.078	0.153	0.161	0.084
I-statistic	4.743	1.612	2.262	1.126	2.638	2.456	3.470	1.164	1.108
GT *p*-value	0.463	0.465	0.505	0.495	0.488	0.495	0.464	0.479	0.489
$c_\alpha = 4$									
Mean	−1.885	1.166	−1.160	0.594	0.373	0.616	0.440	0.399	0.302
Bias	0.115	−0.084	−0.160	0.094	−0.027	0.016	−0.060	−0.101	0.052
RMSE	0.359	0.220	0.266	0.188	0.090	0.077	0.160	0.148	0.104
I-statistic	6.385	1.974	2.915	1.229	3.964	3.469	4.960	1.280	1.183
GT *p*-value	0.454	0.464	0.478	0.469	0.514	0.485	0.460	0.473	0.461

The *I*-statistic is calculated following Raftery and Lewis (1992). GT *p*-value denotes the *p*-value of the Geweke (1992) test.

5.6. Simulation Results for the Correlated Random Effects Model

We summarize the Monte Carlo simulation results for the correlated random effects model and the three configurations $c_\alpha = \{1; 2; 4\}$ in Table 4.

The results in Table 4 suggest that the proposed approach works well in small samples even with endogenous cross-sectional effects when conditioning on individual-specific variable means. We have seen that the correlations between x_2 and α are relatively strong even in the case of $c_\alpha = 1$. In that case, the biases of the parameters amount to less than 10% on average. The root-mean-squared error (RMSE) is relatively highest for the coefficients on the endogenous variable, $\{\beta_{12}; \beta_{22}\}$, and it amounts to less than one-fifth for each of those. Clearly, both the biases and the RMSEs tend to be somewhat larger with a higher degree of endogeneity (a larger value of c_α). However, as said before, the degree of correlation studied here is rather strong, which is supportive of the proposed procedure.

While we illustrated that a consideration of correlated random effects is possible in Table 4, it is the purpose of Table 5 to document the consequences of disregarding correlated random effects when they are present.

As in Table 4, we focus on the case of $\{N, T\} = \{100, 5\}$, and, for the sake of brevity, we summarize the results for the case of $c_\alpha = 4$, where the correlated-random-effects assumption is relatively important. A comparison of the respective rows in the table indicates that both the bias and the RMSE on $\{\beta_{11}, \beta_{12}, \beta_{21}, \beta_{22}\}$ are much higher in Table 5 than in Table 4. Hence, the merits of considering a correlated-random-effects version of the model in practice are obvious.

6. CONCLUSION

This paper analyzes a Bayesian estimation procedure for bivariate and, eventually, higher-variate panel probit models with spatial interdependence in the dependent variable. Such models could be interesting to use for an array of empirical problems where contagion or spillovers in a broad sense are important, the choices are not mutually exclusive, and there is time variation in those choices. Examples are discrete preferential policy choices of countries (e.g., with respect to trade agreement and/or investment agreement membership), discrete global-market-participation decisions of firms as exporters and/or multinational firms, discrete market-entry decisions of firms in a set of markets (such as countries and/or products), discrete

Table 5. Results for Non-CRE-Variant in CRE World for $c_\alpha = 4$; $N = 100$ and $T = 5$.

	β_{11}	β_{12}	β_{21}	β_{22}	λ_1	λ_2	τ	α_1	α_2
True	−2	1.25	−1	0.5	0.4	0.6	0.5	0.5	0.25
$c_\alpha = 4$									
Mean	−2.234	1.616	−1.238	0.768	0.383	0.620	0.474	0.451	0.308
Bias	−0.234	0.366	−0.238	0.268	−0.017	0.020	−0.026	−0.049	0.058
RMSE	0.459	0.457	0.347	0.324	0.088	0.080	0.180	0.135	0.106
I-statistic	8.865	2.697	3.459	1.371	4.469	3.971	5.673	1.416	1.212
GT *p*-value	0.482	0.493	0.490	0.523	0.518	0.515	0.504	0.476	0.479

The *I*-statistic is calculated following Raftery and Lewis (1992). GT *p*-value denotes the *p*-value of the Geweke (1992) test.

consumption decisions of households with regard to certain products, discrete portfolio-acquisition decisions of investors, etc. All of these choices are ones where earlier empirical work had identified independently the existence of contagious effects and the interdependence between those choices. The approach presented in this paper is capable of treating the features of contagion or spillovers and cross-issue correlation simultaneously.

For estimation, the paper proposes a Bayesian spatial bivariate panel probit model. An advantage of this estimation procedure relative to standard maximum-likelihood estimation is that it can be used with large, interdependent cross-sections of data that are repeatedly observed over relatively short time periods. Our Monte Carlo simulation study suggests that the procedure works well even in small to moderately large samples.

NOTES

1. In earlier research—mostly cross-section—alternatives to Bayesian nonlinear probability model estimation had been proposed: see McMillen (1992) for expectation-maximization methods; see Beron and Vijverberg (2004) for simulated maximum likelihood methods; and Klier and McMillen (2008) for generalized methods of moments procedures.
2. The spillover effects are referred to as *global*, because the reduced form of the model involves an infinite number of cross-sectional effects and associated repercussions in the cross-sectional system.
3. In principle, the weights w_{ijt} could be specific to equation m.
4. Note that $x_{m,it}$ may contain time averages of some or all of the time-variant covariates. In the latter case, it is sufficient for the time-variant variables in $x_{m,it}$ to be singly exogenous with only $E[x_{m,it}\nu_{m,it}] = 0$.
5. With a time-invariant, normalized, $N \times N$ spatial weights matrix, $W_{TN} = I_T \otimes W_N$, where I_T is an identity matrix of dimension T and $W_N = (w_{ij})$.
6. For more details, we refer the reader to LeSage and Pace (2009, pp. 136–137).
7. In this case, Σ is symmetric with unitary diagonal and contains $M(M-1)/2$ unknown off-diagonal elements.

ACKNOWLEDGMENTS

The authors would like to thank an anonymous reviewer, Cheng Hsiao, and Jaya Krishnakumar for numerous helpful comments on earlier versions of the manuscript. Moreover, we are grateful to the participants of the *Advances in Econometrics Conference* 2015 at Baton Rouge and the 26th (EC)2 Conference on *Theory and Practice of Spatial Econometrics.*

REFERENCES

Albert, J. H., & Chib, S. (1993). Bayesian analysis of binary and polychotomous response data. *Journal of the American Statistical Association, 88*(422), 669–679.

Altonji, J., Elder, T., & Taber, C. (2005). Selection on observed and unobserved variables: Assessing the effectiveness of catholic schools. *Journal of Political Economy, 113*(1), 151–184.

Anselin, L. (1988). *Spatial econometrics methods and models.* Dordrecht: Kluwer.

Beron, K. J., & Vijverberg, W. P. M. (2004). Probit in a spatial context: A Monte Carlo analysis. In L. Anselin, R. J. G. M. Florax, & S. J. Rey (Eds.). *Advances in spatial econometrics. Methodology, tools and applications.* Berlin: Springer.

Börsch-Supan, A., Hajivassiliou, V., Kotlikoff, L. J., & Morris, J. N. (1992). Health, children, and elderly living arrangements: A multi-period-multinomial probit model with unobserved heterogeneity and autocorrelated errors. In D. Wise (Ed.), *Topics in the economics of aging* (pp. 79–108). Chicago, IL: Chicago University Press.

Chamberlain, G. (1982). Multivariate regression models for panel data. *Journal of Econometrics, 18*(1), 5–46.

Egger, P. H., & Wamser, G. (2013). Multiple faces of preferential market access: Their causes and consequences. *Economic Policy, 28*(73), 145–187.

Geweke, J. (1991). Efficient simulation from the multivariate normal and Student t-distributions subject to linear constraints. *Computer sciences and statistics proceedings of the 23d symposium on the interface* (pp. 571–578).

Geweke, J. (1992). Evaluating the accuracy of sampling-based approaches to calculating posterior moments. In J. M. Bernardo, J. O. Berger, A. P. Dawid, & A. F. M. Smith (Eds.). *Bayesian statistics.* Oxford: Clarendon Press.

Greene, W. H. (1984). Estimation of the correlation coefficient in a bivariate probit model using the method of moments. *Economics Letters, 16*(3–4), 285–291.

Greene, W. H. (1996). *Marginal effects in the bivariate probit model.* NYU Working Paper No. EC-96-11.

Greene, W. H. (2003). *Econometric analysis.* Upper Saddle River, NJ: Prentice-Hall.

Haque, R., & Haque, M. (2009). *Gender, ethnicity and employment.* Heidelberg: Physica Verlag.

Jones, A. M. (2007). *Applied econometrics for health economists* (2nd ed.). Oxford: Radcliffe Publishing.

Johnson, L., & Hensher, D. (1982). Application of multinomial probit to a two-period panel data set. *Transportation Research A, 16A*(5–6), 457–464.

Kapoor, M., Kelejian, H. H., & Prucha, I. R. (2007). Panel data models with spatially correlated error components. *Journal of Econometrics, 140*(1), 97–130.

Keane, M. P. (1992). A note on identification in the multinomial probit model. *Journal of Business and Economic Statistics, 10*(2), 193–200.

Keane, M. P. (1997). Modeling heterogeneity and state dependence in consumer choice behavior. *Journal of Business and Economic Statistics, 15*(3), 310–327.

Kelejian, H. H., & Prucha, I. R. (2010). Specification and estimation of spatial autoregressive models with autoregressive and heteroskedastic disturbances. *Journal of Econometrics*, *157*(1), 53–67.

Klier, T., & McMillen, D. P. (2008). Clustering of auto supplier plants in the United States: Generalized method of moments spatial logit for large samples. *Journal of Business and Economic Statistics*, *26*(4), 460–471.

Koop, G. (2003). *Bayesian econometrics*. Chichester: Wiley.

Lacombe, D. J., & LeSage, J. P. (2015). Use and interpretation of spatial autoregressive probit models. *Annals of Regional Science*. doi:10.1007/s00168-015-0705-x

LeSage, J. P. (2000). Bayesian estimation of limited dependent variable spatial autoregressive models. *Geographical Analysis*, *32*(1), 19–35.

LeSage, J. P., & Pace, R. K. (2009). *Introduction to spatial econometrics*. Boca Raton, FL: CRC Press/Taylor & Francis.

LeSage, J. P., Pace, R. K., Lam, N., Campanella, R., & Liu, X. (2011). New Orleans business recovery in the aftermath of Hurricane Katrina. *Journal of the Royal Statistical Society: Series A (Statistics in Society)*, *174*, 1007–1027.

McMillen, D. P. (1992). Probit with spatial autocorrelation. *Journal of Regional Science*, *32*(3), 335–348.

Mulkay, B. (2014). *Bivariate probit estimation for panel data: A two-step Gauss-Hermite Quadrature approach with an application to product and process innovations for France*. Unpublished manuscript, Université Montpellier.

Mundlak, Y. (1978). On the pooling of time series and cross section data. *Econometrica*, *46*(1), 69–85.

Munkin, M. K., & Trivedi, P. K. (2008). Bayesian analysis of the ordered probit model with endogenous selection. *Journal of Econometrics*, *143*(2), 334–348.

Raftery, A. E., & Lewis, S. M. (1992). How many iterations in the Gibbs sampler? In J. M. Bernardo, J. O. Berger, A. P. Dawid, & A. F. M. Smith (Eds.). *Bayesian Statistics*. Oxford: Clarendon Press.

Wooldridge, J. A. (1995). Selection corrections for panel data models under conditional mean independence assumptions. *Journal of Econometrics*, *68*(1), 115–132.

ESTIMATING BINARY SPATIAL AUTOREGRESSIVE MODELS FOR RARE EVENTS

Raffaella Calabrese[a] and Johan A. Elkink[b]

[a] *Business School, University of Edinburgh, Edinburgh, UK*
[b] *School of Politics and International Relations, University College Dublin, Dublin*

ABSTRACT

The most used spatial regression models for binary-dependent variable consider a symmetric link function, such as the logistic or the probit models. When the dependent variable represents a rare event, a symmetric link function can underestimate the probability that the rare event occurs. Following Calabrese and Osmetti (2013), we suggest the quantile function of the generalized extreme value (GEV) distribution as link function in a spatial generalized linear model and we call this model the spatial GEV (SGEV) regression model. To estimate the parameters of such model, a modified version of the Gibbs sampling method of Wang and Dey (2010) is proposed. We analyze the performance of our model by Monte Carlo simulations and evaluate the prediction accuracy in empirical data on state failure.

Spatial Econometrics: Qualitative and Limited Dependent Variables
Advances in Econometrics, Volume 37, 145–166

ISSN: 0731-9053/doi:10.1108/S0731-905320160000037012

Keywords: Rare events; spatial econometrics; probit, GEV

JEL classifications: C21; C25

1. INTRODUCTION

In this work, we analyze rare binary spatial events, that is, binary-dependent variable with spatial dependencies and with a very small number of ones in the sample, usually lower than 5%. In forecasting applications ranging from epidemiology, finance, international relations, to natural disasters, rare events and interdependencies between these events are common. Both the rare event nature of the dependent variable and the spatial autoregressive component generate challenges for the statistical estimation of the model parameters.

When dealing with binary rare events without spatial effects, conventional classification methods, such as logit or probit models, tend to strongly favor the majority class because they are built upon the assumption that every class to be predicted has enough representatives in the data set (Hand, Whitrow, Adams, Juszczak, & Weston, 2008). Different authors (e.g., Calabrese & Osmetti, 2013; King & Zeng, 2001a, b; Wang & Dey, 2010) have shown that a symmetric link function leads to very low or even no detection of the minority class when the dependent variable is a rare event.

Some solutions have been proposed to improve the prediction quality of such models for binary rare events without spatial interdependence. King and Zeng (2001a, 2001b) have suggested a correction of the intercept of the logistic regression based on case-control sampling. According to Weiss (2004), this proposal has several drawbacks. A different approach has been suggested by Wang and Dey (2010) and Calabrese and Osmetti (2013), based on a flexible skewed link function given by the generalized extreme value (GEV) distribution. This particular distribution is chosen for two main reasons. First, it allows to assign more weight to the information on the minority class. Second, if the minority class is represented by the ones, the characteristics of the rare events are given by the right tail of the response curve. The variable used in the literature to model the tail of a distribution is the GEV random variable (Kotz & Nadarajah, 2000).

The GEV distribution is characterized by three parameters: a location parameter, a scale parameter, and a shape parameter. The main advantage of the GEV distribution is its flexibility – it can be negative and positive skewed. In the first case, more weight is given to the left tail of the response curve and this is more convenient if the minority class is represented by the zeroes. When the GEV link function is positive skewed, the values ones of the dependent variable get more weight, so the minority class should be given by the ones.

Based on our knowledge, this is the first manuscript that analyses the drawbacks caused by a symmetric link function in a spatial regression model for binary rare events. Binary spatial choice models are sufficiently important that LeSage and Pace (2009, Chapter 10) focus an entire chapter on this topic. In this context, the most used models are probit or logit functional forms with spatial interdependence. Different approaches have been proposed in the literature to estimate these models, for example, the Gibbs sampling method (LeSage, 2000), the expectation-maximization algorithm (McMillen, 1992), the generalized method of moments (Klier & McMillen, 2008; Pinkse & Slade, 1998) and recursive importance sampling (Beron & Vijverberg, 2004). Fleming (2004) and Calabrese and Elkink (2014) compare the properties of these estimators, both theoretically and by Monte Carlo simulations.

To improve the detection of the minority class and following Calabrese and Osmetti (2013), we propose the quantile function of the GEV distribution as link function in a spatial generalized linear model and we call this model the Spatial GEV (SGEV) regression model. To estimate the parameters of such model, a modified version of the Gibbs sampling method of LeSage (2000) and Wang and Dey (2010) is proposed. LeSage (2000) proposes a Gibbs sampler for estimating binary-dependent variable models with spatial interdependence, which comparative analysis shows is one of the best estimators available in this context (Calabrese & Elkink, 2014).[1] Wang and Dey (2010) propose a Gibbs sampler for rare events using the GEV distribution. We merge the two efforts to develop a new estimator for rare events with spatial autocorrelation.

The SGEV estimator will be evaluated in a series of Monte Carlo simulations, comparing the performance to a number of existing estimators Klier and McMillen (2008) and LeSage (2000) for similar data structures, where we evaluate the accuracy of the prediction. In so doing, this research makes a significant contribution to the literatures in spatial econometrics and rare events modeling.

The proposed estimator is of particular relevance to several areas, such as natural science, epidemiology, political science, or credit risk. Even if natural disasters (Frei & Schar, 1998; LeSage et al., 2011) or epidemics (Roberts, 2000) occur infrequently, their forecasting is a mandatory activity to reduce the level of risk and damage. In credit risk analysis, there are several contexts where the detection of the minority class is pivotal. Moreover, our proposal could be particularly useful to measure credit contagion, that is, how the failure of a debtor to fulfill his or her debt obligation can affect the failure propensity of another debtor, on different types of portfolio. For example, if we consider loans to firms, the interdependence is given by the presence of business relations among different firms (Barro & Basso, 2010). As house prices are affected by house locations, credit contagion is important to estimate the failure propensity of a mortgage loan (Zhu & Kelley Pace, 2014). Credit contagion can also be measured on banks as opposed to obligors, such that this approach contributes to the topical literature on systemic risk (Calabrese, Elkink, & Giudici, 2014).

Aside from the literature in economics and banking, there are countless application areas in the social sciences more generally. For example, in the political science literature, rare events data with spatial or network interdependencies can be found in the study of civil war or interstate conflict (e.g., Gleditsch & Ward, 2013), of currency crisis (Novo, 2003), or of state failure (King & Zeng, 2001a, b). The change of political regime from autocracy to democracy is another example where the occurrence of the transition is rare, while they can be expected to be spatially and temporally correlated (Elkink, 2011; Gleditsch & Ward, 2006). The interdependence here can be spatial, specified in an exogenously given spatial weights matrix, or based on some alternative network structure such as trade relations or cultural similarity matrices. Following King and Zeng (2001b), who demonstrate the relevance of a rare events estimator by predicting state failure, we provide an empirical application of the SGEV model using updated data on state failure.

Section 2 provides a brief overview of binary regression models with spatially interdependent data. Section 3 outlines the estimation complications arising from the nature of rare events data and proposes the use of an asymmetric link function in the binary regression model. Section 4 proposes the Spatial GEV model for the estimation of rare events data with spatial or network interdependence. Section 5 provides a Monte Carlo analysis to evaluate the statistical performance of the proposed estimator. An initial empirical application is presented in Sections 6 and 7 concludes.

2. SPATIAL BINARY REGRESSION MODELS

A widely used representation of a regression model for a binary response Y is the latent response model (Verbeek, 2008). A continuous variable Y^* is the dependent variable with the observation mechanism

$$Y_i = \begin{cases} 1, & Y^* > 0 \\ 0, & \text{otherwise.} \end{cases} \tag{1}$$

A linear model is specified for this latent response, so the model specification is

$$\mathbf{Y}^* = \rho \mathbf{W} \mathbf{Y}^* + \mathbf{X}\boldsymbol{\beta} + \boldsymbol{\varepsilon}, \tag{2}$$

where the error term $\boldsymbol{\varepsilon}$ can follow a multivariate normal distribution in a probit model or a multivariate logistic distribution in a logit model. **W** is a spatial lag weights matrix, ρ the associated scalar parameter, **X** a matrix of exogenous variables, and $\boldsymbol{\beta}$ the associated regression coefficients. **W** is typically a normalized matrix, whereby all rows add up to one and the diagonal is zero, but see Neumayer and Plümper (2016) for a critique on this convention. For a spatial stationary process, $-1 < \rho < 1$.[2] This corresponds to the lattice perspective on spatial data (Anselin, 2002, p. 255),[3] which can be directly applied to any other (social) network data – any application where the dependent variable represents a binary characteristic of the nodes and the edges (i.e., **W**) are exogenously given.

From the model (2), the binary spatial autoregressive (BSAR) model is obtained

$$\mathbf{Y}^* = (I - \rho \mathbf{W})^{-1}(\mathbf{X}\boldsymbol{\beta} + \boldsymbol{\varepsilon}) = \mathbf{A}^{-1}\mathbf{X}\boldsymbol{\beta} + \mathbf{e}, \tag{3}$$

with $\mathbf{A} = I - \rho \mathbf{W}$ and $\mathbf{e} = \mathbf{A}^{-1}\boldsymbol{\varepsilon}$ (see also, Fleming, 2004; McMillen, 1992, 1995).

The variance of the error term follows as:

$$\text{var}(\mathbf{e}) = \text{var}\left[\mathbf{A}^{-1}\boldsymbol{\varepsilon}\right] = A^{-1}\boldsymbol{\varepsilon}\boldsymbol{\varepsilon}'\left[\mathbf{A}^{-1}\right]'. \tag{4}$$

The inherent heteroskedasticity present in matrix (4) renders standard binary regression models inconsistent and inefficient (McMillen, 1992), a problem which has been addressed in the literature by the development of various different estimators for BSAR models. We can identify five main estimators of the spatial autocorelation parameter ρ in this context (see also, Fleming, 2004; LeSage & Pace, 2009).

In the first method, McMillen (1992, 1995) uses an expectation-maximization (EM) algorithm. The latent variable Y^* is replaced with its expected value and the maximum likelihood (ML) method is applied. Given the difficulty of estimating both the $\boldsymbol{\beta}$ and $\boldsymbol{\varepsilon\varepsilon}'$, McMillen (1992) introduces the assumption of homogeneity for the disturbances $\boldsymbol{\varepsilon}$, assuming that $\boldsymbol{\varepsilon\varepsilon}' = I$. Analogous to McMillen (1992), LeSage (2000) also replaces the latent variable Y^* with its expected value, but a Gibbs sampling approach is applied for the parameter estimation. Furthermore, LeSage (2000) removes the assumption of homogeneity, that is, $\boldsymbol{\varepsilon\varepsilon}' = \sigma_\varepsilon^2\mathbf{V}$ where $\mathbf{V} = \text{diag}(v_1, v_2, \ldots, v_n)$ and v_i with $i = 1, 2, \ldots, n$ are the variance parameters to be estimated. In the third method, since the likelihood function is a multivariate normal distribution, Beron and Vijverberg (2004) suggest to apply recursive importance sampling (RIS) to the ML estimation. Pinkse and Slade (1998) apply a generalized method of moments (GMM) estimator. Finally, Klier and McMillen (2008) suggest an approximation of the method proposed by Pinkse and Slade (1998), whereby an extrapolation is applied based on the estimate of β when $\rho = 0$.

Calabrese and Elkink (2014) analyze the properties of the above estimators by Monte Carlo simulations and an empirical application. This study shows that the Gibbs sampler performs best for low values of the spatial autocorrelation parameter and the RIS estimator for high values of ρ. The computationally much more efficient linearized GMM estimator of Klier and McMillen (2008) performs well under low autocorrelation and large sample size conditions. Because of these properties, we propose a modified version of the Gibbs sampling approach to binary spatial autoregression models, modified for rare events data using an asymmetric link function.

3. RARE EVENTS AND SYMMETRIC LINK FUNCTIONS

Let Y be a Bernoulli random variable with parameter $\pi = P\{Y = 1\}$ and $\mathbf{x}$ a covariate vector. The most used regression models for a binary-dependent variable are the generalized linear models (GLMs). In GLMs, the link function $g(\cdot)$ is a monotonic function such that

$$g(\pi) = \beta'\mathbf{x},$$

where π is the probability of observing the rare event.

For simplicity, the most used link functions are symmetric functions. For example, in the logistic regression model, the link function $g(\cdot)$ is the quantile function of a logistic random variable

$$g(\mathbf{x}) = \text{logit}(\pi(\mathbf{x})) = \ln\left(\frac{\pi(\mathbf{x})}{1 - \pi(\mathbf{x})}\right) = \beta'\mathbf{x},$$

which is a symmetric function.

In the probit model, the link function $g(\cdot)$ is the quantile function of a standard normal random variable, which is also symmetric

$$g(\mathbf{x}) = \Phi^{-1}(\beta'\mathbf{x}).$$

When the link function is symmetric, the response curve $\pi(\mathbf{x})$ approaches zero at the same rate it approaches one. This corresponds to the assumption that the same amount of information is included in the observed zeros and ones of the dependent variable Y. On the contrary, if Y is a rare event with a low number of ones in the sample, the observed ones are more informative than the observed zeros and should be weighted accordingly in the estimation of the model (Calabrese & Osmetti, 2013; King & Zeng, 2001b). Weighting the zero and one observations equally, when the dependent variable Y is a rare event, by using a GLM with a symmetric link function, potentially underestimates the probability π for the observed ones (Calabrese & Osmetti, 2015; King & Zeng, 2001b).

Furthermore, when the probability of an event is low and the sample size reasonably large, the binomial distribution can be, and commonly is, approximated by a Poisson distribution (Falk, Hüsler, & Reiss, 2010, pp. 4–5), which is a skewed distribution. It is therefore more consistent to also choose an asymmetric link function for binary regression models dealing with such rare events.

In order to overcome these drawbacks, different methods have been proposed in the literature. The most widely used approach is choice-based or case-control sampling with a correction on the parameter estimates (David, Pirog-Good, & Sickles, 1986; King & Zeng, 2001a; Manski & Lerman, 1977; McCullagh & Nelder, 1989; Scott & Wild, 1986). In the survival analysis context, the cure model (Lambert & Thompson, 2007) and the mixture hazard model (Almanidis & Siclles, 2015) are also used. Instead, Wang and Dey (2010) and Calabrese and Osmetti (2013) propose to focus the attention on the right tail of the response curve that represents the feautures of ones.

Since the GEV distribution function is used in the literature (e.g., Falk, et al., 2010; Kotz & Nadarajah, 2000) to represent the tail of a random variable, Wang and Dey (2010) and Calabrese and Osmetti (2013) propose the quantile function of a GEV random variable as a link function in a GLM. The main difference between these two proposals is that Wang and Dey (2010) use a Bayesian approach to estimate β and the shape parameter of the GEV distribution and Calabrese and Osmetti (2013) estimate β by the ML method, while they keep the shape parameter fixed. Instead of estimating the shape parameter, Calabrese and Osmetti (2013) propose to fit as many models as the number of chosen values of the shape parameter and select the model that yields the highest predictive accuracy.

4. THE SPATIAL GENERALIZED EXTREME VALUE REGRESSION MODEL

The aim of this section is to propose a new spatial regression model for binary responses with unequal sample frequencies of the two outcomes that overcome the drawbacks outlined in Section 3. Following Wang and Dey (2010) and Calabrese and Osmetti (2013), we consider a quantile function of a GEV distribution as the link function in a binary regression model and extend this to model spatial interdependence. Hence, we propose the spatial generalized extreme value (SGEV) regression model

$$\pi(\mathbf{x}) = \exp\left\{-\left[1 + \tau\mathbf{D}^{-1}\mathbf{A}^{-1}\mathbf{X}\beta\right]_{+}^{-1/\tau}\right\}, \tag{5}$$

where $x_{+} = \max(x, 0)$ and $\mathbf{D} = \text{diag}(\boldsymbol{\sigma}_{\mathbf{e}})$ is the diagonal matrix, with elements $\boldsymbol{\sigma}_{\mathbf{e}}$ that represent the root square of the diagonal elements in matrix (4).

Since a GEV response curve can be asymmetric, the underestimation of $P\{Y = 1\}$ for the observation equal to one may be overcome. Another advantage of the GEV distribution is that it is very flexible with the tail shape parameter τ controlling the shape and size of the tails, with three different families of distributions subsumed under it. The Type II (Fréchet-type distribution) and the Type III (Weibull-type distribution) classes of the extreme value distribution correspond, respectively, to the case where

$\tau > 0$ and $\tau < 0$, while the Type I class (Gumbel-type distribution) arises in the limit as $\tau \to 0$, Fréchet and Weibull distributions are related by a change of sign. For $\tau \to 0$ and $\rho = 0$, the SGEV regression model becomes the response curve of the log-log model (e.g., Agresti, 2002).

The main estimators proposed in the literature for spatial regression models are analyzed in Section 2. Since the Gibbs sampling approach (LeSage, 2000) provides accurate estimates of the parameter ρ under a wide range of different Monte Carlo parameters (Calabrese & Elkink, 2014), we propose a modified version of this method to estimate the SGEV model (5). We make use of the Gibbs sampler for the non-spatial GEV model proposed by Wang and Dey (2010). While LeSage (2000) makes use of the Metropolis-Hastings algorithm for the estimation of the spatial parameter ρ, Wang and Dey (2010) use this algorithm for all model parameters. We follow Wang and Dey (2010)'s approach, which provides more accurate and computationally more efficient results.[4]

The joint posterior distribution of the parameter vector $\boldsymbol{\theta} = [\boldsymbol{\beta}', \tau, \rho]'$ is given by

$$\phi(\boldsymbol{\theta}/\mathbf{y}, \mathbf{X}) \propto L(\mathbf{y}/\mathbf{X}, \boldsymbol{\theta}) \nu(\boldsymbol{\theta}),$$

where the likelihood

$$L(\mathbf{y}/\mathbf{X}, \boldsymbol{\theta}) = \prod_{i=1}^{N} \left\{ \pi_i(\boldsymbol{\theta})^{y_i} [1 - \pi_i(\boldsymbol{\theta})]^{1-y_i} \right\} \tag{6}$$

and $\pi(\cdot)$ is defined in Eq. (5).[5] To assign the priors of the SGEV model, we use LeSage (2000)'s assumption that the priors are independent

$$\nu(\boldsymbol{\theta}) = \nu(\rho, \boldsymbol{\beta}, \rho) = \nu(\rho)\nu(\boldsymbol{\beta})\nu(\mathbf{V}),$$

where we follow Wang and Dey (2010) in assigning a relatively uninformative prior distribution of $N(0, 100)$ to all parameters. Using the estimates of a non-spatial log-log model as the initial values $\boldsymbol{\beta}_0$, the correlation between $\mathbf{y}$ and $\mathbf{Wy}$ as the initial value ρ_0, and $\tau_0 = 0$, all estimates are updated in each Markov chain Monte Carlo (MCMC) iteration through the Metropolis-Hastings algorithm.

The Metropolis-Hastings algorithm (Hastings, 1970) proceeds as follows. For each θ_j, let the value $\theta^*_{j,t+1} = \theta_{j,t} + cZ$ be generated, where Z is a draw from a standard normal distribution, c is a known constant, and t refers to the sampling iteration. Defining the log-likelihood $l(\mathbf{y}/\mathbf{X},\boldsymbol{\theta}) = \log\left[L(\mathbf{y}/\mathbf{X},\boldsymbol{\theta})\right]$, the acceptance probability

$$a = \min\left\{1, \frac{l\left(\mathbf{y}/\mathbf{X},\boldsymbol{\theta}^*_{t+1}\right)\nu(\boldsymbol{\theta})}{l\left(\mathbf{y}/\mathbf{X},\boldsymbol{\theta}_{t+1}\right)\nu(\boldsymbol{\theta})}\right\},$$

where $\boldsymbol{\theta}^*_{t+1} = \boldsymbol{\theta}_{t+1}$, except for parameter $\theta^*_{j,t+1}$. A value m is drawn from a continuous uniform distribution with support [0, 1]. If $m < a$, the next draw from the density function (6) is given by $\theta_{j,t+1} = \theta^*_{j,t+1}$, otherwise the draw is taken to be the current value $\theta_{j,t+1} = \theta_{j,t}$. Where the parameter is constrained, Z is drawn from a truncated standard normal distribution – in our application this holds for ρ, which is constrained to the $[-1, 1]$ interval. For computational efficiency reasons and following Thomas (2007), we dynamically adapt c throughout the chain for each parameter in $\boldsymbol{\theta}$, such that the acceptance rate of the Metropolis-Hastings algorithm is approximately 20%.[6]

5. MONTE CARLO SIMULATIONS

In order to evaluate the performance of the proposed estimator, we perform Monte Carlo analyses whereby the estimator is applied to data of which the underlying data generation mechanism, and its associated parameters, are known. While the Monte Carlo analysis in Calabrese and Elkink (2014) focuses primarily on the estimation of the intensity of the spatial autocorrelation, ρ, we focus primarily on the prediction quality of the estimator.

The data generation process results in four continuous independent variables, with for each $X \sim N(0, 4\sigma_\varepsilon)$, with $\sigma_\varepsilon = 1$. The residuals vector $\boldsymbol{\varepsilon}$ is generated from a multivariate normal distribution $N_n(\mathbf{0}, \mathbf{I})$.

We performed the simulations using $N = 500$ as sample size and a parameter vector $\boldsymbol{\beta} = [0, 1, 1, -1, -1]'$. The level of spatial autocorrelation is varied from entirely absent to high autocorrelation, $\rho \in \{0, 0.1, 0.45, 0.8\}$. Finally, as we handle two-class classification problems with highly unbalanced class sizes, the dependent variable Y is constructed by applying a threshold different from the zero in Eq. (1), such that the proportion of ones is predetermined, in these simulations to 20% and 5%. We thus end up with eight different configurations of the data generation parameters. We perform estimations on 60 replications of each parameter configuration.

In order to generate the matrix **W**, we apply the method suggested by Beron and Vijverberg (2004, p. 179). We assign each observation randomly to a coordinate in the unit square using a uniform distribution. For each observation, those observations that are within a fixed radius, excluding the observation itself, are considered neighbours. The radius d is set such that the average number of neighbours for each observation is approximately 5, identical to Beron and Vijverberg (2004), which implies $d=0.06$ for $N=500$.

The main aim of the SGEV model is to improve the accuracy of predicting the rare events, the ones. Hence, the applications of our proposal are classification problems where performing an incorrect prediction of the rare event may have grave consequences. For example, in mushroom classification, judging a poisonous mushroom to be edible is far worse than judging an edible mushroom to be poisonous. In the context of our empirical example, the prediction of state failure, it is also reasonable to assume that it is more important not to miss a potential future failed state than that it is to slightly overestimate the probability of state failure for a state that is less at risk. A similar rationale applies to the risk of bank defaults, currency defaults or default on credits, where (central) banks will be more concerned with correctly identifying those cases that are truly at risk than with incorrectly identifying some cases as at risk while they are not. Applying a similar logic to credit defaults, Calabrese and Osmetti (2013) therefore calculate the mean absolute error (MAE^+) and mean-squared error (MSE^+) for the subset of cases where $Y=1$

$$\text{MAE}^+ = \frac{1}{N} \sum_{\{y_i=1\}} [y_i - \hat{\pi}_i], \quad \text{MSE}^+ = \frac{1}{N} \sum_{\{y_i=1\}} [y_i - \hat{\pi}_i]^2. \tag{7}$$

We compare the SGEV model with the predictive performance of the estimators proposed by Klier and McMillen (2008) (denoted as KM) and LeSage (2000) (denoted as GibbsT). Within a certain range of values of the shape parameter τ, the usual regularity conditions for the estimator of this parameter do not hold (Smith, 1985). For this reason, we report the results of the SGEV model with the estimation of τ (denoted as SGEV), as explained in the previous section, and fixing the parameter τ to 25 (denoted

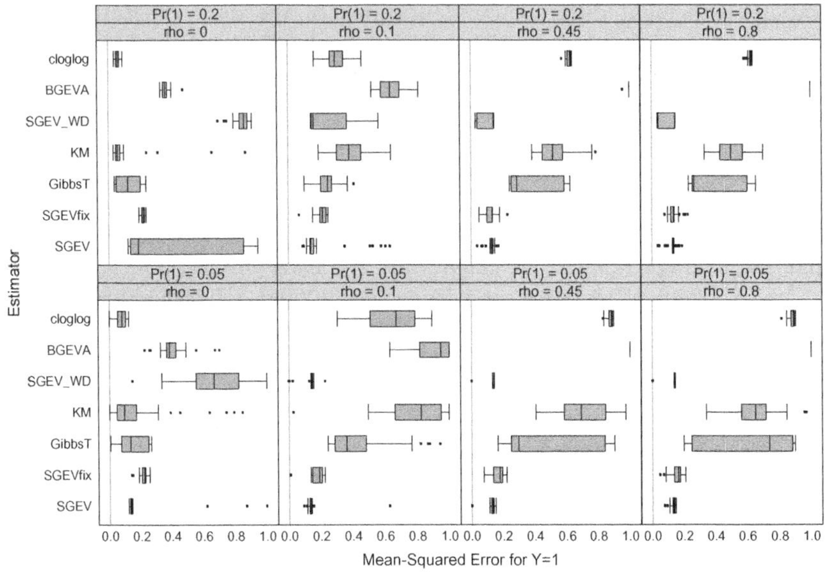

Fig. 1. Distribution of the MSE^+ for $y=1$ Defined in Eq. (7) for Different Configurations of the Parameters, across 60 Replications.

as SGEVfix).[7] Finally, three GLMs with asymmetric link functions that ignore the spatial interdependence are considered: the cloglog model, the GEV model proposed by Calabrese and Osmetti (2015)[8] (denoted as BGEVA) and the GEV model proposed by Wang and Dey (2010) (denoted as GEV_WD).[9]

The plot in Fig. 1 provides a graphical depiction of the MSE^+ defined in Eq. (7). This plot shows that for 20% of ones, the SGEV model outperforms the other models when the spatial autocorrelation ρ increases. When the sample is strongly unbalanced (i.e., 5% of ones) and in the presence of spatial interdependence, the accuracy of identifying the ones in the data set is notably better for the SGEV estimator. This is of course not surprising, given that the proposed model is designed to address the prediction of rare events in the presence of spatial interdependence.

While we emphasise the importance of correctly predicting high probabilities for the rare outcome of $Y=1$, the estimator still needs to classify the cases for both positive and negative outcomes. In other words, while we can prioritize a low true positive rate over a low false positive rate, we still need to make sure that our classifier identifies both negative and positive

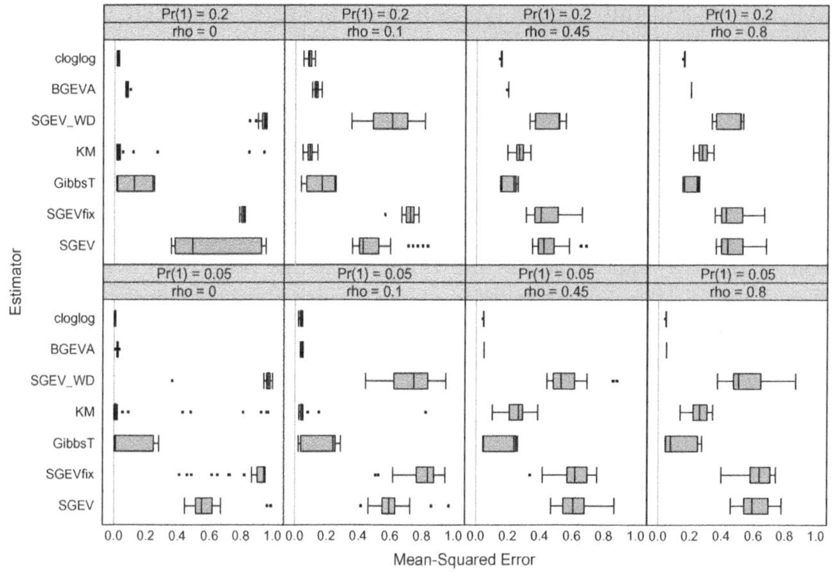

Fig. 2. Distribution of the Mean-Squared Error for Different Configurations of the Parameters, across 60 Replications.

cases. The plot in Fig. 2 therefore provides the overall Mean Squared Error, including both $y_i = 1$ and $y_i = 0$ cases. It is clear from this plot that, while positive cases are generally better identified by the SGEV estimator, this is combined with a relatively high false positive rate.

Since the prediction of ones and zeros can be sensitive to the choice of the prediction threshold – the predicted probability $P(Y = 1)$ above which we predict a 1 – alternative statistics are available that consider the entire range of potential threshold values. A common procedure is to sort all predicted values $\hat{y}^*$, then move the decision threshold along the range of values, and plot the proportion of correctly classified ones against the proportion of incorrectly classified ones. This is referred to as the receiver operating characteristic (ROC) curve (see, e.g., Hand & Anagnostopoulos, 2014) and is often used to compare the classification quality of different models or algorithms. The curve will generally be above the 45° diagonal line, since otherwise we could simply create a better classifier by swapping the labelling of the predictions. The further the ROC curve from the diagonal line, the better the classifier. A numerical indicator for this prediction quality is the area under curve (AUC) statistic, which is the area under the

ROC curve, and thus ranges typically from 0.5 to 1 – an AUC below 0.5 indicates a classifier performing worse than random classification of cases.

The AUC statistic suffers from a number of deficiencies as a measure to evaluate the performance of different estimators. A particular feature of the statistic that is of concern to our Monte Carlo study is the fact that this statistic amounts to a weighted average minimum loss measure. This average loss is determined by the relative cost of misclassifying zeros or ones, whereby the cases are weighted depending on the cumulative density function of the two classes across the range of scores (i.e., $F_0(t) = \Pr[\hat{y}^*(\mathbf{x}) < t | Y = 0]$ and $F_1(t) = \Pr[\hat{y}^*(\mathbf{x}) < t | Y = 1]$, with score $\hat{y}^*(\mathbf{x})$ the prediction of the classifier and t the threshold value) (Hand, 2009, pp. 108–111). In other words, the relative cost of misclassifying ones or zeros – and thus the evaluation of the relative performance of the classifier – are dependent on the classifier used, as opposed to being dependent on the underlying application, which is incoherent. Hand (2009) and Hand and Anagnostopoulos (2013, 2014) outline this complication and provide an alternative to the AUC score, the so-called H-index, which addresses this deficiency. The H-index has a range of 0–1, with high values indicating improved performance. We use the `hmeasure` package in R (Anagnostopoulos & Hand, 2012) to calculate the H-index statistics, the results of which are summarized in Fig. 3.

Coherently with the results shown in Fig. 1, we again see a relatively better performance for the SGEV model compared to the others in Fig. 3, when the sample is strongly imbalanced and the spatial autocorrelation parameter ρ increases.

6. EMPIRICAL APPLICATION TO STATE FAILURE

We investigate the performance on empirical data by using an application from comparative politics, on state failure. State failure refers to a state losing the capacity to control its territory and implement domestic policies, due to, for example, civil war. The prediction of state failure is also the core example of the earlier work on models for rare events by King and Zeng (2001a).

State failures can be expected to be "contagious" for a number of reasons (Iqbal & Starr, 2008). Indeed, there is extensive research on the spatial diffusion of civil war (see, e.g., Buhaug & Gleditsch, 2008; Starr, Darmofal & Iqbal, 2008). Instability in one country and lack of capacity by the state can

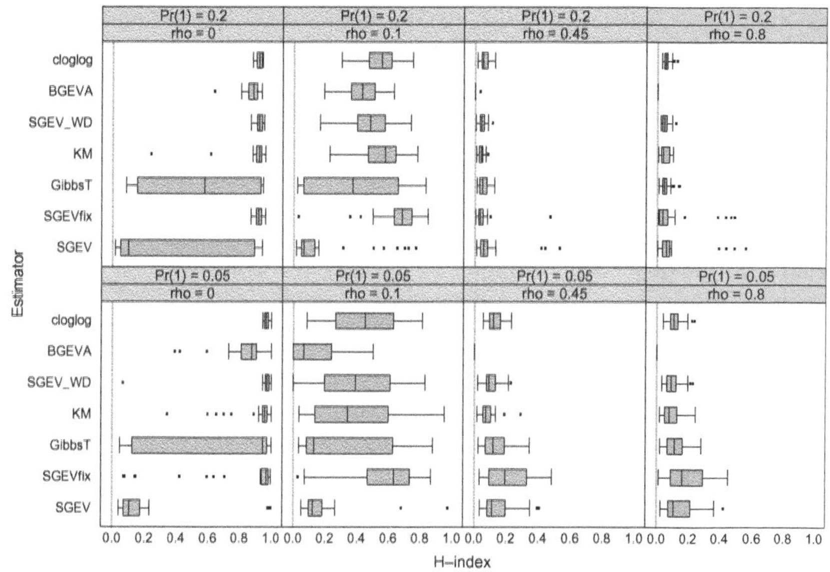

Fig. 3. Distribution of the *H*-Index, for Different Configurations of the Parameters, across 60 Replications.

create a safe haven for potential rebels in a neighboring country. Civil conflict is often related to ethnic divisions, which tend to cross national boundaries. Reduced state capacity due to extreme natural events, such as droughts, will also typically affect adjacent countries. Finally, rebellion and civil war in a neighboring country can act as an example for groups within a country. Such effects are clearly visible in, for example, the Arab Spring in 2011, when rebellious behavior in one state soon affected similar acts in a wide region. The spatial clustering of instability and civil war is well established, but the debate on the causal explanations of this clustering ongoing.

To test the model on data related to state failure, we use a definition of **W** that is based on the inverse distance between two states, whereby the distance is defined as the shortest distance between the two state borders. Since the inverse of the distance is undefined when the distance is zero, and because the inverse has a very fast decay, with slightly larger distances having minimal effect, we use a slowly decaying function by distance, $w_{ijt} = 1/(d_{ijt} + 100)$, with $w_{iit} = 0$ and d_{ijt} the minimum geographical distance between countries i and j at time t.[10] This **W** matrix is a block-diagonal matrix, with the inverse distances on the blocks along the diagonal and zeros otherwise – that is, one block for each time period t. This $\mathbf{W}$ is subsequently normalized such that all rows add up to one.

The model specification we use is inspired by, but does not closely follow Goldstone et al. (2010). In their replication data, specific matched samples are used to address the rare events nature of the data, while we estimate our models on a full data set of all countries and years where we have data on the relevant variables. All independent variables are lagged by one year relative to the dependent variable. To account for world-wide shocks, year dummies are included. The independent variables are sourced from the *Nations, Development, and Democracy* data set by Wejnert (2007) and the data used is from 1975 onwards.

Table 1 provides the regression estimates for the four models on identical data,[11] with in addition the H-index measure of prediction quality. Strikingly, while for the Monte Carlo analysis the SGEV estimator performed well in the presence of spatial autocorrelation, in this empirical data the results appear weaker – for the within-sample prediction of the outcome variable, the H-index suggests a marginally better classifier than logistic regression without accommodation of spatial or skewed effects.

The estimate for the autoregression parameter ρ by the regular Gibbs sampler, which it is generally good at estimating (Calabrese & Elkink, 2014),

Table 1. Regressions Explaining State Failure.
State failure as classified in Goldstone et al. (2010), using a slowly decaying inverse of the distance to define the adjacency matrix.

	Logistic	Gibbs	BGEVA	SGEVfix	SGEV
Intercept	−17.08	−3.50	−3.69	−6.43	−134.78
Polity IV	−0.03	−0.01	−0.04	−6.48	−0.34
Polity IV squared	−0.01	−0.02	−0.02	5.43	5.25
Log of infant mortality	0.17	0.44	0.51	−41.97	−4.09
Log of GDP per capita	−0.51	0.06	−0.02	3.76	−4.88
ρ		−0.17		−0.10	0.28
τ			25.00	25.00	126.92
N	1,653	324	324	324	324
H-index	0.467	0.432	0.433	0.471	0.471

Notes: Models include year fixed effects and the dependent variable is observed at $t+1$. For the BGEVA and SGEVfix models, τ is fixed a priori.

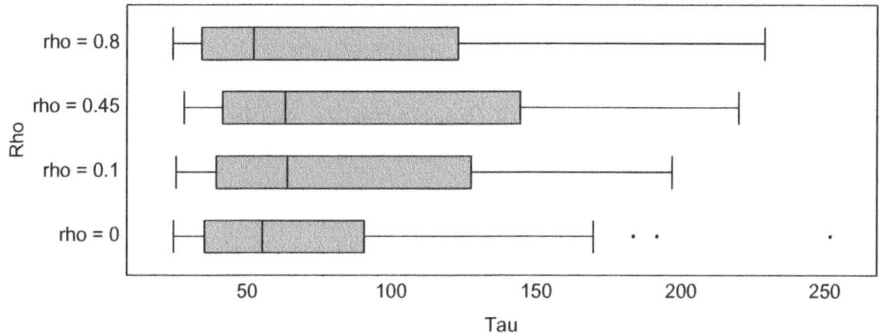

Fig. 4. Distribution of the Estimates of τ, for Different Configurations of the Parameters, across 60 Replications.

suggests an absence of, or even negative spatial autocorrelation – the 95% Highest Posterior Density interval is $[-0.37, 0.22]$, with 82% of the posterior samples providing an estimate of ρ below zero. The same negative coefficient is identified by the SGEV estimator when τ is fixed. The weak predictive results of the SGEV estimator might therefore be due to lack of actual spatial autocorrelation in this data, at least when the spatial contiguity matrix is defined as a matrix of inverse distances between countries.

While the paper is primarily concerned with the accurate prediction of the rare event, the empirical results do raise the question whether the estimation of τ in particular is problematic. Fig. 4 provides some insight into the performance of the SGEV estimator when it comes to correctly identifying the shape parameter τ. Strikingly, under the absence of any spatial autocorrelation, the estimates of τ are reasonably accurate, albeit with high variance. Under spatial autocorrelation, however ($\rho = 0.5$), the estimates of τ are nearly always zero, which is the initial value τ_0.

7. CONCLUSION

In this paper, we propose a spatial regression model for highly imbalanced binary data, that is, data whereby the classification categories are not approximately equally represented. Specifically, the category less represented is considered a rare event with its percentage in the sample lower than 5%. In this context, a symmetric link function, such as the logit or the probit function can underestimate the probability that the rare event occurs. To overcome this drawback, a generalized linear model with a flexible link function given by the GEV distribution is proposed in the literature (Calabrese & Osmetti, 2013; Wang & Dey, 2010).

Many applications where such rare events occur also contain spatial or network interdependencies. Examples include systemic risk for banks, eruption of international conflict, or currency crises. We therefore propose a generalized linear model based on the GEV distribution, taking into account spatial or network interdependence, the SGEV model. We provide a modified version of the Gibbs sampling method LeSage (2000) and Wang and Dey (2010) to estimate the parameters of the proposed model. The shape parameter of the GEV distribution regulates the skewness. In this paper, we both estimate the shape parameter and fix it in order to obtain lower errors.

Monte Carlo simulations are used to evaluate the performance of the SGEV model. We compare the predictive accuracy of our proposal with that of the spatial Gibbs sampler LeSage (2000) and the linearized GMM Klier and McMillen (2008). The current implementation provides a high true positive rate – the rare events are generally correctly identified – but also a relatively high false positive rate. The H-index however, which is used for the evaluation of the overall prediction quality for imbalanced samples, shows a slightly better performance of our estimator than existing estimators, in the presence of spatial autocorrelation.

A brief example from the political science literature is used to demonstrate the applicability of the model, namely by investigating the rare occurrence of state failure. This is based on the data used in published work on rare events. The SGEV estimator outperforms the other estimators as measured by the H-index. Future work will include applications to systemic risk for banks and credit risk. Furthermore, future research should be able to improve the estimation of the shape parameter τ. One direction of research in this regard might be the use of Bayesian model selection. Finally, while this paper, in line with Calabrese and Elkink (2014), focuses on the spatial autoregressive model, a similar extension can also be developed for the spatial error model, whereby the network interdependence is modeled in the error term as opposed through the spatially lagged-dependent variable.

NOTES

1. See LeSage, Kelley Pace, Lam, Campanella, and Liu (2011) for a corrected, more recent version of this estimator. The estimator proposed below is based largely on Wang and Dey (2010) and therefore not affected by these corrections.
2. When **W** is normalized and maximum likelihood is applied, Anselin (1982) proves that $1/\omega_{\min} < \rho < 1$ to ensure invertibility of $(I - \rho\mathbf{W})$, where $\omega_{\min}$ is the minimum eigenvalue of **W**.
3. The alternative, geostatistics, perspective concerns spatial data where space is seen as continuous and observations measured at specific coordinates (Anselin, 2002, p. 255; Bivand, 1998).
4. This will also allow further improvements, since there is a flourishing literature on optimizing Metropolis-Hastings algorithms (e.g., Angelino, Kohler, Waterland, Seltzer & Adams, 2014; Korattikara, Chen, & Welling, 2014; Maclaurin & Adams, 2014).
5. We assume $\boldsymbol{\varepsilon\varepsilon}' = \sigma_\varepsilon^2 I$. The parameter σ_ε^2 is kept fixed, because of lack of identifiability when simultaneously estimating the error variance and the linear regression coefficients in a latent variable model – similar to probit and logit regressions.
6. We constrain c to remain in the $[0.0005, 10]$ interval.
7. We considered different values of the parameter τ and we chose the one that shows the best predictive performance.
8. The R package BGEVA (Marra, Calabrese & Osmetti, 2013) is used to estimate the GEV model.
9. Analogously to LeSage (2000) we consider a maximum number of loops equal to 3,000 for the Gibbs estimator.
10. The minimum distance is calculated using the `cshapes` package in R (Weidmann & Gleditsch, 2010).
11. For computational efficiency reasons, the data is a subset of the overall data set.

REFERENCES

Agresti, A. (2002). *Categorical data analysis* (2nd ed.). New York, NY: Wiley.

Almanidis, P., & Sicles, R. C. (2015). *Banking crises, early warning models, and efficiency*. Working Paper.

Anagnostopoulos, C., & Hand, D. J. (2012). *hmeasure: The H-measure and other scalar classification performance metrics*. R package version 1.0.

Angelino, E., Kohler, E., Waterland, A., Seltzer, M., & Adams, R. P. (2014). *Accelerating MCMC via parallel predictive prefetching*. arXiv preprint arXiv:1403.7265.

Anselin, L. (1982). A note on small sample properties of estimators in a first-order spatial autoregressive model. *Environment and Planning*, *14*(1), 1023–1030.

Anselin, L. (2002). Under the hood. Issues in the specification and interpretation of spatial regression models. *Agricultural Economics*, *27*, 247–267.

Barro, D., & Basso, A. (2010). Credit contagion in a network of firms with spatial interaction. *European Journal of Operational Research*, *205*, 459–468.

Beron, K. J., & Vijverberg, W. P. M. (2004). Probit in a spatial context: A Monte Carlo analysis. In L. Anselin, R. J. G. M. Florax, & S. J. Rey (Eds.). *Advances in spatial econometrics. Methodology, tools and applications* (pp. 169–195). Berlin: Springer.

Bivand, R. (1998). A review of spatial statistical techniques for location studies. Paper presented at the CEPR symposium on New Issues in Trade and Location (2277), Lund, Sweden, 28–30 August, 1998.

Buhaug, H., & Gleditsch, K. S. (2008). Contagion or confusion? why conflicts cluster in space. *International Studies Quarterly*, *52*(2), 215–233.

Calabrese, R., & Elkink, J. A. (2014). Estimators of binary spatial autoregressive models: A Monte Carlo study. *Journal of Regional Science*, *54*(4), 664–687.

Calabrese, R., Elkink, J., & Giudici, P. (2014). *Measuring bank contagion in Europe using binary spatial regression models*. Technical report, Department of Economics and Management, University of Pavia.

Calabrese, R., & Osmetti, S. A. (2013). Modelling small and medium enterprise loan defaults as rare events: The generalized extreme value regression model. *Journal of Applied Statistics*, *40*, 1172–1188.

Calabrese, R., & Osmetti, S. (2015). Improving forecast of binary rare events data: A GAM-based approach. *Journal of Forecasting*, *34*(3), 230–239.

David, H. G., Pirog-Good, M. A., & Sickles, R. C. (1986). An analysis of youth crime and employment patterns. *Journal of Quantitative Criminology*, *2*(3), 219–236.

Elkink, J. A. (2011). The international diffusion of democracy. *Comparative Political Studies*, *44*(12), 1651–1674.

Falk, M., Hüsler, J., & Reiss, R.-D. (2010). *Laws of small numbers: Extremes and rare events*. Basel: Springer.

Fleming, M. M. (2004). Techniques for estimating spatially dependent discrete choice models. In L. Anselin, R. J. G. M. Florax, & S. J. Rey. *Advances in spatial econometrics. Methodology, tools and applications* (pp. 145–167). Berlin: Springer.

Frei, C., & Schar, C. (1998). A precipitation climatology of the Alps from high-resolution reain-gauge observations. *International Journal of Climatology*, *18*, 873–900.

Gleditsch, K. S., & Ward, M. D. (2006). Diffusion and the international context of democratization. *International Organization*, *60*(4), 911–933.

Gleditsch, K. S., & Ward, M. D. (2013). Forecasting is difficult, especially about the future: Using contentious issues to forecast interstate disputes. *Journal of Peace Research*, *50*(1), 17–31.

Goldstone, J. A., Bates, R. H., Epstein, D. L., Gurr, T. R., Lustik, M. B., Marshall, M. G., Ulfelder, J., & Woodward, M. (2010). A global model for forecasting political instability. *American Journal of Political Science*, *51*(1), 190–208.

Hand, D. J. (2009). Measuring classifier performance: A coherent alternative to the area under the ROC curve. *Machine Learning*, *77*, 103–123.

Hand, D. J., & Anagnostopoulos, C. (2013). When is the area under the receiver operating characteristic curve an appropriate measure of classifier performance? *Pattern Recognition Letters*, *13*, 492–495.

Hand, D. J., & Anagnostopoulos, C. (2014). A better Beta for the *H* measure of classification performance. *Pattern Recognition Letters*, *40*, 41–46.

Hand, D. J., Whitrow, C., Adams, N. M., Juszczak, P., & Weston, D. (2008). Performance criteria for plastic card fraud detection tools. *Journal of Operational Research Society*, *59*(7), 956–962.

Hastings, W. K. (1970). Monte Carlo sampling methods using Markov chains and their applications. *Biometrika*, *57*, 97–109.

Iqbal, Z., & Starr, H. (2008). Bad neighbors: Failed states and their consequences. *Conflict Management and Peace Science*, *25*, 315–331.

King, G., & Zeng, L. (2001a). Explaining rare events in international relations. *International Organization*, *55*, 693–715.

King, G., & Zeng, L. (2001b). Logistic regression in rare events data. *Political Analysis*, *9*, 137–163.

Klier, T., & McMillen, D. P. (2008). Clustering of auto supplier plants in the United States: Generalized method of moments spatial logit for large samples. *Journal of Business & Economic Statistics*, *26*(4), 460–471.

Korattikara, A., Chen, Y., & Welling, M. (2014). Austerity in MCMC land: Cutting the Metropolis-Hastings budget. arXiv preprint arXiv:1304.5299.

Kotz, S., & Nadarajah, S. (2000). *Extreme value distributions. Theory and applications*. London: Imperial College Press.

Lambert, P. C., & Thompson, J. R. (2007). Estimating and modeling the cure fraction in population-based cancer survival analysis. *Biostatistics*, *8*(3), 576–594.

LeSage, J. P. (2000). Bayesian estimation of limited dependent variable spatial autoregressive models. *Geographical Analysis*, *32*(1), 19–35.

LeSage, J. P., & Kelley Pace, R. (2009). *Introduction to spatial econometrics*. CRC Press.

LeSage, J. P., Kelley Pace, R., Lam, N., Campanella, R., & Liu, X. (2011). New Orleans business recovery in the aftermath of Hurricane Katrina. *Journal of the Royal Statistical Society: Series A (Statistics in Society)*, *174*(4), 1007–1027.

Maclaurin, D., & Adams, R. P. (2014). Firefly Monte Carlo: Exact MCMC with subsets of data. arXiv preprint arXiv:1403.5693.

Manski, C. F., & Lerman, S. R. (1977). The estimation of choice probabilities from choice-based samples. *Econometrica*, *45*(8), 1977–1988.

Marra, G., Calabrese, R., & Osmetti, S. A. (2013). Package 'bgeva: Generalized extreme value additive modelling for binary rare events data'. https://cran.r-project.org/web/packages/bgeva.pdf

McCullagh, P., & Nelder, J. A. (1989). *Generalized linear models* (2nd ed.). New York, NY: Chapman & Hall.

McMillen, D. P. (1992). Probit with spatial autocorrelation. *Journal of Regional Science*, *32*(3), 335–348.

McMillen, D. P. (1995). Spatial effects in probit models: A Monte Carlo investigation. In L. Anselin & R. J. G. M. Florax (Eds.). *New directions in spatial econometrics* (pp. 189–228). Berlin: Springer Verlag.

Neumayer, E., & Plümper, T. (2016). W. *Political Science Research and Methods*, *4*(1), 175–193.

Novo, Á. A. (2003). *Contagious currency crisis: A spatial probit approach*. Working Papers Banco de Portugal, Economics and Research Department. http://EconPapers.repec.org/RePEc:ptu:wpaper:w200305

Pinkse, J., & Slade, M. E. (1998). Contracting in space: An application of spatial statistics to discrete-choice models. *Journal of Econometrics*, *85*, 125–154.

Roberts, S. J. (2000). Extreme value statistics for novelty detection in biomedical data processing. *Science, Measurement and Technology, IEE Proceedings*, *147*, 363–367.

Scott, A., & Wild, C. (1986). Fitting logistic models under case-control or choice based sampling. *Journal of the Royal Statistical Society. Series B (Methodological)*, *48*(2), 170–182.

Smith, R. L. (1985). Maximum likelihood estimation in a class of non-regular cases. *Biometrika*, *72*, 67–90.

Starr, H., Darmofal, D., & Iqbal, Z. (2008). Civil war: Spatiality, contagion, and diffusion. Paper presented at the Spatial and Network Analysis of Conflict conference.

Thomas, T. S. (2007). A primer for Bayesian spatial probits, with an application to deforestation in Madagascar. Companion Paper for the World Bank Policy Research Report on Forests, Environment, and Livelihoods. http://www.timthomas.net

Verbeek, M. (2008). *A guide to modern econometrics*. Chichester: Wiley.

Wang, X., & Dey, D. K. (2010). Generalized extreme value regression for binary response data: An application to B2B electronic payments system adoption. *Annals of Applied Statistics*, *4*(4), 2000–2023.

Weidmann, N. B., & Gleditsch, K. S. (2010). Mapping and measuring country shapes: The cshapes package. *The R Journal*, *2*(1), 18–24.

Weiss, G. M. (2004). Mining with rarity: A unifying framework. *ACM SIGKDD Explorations Newsletter*, *6*(1), 7–19.

Wejnert, B. (2007). *Nations, Development, and Democracy, 1800-2005*. Inter-university Consortium for Political and Social Research, Ann Arbor, NY. http://doi.org/10.3886/ICPSR20440.v1

Zhu, S., & Kelley Pace, R. (2014). Modeling spatially interdependent mortgage decisions. *Journal of Real Estate Finance and Economics*, *49*(4), 598–620.

A MULTIVARIATE SPATIAL ANALYSIS FOR ANTICIPATING NEW FIRM COUNTS

Yiyi Wang[a], Kara M. Kockelman[b] and Paul Damien[c]

[a]*Civil Engineering Department, Montana State University, Bozeman, MT, USA*

[b]*Department of Civil, Architectural, and Environmental Engineering, The University of Texas at Austin, TX, USA*

[c]*Department of Information Risk and Operations Management, The University of Texas at Austin, TX, USA*

ABSTRACT

This paper analyzes county-level firm births across the United States using a spatial count model that permits spatial dependence, cross-correlation among different industry types, and over-dispersion commonly found in empirical count data. Results confirm the presence of spatial autocorrelation (which can arise from agglomeration effects and missing variables), industry-specific over-dispersion, and positive, significant cross-correlations. After controlling for existing-firm counts in 2008 (as an exposure term), parameter estimates and inference suggest that a younger work force and/or clientele (as quantified using each county's median-age values) is associated with more firm births (in 2009). Higher

Spatial Econometrics: Qualitative and Limited Dependent Variables
Advances in Econometrics, Volume 37, 167–193

ISSN: 0731-9053/doi:10.1108/S0731-905320160000037014

population densities is associated with more new basic-sector firms, while reducing retail-firm starts. The modeling framework demonstrated here can be adopted for a variety of settings, harnessing very local, detailed data to evaluate the effectiveness of investments and policies, in terms of generating business establishments and promoting economic gains.

Keywords: Firm birth; spatial count model; multivariate response; conditional autoregressive

JEL classification: M13; C11; C30; C35

1. INTRODUCTION

The number of business establishments, aggregated at a certain geography level, is a key input parameter to the many decisions made in the public and private sectors. From an economic perspective, new firms/companies indicate the vitality of entrepreneurship and overall economic well-being (Sadeghi, 2008) and influence policies such as tax incentives or regulatory measures to modify the markets (Harger & Ross, 2014). From a planning perspective, firm locations, in a disaggregated form of firm counts, affect travel patterns (Levinson, 1998; Mercado, Paez, Farber, Roorda, & Morency, 2012; O'Kelly & Lee, 2005) and residential location choice (Paleti, Bhat, & Pendyala, 2013), which measurably shape the job-housing balance and level of accessibility of cities and towns. Therefore, it is of both theoretical and practical value to explore the methods for anticipating where firms are and what industry types they fall into.

There are two fundamental methods that can be used. The first method focuses on the location choice of individual firms and typically employs the utility-maximization-based discrete choice theory (Basile, Castellani, & Zanfei, 2008; Draganska et al., 2008; Siedschlag & Zhang, 2015) or its variant that incorporates value chain and organization theory (Alcacer & Delgado, 2013; Henderson & Ono, 2008). While the notion of predicting where (or which zone) a firm of given attributes would locate is attractive, the estimation scheme can become excruciatingly difficult to handle, due to the sheer number of zones or choice options (Bhat, Paleti, & Palvinder, 2014). In contrast, the second method circumvents this challenge by analyzing the aggregates of firms within a certain geography, instead of individual location choice, through the lens of econometric techniques designed for count responses (Bhat et al., 2014; Brown, Lambert, & Raymond, 2009; Cincera, 1998). Such an aggregates-based method has practical values too, as many macro-level decisions rely on aggregated firm counts, and travel demand models regularly use employment aggregates by industry type to impute trips generated at the zone level (An & Chen, 2007; Ewing & Cervero, 2001; Kitamura, Chen, Pendyala, & Narayanan, 2000; Zhao & Kockelman, 2002; Zhang, Southworth, Xiong, & Sonnenberg, 2012).

This study falls under the second, aggregates-based method and develops a new model for simultaneously estimating firm counts, by three industry types at the county level, while capturing spatial dependence, interactions among different industry types that emerge locally, and interactions among different industry types that trend over space. Capturing these two different forms of interactions offers behavioral advantages because each industry sector can influence all businesses that co-locate in the same zone, thanks to, for example, agglomeration effects, while impacting jobs creation in nearby zones via network effects (e.g., greater accessibility and shipping convenience). Incorporating such behaviors helps the model mimic the nuanced ways in which industries operate and thereby increase a model's predictive power.

This work's main contribution is a new way of examining multivariate spatial data, with enhanced behavioral realism and a modeling framework that may be scaled up for higher dimension problems. Models of this type can be easily adapted to study a variety of multivariate spatial data, such as crime counts, vehicle ownership levels, and technological advances. The paper contains a review of the firm ecology literature described in Section 2, followed by a Section 3 that summarizes socio-economic data obtained from the U.S. Census and the response variables retrieved from the Statistics of U.S. Businesses surveys. The modeling framework is reported in Section 4, and coefficient estimates and elasticities are presented and assessed in Section 5. Section 6 suggests future work.

2. LITERATURE REVIEW

The study of firm births and deaths, falls within the literature of organization ecology, a branch of study introduced by Hannan and Freeman (1977), who identified the four strands associated with "the population ecology of organizations": inertia and resistance to change (deemed a by-product of the need of a firm to be reliable and accountable), age dependence (i.e., the risk of mortality tends to decline as an organization grows but then shoots up once the organization has depleted its initial resources), niche theory (which explains those varying organizational structures in different industries given the two distinct sets of generalists and specialists within organizations), and density dependence (which predicts that the rates of births and deaths depend on the density of the organizations in the market).

Reynolds, Miller, and Maki (1995) examined firm births and deaths during a 12-year period (from 1976 to 1988) using a pooled OLS regression across U.S. counties. They concluded that higher shares of mid-career, educated adults are associated with higher firm-birth rates (computed as the number of new firms divided by the total number of firms) across all time periods, and that economic diversity (measured as firm count per employee plus an occupational diversity index) also tends to contribute to higher levels of firm births and deaths. Higher personal wealth also exerted a positive impact on firm births, presumably due to an increase in consumer demand on service and retail activities. The absence of work unions and the presence of work laws were also associated with an elevated birth rate of firms in a significant way, as is higher population growth. By contrast, the following factors were shown to yield marginal or no effects on firm births: unemployment rates, input and production costs (of the economic system), national transportation access (measured by distance to the nearest airports), the size of economic systems (i.e., total population, total work force, and total number of establishments), and a host of research and development (R&D) variables (measured by numbers of post-college, professional, and technical employees; patents granted; and doctorates granted per 1,000 square miles).

Brown et al. (2009) examined the birth and death of manufacturing firms for U.S. counties in the contiguous 48 states, using a standard negative binomial model with lagged spatial effects. In other words, spatial ripple effects enter the mean birth (or death) rates (μ_i) by $\mu_i = \exp(\beta' x_i) \prod_{j \neq i} y_j^{\rho w_{ij}} = \exp\left(\beta' x_i + \rho \sum_{j \neq i} w_{ij} \ln(y_j)\right)$, where μ_i is the expected mean at location I, x_i represents a vector of covariates observed at that location, β's capture the effects of these covariates on the mean, y_j is the observed birth (or death) counts for a neighboring location j, w_{ij} describes the distance between location i and j, and ρ measures the strength of spatial dependence. Results suggested that agglomeration economies, including both local agglomeration (measured by the percentage of manufacturing establishments with less than 10 employees and shares of employment in each county) and economies of scale (captured by the percentage of manufacturing establishments with more than 100 employees and the total number of establishments divided by county area) tended to be associated with increases in firm births. Higher median-household income was also estimated to contribute to firm births.

Alsaaty (2012) investigated the birth and death cycle of micro firms (defined as employer firms with less than 20 people) in the United States, and maintained that the survival rate of micro firms in the United States is approximately 10 percent and depends on states, industries, and entrepreneurs. He also suggested several influencing factors, including the population of the state, the budget situation of the state, the level of economic development (gauged by indicators such as the output of goods and services), and the intensity of the state's industrial (or service) base.

In a recent effort, Bhat, Paleti, and Castro (2014) proposed a multivariate count model for estimating county-level sums of new firms by industry sectors across the 254 counties in Texas. The model was casted in a generalized ordered response (GOR) framework through a latent variable measuring the growth intensity of firms of a given industry at a given county. The study controlled for an array of covariates pertaining to agglomeration economies, transportation infrastructure, county-level demographics, and human capital while allowing for the spatial dependence among neighboring counties, cross-correlations among the 11 industry sectors considered, as well as over-dispersion and excess zeroes. Model estimation was conducted using the composite marginal likelihood (CML) approach. Results found that agglomeration economies (proxied by population density, population change, number of existing businesses, etc.) and fiscal factors (measured by property tax rates and total government expenditure) are strong predictors of county-level demand for new firms across industry types, whereas road infrastructure and land use characteristics mainly affect the firm growth through the supply side.

This paper proposed an alternative way for analyzing geo-referenced, multivariate count responses through a flexible framework that is scalable to higher dimension response levels. The model was built upon the multivariate conditional autoregressive (MCAR) model, as appeared in Wang and Kockelman (2013), to analyze the number of new firms by industries (i.e., base, service, and retail) across counties in the contiguous 48 states. To group new firms by industries is not only of theoretical interest (so that the research problem can be cast in a multivariate setting), but also of behavioral realism, as different industries tend to exhibit different organizational structures and growth patterns (Hannan & Freeman, 1977).

The following sections discuss the data sets for a selected sample of the 3,109 U.S. counties in the contiguous 48 states, the modeling framework, and estimation results and inference.

3. DATA SETS

This study relies on a U.S. county-level firm-birth data set across three industry types from 2008 to 2009. Firm births are characterized by the number of new establishments, which are available annually from the Statistics of U.S. Businesses, as part of the data reservoir from the U.S. Census Bureau (http://www.census.gov//econ/susb/data/download_susb2009.html). The 2007 North American Industry Classification System (NAICS) code was used to group these business establishments into 19 industry sectors (based on its first two digits). These industry sectors were later grouped by the authors into three broader industry types: basic, retail, and service, as shown in Table 1. Basic jobs refer to those involved in industries driven largely by external demands, from outside the region (Quintero, 2007). These include agriculture, manufacturing, and wholesale trade, since their products tend to be transported outside the source regions. Non-basic industries primarily sell their goods and services locally and consist of two major categories: retail trade (e.g., grocery stores and shopping centers) and service (e.g., information, finance, and insurance, etc.).

The number of new establishments (in basic, retail, and service industries) in each U.S. county from 2008 to 2009 serves as the response vector here. Figs. 1–3 illustrate the spatial distribution of the three new-establishment counts.

As an exploratory study, this research only controlled for those social-economic variables that are regularly reported by public data sources. These covariates represent customer base (e.g., population and population density), human capital (measured by median age of population), economic vitality (proxied by share of vacant housing units, share of impoverished families, and median annual income for workers 16 years and older), and land use characteristics expressed as an indicator variable to distinguish metropolitan counties from non-metro areas based on the rural-urban continuum coding (United States Department of Agriculture Economic Research Service [USDA], 2003). The data used to generate covariates come from the U.S. Census 2010 summary files, which focus on social,

Table 1. NAICS 2007 Definition of Industry Classification and General Codes.

NAICS Code	NAICS Industry Description	General Class
11	Agriculture, forestry, fishing, and hunting	1
21	Mining, quarrying, and oil & gas extraction	1
22	Utilities	3
23	Construction	3
31–33	Manufacturing	1
42	Wholesale trade	1
44–45	Retail trade	2
48–49	Transportation and warehousing	1
51	Information	3
52	Finance and insurance	3
53	Real estate and rental & leasing	3
54	Professional, scientific, and technical services	3
55	Management of companies and enterprises	3
56	Administrative support, waste management, and remediation services	3
61	Educational services	3
62	Health care and social assistance	3
71	Arts, entertainment, and recreation	3
72	Accommodation and food services	3
81	Other services (except public administration)	3

Note: General classes are basic (class 1), retail (class 2), and service (class 3) industries. More NAICS information can be found at http://www.census.gov/cgi-bin/sssd/naics/naicsrch?chart=2007.

economic, and housing characteristics of the U.S. population. The data was collected using the Census short form (Summary Files 1 and 2) and the long-form questionnaire (Summary File 3) from a sample of 19 million housing units, about 1 in 6 households nationwide. Unemployment rates and educational attainment may also influence economic growth and thus new-firm starts, but these variables are only available for about 800 of the nation's 3,200 counties, and hence were not controlled for here.

Summary statistics for all the covariates (including exposure metrics) used are summarized in Table 2. Covariates include shares of vacant

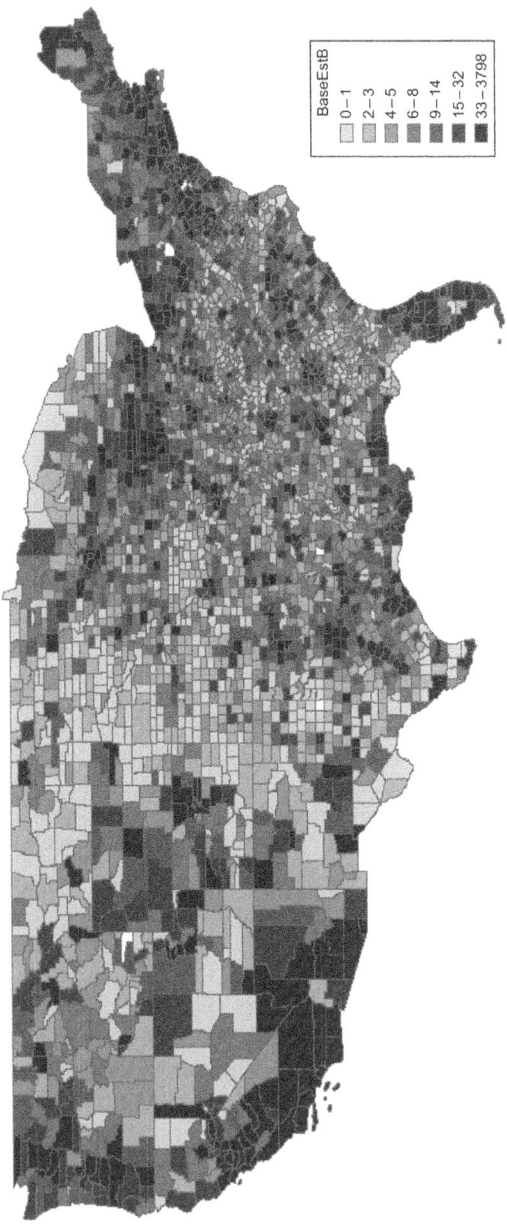

Fig. 1. New Basic Establishments across U.S. Counties in the Contiguous 48 States during 2008–2009.

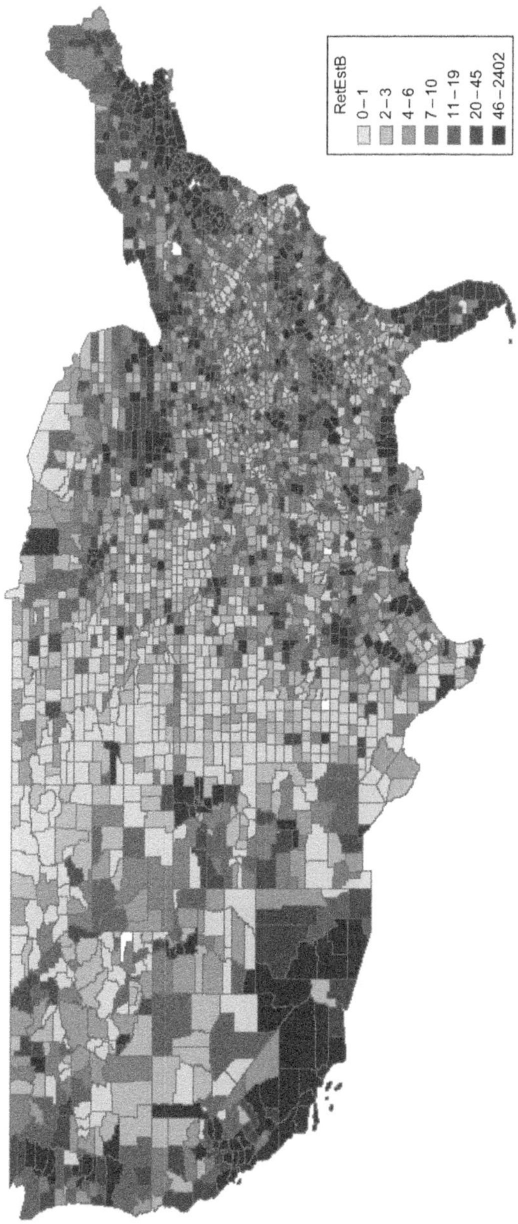

Fig. 2. New Retail Establishments across U.S. Counties in the Contiguous 48 States during 2008–2009.

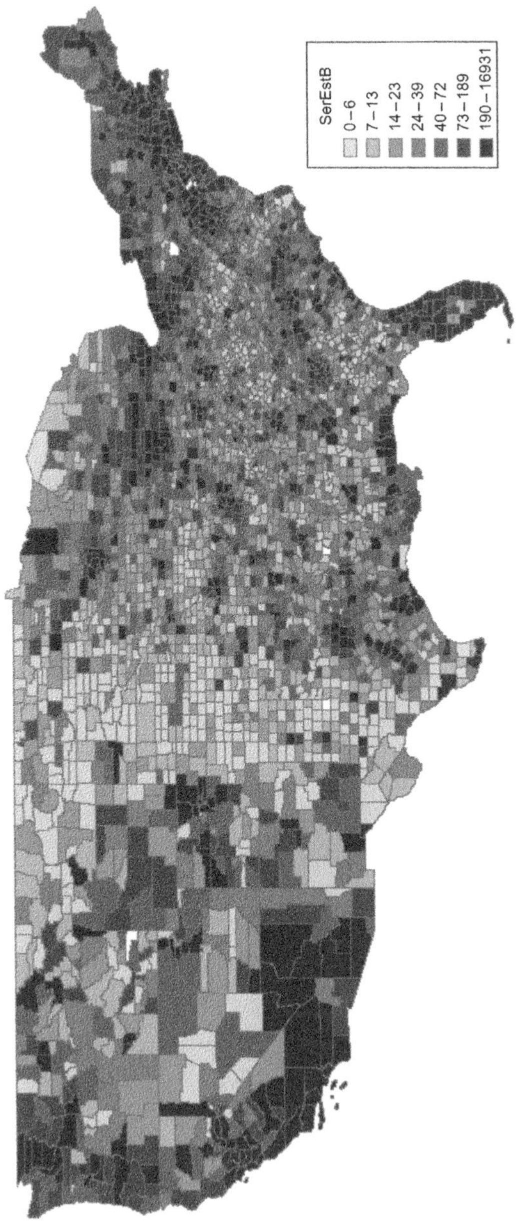

Fig. 3. New Service Establishments across U.S. Counties in the Contiguous 48 States during 2008−2009.

Table 2. Summary Statistics of Covariates for the Firm-Birth Model.

	Mean	Stdev	Min	Max	Median
Potential exposure measures					
Land area (sq. miles)	950.84	1304.02	2.00	20,057.11	610.31
Total establishments	2,180	7,248	1	218,787	517
Total jobs	37,476	138,060	0	3,909,096	6,741
Covariates					
VacantHousing (share)	0.162	0.098	0.038	0.074	0.013
MedianAge (years)	40.37	5.03	22.40	62.70	40.30
Families in Poverty (share)	0.11	0.06	0.00	0.45	0.10
MedAnnIncome per worker	25,466	5,047	5,559	59,672	24,934
MetroIndex (indicator)	0.35	0.48	0.00	1.00	0.00
Pop Density (persons per acre)	0.40	2.70	0.00	108.51	0.07
Response variables					
New basic estab.	23	99.25	0	3798	6
New retail estab.	25	88.44	0	2402	6
New service estab.	153	574.19	0	16,931	28

housing units (VacantHousing), median age of county residents (MedianAge), shares of families living below the poverty line (Families in Poverty), median annual income of working people older than 16 years, and population density (Pop Density). As mentioned earlier, the three response variables (per county) are the number of new firms in basic, retail, and service industries in from 2008 to 2009.

As with most (spatial) count models, a size or exposure measure (like land area or annual payroll) can be used in the firm-birth model. County size, population, existing employment, and existing-firm counts (number of establishments) were entered in the model, respectively, as the exposure measures for the rate of new-firm starts. Existing-firm counts yielded the best goodness-of-fit and parameter inference among the four candidates and hence was chosen as the exposure term in the final model shown in Table 3. Estimating the associated coefficient for the exposure term is appropriate, since one does not normally expect or find simple proportionality between the exposure term and number of new firms, or in the context of traffic crashes, between traffic volume and crash frequency. Here, the exposure measure used in the tri-variate firm-birth model is the total number of business establishments in the same industry category as the response

Table 3. Model Results for the Firm-Birth Model with Three-Level Responses.

	Parameter	Estimates	Pseudo-*T*-Stats	2.50%	Median	97.50%	Elasticity
Constant	Basic (1)	−7.441	−8.09	−8.934	−7.333	−5.777	
	Retail (2)	−3.792	−7.00	−4.712	−3.832	−2.816	
	Service (3)	−2.833	−2.66	−4.708	−2.998	−0.756	
Exposure term (new firms): γ	1	0.884	9.59	0.596	0.823	0.943	
	2	1.068	28.5	0.990	1.076	1.124	
	3	1.015	27.8	0.940	1.019	1.080	
VacantHousing	1	−0.041	−1.98	−0.131	−0.052	0.003	−0.05
	2	0.011	2.06	0.001	0.011	0.021	0.02
	3	0.010	2.18	0.001	0.010	0.019	0.02
MedianAge	1	−0.006	−1.95	−0.024	−0.006	0.014	−0.003
	2	−0.016	−2.37	−0.029	−0.015	−0.004	−0.03
	3	−0.031	−3.16	−0.059	−0.024	−0.005	−0.05
Families in Poverty	1	1.861	1.71	0.772	2.171	4.338	0.07
	2	1.481	1.65	−0.299	1.527	3.093	0.06
	3	−0.875	−1.08	−2.423	−0.893	0.740	−0.02
Metro Index (1 = Metro.)	1	0.051	2.64	0.028	0.043	0.104	0.07
	2						
	3	0.108	1.75	−0.011	0.107	0.232	0.05
Pop Density	1	0.174	3.30	0.071	0.174	0.279	0.07
	2	−0.114	−2.07	−0.222	−0.114	−0.010	−0.02
	3						
ρ_1		0.664	6.53	0.452	0.671	0.843	
ρ_2		0.499	5.05	0.309	0.499	0.694	
ρ_3		0.717	7.10	0.500	0.725	0.891	
η_{012}		0.380	3.74	0.196	0.376	0.582	
η_{013}		0.320	3.73	0.166	0.315	0.502	
η_{023}		0.348	3.87	0.181	0.345	0.534	
η_{112}		0.230	4.13	0.128	0.229	0.347	
η_{113}		0.127	3.19	0.059	0.124	0.215	
η_{123}		0.128	3.16	0.060	0.124	0.214	
τ_{v1}		12.510	11.1	10.410	12.470	14.790	
τ_{v2}		6.835	8.92	5.434	6.798	8.449	

Table 3. (*Continued*)

Parameter	Estimates	Pseudo-*T*-Stats	2.50%	Median	97.50%	Elasticity
τ_{v3}	7.051	9.05	5.632	7.014	8.669	
τ_1	4.555	6.26	3.305	4.490	6.153	
τ_2	4.813	6.21	3.466	4.755	6.487	
τ_3	5.180	7.31	3.947	5.135	6.696	
DIC	7687.3					
Run time: 10.1 hours		# of chains = 2, burn-in = 5,000, # of iterations = 10,000				

variable of interest at the end of 2008. The unknown parameters (i.e., the exponents γ's) associated with these three exposure terms were estimated simultaneously with all other model parameters, using Bayesian techniques.

A tri-variate extension of the MCAR model (Wang & Kockelman, 2013) was applied to analyze firm births during the 2008–2009 period. In the interest of run time, a sample of 1,316 counties in the Midwestern and Western regions of the United States, as shown in Fig. 4, was used to showcase the model.

4. METHODOLOGY

Spatial dependence among neighboring zones can be mainly captured by two fundamental types of models: the spatial autoregressive-type of models, as discussed in Elhorst (2009), LeSage and Pace (2009), and Anselin (1988), and the conditional autoregressive models (CAR) (Besag, 1975). The former contains a wide array of specifications, such as the spatial error models or SEMs (which describe spatial dependence among the error terms and is considered to control for more "subtle" correlation over space), the spatial autoregressive models or SARs (which consider direct spatial interactions among the response variables), and the Spatial Durbin Models or SDMs (which allow for not only a zone's response variable to spillover to influence its neighbors' responses, but also that zone's covariates to spillover to influence its neighbors' responses). The above models have been extended to analyze ordered responses such as crash severity and ozone

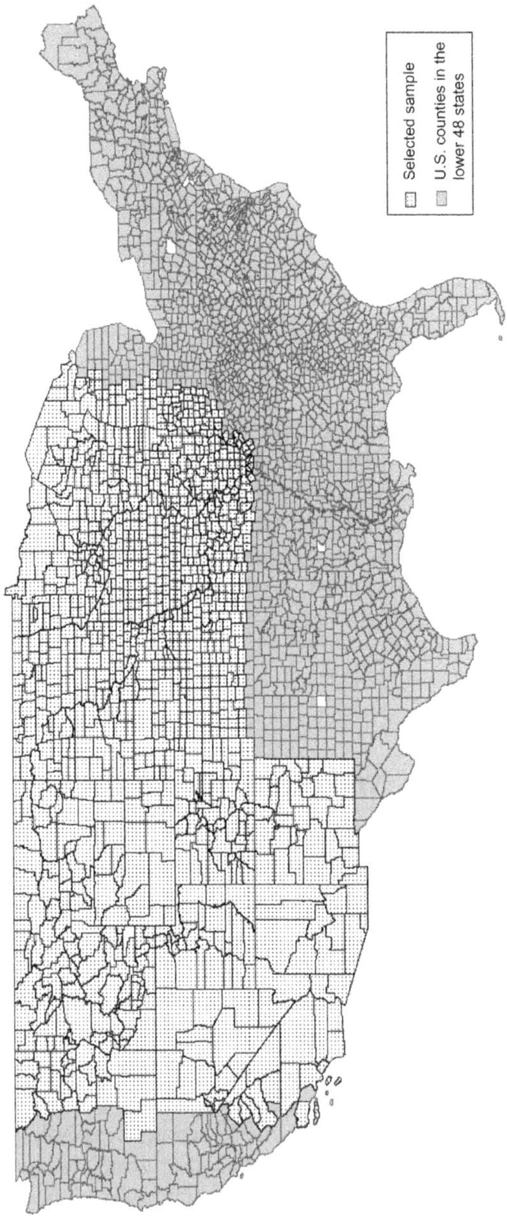

Fig. 4. Selected Sample for the Firm-Birth Model.

concentration (see, e.g., Castro, Paleti, & Bhat, 2012; Song, Ghosh, Miaou, & Mallick, 2006; Wang & Kockelman, 2009) and unordered responses, such as travel mode choice (see, e.g., Bille & Arbia, 2013; Pike, 2014; Sidharthan, Bhat, Pendyala, & Goulias, 2011).

By comparison, CAR models are more commonly used in spatial analysis of count data, thanks to convenient implementation and faster computation under large sample size (see, e.g., Gelfand & Vounatsou, 2003; Miaou, Song, & Mallick, 2003; Pettitt, Weir, & Hart, 2002; Song et al., 2006) as well as open-source software that provides the CAR priors (Spiegelhalter, Thomas, Best, & Lunn, 2003). Cressie (1995) proved that the SAR specification is a special type of CAR model, at least in a continuous-response setting. While it is unclear if the same proposition holds in limited dependent variable settings, some research has shown that the SAR approach can become unwieldy for estimating those variables, especially when data sets grow large (see, e.g., Wang, Kockelman, & Lemp, 2012). Miaou et al. (2003) showed that the SAR model yields parameter estimates similar to those estimated from the CAR model when being applied to analyze georeferenced count data. For all these reasons, this work focused on the CAR specification and extended it to a multivariate setting.

The growth pattern of U.S. firms is cast in a MCAR Poisson-lognormal model with a three-level response. This model extends the standard Poisson model to allow for extra-Poisson variation (via the lognormal component), cross-correlation among different types of firms, and spatial dependence by incorporating random effects, $\boldsymbol{\phi} = (\boldsymbol{\phi}'_1, \boldsymbol{\phi}'_2, \boldsymbol{\phi}'_3)'$, in the mean functions that govern the numbers of new firms by industry type. In the firm-birth context, $\boldsymbol{\phi}_i$ could be the n by 1 vectors of spatial random effects for the latent rates of industry types 1 (basic, e.g., agriculture, mining, and warehousing), 2 (retail), and 3 (service, e.g., information, education, and professional), formally expressed as:

$$y_{ik} \sim \text{Poisson}(\lambda_{ik}), \tag{1}$$

where y_{ik} is the observed firm births by type ($k = 1$ denotes basic, 2 denotes retail, and 3 denotes service) for the ith county in the study region. The (non-negative) mean firm counts for each county and industry type, λ_{ik}, are defined in the second stage:

$$\lambda_{ik} = E_i^{\alpha} \cdot \exp(x_i'\beta_k + \boldsymbol{\phi}_{ik} + u_{ik}), \tag{2}$$

where E_i^{α} is the exposure or scaling term, of total firm establishments (per county), as discussed earlier. The extra-Poisson variation is captured by the random effect u_{ik}, assumed to follow a normal distribution centered at zero and with variance, $1/\tau_{vk}$, specific to industry type k. The random-effect term, u_{ik}, represents heterogeneity due to missing variables that may be inherent to a county, such as entrepreneurship and certain public policies. These random-effect terms appear justified since they were founds to be statistically significant (as shown in Table 3).

Stacking all spatial random terms by industry type renders a column vector of $\boldsymbol{\phi} = (\boldsymbol{\phi}_1', \boldsymbol{\phi}_2', \boldsymbol{\phi}_3')'$, following a multivariate normal distribution (MVN), by construction:

$$\begin{pmatrix} \boldsymbol{\phi}_1 \\ \boldsymbol{\phi}_2 \\ \boldsymbol{\phi}_3 \end{pmatrix} \sim \text{MVN}\left(\begin{pmatrix} \mathbf{0} \\ \mathbf{0} \\ \mathbf{0} \end{pmatrix}, \begin{bmatrix} \Sigma_{11} & \Sigma_{12} & \Sigma_{13} \\ \Sigma_{12}' & \Sigma_{22} & \Sigma_{23} \\ \Sigma_{13}' & \Sigma_{23}' & \Sigma_{33} \end{bmatrix} \right), \tag{3}$$

where the MVN's zero means ensure that the average firm-birth rate for industry type k ($k = 1, 2, 3$) does not shift due to latent random effects, and $\sum_{kl}$ are n by n matrices describing the covariance structure between industry types k and l.

The MCAR structure decomposes the high-dimensional distribution in Eq. (3) into a sequence of lower dimension conditional distributions as such: $p(\boldsymbol{\phi}) = p(\boldsymbol{\phi}_1 | \boldsymbol{\phi}_2, \boldsymbol{\phi}_3) \cdot p(\boldsymbol{\phi}_2 | \boldsymbol{\phi}_3) \cdot p(\boldsymbol{\phi}_3)$. The marginal distribution of $\boldsymbol{\phi}_3$ can be written as: $p(\boldsymbol{\phi}_3) \sim N(0, \Sigma_{33})$ with $\boldsymbol{\Sigma}_{33} = [\tau_3(\mathbf{D} - \rho_3 \mathbf{W})]^{-1}$. The marginal distribution of $(\boldsymbol{\phi}_2, \boldsymbol{\phi}_3)$ can be obtained by removing irrelevant elements (with respect to $\boldsymbol{\phi}_2$ and $\boldsymbol{\phi}_3$) from the full distribution and follows a multivariate normal distribution: $\begin{pmatrix} \boldsymbol{\phi}_2 \\ \boldsymbol{\phi}_3 \end{pmatrix} \sim N\left(\begin{pmatrix} \mathbf{0} \\ \mathbf{0} \end{pmatrix}, \begin{bmatrix} \Sigma_{22} & \Sigma_{23} \\ \Sigma_{23}' & \Sigma_{33} \end{bmatrix} \right)$ and $\boldsymbol{\phi}_2 | \boldsymbol{\phi}_3 \sim N(A_{23}\boldsymbol{\phi}_3, [(D - \rho_2 W)\tau_2]^{-1})$, where A_{23} describes the aspatial correlation between industry types 2 and 3, as well as the spatially lagged correlation between the two industry types, formally: $A_{23} = \eta_{0,23} I + \eta_{1,23} W$.

$\boldsymbol{\phi}_1 | \boldsymbol{\phi}_2, \boldsymbol{\phi}_3 \sim N(A_{13}\boldsymbol{\phi}_3 + A_{12}\boldsymbol{\phi}_2, [(D - \rho_1 W)\tau_1]^{-1})$, where A_{13} and A_{12} capture the aspatial and spatially lagged correlation across industry types 1 and 3, and industry types 1 and 2, respectively, formally: $A_{13} = \eta_{0,23} I + \eta_{1,13} W$ and $A_{12} = \eta_{0,12} I + \eta_{1,12} W$.

The three-level scheme developed here decomposes the massive covariance structure into a series of conditional distributions that allow for spatial autocorrelation (measured by parameters ρ_1, ρ_2, and ρ_3), aspatial cross-correlations (gauged by parameters $\eta_{0,23}$, $\eta_{0,13}$, and $\eta_{0,12}$), and spatially lagged cross-correlations (expressed by parameters $\eta_{1,23}$, $\eta_{1,13}$, and $\eta_{1,12}$). A similar construct has been adopted in Jin, Carlin, and Banerjee (2005) and Wang and Kockelman (2013).

5. RESULTS AND ANALYSIS

The model was estimated jointly in R and WinBUGS on an Intel Core i7 2.80 GHz CPU with 12.0 RAM, with parameter estimates and inference summarized in Table 3. WinBUGS employs Gibbs Sampling to fit statistical models. Thanks to this flexible language, complex (hierarchical) models can be written in a very simple way, once the analyst properly defines the nodes (unknown parameters) and prior distributions. The codes are provided in the appendix.

Firm growth exhibited a strong clustering pattern across all three industries, evidenced by the significant estimates of ρ's. This result echos previous research (Bhat et al., 2014; Brown et al., 2009). The positive spatial dependence implied that production costs decrease as more firms in related industries cluster and that the clusters of competing firms in the same industry invite more suppliers and customers than a single firm could. Shares of vacant housing appear to be associated with an elevated number of new firms in the retail and service industries while showing a negative correlation with firm births in the basic industry. A plausible explanation is that vacant housing may solicit retail and service business and thus create mixed-use development; however, more vacant housing units indicate a smaller population (and presumably a smaller worker population), meaning firms in the basic industry category lack the luxury of abundant workers. Older median age is associated with fewer new firms across all three types of industries, which suggests that a work force's vitality (measured by age) is also a strong factor in firm births. Reynolds et al. (1995) arrived at a similar conclusion. MetroIndex indicator variable tends to be positively associated with higher birth rates of service and basic establishments (with 1 denoting a metropolitan area) but exert a minimal impact on retail firms (hence removed from the final estimation model in Table 3). Population densities are negatively correlated with retail-firm births, probably due to competition between housing and retail as more housing units are occupied by residents (rather than being converted into mixed-use developments). As expected, the three industries exhibit positive cross-correlations and positive, spatially lagged cross-correlations, supporting the notion of agglomeration economies.

This application of the MCAR model for a tri-variate response variable with a relatively large sample size achieved success. Application to the *full set* of U.S. counties ($n = 3{,}109$ counties) is left for future work, due to the daunting computing efforts that arise from inversion of the large covariance matrices when simulating the MCMC chains.

6. CONCLUSIONS

The main purpose of this paper was to showcase the potentials of a multivariate spatial count model for analyzing firm births ($N_{\mathrm{obs}} = 1{,}316$ U.S. counties) of three industry sectors. The model results also help describe firm growth patterns (in basic, retail, and service industries), across the nation's Midwestern and Western regions. The model's exposure term was the total number of establishments in the same industry category as the response variable of interest at the end of 2008.

Like many economic and transportation phenomena, counts of new firms were spatially clustered. Such patterns may reflect the underlying mechanisms that govern firm growth: related firms are predisposed to cluster, thanks to decreased production costs (agglomeration economies), or out of necessity to attract patrons and share supplies amid inter-firm competitions. Interestingly, higher shares of vacant housing appeared to be associated with more new firms in the retail and service industries, but fewer starts of basic-industry firms. After controlling for existing-firm counts (in 2008), a younger (and possibly more vital) work force and/or clientele (as quantified by each county's median-age values) was associated with more firm births (in 2009) in all three categories (with elasticities of −0.003, −0.03, and −0.05 on median age, for basic, retail, and service firm births, respectively). Rising population density contributed to new basic firms, while reducing retail-firm starts. New firm counts exhibited positive aspatial cross-correlations (across industries) and positive, spatially lagged cross-correlations.

In sum, this study explored an alternative econometric approach to simultaneously analyze geo-referenced count responses. The model extended the bivariate conditional autoregressive (CAR) specifications (Jin et al., 2005; Wang & Kockelman, 2013) to a tri-variate case while permitting zone-specific heterogeneity and spatial/aspatial cross-correlations among industry sectors. The application was successful, and the model seemed scalable to situations involving higher dimension of response levels. Nevertheless, a formal proof would be needed to confirm its applicability to settings involving many response levels. Alternatively, Bhat et al. (2014) demonstrated that all count models can be re-casted into utility-maximization-based discrete choice models. Future research could focus on incorporating the spatial lagged covariates and explore ways to describe SAR-type spatial dependence through the current CAR structures.

REFERENCES

Alcacer, J., & Delgado, M. (2013). *Spatial organization of firms and location choices through the value chain.* Working Paper. Retrieved from http://www.hbs.edu/faculty/Publication%20Files/13-025_5f10af16-c871-45b1-9de7-344547febcf5.pdf. Accessed on November 14, 2015.

Alsaaty, F. M. (2012). The cycle of births and deaths of U.S. employer micro firms. *Journal of Management and Marketing Research, 11*, 1–13.

An, M., & Chen, M. (2007). Estimating nonmotorized travel demand. *Transportation Research Record: Journal of the Transportation Research Board, 2002*, 18–25.

Anselin, L. (1988). *Spatial econometrics: Methods and models.* Norwell, MA: Kluwer Academic Publisher.

Basile, R., Castellani, D., & Zanfei, A. (2008). Location choices of multinational firms in europe: The role of EU cohesion policy. *Journal of International Economics, 74*(2), 328–340.

Besag, J. (1975). Statistical analysis of non-lattice data. *Journal of the Royal Statistical Society, Series D, 24*(3), 179–195.

Bhat, C. R., Paleti, R., & Castro, M. (2014). A new utility-consistent econometric approach to multivariate count data modeling. *Journal of Applied Econometrics, 30*(5), 806–825.

Bhat, C. R., Paleti, R., & Palvinder, S. (2014). A spatial multivariate count model for firm location decisions. *Journal of Regional Science, 54*(3), 462–502.

Bille, A. G., & Arbia, G. (2013). *Spatial discrete choice and spatial limited dependent variable models: A review with an emphasis on the use in regional health economics.* arXiv:1302.2267. Retrieved from http://arxiv.org/ftp/arxiv/papers/1302/1302.2267.pdf. Accessed on November 14, 2015.

Brown, J., Lambert, D. M., & Raymond, F. (2009). Firm birth and death in U.S. manufacturing: A regional adjustment model. Presented at the Agricultural & Applied Economics Association Annual Meeting, Milwaukee, Wisconsin. Retrieved from http://ageconsearch.umn.edu/bitstream/49467/2/brownetal_aaea09.pdf

Castro, M., Paleti, R., & Bhat, C. R. (2012). A latent variable representation of count data models to accommodate spatial and temporal dependence: Application to predicting crash frequency at intersections. *Transportation Research Part B, 46*(1), 253–272.

Cincera, M. (1998). Patents, R&D, and technological spillovers at the firm level: Some evidence from econometric count models for panel data. *Journal of Applied Econometrics, 12*(3), 265–280.

Cressie, N. A. (1995). *Statistics for spatial data* (Rev. ed.). New York, NY: Wiley.

Draganska, M., Misra, S., Aguirregabiria, V., Bajari, P., Einav, L., Ellickson, P., ... Zhu, T. (2008). Discrete choice models of firms' strategic decisions. *Marketing Letters, 19*, 399–416.

Elhorst, P. (2009). Spatial panel data models. In M. Fischer & A. Getis (Eds.), *Handbook of applied spatial analysis* (pp. 377–407). Berlin: Springer.

Ewing, R., & Cervero, R. (2001). Travel and the built environment: A synthesis. *Transportation Research Record, 1780*, 87–114.

Gelfand, A. E., & Vounatsou, P. (2003). Proper multivariate conditional autoregressive models for spatial data analysis. *Biostat, 4*(1), 11–15.

Hannan, M., & Freeman, J. (1977). The population ecology of organizations. *American Journal of Sociology, 82*(5), 929–964.

Harger, K., & Ross, A. (2014). *Do capital tax incentives attract new businesses? Evidence across industries from the new markets tax credit*. Retrieved from https://www.aeaweb.org/aea/2015conference/program/retrieve.php?pdfid=999. Accessed on November 14th, 2015.

Henderson, J. V., & Ono, Y. (2008). Where do manufacturing firms locate their headquarters? *Journal of Urban Economics, 63*(2), 431–450.

Jin, X., Carlin, B. P., & Banerjee, S. (2005). Generalized hierarchical multivariate car models for areal data. *Biometrics, 61*, 950–961.

Kitamura, R., Chen, C., Pendyala, R. M., & Narayanan, R. (2000). Micro-simulation of daily activity-travel patterns for travel demand forecasting. *Transportation, 27*(1), 25–51.

LeSage, J., & Pace, R. K. (2009). *Introduction to spatial econometrics*. Boca Raton, FL: CRC Press.

Levinson, D. (1998). Accessibility and the journey to work. *Journal of Transport Geography, 6*(1), 11–21.

Mercado, R. G., Paez, A., Farber, S., Roorda, M. J., & Morency, C. (2012). Explaining transport mode use of low-income persons for journey to work in urban areas: A case study of Ontario and Quebec. *Transportmetrica, 8*(3), 157–179.

Miaou, S.-P., Song, J., & Mallick, B. (2003). Roadway traffic crash mapping: A space-time modeling approach. *Journal of Transportation & Statistics, 6*(1), 33–58.

O'Kelly, M. E., & Lee, W. (2005). Disaggregate journey-to-work data: Implications for excess commuting and jobs-housing balance. *Environment and Planning A, 37*(12), 2233–2252.

Paleti, R., Bhat, C. R., & Pendyala, R. M. (2013). Integrated model of residential location, work location, vehicle ownership, and commute tour characteristics. *Transportation Research Record, 2382*, 162–172.

Pettitt, A., Weir, I. S., & Hart, A. G. (2002). A conditional autoregressive Gaussian process for irregularly spaced multivariate data with application to modeling large sets of binary data. *Statistics and Computing, 12*(4), 353–367.

Pike, S. (2014). Travel mode choice and social and spatial reference groups. *Transportation Research Record, 2412*, 75–81.

Quintero, J. P. (2007). Regional Economic Development: An Economic Base Study and Shift-Share Analysis of Hays County, Texas. An Applied Research Project submitted to the Department of Political Science, Texas State University, San Marcos, Texas.

In partial fulfillment for the Degree of Masters of Public Administration. Retrieved from https://digital.library.txstate.edu/bitstream/handle/10877/3656/fulltext.pdf. Accessed on September 23, 2016.

Reynolds, P. D., Miller, B., & Maki, W. R. (1995). Explaining regional variation in business births and deaths: U.S. 1976–88. *Small Business Economics*, *7*, 389–407.

Sadeghi, A. (2008). The births and deaths of business establishments in the United States. *Monthly Labor Review*, *131*, 3–18. Retrieved from http://www.bls.gov/opub/mlr/2008/12/art1full.pdf. Accessed on September 23, 2016.

Sidharthan, R., Bhat, C. R., Pendyala, R., & Goulias, K. (2011). Model for children's school travel mode choice: Accounting for effects of spatial and social interaction. *Transportation Research Record*, *2213*, 78–86.

Siedschlag, L., & Zhang, X. (2015). Internationalisation of firms and their innovation and productivity. *Economics of Innovation and New Technology*, *24*(3), 183–203.

Song, J. J., Ghosh, M., Miaou, S., & Mallick, B. (2006). Bayesian multivariate spatial models for roadway traffic crash mapping. *Journal of Multivariate Analysis*, *97*(1), 246–273.

Spiegelhalter, D., Thomas, A., Best, N., & Lunn, D. (2003). *WinBUGS user manual version 1.4*. Retrieved from http://voteview.org/manual14.pdf

United States Department of Agriculture Economic Research Service. (2003). *Rural-urban continuum codes*. Retrieved from http://www.ers.usda.gov/data-products/rural-urban-continuum-codes.aspx#.Ut1XuRDn-Uk

Wang, X., & Kockelman, K. (2009). Application of dynamic spatial ordered probit model: Patterns of ozone concentration in Austin, Texas. *Transportation Research Record*, *2136*, 45–56.

Wang, X., Kockelman, K., & Lemp, J. (2012). The dynamic spatial multinomial probit model: Analysis of land use change using parcel-level data. *Journal of Transport Geography*, *24*, 77–88.

Wang, Y., & Kockelman, K. (2013). A poisson-lognormal multivariate conditional-autoregressive model for spatial analysis of area-level pedestrian crashes. *Accident Analysis & Prevention*, *60*, 71–84.

Zhang, L., Southworth, F., Xiong, C., & Sonnenberg, A. (2012). Methodological options and data sources for the development of long-distance passenger travel demand models: A comprehensive review. *Transport Reviews*, *32*(4), 399–433.

Zhao, Y., & Kockelman, K. (2002). The propagation of uncertainty through travel demand models. *Annals of Regional Science*, *36*(1), 145–163.

APPENDIX

WinBUGS Codes

```
model
  {

  for(k in 1 : sumNumNeigh) {
  CC[k] <- C[k]
  }

  for( i in 1 : N )
  {
  Y10[i] ~ dpois(mu1[i])
  Y20[i] ~ dpois(mu2[i])
  Y30[i] ~ dpois(mu3[i])
  log(mu1[i]) <- log(pop[i]) + phi1[i] + V1[i]
  log(mu2[i]) <- log(pop[i]) + phi2[i] + V2[i]
  log(mu3[i]) <- log(pop[i]) + phi3[i] + V3[i]
  V1[i] ~ dnorm(0, tau.v1)
  V2[i] ~ dnorm(0, tau.v2)
  V3[i] ~ dnorm(0, tau.v3)
  }

  for( i in 1 : N )
  {
  beta3[i] <- beta03 + beta13* x1[i] + beta23* x2[i] + beta33* x3[i] + beta43* x4[i] +
  beta53* x5[i] + beta63* x6[i] + beta73* x7[i] + beta83* x8[i] + beta93* x9[i] + beta103*
  x10[i] + beta113* x11[i] + beta123* x12[i]
  mu_phi3[i] <- beta3[i]

  for ( j in 1:N)
  { count3[i, j] <- W[i, j ]*(phi3[j]- beta3[j]) }

  mu_phi2[i] <- beta02 + beta12*x1[i] + beta22*x2[i] + beta32*x3[i] + beta42* x4[i] +
  beta52* x5[i] + beta62* x6[i] + beta72* x7[i] + beta82* x8[i] + beta92* x9[i] + beta102*
  x10[i] + beta112* x11[i] + beta122* x12[i] + eta_023*(phi3[i]- beta3[i])+ eta_123*sum
  (count3[i, ]) # conditional mean for phi_2|phi_3
  m[i] <- 1/num[i]          # scaling factor for variance in each county
```

```
for ( j in 1:N)
{ count12[i, j] <- W[i, j ]*(phi2[j]- mu_phi2[j])} # mean for phi_2, W should be the #unnor-
malized weight matrix

mu_phi1[i]<-beta01+beta11*x1[i] + beta21*x2[i] + beta31*x3[i]+ beta41* x4[i] + beta51*
x5[i] + beta61* x6[i] + beta71* x7[i] + beta81* x8[i] + beta91* x9[i] + beta101* x10[i] +
beta111* x11[i] +beta121* x12[i]+eta_012*(phi2[i]- mu_phi2[i]) + eta_112*sum(count12[i, ]) +
eta_013*(phi3[i]- mu_phi3[i])+eta_113*sum(count3[i, ])
# conditional mean for phi_1|phi_2
                                    # scaling factor for variance in each county
}

beta01 ~ dnorm(0.5, 0.0001)
beta11 ~ dnorm(1, 0.0001)
beta21 ~ dnorm(-1.2, 0.0001)
beta31 ~ dnorm(1.5, 0.0001)
beta41 ~ dnorm(0.5, 0.0001)
beta51 ~ dnorm(0, 0.0001)
beta61 ~ dnorm(-1.2, 0.0001)
beta71 ~ dnorm(1.5, 0.0001)
beta81 ~ dnorm(0.5, 0.0001)
beta91 ~ dnorm(0, 0.0001)
beta101 ~ dnorm(0, 0.0001)
beta111 ~ dnorm(0, 0.0001)
beta121 ~ dnorm(0, 0.0001)

beta02 ~ dnorm(0, 0.0001)
beta12 ~ dnorm(0, 0.0001)
beta22 ~ dnorm(0, 0.0001)
beta32 ~ dnorm(1, 0.0001)
beta42 ~ dnorm(0, 0.0001)
beta52 ~ dnorm(0, 0.0001)
beta62 ~ dnorm(1, 0.0001)
beta72 ~ dnorm(1, 0.0001)
beta82 ~ dnorm(0, 0.0001)
beta92 ~ dnorm(0, 0.0001)
beta102 ~ dnorm(0, 0.0001)
beta112 ~ dnorm(0, 0.0001)
beta122 ~ dnorm(0, 0.0001)
```

```
eta_012 ~ dbeta(8,8) # 0.8
eta_112 ~ dbeta(8,8) #0.5
eta_013 ~ dbeta(8,8) #0.7
eta_113 ~ dbeta(8,8) #0.4
eta_023 ~ dbeta(8,8) #0.1
eta_123 ~ dbeta(8,8) #0.2

tau1 ~ dgamma(9,6)
tau2 ~ dgamma(9,6) #dgamma(alpha, beta)-alpha the shape parameter, beta the
rate parameter
tau.v1 ~ dgamma(3,6)
tau.v2 ~ dgamma(3,6)
tau.v3 ~ dgamma(3,6)
tau3 ~ dgamma(9,6)

rho[1] ~ dbeta(12,4)
rho[2] ~ dbeta(12,8)
rho[3] ~ dbeta(12,4)

phi2[1:N] ~ car.proper(mu_phi2[], CC[], adj[], num[], m[], tau2, rho[2])
phi1[1:N] ~ car.proper(mu_phi1[], CC[], adj[], num[], m[], tau1, rho[1])
phi3[1:N] ~ car.proper(mu_phi3[], CC[], adj[], num[], m[], tau3, rho[3])
}
```

R Codes (to Create Weight Matrix and Read Shapefile and Data into WinBUGS)

```
library(spdep)
library(R2WinBUGS)
library(MASS) # in order to call the mvrnorm() function
library(rgdal)
library(mcmcplots)

input = read.csv("your path.csv", header = TRUE)
shape <- readOGR("your path.shp","OBJECT_ID")
shape <- shape[order(shape$GEOIDint),]
shape_nb <- poly2nb(shape, row.names = shape$GEOIDint,
queen = FALSE)
N = length(shape_nb)#total number of geographic units
```

```
nb2 = nblag(shape_nb, 2)
nb3 = nblag_cumul(nb2)
num = sapply(nb3,length)
adj = unlist(nb3)
sumNumNeigh = length(unlist(nb3))
W = nb2mat(nb3,style = "B",zero.policy = TRUE)# B-binary coding
W1 = nb2mat(nb3,style = "W",zero.policy = TRUE) # W- row-
standardized
# num = sapply(shape_nb,length) # number of neighbors for each unit
# adj = unlist(shape_nb) # neighbor IDs for each unit
# sumNumNeigh = length(unlist(shape_nb))
# W = nb2mat(shape_nb,style = "B",zero.policy = TRUE)# B-binary coding
# W1 = nb2mat(shape_nb,style = "W",zero.policy = TRUE) # W- row-
standardized
# getting non zero weights in the list
s = 1
C = rep(0, sumNumNeigh)
for (i in 1:N) {
  for (j in 1:N) {
    if (W1[i,j] != 0) {C[s] = W1[i,j]
          s = s + 1}
  }
}
Y10 <-input[,15]# greater than 40
Y20 <-input[,16]# between 40 and 20
Y30 <-input[,17]# less than 20
x1 = input[,3]
x2 = input[,4]
x3 = input[,5]
x4 = input[,6]
x5 = input[,7]
x6 = input[,8]
x7 = input[,9]
x8 = input[,10]
x9 = input[,11]
x10 = input[,12]
x11 = input[,13]
x12 = input[,14]
pop = input[,2]
```

```
poi1 <- glm(formula = Y10 ~ offset(log(pop)) + x1 + x2 + x3 + x4 + x5
+ x6 + x7 + x8 + x9 + x10 + x11 + x12, family = "quasipoisson")
beta1.init <- poi1$coefficients

poi2 <- glm(formula = Y20 ~ offset(log(pop)) + x1 + x2 + x3 + x4 + x5
+ x6 + x7 + x8 + x9 + x10 + x11 + x12, family = "quasipoisson")
beta2.init <- poi2$coefficients

poi3 <- glm(formula = Y30 ~ offset(log(pop)) + x1 + x2 + x3 + x4 + x5
+ x6 + x7 + x8 + x9 + x10 + x11 + x12, family = "quasipoisson")
beta3.init <- poi3$coefficients

negbi <- glm.nb(formula = Y30 ~ offset(log(pop)) + x1 + x2 + x3 + x4
+ x5 + x6 + x7 + x8 + x9 + x10 + x11 + x12)
summary(negbi)

# rm(input,W1)

data <- list(Y10 = Y10,Y20 = Y20,Y30 = Y30, N = N,adj = adj,
sumNumNeigh = sumNumNeigh,
num = num, W = W,pop = pop, x1 = x1, x2 = x2, x3 = x3, x4 = x4, x5 = x5,
x6 = x6,x7 = x7, x8 = x8, x9 = x9, x10 = x10, x11 = x11,x12 = x12,
C = C,beta03 = beta3.init[1],beta13 = beta3.init[2],beta23 = beta3.init[3],
beta33 = beta3.init[4],beta43 = beta3.init[5],beta53 = betanit[6],
beta63 = beta3.init[7],beta73 = beta3.init[8],beta83 = beta3.init[9],
    beta93 = beta3.init[10],beta103 = beta3.init[11],beta113 = beta3.init
[12],beta123 = beta3.init[13])
parameters <- c("eta_012", "eta_013","eta_023","eta_112",
"eta_113","eta_123", "beta01", "beta11", "beta21","beta31", "beta41",
"beta51", "beta61","beta71", "beta81", "beta91", "beta101","beta111",
    "beta121", "beta02", "beta12", "beta22","beta32", "beta42",
"beta52", "beta62","beta72", "beta82", "beta92", "beta102","beta112",
    "beta122", "tau2", "tau1","tau3","rho","tau.v1","tau.v2","tau.v3")
inits <- function() {
  list(
beta01 = beta1.init[1],beta11 = beta1.init[2],beta21 = beta1.init[3],
beta31 = beta1.init[4],beta41 = beta1.init[5],beta51 = beta1.init[6],
beta61 = beta1.init[7],beta71 = beta1.init[8],beta81 = beta1.init[9],
beta91 = beta1.init[10],beta101 = beta1.init[11],beta111 = beta1.init[12],
```

```
beta121 = beta1.init[13],beta02 = beta2.init[1],beta12 = beta2.init[2],
beta22 = beta2.init[3],beta32 = beta2.init[4],
beta42 = beta2.init[5],beta52 = beta2.init[6],beta62 = beta2.init[7],
beta72 = beta2.init[8],beta82 = beta2.init[9],beta92 = beta2.init[10],
beta102 = beta2.init[11],beta112 = beta2.init[12],
   beta122 = beta2.init[13])}
result <- bugs(data, inits, parameters, model.file = "the path where the file
in Appendix A is stored.txt", n.chains = 1, n.iter = 4000, n.burnin = 1000,n.
thin = 1, debug = TRUE, DIC = TRUE, bugs.directory = "c:/Program Files/
WinBUGS14/", codaPkg = FALSE)
save(result, file = "the path where you want to save the outputs")
```

A MULTIVARIATE SPATIAL-TIME OF DAY ANALYSIS OF TRUCK CRASH FREQUENCY ACROSS NEIGHBORHOODS IN NEW YORK CITY

Wei Zou[a], Xiaokun Wang[b] and Yiyi Wang[c]

[a]*Rensselaer Polytechnic Institute, Troy, NY, USA*
[b]*Department of Civil and Environmental Engineering, Rensselaer Polytechnic Institute, Troy, NY, USA*
[c]*Civil Engineering Department, Montana State University, Bozeman, MT, USA*

ABSTRACT

To address the safety concerns generated by truck crashes occurred in big cities, this paper analyzes the zip code tabulation area (ZCTA)-based truck crash frequency across four temporal intervals – morning (6:00–10:00), mid-day (10:00–15:00), afternoon (15:00–19:00), and night (19:00–6:00) in New York City in 2010. A multivariate conditional autoregressive count model is used to recognize both spatial and temporal dependences. The results prove the presence of spatial and

Spatial Econometrics: Qualitative and Limited Dependent Variables
Advances in Econometrics, Volume 37, 195–219

ISSN: 0731-9053/doi:10.1108/S0731-905320160000037015

temporal dependencies for truck crashes that occurred in neighboring areas. Built environment attributes such as various types of business establishment density and traffic volume for different types of vehicles, which are important factors to consider for crashes occurred in an urban setting, are also examined in the study.

Keywords: Truck accidents; spatial dependency; time of day effect; count data model; bayesian estimation

JEL classifications: C5

1. INTRODUCTION

Freight transportation is a critical part of the US economy. The 2012 Commodity Flow Survey shows that trucks moved about 8.2 billion tons of goods in the United States (70% of all goods by weight), which worth about $10 trillion (73.7% of all goods by value) (Margreta, Chester, & Grube, 2014). While the use of trucks makes people's life more convenient and connected, it also carries safety concerns. According to the Federal Motor Carrier Safety Administration (2013), 2,757 people were killed (11.6% of total fatal crashes) and 88,000 people were injured in large truck crashes in 2012. The report (2013) also reveals that the estimated costs of commercial motor vehicle crashes increased from 2009 to 2011. In 2011, the costs for fatal, injury, and property damage only crashes were $39 billion, $32 billion, and $16 billion, respectively. The tremendous economics losses and emotional burdens to victims, their families and the society as a whole clearly underscore the importance of truck crash studies for a safer transportation system.

To address the safety concerns, a wide variety of data modeling techniques have been developed to study the determinants of road accident (see Lord & Mannering, 2010 for crash frequency analysis, Savolainen, Mannering, Lord, & Quddus, 2011 for injury severity analysis, and Mannering & Bhat, 2014 for more advanced models). However, the spatial and temporal dependences among neighboring segments are usually ignored in crash modeling, which violates the sample independence assumption and could lead to: (1) inconsistent estimates; (2) efficiency losses; and (3) confounding results with other unmeasured factors (Aguero-Valverde & Jovanis, 2008, 2010; Chiou & Fu, 2015; Cressie, 2015; Dubin, 1988; LeSage & Pace, 2009; Lord & Mannering, 2010; Lord & Persaud, 2000). To this end, this paper analyzes the zip code tabulation area (ZCTA)-based truck crash frequency across four temporal intervals – morning (6:00–10:00), mid-day (10:00–15:00), afternoon (15:00–19:00), and night (19:00–6:00) in New York City in 2010, using a multivariate conditional autoregressive count model, which recognizes both spatial and temporal dependences. Focusing on area-level truck crash counts provides more complete data (compared to studies focusing on intersectional accidents only) and allows for spatial modeling (Morency & Cloutier, 2006).

2. LITERATURE REVIEW

2.1. Truck Crash Studies and the Influencing Factors

Traditional crash analysis can be divided into two groups: (1) crash frequency studies analyzing how likely an accident may occur and (2) injury severity analysis for individual vehicles conditional on the occurred crashes. While many studies include all types of vehicles in the analysis, a truck crash is a complex event with many unique characteristics and confounding influencing factors, thus it is reasonable to separate it from other crash studies. Existing literature on truck crash analysis focus heavily on injury severity analysis for individual large trucks on highways, partly due to the fact that data on highway crashes is more complete and easy to obtain. Khattak, Schneider, and Targa (2003) used ordered probit models to analyze the truck driver's injury severity of large truck crashes in North Carolina, from 1996 to 1998, using the Highway Safety Information System data. The authors found that roll-over crashes tend to generate more severe injuries in single truck crashes, and driver's behavior such as drug use and speeding also increased the accident severity. Golob, Recker, and Leonard (1987) used the Traffic Accident Surveillance and Analysis data to assess the truck-involved freeway accidents severity in Los Angeles area from 1983 to 1984. The result showed that "hit-object" and "rear end" were the most dangerous types of incidents. Zhu and Srinivasan (2011) used the Large Truck Crash Causation Study (LTCCS) data to study the influencing factors of large truck accident severity in 17 states in the United States, from April 2001 to December 2003. The estimates from ordered logit models captured the negative impacts of driver behavior, such as truck driver distraction, alcohol use, and emotional factors, on accident severity. Lemp, Kockelman, and Unnikrishnan (2011) found that accident severity increased with the number of trailers, but fell with the truck length and gross vehicle weight rating. Islam and Hernandez (2013a,b) used both a random parameter ordered probit model and a mixed logit model to analyze the injury severities of multi-vehicle collisions involving large trucks, using a fused national crash datasets. The result shows that the level of injury severity is a result of complex interaction of human factors such as distracted/sleepy driving, female occupants, and seat-belt usage, road and environmental facts such as light condition, road condition such as curved segments and wet surface, vehicle characteristics such as vehicle and traffic condition. The authors also used a mixed logit model to study the large truck crash injury outcomes in Texas, revealing the complex interactions between factors, including driver demographics, traffic flow, roadway geometric features, land use, time characteristics, weather and light conditions, contributed to the different level of injury outcomes (Islam & Hernandez, 2013a,b). Since the above studies focus on the injury severity analysis for individual trucks on highways, only human, vehicle, road, traffic, and accident-specific factors were addressed. Area-level effects from built environment factors such as population density, land use types and business establishment distribution are usually ignored due to the simple and homogeneous land use structure on highways. However, for urban settings, especially for big cities, built environment factors are strong indicators of human and business activities, which lead to direct conflicts between pedestrians/bikers and vehicles, and thus are strongly correlated to pedestrian crash counts and injury severity (Cho, Rodríguez, & Khattak, 2009; Clifton, Burnier, & Akar, 2009; Ewing & Dumbaugh, 2009; Wier, Weintraub, Humphreys, Seto, & Bhatia, 2009; Miranda-Moreno, Morency, & El-Geneidy, 2011; Ukkusuri, Miranda-Moreno, Ramadurai, & Isa-Tavarez, 2012). Similarly, the conflicts between trucks and human/business activities, which are captured by built environment variates, may lead to truck crashes, and should be considered in crash modeling.

2.2. Spatial and Temporal Dependency Analysis

The subjective selection of sample data (temporal and spatial segmentation) for crash studies may result in potential spatial and temporal dependence among observations. Neighboring sites typically have similar environmental and geographical characteristics and may share unobserved effects. For example, road design features influencing crash occurrences at one site may have unobserved "spatial spillover" effects to other sites located proximally. At the same time, the variates affect crash occurrences may change (e.g., the lighting condition) or stay consistent (e.g., road conditions) depending on the time of day. Recently, numerous efforts have been spared to include spatial correlation in the development of collision models (see Wang, Quddus, Ryley, Enoch, & Davison (2012) for a comprehensive review), for both area-wide (Aguero-Valverde, 2013; Aguero-Valverde & Jovanis, 2006, 2008; Amoros, Martin, & Laumon, 2003; Flask & Schneider, 2013; Guo, Wang, & Abdel-Aty, 2010; MacNab, 2004; Noland & Quddus, 2004; Quddus, 2008a, b) and road segments/intersections (Abdel-Aty & Wang, 2006; Aguero-Valverde & Jovanis, 2008, 2010; El-Basyouny & Sayed, 2009; Guo, Wang, & Abdel-Aty, 2010; Mitra, 2009). As to studies accommodating time of day effect/temporal dependence, indicator variables are usually used and employed in the models (Chang & Chen, 2005; Dupont, Papadimitriou, Martensen, & Yannis, 2013; Islam & Hernandez, 2013a, b; Qin, Ivan, Ravishanker, Liu, & Tepas, 2006). However, such an modeling approach does not account for the heterogeneity in variable effects during different time periods (Pahukula, Hernandez, & Unnikrishnan, 2015) and a possible solution is to estimate separate univariate count models for each time period (Mannering & Bhat, 2014). Recently, Pahukula, Hernandez, and Unnikrishnan (2015) studied the time of days effect for crashes involving large trucks occurring on urban freeways in Texas, from year 2006 to 2010. The results from five several random parameter models of different time of the day have demonstrated the traffic flow, light conditions, surface conditions, time of year, and percentage of trucks on the road influence the injury severity differently during different times of the day. However, since the unobserved factors across different time periods are likely to affect multiple dependent variables (i.e., crash counts at different times of day) simultaneously (Mannering & Bhat, 2014), the separated univariate count models are not the optimum approach. A number of studies also began to explore the spatial and temporal correlations simultaneously. Castro, Paleti, and Bhat (2012) proposed a latent variable-based generalized ordered response framework for count data models, in which spatial dependence is introduced by a spatial structure on the latent continuous variables, and temporal dependence is captured in the error term of the latent variable. Chiou and Fu (2015) developed a multinomial generalized Poisson model with error components and spatiotemporal dependence (ST-EMGP) that not only model crash count and injury severity simultaneously, but also accommodates spatial and temporal dependence. The above studies focus on a longer temporal segment (in years), however, the time of day effect is not studied.

Recent years offer a rising number of research studies on multivariate models that captured and proved the inter-related nature in crash data's multiple dependent variables. Examples include multivariate count models accommodating different crash type (Kim, Washington, & Oh, 2006), injury severities (Barua, El-Basyouny, & Islam 2014; Chiou & Fu, 2013; Chiou, Fu, & Chih-Wei, 2014; Eluru, Paleti, Pendyala, & Bhat, 2010; Narayanamoorthy,

Paleti, & Bhat, 2013; Rana, Sikder, & Pinjari, 2010; Yamamoto & Shankar, 2004; Yasmin, Eluru, Pinjari, & Tay, 2014), temporal and spatial dependencies (Aguero-Valverde, 2013; Bhat, Born, Sidharthan, & Bhat 2014; Castro, Paleti, & Bhat, 2012; Chiou, Fu, & Chih-Wei, 2014; Mohammadi, Samaranayake, & Bham, 2014; Narayanamoorthy, Paleti, & Bhat, 2013; Quddus, 2008a, 2008b; Wang & Kockelman, 2013).

Built on existing multivariate models, this paper aims to contribute to the literature by conducting a comprehensive analysis on truck accidents in an urban setting (compared to highway intersections) – New York City, accounting for spatial autocorrelation, zone-specific heterogeneity, and integrates the time of day dependency using a multivariate structure. To do so, a recently developed multivariate count model (Wang & Kockelman, 2013) is applied to the 2010 truck crash data in New York City, together with other built environment, business pattern and traffic attributes.

3. DATA DESCRIPTION

The sample data was drawn from the following four primary data sources in 2010: (1) the state maintained incident data (NYSDOT, 2014), (2) the publicly available smart location data (US EPA, 2014), (3) ZIP code Business Pattern data from the New York City Geodatabase (The William and Anita Newman Library, 2015), and (4) the BEST Practices Model (BPM) data (Brinckerhoff, 2009). The integration of these four datasets allows the examination of a wide range of factors comprehensively, including crash attributes, built environment factors, land use characteristics, and traffic information.

The original incident data is provided by the New York State Department of Transportation with three separate files: the event information, the involved vehicles' characteristics, and the contributing factors for the incident. In this study, a "truck crash" is defined as a collision involving at least a truck, which maybe a truck-only crash or a collision between a truck and a motor vehicle. Collisions between a truck and a pedestrian/bicyclist are not included in the study as pedestrian/bicyclists tend to be more vulnerable in a truck-related crash and should be studied separately. The types of trucks analyzed in this study includes: small wheel trucks, delivery trucks, dump trucks, flatbed trucks, stake trucks, tank trucks, refrigerated trucks, tow trucks, van trucks, utility trucks, and other unknown trucks, based on the classification of vehicle body type code provided in the NYS Incident Vehicle Data File.

The smart location data is developed and maintained by the Environmental Protection Agency (EPA) in 2013. It includes various built environment information such as land use, urban design, demographics, and transit services, generated from data sources, including Census of Population and Economic Census, and American Community Survey. The majority of the information was collected in 2010.

The ZIP Code Business Patterns (ZBP) data are generated from the 2013 US Census ZIP code Business Pattern database, they are included in the NYC Geodatabase maintained by the Geospatial Serviced Team in the GIS Lab at the Newman Library at Baruch College, City University of New York, the data include number and percentage of business establishments by the North American Industrial Classification System (NAICS) code for each ZIP code area.

The BPM data is developed by the New York Metropolitan Transportation Council (NYMTC) with road traffic volume on major links in New York State during four time blocks: (1) AM, from 6:00 to 10:00 AM, (2) Mid-day (MD), from 10:00 AM to 3:00 PM, (3) PM, from 3:00 to 7:00 PM, and (4) Nighttime (NT), from 7:00 PM to 6:00 AM. To ensure the consistency in modeling estimation, the traffic volumes on links within a ZCTA are aggregated and then the hourly traffic volume is derived for each time block.

The information was then compiled with the smart location data and the BPM data by using the "joint attributes by location" function in QGIS (Gandhi, 2014). The Thiessen polygons are then generated based on New York City Census Zip Code Tabulation Areas (ZCTA) centroids, and the accident frequency within each polygon is estimated accordingly. The Thiessen polygons are used to ensure that locations with high crash frequencies, for example, highway intersections along the census tract corners, can be assigned properly within a polygon. After filtering out irrelevant and incomplete information, an accident frequency analysis dataset with 188 Thiessen polygons was used for model estimation, with a frequency count ranging from 1 to 22 accidents per ZCTA, as shown in Fig. 1(a) and (b). The plots (one for each time period) also reveals that clustering effects in the accident frequency among the neighboring segments for all four time periods, implying potential spatial correlation among them.

The truck crash distributions across different times of the day are presented in Fig. 2. The majority of the crashes occurred during day time (7:00–17:00) and the MD category (10:00–15:00) accounts for about 30% of the total crash occurrence. Table 1 summarizes the statistics for the built environment and traffic volume attributes. The ZBP data's original 17 categories of business establishment are re-grouped into four categories

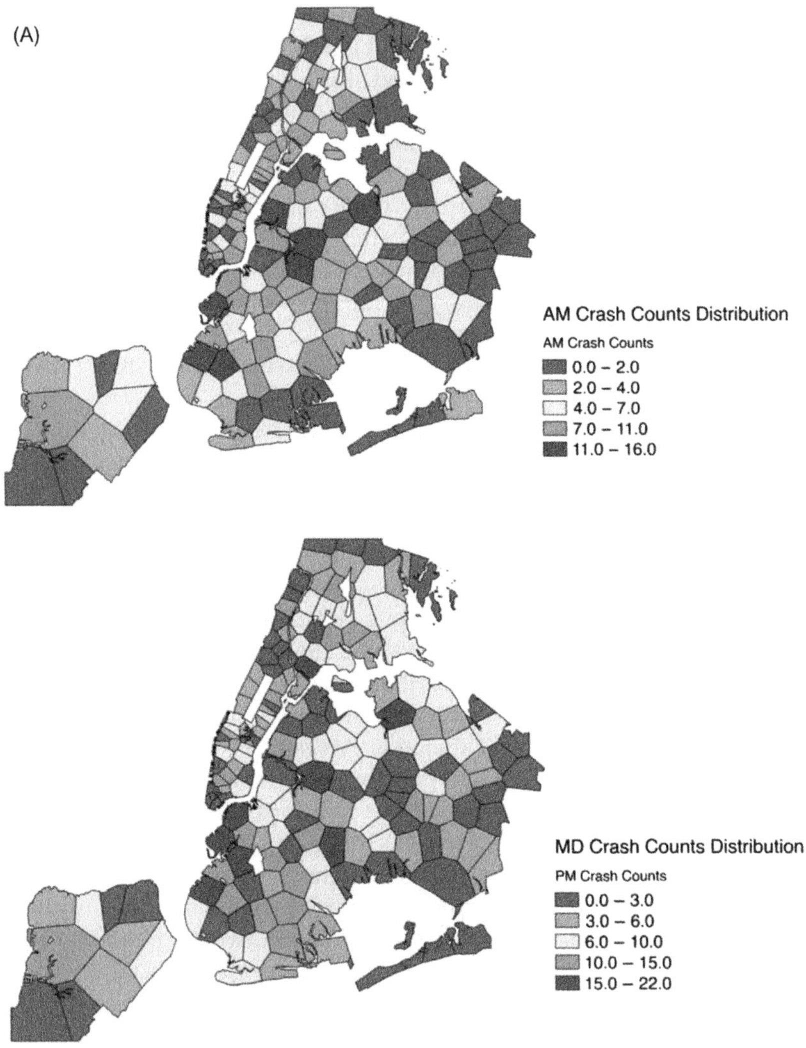

Fig. 1. (a) Accident Frequency Distribution of Truck Crashes (AM, MD); (b) Accident Frequency Distribution of Truck Crashes (PM, NT).

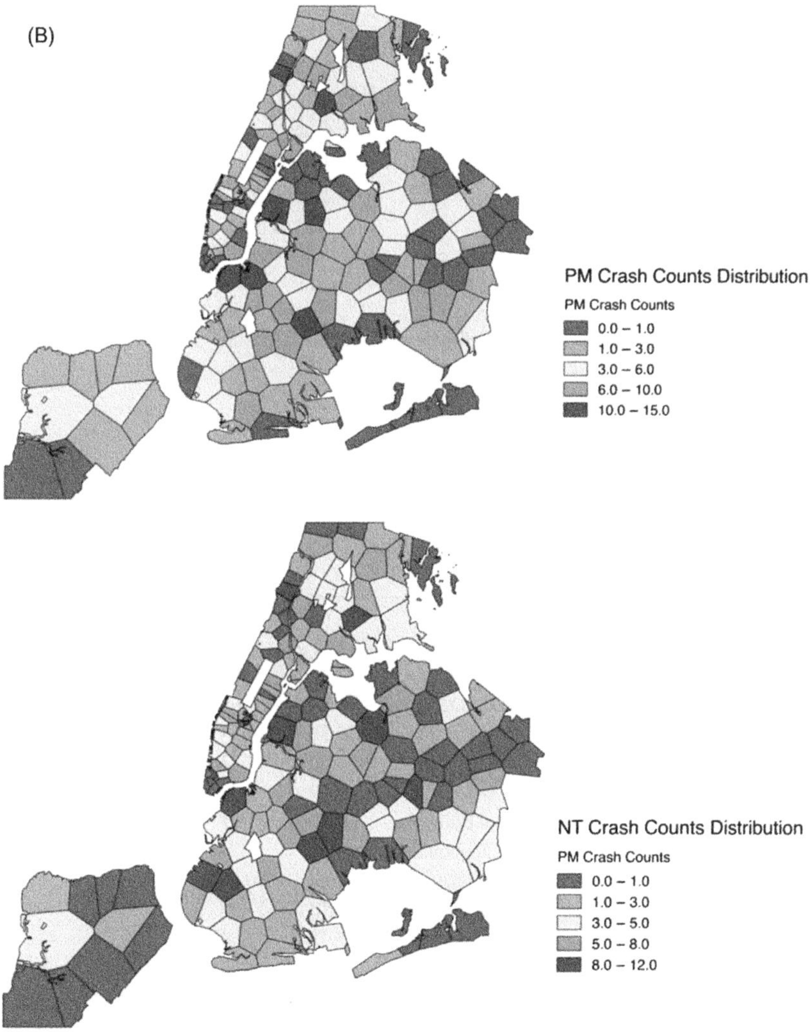

Fig. 1. (*Continued*)

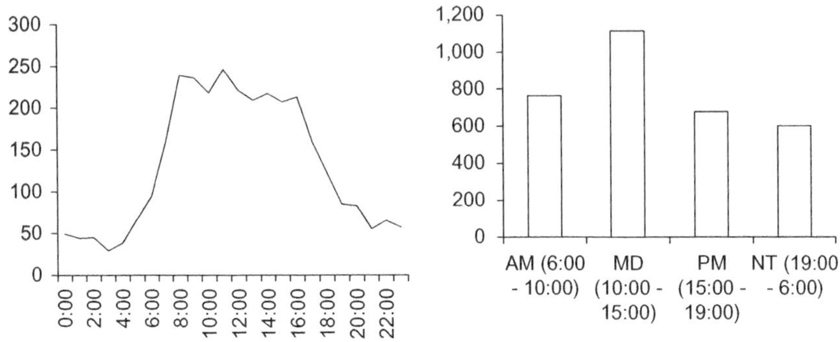

Fig. 2. Accident Frequency Distribution of Truck Crashes at Different Times of the Day.

Table 1. Summary Statistics of the Model Attributes.

	Business Establishment Density	Mean	Standard Deviation	Minimum	Maximum
Group 1	Mining	7.40	5.89	0.00	27.44
	Utilities	1.95	2.03	0.00	13.06
	Construction	5.34	4.94	0.00	37.03
	Manufacturing	16.77	7.68	0.00	50.00
	Total	29.38	14.14	0.00	62.91
Group 2	Information	8.10	4.83	0.00	24.31
	Finance	9.09	7.52	0.00	45.45
	Real estate	0.41	1.05	0.00	11.76
	Professional	4.24	5.74	0.00	75.00
	Management	1.64	0.88	0.00	6.34
	Total	16.13	13.49	0.00	49.82
Group 3	Wholesale	3.15	5.34	0.00	47.37
	Retail	1.76	1.76	0.00	9.10
	Transportation	4.84	6.25	0.00	41.26
	Total	8.76	7.65	0.00	51.71
Group 4	Administration	11.62	6.41	0.00	60.00
	Education	1.75	1.95	0.00	10.31
	Health care	9.96	3.54	0.00	25.00
	Entertainment	11.72	3.52	0.00	21.74
	Accommodation	0.19	0.20	0.00	1.38
	Total	24.05	18.10	0.00	51.41
	Time of day variates				
	AM	26,344	21,400	0	121,126
	MD	9,486	7,652	0	42,438

Table 1. (*Continued*)

	Business Establishment Density	Mean	Standard Deviation	Minimum	Maximum
Hourly commercial vehicle traffic volume (truck + commercial vans)	PM	10,060	8,820	0	52,851
	NT	28,094	22,889	0	127,228
Percentage of hourly automobile volume (HOV + SOV)	AM	0.404	0.242	0.000	0.940
	MD	0.438	0.253	0.000	0.964
	PM	0.472	0.262	0.000	0.979
	NT	0.442	0.269	0.000	0.981
Percentage of hourly bus and taxi traffic volume	AM	0.033	0.036	0.000	0.218
	MD	0.033	0.036	0.000	0.218
	PM	0.036	0.035	0.000	0.215
	NT	0.020	0.026	0.000	0.179

according to their business nature. The four groups are dominated by manufacturing (16.77 establishments per acre), information (8.1 establishments per acre) and finance (9.09 establishments per acre), wholesale (3.15 establishments per acre) and transportation (4.84 establishments per acre), and administration (11.62 establishments per acre) and health care (9.96 establishments per acre) and entertainments (11.72 establishments per acre), respectively (Table 1).

4. METHODOLOGY

To model spatial interactions, autoregressive models are commonly used by incorporating the dependence effect into the covariance structure either explicitly or implicitly (Wall, 2004). Two widely used autoregressive models in literature are known as the conditional autoregressive model (CAR) (Anselin, 2013; Elhorst, 2014; Whittle, 1954), and the simultaneously autoregressive model (SAR) (Besag, 1974). While both methods rely on defining a neighborhood structure based on the shape of the study area (e.g., whether two regions share a common border or not), a CAR model obeys the spatial version of the Markov property, making it more appropriate for situations with first-order dependency (e.g., local spatial correlations); and a SAR model fits better when there are second-order dependencies (i.e., more global spatial autocorrelations) (Shekhar & Xiong, 2008). With simpler structure and faster computation speed, CAR models are more commonly used in spatial analysis of count data (Gelfand & Vounatsou, 2003; Gschlößl & Czado, 2008; Miaou, Song, & Mallick, 2003; Pettitt, Weir, & Hart, 2002; Song, Ghosh, Miaou, & Mallick 2006).

The conditional autoregressive models (CAR) were initiated by Besag (1975) and further developed into multivariate conditional autoregressive (MCAR) models (Mardia, 1988). While most previous MCAR models use precision matrix to specify the model structure, a more generalized version of MCAR model is developed by Jin, Carlin, and Banerjee (2005) working directly with the covariance matrix. The model is further developed by Wang et al. (2012) to extend the application for count data and account for region-specific heterogeneity. There are two stages in the modeling framework:

In the first stage, a Poisson process is used to model the count of crash frequency:

$$\lambda_{ik} = Poisson\,(\lambda_{ik})$$

where y_{ik} is the observed truck crash frequency by different time of day intervals, ($k = 1, 2, 3, 4$) for the ith ZCTA; λ_{ik} refers to the mean crash rates.

The second stage of the model describes the mean crash rate λ_{ik}:

$$\lambda_{ik} = E_{ik}^{\alpha}\exp(x_i'\beta_k + \phi_{ik} + \mu_{ik}),$$

where E_{ik} is the exposure measure of truck crashes, in this study, the hourly total traffic volume for truck and commercial vehicle is used, and it is assumed to have a linear relationship with the truck crashes (i.e., $\alpha = 1$); x_i refers to a column vector of covariates (including a constant term); β_k is a vector of the corresponding parameter coefficients specific to type k; μ_{ik} denotes the heterogeneity for ZCTA i during time of day interval k, which is not explained by the spatial effect ϕ_{ik}, and for a lognormal spatial model, it is assumed to follow a normal distribution $N(0, \sigma_{\mu k}^2)$, where all $\sigma_{\mu k}^2$ are assumed to follow a gamma distribution Gamma (θ, θ); ϕ_{ik} represents the spatial random effect defined by the following MCAR structure (Jin, Carlin, & Banerjee, 2005):

$$\begin{pmatrix} \phi_1 \\ \phi_2 \\ \phi_3 \\ \phi_4 \end{pmatrix} \sim N\left[\begin{pmatrix} 0 \\ 0 \\ 0 \\ 0 \end{pmatrix}, \begin{pmatrix} \Sigma_{11} & \Sigma_{12} & \Sigma_{13} & \Sigma_{14} \\ \Sigma_{12}' & \Sigma_{22} & \Sigma_{23} & \Sigma_{24} \\ \Sigma_{13}' & \Sigma_{23}' & \Sigma_{33} & \Sigma_{34} \\ \Sigma_{14}' & \Sigma_{24}' & \Sigma_{34}' & \Sigma_{44} \end{pmatrix}\right],$$

where ϕ_1 refers to the spatial random effects for the AM (6:00–10:00) crashes across the ZCTAs; ϕ_2 refers to the spatial random effects for the MD (10:00–15:00) crashes across the ZCTAs; ϕ_3 refers to the spatial random effects for the PM (15:00–19:00) crashes across the ZCTAs; ϕ_4 refers to the spatial random effects for the NT (19:00–6:00) crashes across the ZCTAs; Σ_{kl} is the covariance matrices between each pair of the time of day crash counts.

According to the multivariate normal theory:

$$\begin{aligned}
&\phi_1|\phi_2,\phi_3,\phi_4 \sim N(A_{12}\phi_2 + A_{13}\phi_3 + A_{14}\phi_4,[\tau_1(D-\rho_1 W)]^{-1})\\
&\phi_2|\phi_3,\phi_4 \sim N(A_{23}\phi_3 + A_{24}\phi_4,[\tau_2(D-\rho_2 W)\tau_2]^{-1})\\
&\phi_3|\phi_4 \sim N(A_{34}\phi_4,[\tau_3(D-\rho_3 W)\tau_3]^{-1})\\
&\phi_4 \sim N(0[(D-\rho_4 W)\tau_4]^{-1})
\end{aligned},$$

where A_{ij} describes the aspatial correlation between response types i and j, as well as the spatially lagged correlation between the two response types, formally:

$$A_{ij} = \eta_{0,ij}I + \eta_{1,ij}W.$$

Scalars τ_i as scale parameters; ρ_i refers to the spatial autocorrelation coefficients for the crash counts in time of day period I; η_0 refers to the aspatial cross correlation and η_1 refers to the spatially lagged cross correlation; W refers to the n by n unnormalized weight matrix, which is defined by first-ordering contiguity; D refers to a diagonal matrix with the ith diagonal element representing the ith row sum of W.

Similarly, the logarithmic mean crash rates $\ln(\lambda_{ik})$ can be expressed by the above MCAR structure with:

$$\begin{aligned}
Z_1 &= \ln(\lambda_{i1}),\\
Z_2 &= \ln(\lambda_{i2}),\\
Z_3 &= \ln(\lambda_{i3}),\\
Z_4 &= \ln(\lambda_{i4}),
\end{aligned}$$

$$Z_1|Z_2,Z_3,Z_4 \sim N(\ln(E) + X\cdot\beta_1 + u_1 + (\eta_{012}I + \eta_{112}W)(Z_2 - \ln(E)$$
$$- X\cdot\beta_2 - u_2) + (\eta_{013}I + \eta_{113}W)(Z_3 - \ln(E) - X\cdot\beta_3 - u_3)$$
$$+ (\eta_{014}I + \eta_{114}W)(Z_4 - \ln(E) - X\cdot\beta_4 - u_4), [\tau_1(D - \rho_1 W]^{-1}),$$
$$Z_2|Z_3,Z_3 \sim N(\ln(E) + X\cdot\beta_2 + u_2 + (\eta_{023}I + \eta_{123}W)(Z_3 - \ln(E) - X\cdot\beta_3 - u_3)$$
$$+ (\eta_{024}I + \eta_{124}W)(Z_4 - \ln(E) - X\cdot\beta_4 - u_4), [\tau_2(D - \rho_2 W]^{-1}),$$
$$Z_3|Z_4 \sim N(\ln(E) + X\cdot\beta_3 + u_3 + (\eta_{034}I + \eta_{134}W)(Z_4 - \ln(E) - X\cdot\beta_4$$
$$- u_4, [\tau_3(D - \rho_3 W]^{-1}),$$
$$Z_4 \sim N(\ln(E) + X\cdot\beta_4 + u_4, [\tau_4(D - \rho_4 W]^{-1}).$$

After the conditional distributions for the mean crash rates (i.e., $Z = (Z_1, Z_2, Z_3, Z_4)$ have been specified, the model was estimated using Bayesian Markov Chain Monte Carlo techniques and the open-source WinBUGS software package was used (Spiegelhalter, Thomas, Best, & Lunn, 2003). For the sampling scheme, the posterior distribution $p(\beta,u,Z,\tau,\alpha,\eta|Y)$ can be specified as:

$$p(\beta,u,Z,\tau,\rho,\eta|Y)$$
$$\propto L(Y|\beta,u,Z,\tau,\rho,\eta)\cdot\pi(\beta)\cdot\pi(u)\cdot\pi(Z)\cdot\pi(\beta)\cdot\pi(\tau)\cdot\pi(\rho)\cdot\pi(\eta)$$
$$\propto L(Y|\beta,u,Z,\tau,\rho,\eta)\cdot p(Z_1|Z_2,Z_3,Z_4,\beta,u,\tau,\rho,\eta)\cdot p(Z_2|Z_3,Z_4,\beta,u,\tau,\rho,\eta)\cdot$$
$$p(Z_3|Z_4,\beta,u,\tau,\rho,\eta)\cdot p(Z_4,\beta,u,\tau,\rho,\eta)\cdot\pi(\beta)\cdot\pi(u)\cdot\pi(Z)\cdot\pi(\beta)\cdot\pi(\tau)\cdot\pi(\rho)\cdot\pi(\eta).$$

The estimated parameters and their prior assumptions are summarized in Table 2.

When using WinBUGS, only the data and model specification are required. WinBUGS employs graphical models to simulate Bayesian draws; with built-in samplers, it will automatically select the most efficient and appropriate algorithm and implement the MCMC process so the users don't have to apply any transformation or estimate the full conditional probabilities. Rannala and Yang (2015), Ntzoufras (2011), Lunn, Thomas, Best, and Spiegelhalter (2000), and Rannala and Yang (2015) have provided some insightful review for the use of the software.

Table 2. Summary of Estimated Parameters and Prior Assumptions.

Estimated Parameters	Prior Distribution
$\beta_1\ \beta_2\ \beta_3\ \beta_4$	Flat normal: $N(0, 0.00001)$
$\tau_1\ \tau_2\ \tau_3\ \tau_4$	Diffused Gamma: Gamma (1,0.1)
$\rho_1\ \rho_2\ \rho_3\ \rho_4$	Uniform: $U(0,1)$
$\eta_{012}\ \eta_{013}\ \eta_{014}\ \eta_{023}\ \eta_{024}\ \eta_{034}\ \eta_{112}\ \eta_{113}\ \eta_{114}\ \eta_{123}\ \eta_{124}\ \eta_{134}$	Diffused normal: $N(0,0.001)$
$u_1\ u_2\ u_3\ u_4$	Normal: $N(0, \sigma_u^2)$
σ_u^2	Gamma: Gamma (3,6)

Table 3. Summary Statistics of the Model Attributes.

Continuous target distribution	
Conjugate	Direct sampling using Gibbs Sampling
Log-concave	Derivative-free adaptive rejection sampling
Non-log-concave(restricted range)	Slice sampling
Non-log-concave (unrestricted range)	Metropolis-Hastings
Discrete target distribution	
Finite upper bound	Inversion of cumulative distribution
Shifted Poisson	Direct sampling using Gibbs Sampling

There are three major steps involved in a typical WinBUGS estimation:

Step 1: User provides the data and specifies the model using the BUGS language or a graphical interface called Doodle bugs.

Step 2: WinBUGS will simulate a series of data from a Markov Chain that is constructed so that its stationary distribution is the posterior. It will attempt to use the most efficient and appropriate sampling scheme for each stochastic variable. Table 3 presents the current sampling scheme used in WinBUGS in order of precedence. When conjugate priors are used (i.e., prior and posterior are coming from the same type of distribution and thus the full conditional distribution can be derived analytically), the primary algorithm used for continuous target posterior distribution is Gibbs Sampling. If the full conditional distribution is not available in closed form for any estimating parameters, more general sampling methods such as adaptive rejection sampling, slicing, and Metropolis-Hastings algorithm will be used. The MH algorithm is based on a symmetric normal proposal distribution, whose standard deviation will be changed over the first 4,000 iterations to obtain an acceptance rate between 20% and 40% (Spiegelhalter, Thomas, Best, & Lunn, 2003).

Step 3: WinBUGS will assess the convergence of MCMC to make sure that the output samples are coming from the stationary distribution of the Markov Chain.

5. ESTIMATION RESULTS

The summary of the model estimates is presented in Table 4. For all attributes, both statistical significance (*p*-value) and practical significance (elasticity) are estimated, and included in the last two columns of the table. The elasticity for variable *i* refers to the average percentage change in the mean truck crash counts (averaged across 188 ZCTAs) per one percent change in variable *i*, while holding all other covariate values constant.

5.1. Spatial and Temporal Correlation

As shown in Table 4, all spatial and temporal characteristics yield statistically significant associations with truck crash counts. The autocorrelation estimates (ρ) capture the unobserved attributes that are continuous in space, such as land use intensity and congestion, and may lead to dependency between crash counts in neighboring ZCTAs. The spatial clustering effect tends to be higher for PM (0.99) and NT (0.99) crash counts, followed by crash counts for the AM (0.75) and MD (0.58) periods. Similarly, the aspatial time of day dependency, as a result of unobserved attributes that are continuous in time (e.g., unusual site conditions, light conditions), is captured by the positive associations between the error terms of each pair of time of day attributes (η_0). For example, η_{-012} indicates that higher crash counts in the AM period are likely to co-exist with higher crash counts in the MD period, same with all other pairs. Noted that there is a delay for the effect of time of day dependence. For example, η_{-013} and η_{-014} are higher than η_{-012}, suggesting that it takes time for the temporal dependence to take place, which may be a result of more cautious driving

Table 4. Summary of the Model Estimates.

Variable		Time of Day	Mean	SD	*p*-Value	Elasticity
Constant		1 (6:00–10:00)	−0.0509	0.717	0.944	
		2 (10:00–15:00)	−1.2720	0.233	0.000	
		3 (15:00–19:00)	0.6813	0.010	0.000	
		4 (19:00–6:00)	0.8757	0.029	0.000	
Business establishment density	Mining, utilities, construction, manufacturing	1	−0.021	0.010	0.036	−3.232
		2	0.025	0.004	0.000	0.928
		3	0.030	0.000	0.000	2.327
		4	0.016	0.001	0.000	0.471
	Information, finance, real estate, professional, management	1	−0.005	0.013	0.713	−0.251
		2	0.075	0.003	0.000	0.072
		3	0.002	0.001	0.003	0.202
		4	−0.006	0.001	0.000	−0.016
	Wholesale, retail, transportation	1	−0.008	0.019	0.678	−0.655
		2	0.095	0.010	0.000	1.436
		3	0.007	0.002	0.000	0.767
		4	−0.006	0.001	0.000	−0.053
	Admin, edu, health, arts, accomm	1	−0.018	0.007	0.014	−0.505
		2	0.035	0.007	0.000	0.765
		3	0.009	0.002	0.000	0.106
		4	0.000	0.001	0.794	0.007
Traffic volume ratio	Auto	1	−1.080	0.361	0.003	−0.43
		2	3.952	0.418	0.000	1.693
		3	−0.113	0.045	0.012	−0.053
		4	−0.665	0.028	0.000	−0.294
	Pub	1	−10.570	4.204	0.013	−0.343
		2	−1.537	2.491	0.538	−0.125
		3	0.233	0.889	0.794	0.008
		4	−3.903	0.513	0.000	−0.373

Table 4. *(Continued)*

Variable		Time of Day	Mean	SD	*p*-Value	Elasticity
Spatial autocorrelation	ρ [1]		0.745	0.107	0.000	
	ρ [2]		0.579	0.102	0.000	
	ρ [3]		0.993	0.004	0.000	
	ρ [4]		0.993	0.003	0.000	
Time of day dependence	η_012		0.494	0.121	0.000	
	η_013		0.657	0.132	0.000	
	η_014		0.720	0.077	0.000	
	η_023		0.350	0.047	0.000	
	η_024		0.752	0.039	0.000	
	η_034		0.567	0.003	0.000	
Spatial lag cross-correlation	η_112		0.419	0.123	0.001	
	η_113		0.138	0.007	0.000	
	η_114		0.195	0.016	0.000	
	η_123		0.411	0.002	0.000	
	η_124		0.493	0.002	0.000	
	η_134		0.110	0.000	0.000	
DIC	2,878	Burn-in period	3,000			
# of Iterations	6,000	# of Chains	1			

right after an accident, and the fact that an accident's neighboring effect needs sometime to propagate. The general time of day effect on crash counts are also revealed by the constant terms estimated in the model: more crashes tend to occur in the PM and NT periods, which is consistent with the results shown in Section 3. The spatial lag correlation across different times of the day (i.e., the spatial lag across-correlation) is revealed by the estimates of η_1. The strongly positive estimates indicate that after controlling for the spatial autocorrelation across the ZCTAS (local spatial correlation) from missing variables, the cross-correlation among different time of day periods also exist. Possible contributing factors include terrain features, weather conditions and demographic characteristics.

5.2. Built Environment and Business Establishment

The study hypothesizes that the built environment attributes also affect truck crash occurrence. Intuitively, areas with more active business activities will attract more traffic and generate more vehicle interactions, and thus are likely to have a higher percentage of crashes. After controlling for exposure (the traffic volume of truck and commercial vehicles), higher business establishment densities for large-scale heavy industries (Mining, utilities, construction, and manufacturing) are estimated to increase truck crash rates during MD – NT periods, and lower the crash counts in the AM period. The estimates are both statistically significant and practically meaningful (with high elasticity). For example, one percent increase in the business establishment density for industries involving mining, utilities, construction, or manufacturing businesses will decrease the MD crash counts by 0.93% and PM crash counts by 2.33%. Similar trends are found in the estimates for the density of public-oriented industries (administrative, educational, health, arts, and accommodation), however, the findings for this category is less practically meaningful with lower elasticity estimates. The result may come from the fact that large-scale heavy industries tend to have more complex interactions with trucks (e.g., for deliveries), and higher exposure of these activities tends to occur during day time business hours. For group two (Information, finance, real estate, professional, management) and three (Wholesale, retail, transportation), the business establishment density covariates yielded mixed effects on crash frequency: the effects are not statistically significant for AM crash counts; and they contributed to MD and PM crash counts positively and to NT crash counts negatively. However, the effects are not practically meaningful for the NT period for small elasticities estimated. The results are reasonable as these industries are more commercial and customer oriented, resulting in more conflicts during MD and PM periods.

5.3. Traffic Volume

The estimate of the auto (HOV + SOV) variable shows that truck crash counts decreases with the number of passenger vehicles on road during AM, PM, and NT periods, and increases during MD period. The contributing effects of traffic volume of bus and taxi on crash counts seem to be consistent for all time periods: the crash frequency tends to decrease with the number of buses and taxies on road. The estimated elasticity shows that with a one percent increase in the percentage of bus and taxi's traffic volume, the crash counts in the AM, MD and NT periods will decrease 0.34%, 0.12% and 0.37% respectively. The MD estimate shows a positive effect, however, since it is not practically meaningful, its effect may be neglected. Such findings are not surprising as drivers tend to be more careful when there is more traffic on road and crashes occur less frequently when the average driving speed is lower on road (Wang & Abdel-Aty, 2006).

5.4. Model Fit

To validate the spatial crash count model, estimation performances were compared to a simple Poisson-lognormal multivariate model. The Deviance Information Criteria (DIC) is used to evaluate the goodness-of-fit of the model, which is common in the Bayesian modeling literature (Spiegelhalter, Best, Carlin, & Van Der Linde, 2002). The metric (smaller DIC) suggests that the addition of spatial and temporal dependence effects increased the explanatory power of the model, and the MCAR model (DIC = 2,878) outperforms the traditional simple model (DIC = 2,987).

6. CONCLUSION

Using a four-level Poisson-lognormal CAR model, this study examined the effects of ZCTA-level characteristics on truck crash counts in New York

City in AM, MD, PM, and NT four periods, while reflecting spatial correlations.

The analysis shed light on patterns of truck accidents relative to the built environment characteristics, spatial correlations and time of day dependencies. The spatial clustering effects identified in this study point to the existence of missing variables that trend in space and possibly a "neighboring effect." The time of day dependence effect exhibited by the results here suggests that crash counts are indeed correlated across different times of the day. Additionally, the results reveal that the crash rates in MD and PM periods rise with the densities of commercial- and customer-oriented industries since the conflicts tend to be most severe during those periods. In the meantime, crash counts from MD to NT are predicated to rise as the density of heavy and large-scale industries increases, perhaps due to more delivery activities occur during that time and result in more exposure and complexities. The above findings could provide policy insights for planners and transportation engineers, for example, better safety measures and law enforcements may be applied to areas with high business establishment densities, especially during afternoon peaks and night times. Last but not least, it appears that areas with high traffic volume are safer with fewer crash counts as a result of a lower average driving speed, especially when more buses and taxies are involved.

The analysis is not without limitations. First, the data on built environment attributes are limited. The crash rate is also influenced by many relatively complex land use characteristics, not included in this study's set of covariates. Next, the current study focus on the time of day effect only, while the temporal dependency in multiple years should also be investigated when panel data are available. Furthermore, because this model uses aggregate data for each ZCTA, the estimated parameters cannot be generalized to apply at an individual accident record level. The results more strongly suggest a direction for future research and investigation, more data and analysis are needed before these results can be translated into concrete policy recommendations.

REFERENCES

Abdel-Aty, M., & Wang, X. (2006). Crash estimation at signalized intersections along corridors: Analyzing spatial effect and identifying significant factors. *Transportation Research Record: Journal of the Transportation Research Board, 1953*, 98–111.

Administration, F. M. C. S. (2013). Commercial Motor Vehicle Facts – 2013.

Aguero-Valverde, J. (2013). Multivariate spatial models of excess crash frequency at area level: Case of Costa Rica. *Accident Analysis & Prevention*, *59*, 365–373.

Aguero-Valverde, J., & Jovanis, P. (2008). Analysis of road crash frequency with spatial models. *Transportation Research Record: Journal of the Transportation Research Board*, *2061*, 55–63.

Aguero-Valverde, J., & Jovanis, P. (2010). Spatial correlation in multilevel crash frequency models: Effects of different neighboring structures. *Transportation Research Record: Journal of the Transportation Research Board*, *2165*, 21–32.

Aguero-Valverde, J., & Jovanis, P. P. (2006). Spatial analysis of fatal and injury crashes in Pennsylvania. *Accident Analysis & Prevention*, *38*(3), 618–625.

Amoros, E., Martin, J. L., & Laumon, B. (2003). Comparison of road crashes incidence and severity between some French counties. *Accident Analysis & Prevention*, *35*(4), 537–547.

Anselin, L. (2013). *Spatial econometrics: Methods and models*. New York, NY: Springer Science & Business Media.

Barua, S., El-Basyouny, K., & Islam, M. T. (2014). A full Bayesian multivariate count data model of collision severity with spatial correlation. *Analytic Methods in Accident Research*, *3*, 28–43.

Besag, J. (1974). Spatial interaction and the statistical analysis of lattice systems. *Journal of the Royal Statistical Society. Series B (Methodological)*, *36*(2), 192–236.

Besag, J. (1975). Statistical analysis of non-lattice data. *The Statistician*, *24*(3), 179–195.

Bhat, C. R., Born, K., Sidharthan, R., & Bhat, P. C. (2014). A count data model with endogenous covariates: Formulation and application to roadway crash frequency at intersections. *Analytic Methods in Accident Research*, *1*, 53–71.

Brinckerhoff, P. (2009). New York best practice model (NYBPM) for regional travel demand forecasting.

Castro, M., Paleti, R., & Bhat, C. R. (2012). A latent variable representation of count data models to accommodate spatial and temporal dependence: Application to predicting crash frequency at intersections. *Transportation Research Part B: Methodological*, *46*(1), 253–272.

Chang, L.-Y., & Chen, W.-C. (2005). Data mining of tree-based models to analyze freeway accident frequency. *Journal of Safety Research*, *36*(4), 365–375.

Chiou, Y.-C., & Fu, C. (2013). Modeling crash frequency and severity using multinomial-generalized Poisson model with error components. *Accident Analysis & Prevention*, *50*, 73–82.

Chiou, Y.-C., & Fu, C. (2015). Modeling crash frequency and severity with spatiotemporal dependence. *Analytic Methods in Accident Research*, *5*, 43–58.

Chiou, Y.-C., Fu, C., & Chih-Wei, H. (2014). Incorporating spatial dependence in simultaneously modeling crash frequency and severity. *Analytic Methods in Accident Research*, *2*, 1–11.

Cho, G., Rodríguez, D. A., & Khattak, A. J. (2009). The role of the built environment in explaining relationships between perceived and actual pedestrian and bicyclist safety. *Accident Analysis & Prevention*, *41*(4), 692–702.

Clifton, K. J., Burnier, C. V., & Akar, G. (2009). Severity of injury resulting from pedestrian–vehicle crashes: What can we learn from examining the built environment? *Transportation Research Part D: Transport and Environment*, *14*(6), 425–436.

Cressie, N. (2015). *Statistics for spatial data*. John Wiley & Sons.

Dubin, R. A. (1988). Estimation of regression coefficients in the presence of spatially autocorrelated error terms. *The Review of Economics and Statistics*, 466–474.

Dupont, E., Papadimitriou, E., Martensen, H., & Yannis, G. (2013). Multilevel analysis in road safety research. *Accident Analysis & Prevention, 60*, 402–411.

El-Basyouny, K., & Sayed, T. (2009). Urban arterial accident prediction models with spatial effects. *Transportation Research Record: Journal of the Transportation Research Board, 2102*, 27–33.

Elhorst, J. P. (2014). Spatial panel data models. *Spatial Econometrics*, 37–93.

Eluru, N., Paleti, R., Pendyala, R., & Bhat, C. (2010). Modeling injury severity of multiple occupants of vehicles: Copula-based multivariate approach. *Transportation Research Record: Journal of the Transportation Research Board, 2165*, 1–11.

Ewing, R., & Dumbaugh, E. (2009). The built environment and traffic safety a review of empirical evidence. *Journal of Planning Literature, 23*(4), 347–367.

Flask, T., & Schneider, W. (2013). A Bayesian analysis of multi-level spatial correlation in single vehicle motorcycle crashes in Ohio. *Safety Science, 53*, 1–10.

Gandhi, U. (2014). QGIS tutorials and tips.

Gelfand, A. E., & Vounatsou, P. (2003). Proper multivariate conditional autoregressive models for spatial data analysis. *Biostatistics, 4*(1), 11–15.

Golob, T. F., Recker, W. W., & Leonard, J. D. (1987). An analysis of the severity and incident duration of truck-involved freeway accidents. *Accident Analysis & Prevention, 19*(5), 375–395.

Gschlößl, S., & Czado, C. (2008). Does a Gibbs sampler approach to spatial Poisson regression models outperform a single site MH sampler? *Computational Statistics & Data Analysis, 52*(9), 4184–4202.

Guo, F., Wang, X., & Abdel-Aty, M. A. (2010). Modeling signalized intersection safety with corridor-level spatial correlations. *Accident Analysis & Prevention, 42*(1), 84–92.

Islam, M., & Hernandez, S. (2013a). Large truck–involved crashes: Exploratory injury severity analysis. *Journal of Transportation Engineering, 139*(6), 596–604.

Islam, M., & Hernandez, S. (2013b). Modeling injury outcomes of crashes involving heavy vehicles on Texas highways. *Transportation Research Record: Journal of the Transportation Research Board, 2388*, 28–36.

Jin, X., Carlin, B. P., & Banerjee, S. (2005). Generalized hierarchical multivariate CAR models for areal data. *Biometrics, 61*(4), 950–961.

Khattak, A. J., Schneider, R. J., & Targa, F. (2003). "*Risk factors in large truck rollovers and injury severity: Analysis of single-vehicle collisions.*" Transportation Research Record.

Kim, D.-G., Washington, S., & Oh, J. (2006). Modeling crash types: New insights into the effects of covariates on crashes at rural intersections. *Journal of Transportation Engineering, 132*(4), 282–292.

Lemp, J. D., Kockelman, K. M., & Unnikrishnan, A. (2011). Analysis of large truck crash severity using heteroskedastic ordered probit models. *Accident Analysis & Prevention, 43*(1), 370–380.

LeSage, J. P., & Pace, R. K. (2009). *Introduction to Spatial Econometrics*. Boca Raton, FL: CRC Press, Taylor & Francis Group.

Lord, D., & Mannering, F. (2010). The statistical analysis of crash-frequency data: A review and assessment of methodological alternatives. *Transportation Research Part A: Policy and Practice, 44*(5), 291–305.

Lord, D., & Persaud, B. N. (2000). Accident prediction models with and without trend – Application of the generalized estimating equations procedure. *Highway and Traffic Safety: Crash Data, Analysis Tools, and Statistical Methods, 1717*, 102–108.

Lunn, D. J., Thomas, A., Best, N., & Spiegelhalter, D. (2000). WinBUGS-a Bayesian modelling framework: Concepts, structure, and extensibility. *Statistics and Computing*, *10*(4), 325–337.

MacNab, Y. C. (2004). Bayesian spatial and ecological models for small-area accident and injury analysis. *Accident Analysis & Prevention*, *36*(6), 1019–1028.

Mannering, F. L., & Bhat, C. R. (2014). Analytic methods in accident research: Methodological frontier and future directions. *Analytic Methods in Accident Research*, *1*, 1–22.

Mardia, K. (1988). Multi-dimensional multivariate Gaussian Markov random fields with application to image processing. *Journal of Multivariate Analysis*, *24*(2), 265–284.

Margreta, M., Chester, F., & Grube, R. (2014). *U.S. freight on the move: Highlights from the 2012 commodity flow survey preliminary data*. Bureau of Transportation Statistics.

Miaou, S.-P., Song, J. J., & Mallick, B. K. (2003). Roadway traffic crash mapping: A space-time modeling approach. *Journal of Transportation and Statistics*, *6*, 33–58.

Miranda-Moreno, L. F., Morency, P., & El-Geneidy, A. M. (2011). The link between built environment, pedestrian activity and pedestrian–vehicle collision occurrence at signalized intersections. *Accident Analysis & Prevention*, *43*(5), 1624–1634.

Mitra, S. (2009). Spatial autocorrelation and Bayesian spatial statistical method for analyzing intersections prone to injury crashes. *Transportation Research Record: Journal of the Transportation Research Board*, *2136*, 92–100.

Mohammadi, M. A., Samaranayake, V. A., & Bham, G. H. (2014). Crash frequency modeling using negative binomial models: An application of generalized estimating equation to longitudinal data. *Analytic Methods in Accident Research*, *2*, 52–69.

Morency, P., & Cloutier, M. (2006). From targeted "black spots" to area-wide pedestrian safety. *Injury Prevention*, *12*(6), 360–364.

Narayanamoorthy, S., Paleti, R., & Bhat, C. R. (2013). On accommodating spatial dependence in bicycle and pedestrian injury counts by severity level. *Transportation Research Part B: Methodological*, *55*, 245–264.

Noland, R. B., & Quddus, M. A. (2004). A spatially disaggregate analysis of road casualties in England. *Accident Analysis & Prevention*, *36*(6), 973–984.

Ntzoufras, I. (2011). *Bayesian modeling using WinBUGS*. New York: John Wiley & Sons.

NYSDOT, N. Y. S. D. o. T. (2014). New York State Department of motor vehicles.

Pahukula, J., Hernandez, S., & Unnikrishnan, A. (2015). A time of day analysis of crashes involving large trucks in urban areas. *Accident Analysis & Prevention*, *75*, 155–163.

Pettitt, A. N., Weir, I., & Hart, A. G. (2002). A conditional autoregressive Gaussian process for irregularly spaced multivariate data with application to modelling large sets of binary data. *Statistics and Computing*, *12*(4), 353–367.

Qin, X., Ivan, J. N., Ravishanker, N., Liu, J., & Tepas, D. (2006). Bayesian estimation of hourly exposure functions by crash type and time of day. *Accident Analysis & Prevention*, *38*(6), 1071–1080.

Quddus, M. A. (2008a). Modelling area-wide count outcomes with spatial correlation and heterogeneity: An analysis of London crash data. *Accident Analysis & Prevention*, *40*(4), 1486–1497.

Quddus, M. A. (2008b). Time series count data models: An empirical application to traffic accidents. *Accident Analysis & Prevention*, *40*(5), 1732–1741.

Rana, T., Sikder, S., & Pinjari, A. (2010). Copula-based method for addressing endogeneity in models of severity of traffic crash injuries: Application to two-vehicle crashes.

Transportation Research Record: Journal of the Transportation Research Board, 2147, 75–87.

Rannala, B., & Yang, Z. (2015). "*Efficient Bayesian species tree inference under the multi-species coalescent*." arXiv preprint arXiv:1512.03843.

Savolainen, P. T., Mannering, F. L., Lord, D., & Quddus, M. A. (2011). The statistical analysis of highway crash-injury severities: A review and assessment of methodological alternatives. *Accident Analysis & Prevention, 43*(5), 1666–1676.

Shekhar, S., & Xiong, H. (2008). *Encyclopedia of GIS*. New York, NY: Springer Science & Business Media.

Song, J. J., Ghosh, M., Miaou, S., & Mallick, B. (2006). Bayesian multivariate spatial models for roadway traffic crash mapping. *Journal of Multivariate Analysis, 97*(1), 246–273.

Spiegelhalter, D., Thomas, A., Best, N., & Lunn, D. (2003). WinBUGS user manual, version.

Spiegelhalter, D. J., Best, N. G., Carlin, B. P., & Van Der Linde, A. (2002). Bayesian measures of model complexity and fit. *Journal of the Royal Statistical Society: Series B (Statistical Methodology), 64*(4), 583–639.

The William and Anita Newman Library. (2015). *NYC geodatabase*. New York, NY: Newman Library, Baruch College CUNY.

Ukkusuri, S., Miranda-Moreno, L. F., Ramadurai, G., & Isa-Tavarez, J. (2012). The role of built environment on pedestrian crash frequency. *Safety Science, 50*(4), 1141–1151.

US EPA, U. S. E. P. A. (2014). Smart location database.

Wall, M. M. (2004). A close look at the spatial structure implied by the CAR and SAR models. *Journal of Statistical Planning and Inference, 121*(2), 311–324.

Wang, C., Quddus, M. A., Ryley, T., Enoch, M., & Davison, L. (2012). Spatial models in transport: A review and assessment of methodological issues. Transportation Research Board 91st Annual Meeting.

Wang, X., & Abdel-Aty, M. (2006). Temporal and spatial analyses of rear-end crashes at signalized intersections. *Accident Analysis and Prevention, 38*, 1137–1150.

Wang, Y., & Kockelman, K. M. (2013). A Poisson-lognormal conditional-autoregressive model for multivariate spatial analysis of pedestrian crash counts across neighborhoods. *Accident Analysis & Prevention, 60*, 71–84.

Whittle, P. (1954). On stationary processes in the plane. *Biometrika, 41*(3/4), 434–449.

Wier, M., Weintraub, J., Humphreys, E. H., Seto, E., & Bhatia, R. (2009). An area-level model of vehicle-pedestrian injury collisions with implications for land use and transportation planning. *Accident Analysis & Prevention, 41*(1), 137–145.

Yamamoto, T., & Shankar, V. N. (2004). Bivariate ordered-response probit model of driver's and passenger's injury severities in collisions with fixed objects. *Accident Analysis & Prevention, 36*(5), 869–876.

Yasmin, S., Eluru, N., Pinjari, A. R., & Tay, R. (2014). Examining driver injury severity in two vehicle crashes – A copula based approach. *Accident Analysis & Prevention, 66*, 120–135.

Zhu, X., & Srinivasan, S. (2011). A comprehensive analysis of factors influencing the injury severity of large-truck crashes. *Accident Analysis & Prevention, 43*(1), 49–57.

PART IV
CONTINUOUS DEPENDENT VARIABLES – MAXIMUM LIKELIHOOD

GROUP INTERACTION IN RESEARCH AND THE USE OF GENERAL NESTING SPATIAL MODELS

Peter Burridge[a], J. Paul Elhorst[b] and Katarina Zigova[c]

[a]Department of Economics and Related Studies, University of York, York, YO10 5DD, UK
[b]Faculty of Economics and Business, P.O. Box 800, 9700 AV Groningen, University of Groningen, The Netherlands
[c]Department of Economics, University of Konstanz, Box 138, D-78457 Konstanz, Germany

ABSTRACT

This paper tests the feasibility and empirical implications of a spatial econometric model with a full set of interaction effects and weight matrix defined as an equally weighted group interaction matrix applied to research productivity of individuals. We also elaborate two extensions of this model, namely with group fixed effects and with heteroskedasticity. In our setting, the model with a full set of interaction effects is overparameterised: only

Spatial Econometrics: Qualitative and Limited Dependent Variables
Advances in Econometrics, Volume 37, 223–258

ISSN: 0731-9053/doi:10.1108/S0731-905320160000037016

the SDM and SDEM specifications produce acceptable results. They imply comparable spillover effects, but by applying a Bayesian approach taken from LeSage (2014), we are able to show that the SDEM specification is more appropriate and thus that colleague interaction effects work through observed and unobserved exogenous characteristics common to researchers within a group.

Keywords: Spatial econometrics; identification; heteroskedasticity; group fixed effects; interaction effects; research productivity

JEL classifications: C21; D85; I23; J24

1. INTRODUCTION

For reasons to be identified in this paper, a linear spatial econometric model with a full set of interaction effects, namely, among the dependent variable, the exogenous variables and among the disturbances, is almost never used in empirical applications. The introductory textbook in spatial econometrics by LeSage and Pace (2009) illustrates this. In their overview of spatial econometric models, they duly consider all extensions of the linear regression model $\mathbf{Y} = \mathbf{X}\boldsymbol{\beta} + \boldsymbol{\varepsilon}$ in which $\mathbf{X}$ is exogenous and $\boldsymbol{\varepsilon}$ is an *i.i.d.* disturbance, except the model with a full set of interaction effects. The spatial autoregressive (SAR) model contains a spatially lagged-dependent variable $\mathbf{WY}$, where the symbol $\mathbf{W}$ represents the weights matrix arising from the spatial arrangement of the geographical units in the sample. The spatial error model (SEM) contains a spatially autocorrelated disturbance, $\mathbf{U}$, usually constructed via the spatial autoregression, $\mathbf{U} = \lambda\mathbf{WU} + \boldsymbol{\varepsilon}$. The model with both a spatially lagged-dependent variable, $\mathbf{WY}$, and a spatially autocorrelated disturbance, $\mathbf{WU}$, is denoted by the term SAC in LeSage and Pace (2009, p. 32), though this acronym is not explained.[1] The spatial lag of $\mathbf{X}$ model (SLX) contains spatially lagged exogenous variables, $\mathbf{WX}$; the spatial Durbin model (SDM) a spatially lagged-dependent variable and spatially lagged exogenous variables, $\mathbf{WY}$ and $\mathbf{WX}$; and the spatial Durbin error model (SDEM) spatially lagged exogenous variables and a spatially autocorrelated error term, $\mathbf{WX}$ and $\mathbf{WU}$. The model with a spatially lagged-dependent variable, spatially lagged exogenous variables and a spatially autocorrelated disturbance is in fact mentioned, namely on page 53, but not taken seriously to judge from the fact that all equations in the book are numbered, except this one.

Part of the motivation for this paper is to take the opportunity to challenge two popular misconceptions about models of this type that have arisen in spatial econometrics. The first of these erroneous views holds that the parameters of a linear regression model specified to include interaction effects among the dependent variable, the exogenous variables and among the disturbances cannot be identified. A possible cause of this mistake could be a loose reading of Manski (1993), who demonstrated the failure of identification in an equation in which the endogenous peer effect was assumed to operate via the group means of the dependent variable, labeling his result "the reflection problem". The second misconception goes back to Anselin and Bera (1998), according to whom an additional identification requirement when applying ML estimators is that the spatial weights matrix of the spatially lagged-dependent variable must be different from the spatial weights matrix of the spatially autocorrelated disturbance, though without formally deriving this identification restriction, either in that study or any related work.

Lee, Liu, and Lin (2010) are the first who provide formal proofs and conditions under which the parameters of a linear regression model specified with interaction effects among the dependent variable, among the exogenous variables and among the disturbances are identified. Importantly, their proofs are limited to a spatial weights matrix that is specified as an equally weighted group interaction matrix with a zero diagonal. This is a block diagonal matrix where each block represents a group of units that interact with each other but not with members of other groups. In that case, the value of all off-diagonal elements within a block equals $w_{ij} = 1/(n_r - 1)$, where n_r denotes the number of units in group r. Despite the fact that such a group interaction matrix is not very popular in applied spatial econometric research, Lee, Liu, and Lin's findings make clear that Manski's reflection problem does not carry over to the case in which the endogenous peer effect operates via the mean of each individual's peers, since this mean is different for each individual, and that Anselin and Bera's (1998) identification restriction is unnecessary.

On the other hand, notice that the difference between this form of interaction matrix and the "group mean" version that leads to Manski's reflection problem can be very small: in the latter, the matrix would not have a zero diagonal, each element being equal to $w^*_{ij} = 1/n_r$. Furthermore, as Lee et al. (2010, p. 156) note, if the groups are large, identification will be weak. This problem may worsen if group fixed effects are included, which Lee et al. (2010) put forward as an important model extension. In a footnote, they (*ibid.*, p. 147) motivate this extension as a first step towards capturing endogenous group formation. Moreover, back in 1988, Anselin (1988, pp. 61–65) advocated a "General model" with all types of interaction effects and heteroskedastic disturbances, though without providing conditions under which the parameters of this model are identified. Lee et al. (2010) establish identification for a model in which the spatial weights matrix has a group interaction form, by introducing explicit rank conditions. The parameters of Anselin's general model will be identified under an extended set of similar such conditions, the function of which is primarily to rule out rogue special cases. Some of these conditions are discussed in Section 2.1, but in this paper our main purpose is to address the empirical usefulness of the heteroskedastic counterpart of the model in Lee et al. (2010), since this turns out to be strongly supported by the data.

Altogether, then, we aim to test the feasibility, empirical implications and relevance of a group interaction model with a full set of interaction effects, as well as the extensions with group fixed effects as proposed in Lee et al. (2010) and heteroskedastic disturbances as proposed in Anselin (1988). We designate these models as the general nesting spatial (GNS) model, the group fixed effects GNS (GFE-GNS) model, and the Heteroskedastic GNS (HGNS) model. For this purpose, we use data that encompass all scientists employed at economics, business, and finance departments of 83 universities in Austria, Germany and German speaking Switzerland to identify the type and to estimate the extent of research interactions among colleagues within a university on individual research productivity.

Our findings throw new light on the seminal works of Anselin (1988), Anselin and Bera (1998), LeSage and Pace (2009), Lee et al. (2010) and many empirical studies adopting one or more of the models explained in these works. Firstly, in our setting the well-known SAR, SEM, SLX and SAC models demonstrably lead to incorrect inferences based on the direct and indirect effects estimates that can be derived from the point estimates of the different models. Interestingly, the group interaction model is one of the few models for which convenient explicit expressions for these direct and indirect effects estimates can be derived, as we will show. Secondly, the GNS model appears to be overparameterised; the significance of the coefficient estimates in this model is lower than in the nested SDM and SDEM models. Thirdly, only the SDM and SDEM specifications produce acceptable results. Apparently, in our case, interaction effects among both the dependent variable and the error terms do not perform well together, though not for reasons of identification as suggested by Anselin and Bera (1998) but for reasons of overfitting. Fourthly, the extension with GFE appears to have little empirical relevance. This is due to high correlation between the **X** and the **WX** variables that arises after transformation by group-demeaning, as we will show both mathematically and empirically. By contrast, the extension with heteroskedasticity appears to have more empirical relevance, bringing us back to the seminal work of Anselin (1988). Finally, the findings of our empirical application show that the kind and magnitude of interaction effects driving research productivity of scientific communities are in line with previous studies on peer effects in academia using a natural experiment setting (Borjas & Doran, 2014; Waldinger, 2011).

The remainder of this paper is organised as follows. Section 2 sets out the GNS model, its basic properties, and the two extensions. Section 3 describes the Matlab routines to find the optimum of the log-likelihood function. After a description of our data, our measure of research productivity, and its potential determinants in Section 4, Section 5 reports and reviews the results of our empirical analysis. The paper concludes with a summary of the main results in Section 6.

2. THE GNS MODEL AND ITS EXTENSIONS

The model with both group specific effects and heteroskedastic disturbances is closely related to those treated by Anselin (1988), Bramoullé Djebbari, and Fortin (2009), and Lee et al. (2010). This model can be viewed either as a generalisation of the "General Model" in Anselin (1988) with group specific effects, restricted here to the group interaction setting, or as a generalisation of the group interaction model of Lee et al. (2010) expanded to allow for heteroskedastic disturbances. In notation that adapts Anselin's to the group interaction setting of Lee et al. (2010), the extended GNS model is, for the rth group:

$$\begin{aligned} \mathbf{Y}_r &= \rho_0 \mathbf{W}_r \mathbf{Y}_r + \mathbf{1}_{n_r}\delta_{r0} + \mathbf{X}_r\boldsymbol{\beta}_0 + \mathbf{Q}_r\mathbf{X}_r\boldsymbol{\gamma}_0 + \mathbf{U}_r, \\ \mathbf{U}_r &= \lambda_0 \mathbf{M}_r \mathbf{U}_r + \boldsymbol{\varepsilon}_r \\ & E\{\boldsymbol{\varepsilon}_r\} = \mathbf{0}_{n_r}, \qquad E\{\boldsymbol{\varepsilon}_r\boldsymbol{\varepsilon}_r'\} = \boldsymbol{\Omega}_r, \\ \omega_{r,ii} &= h_r(\boldsymbol{\alpha}_0, \mathbf{Z}_{r,i}) > 0, \quad \omega_{r,ij} = 0, \quad i \neq j, i,j = 1,\ldots,n_r, \\ r &= 1,\ldots,\bar{r} \end{aligned} \quad . \qquad (1)$$

where n_r is the size of the rth group, $\bar{r}$ is the number of groups, $\mathbf{1}_{n_r} = [1,1,\ldots,1]'$ is an $n_r \times 1$ vector, $[\mathbf{1}_{n_r} \vdots \mathbf{X}_r \vdots \mathbf{Q}_r\mathbf{X}_r]$ is a matrix of n_r rows with full column rank with elements that are independent of the shocks, $\boldsymbol{\varepsilon}_r$, and $\mathbf{Y}_r$ is an $n_r \times 1$ vector of observations of the dependent variable, and $\omega_{r,ii}$ is an element of the $n_r \times n_r$ matrix $\boldsymbol{\Omega}_r$. When the GFE, $1_{n_r}\delta_{r0}$, are absent, they are replaced by a single intercept common to all groups, $\mathbf{1}_{n_r}\delta_0$. The inclusion of group-specific fixed effects, as in Lee et al. (2010), requires the model to be transformed to avoid the incidental parameter problem, while also ruling out the estimation of the effects of exogenous covariates that are constant within groups. For this reason, it seems appropriate to separate these two cases when discussing this extension. We start with the model without group-specific fixed effects, and then consider within-group interactions in the disturbance. The $n_r \times n_r$ matrices of non-negative constants, $\mathbf{W}_r, \mathbf{Q}_r$, and $\mathbf{M}_r$ are of the form $\mathbf{W}_r = \mathbf{Q}_r = \mathbf{M}_r = \frac{1}{n_r - 1}[\, \mathbf{1}_{n_r}\mathbf{1}'_{n_r} - \mathbf{I}_{n_r}]$, as in Lee et al. (2010). It will be assumed that the matrices $[\mathbf{I}_{n_r} - \rho_0\mathbf{W}_r] = \mathbf{A}_r$ and $[\mathbf{I}_{n_r} - \lambda_0\mathbf{M}_r] = \mathbf{B}_r$ are non-singular with inverses as given later in the paper. Further, it is assumed that there is no redundancy in the parameters – that is, there is no common factor restriction relating $\boldsymbol{\beta}_0$, $\boldsymbol{\gamma}_0$ and ρ_0 of the form discussed by Lee et al. (2010, p. 153).

The variables, $\mathbf{Z}_{r,i}$ that determine the pattern of heteroskedasticity are assumed to be observed without error, while the associated parameters, $\boldsymbol{\alpha}$, must be estimated. In our application, $\mathbf{Z}_{r,i} = [1, n_r]$ and $h_r(\boldsymbol{\alpha}_0, \mathbf{Z}_{r,i}) = \alpha_{01} + \alpha_{02}n_r$ so that the disturbances have variance proportional to group size. In the homoskedastic model $\alpha_{02} = 0$ and $\alpha_{01} = \sigma^2$, which yields $\boldsymbol{\Omega} = \sigma^2\mathbf{I}$. Since only university-specific and not researcher-specific determinants are used to model heteroskedasticity, the subscript i of $\mathbf{Z}_{r,i}$ may also be dropped. The Normal likelihood, first-order conditions and information matrix corresponding to Eq. (1), for the homoskedastic case are set out in Lee et al. (2010, p. 151), and for the heteroskedastic case without GFE in Anselin (1988, pp. 61–65). These models can be estimated by ML or QML. In the first case, the disturbances are assumed to be Normally distributed. In the second case, it is required that some absolute moment higher than the 4th exists.

2.1. Case 1: No Group-Specific Fixed Effects

Write $N = \sum_{r=1}^{\bar{r}} n_r$ for the total sample size, and $\mathbf{W}$, $\mathbf{Q}$, $\mathbf{M}$, $\boldsymbol{\Omega}$, $\mathbf{A}$ and $\mathbf{B}$ for the $N \times N$ block-diagonal matrices with diagonal blocks given by $\mathbf{W}_r$, $\mathbf{Q}_r$, and so on, for $r = 1, \ldots, \bar{r}$ and similarly $\mathbf{X}$ for the matrix of exogenous regressors. For convenience, write the full parameter vector as

$\boldsymbol{\theta}_0 = \left(\delta_0, \boldsymbol{\beta}'_0, \boldsymbol{\gamma}'_0, \lambda_0, \rho_0, \boldsymbol{\alpha}'_0\right)' = \left(\boldsymbol{\beta}^{*\prime}_0, \lambda_0, \rho_0, \boldsymbol{\alpha}'_0\right)'$ and suppose it is an interior point in the compact space $\mathcal{T}$. Then, writing $\mathbf{X}^* = (\mathbf{1}:\mathbf{X}:\mathbf{QX})$ so that the exogenous part of the mean function of the model can be written compactly as $\mathbf{X}^*\boldsymbol{\beta}^*_0$ and writing $\boldsymbol{\eta} = \boldsymbol{\Omega}^{-1/2}\boldsymbol{\varepsilon}$ so that the N-dimensional random vector $\boldsymbol{\eta}$ has mean $\mathbf{0}$ and covariance matrix $\mathbf{I}_N$, the Normal log-likelihood takes the form

$$l(\mathbf{Y}, \mathbf{X}, \mathbf{W}, \mathbf{Q}, \mathbf{M}, \boldsymbol{\theta}) = -\frac{N}{2}\ln 2\pi - \frac{1}{2}\ln|\boldsymbol{\Omega}| + \ln||\mathbf{A}|| + \ln||\mathbf{B}|| - \frac{1}{2}\boldsymbol{\eta}'\boldsymbol{\eta} \quad (2)$$

in which the sum of squares term is

$$\boldsymbol{\eta}'\boldsymbol{\eta} = \boldsymbol{\varepsilon}'\boldsymbol{\Omega}^{-1}\boldsymbol{\varepsilon},$$
$$\text{where } \boldsymbol{\varepsilon} = \mathbf{B}\left(\mathbf{AY} - \mathbf{X}^*\boldsymbol{\beta}^*_0\right) = \mathbf{BU}.$$

It follows that for given $(\tilde{\lambda}, \tilde{\rho}, \tilde{\boldsymbol{\alpha}}')$ the ML estimator of $\boldsymbol{\beta}^*$ when it exists, is given by GLS as

$$\tilde{\boldsymbol{\beta}}^* = \left(\mathbf{X}^{*\prime}\tilde{\mathbf{B}}'\tilde{\boldsymbol{\Omega}}^{-1}\tilde{\mathbf{B}}\mathbf{X}^*\right)^{-1}\mathbf{X}^{*\prime}\tilde{\mathbf{B}}'\tilde{\boldsymbol{\Omega}}^{-1}\tilde{\mathbf{B}}\tilde{\mathbf{A}}\mathbf{Y}. \quad (3)$$

In the homoskedastic model, we have $\boldsymbol{\Omega} = \sigma^2\mathbf{I}$, as a result of which the matrix $\tilde{\boldsymbol{\Omega}}$ drops out of Eq. (3). Consequently, the variance parameter σ^2 can be solved from its first-order maximizing condition and its solution substituted in the log-likelihood function. In the heteroskedastic case, the first-order maximizing conditions do not give a closed form solution for $\tilde{\boldsymbol{\alpha}}$ in terms of the residual vector associated with Eq. (3), $\tilde{\boldsymbol{\varepsilon}}(\tilde{\lambda}, \tilde{\boldsymbol{\alpha}}, \tilde{\rho})$. Nevertheless, concentration with respect to $\boldsymbol{\beta}^*$ remains helpful both computationally and analytically. The concentrated log-likelihood function of $(\rho, \lambda, \boldsymbol{\alpha})$ is

$$\ln L(\rho, \lambda, \boldsymbol{\alpha}) = -\frac{N}{2}\ln 2\pi - \frac{1}{2}\ln|\boldsymbol{\Omega}| + \ln||\mathbf{A}|| + \ln||\mathbf{B}|| - \frac{1}{2}\tilde{\boldsymbol{\varepsilon}}'\boldsymbol{\Omega}^{-1}\tilde{\boldsymbol{\varepsilon}}. \quad (4)$$

Lee et al. (2010) make the following assumptions to prove consistency of the (Q)ML estimator of the parameters in this model. Each group, r, is of fixed size, n_r, and upper bounded. This implies that the sample can only grow without limit by the addition of more groups, that is, as $\bar{r} \to \infty$. In addition, these groups should be of different sizes, a condition that is also required for consistent estimation of $\boldsymbol{\alpha}$. It is possible, though laborious, to show directly via the rank of the relevant sub-matrix of the information matrix $\mathcal{I}(\boldsymbol{\theta})$ that in the case $\bar{r} = 2$, $\boldsymbol{\alpha}$ is identified provided $n_1 \neq n_2$. The matrix $\mathbf{X}^{*\prime}\mathbf{B}'\boldsymbol{\Omega}^{-1}\mathbf{B}\mathbf{X}^*$ has full rank, and $\lim_{\bar{r} \to \infty} \{\frac{1}{\bar{r}}\mathbf{X}^{*\prime}\mathbf{B}'\boldsymbol{\Omega}^{-1}\mathbf{B}\mathbf{X}^*\}$ exists and is non-singular. These conditions require boundedness of the row and column sums of the weight matrices $\mathbf{W}_r$ and of the inverses $\mathbf{A}^{-1}$ and $\mathbf{B}^{-1}$, each of which is automatically satisfied by the normalised weights assumed above. Lee (2007) derives additional conditions that need to be satisfied in case the spatial weights matrix is not row-normalised. The rank condition for identification of $\boldsymbol{\beta}^*$ also implies that the columns of $\mathbf{X}$ and $\mathbf{QX}$ must not be collinear if both are to have non-zero coefficients; by considering the case, $\bar{r} = 2$, and assuming $n_1 \neq n_2$ it can be shown that any such covariates must vary over the members of at least one of the groups. However, the rank and existence conditions just stated cover such cases.

Further, Lee et al. (2010) deal with the need to bound linear and quadratic forms involving the exogenous regressors by treating these as fixed constants, remarking that this is just a matter of convenience (Lee et al., 2010, note 16) and would be easily generalised to include stochastic regressors; hence we just repeat this assumption here.

Finally, they assume the shocks are *i.i.d.* with zero mean, constant variance, and that some absolute moment higher than the 4th exists. This last can be modified to suit the heteroskedastic case, perhaps most simply by assuming an underlying *i.i.d.* random variable with mean zero and unit variance and enough higher moments that is simply scaled up by the required non-stochastic function, that is by $(\alpha_{01} + \alpha_{02}n_r)^{1/2}$. If the underlying variable is Normally distributed, then the limiting covariance matrix of $\tilde{\boldsymbol{\theta}}$ coincides with the limit of the inverse of the information matrix; if not, then a correction matrix involving 3rd and 4th moments is required. We now focus below on ML estimation of the different models.

2.2. Case 2: Including Group-Specific Fixed Effects

If the group intercepts, δ_{r0}, vary across groups $r = 1, \ldots, \bar{r}$, the data must be transformed to avoid the growth in the number of parameters with sample size, the so-called incidental parameter problem. Lee et al. (2010) solve this problem by introducing an orthonormal transformation, which they label by the matrix $\mathbf{F}$. However, by closer inspection of $\mathbf{F}$, we show below that an acute problem of multicollinearity is likely to be induced by its use.

Because of the very simple form of the group interaction matrices in the present case, the GFE could be also eliminated by deviation from the group means as in a standard panel data model. However, as this would induce dependence in the transformed disturbances, Lee et al. (2010) use the alternative $\mathbf{F}$ transformation. This transformation decreases the number of observations by one for each group r. Let $\mathbf{J}_{n_r}$ denote the deviation from group mean operator for group r, that is $\mathbf{J}_{n_r} = [\mathbf{I}_{n_r} - n_r^{-1}\mathbf{1}_{n_r}\mathbf{1}'_{n_r}]$, and introduce the orthonormal decomposition $(\mathbf{F}_{n_r}, \mathbf{1}_{n_r}/\sqrt{n_r})$, such that $\mathbf{J}_{n_r} = \mathbf{F}_{n_r}\mathbf{F}'_{n_r}$, $\mathbf{F}'_{n_r}\mathbf{F}_{n_r} = \mathbf{I}_{n_r-1}$ and $\mathbf{F}'_{n_r}\mathbf{1}_{n_r} = \mathbf{0}_{n_r-1}$. An explicit solution for the $n_r \times (n_r - 1)$ matrix $\mathbf{F}_{n_r}$ is easily seen to be

$$\mathbf{F}_{n_r} = \begin{bmatrix} 0 & 0 & \cdots & 0 & -\sqrt{\dfrac{n_r-1}{n_r}} \\ \vdots & \vdots & & -\sqrt{\dfrac{n_r-2}{n_r-1}} & \sqrt{\dfrac{1}{n_r(n_r-1)}} \\ \vdots & 0 & & \sqrt{\dfrac{1}{(n_r-1)(n_r-2)}} & \vdots \\ 0 & -\sqrt{\dfrac{2}{3}} & & \vdots & \vdots \\ -\sqrt{\dfrac{1}{2}} & \sqrt{\dfrac{1}{6}} & & \vdots & \vdots \\ \sqrt{\dfrac{1}{2}} & \sqrt{\dfrac{1}{6}} & \cdots & \sqrt{\dfrac{1}{(n_r-1)(n_r-2)}} & \sqrt{\dfrac{1}{n_r(n_r-1)}} \end{bmatrix}. \tag{5}$$

To exploit this transformation, observe that because $\mathbf{F}'_{n_r}\mathbf{1}_{n_r} = \mathbf{0}$ it follows that $\mathbf{F}'_{n_r}\mathbf{B}_r = \left(1 + \frac{\lambda_0}{n_r-1}\right)\mathbf{F}'_{n_r}$ and similarly $\mathbf{F}'_{n_r}\mathbf{A}_r = \left(1 + \frac{\rho_0}{n_r-1}\right)\mathbf{F}'_{n_r}$ so that the relation

$$\boldsymbol{\varepsilon}_r = \mathbf{B}_r\left(\mathbf{A}_r\mathbf{Y}_r - \mathbf{X}_r^*\boldsymbol{\beta}_0^*\right) \tag{6}$$

transforms to

$$\begin{aligned}\mathbf{F}'_{n_r}\boldsymbol{\varepsilon}_r &= \mathbf{F}'_{n_r}\mathbf{B}_r\left(\mathbf{A}_r\mathbf{Y}_r - \mathbf{X}^*_r\boldsymbol{\beta}^*_0\right)\\ &= \left(1+\tfrac{\lambda_0}{n_r-1}\right)\mathbf{F}'_{n_r}\left(\mathbf{A}_r\mathbf{Y}_r - \mathbf{X}^*_r\boldsymbol{\beta}^*_0\right)\\ &= \left(1+\frac{\lambda_0}{n_r-1}\right)\left(1+\frac{\rho_0}{n_r-1}\right)\mathbf{F}'_{n_r}\mathbf{Y}_r - \left(1+\frac{\lambda_0}{n_r-1}\right)\mathbf{F}'_{n_r}\mathbf{X}^*_r\boldsymbol{\beta}^*_0. \end{aligned} \tag{7}$$

Defining the transformed objects, $\mathbf{Y}^*_r = \mathbf{F}'_{n_r}\mathbf{Y}_r$, $\mathbf{X}^{**}_r = \mathbf{F}'_{n_r}\mathbf{X}^*_r$, together with $\boldsymbol{\beta}^{**}_0$ being $\boldsymbol{\beta}^*_0$ with the fixed effect removed, then we obtain the transformed structure, without GFE

$$\left(1+\frac{\lambda_0}{n_r-1}\right)\left(1+\frac{\rho_0}{n_r-1}\right)\mathbf{Y}^*_r - \left(1+\frac{\lambda_0}{n_r-1}\right)\mathbf{X}^{**}_r\boldsymbol{\beta}^{**}_0 = \boldsymbol{\varepsilon}^*_r \text{ say.} \tag{8}$$

Here, the rth block is of dimension $n_r - 1$, and $E\{\boldsymbol{\varepsilon}^*_r\boldsymbol{\varepsilon}^{*'}_r\} = \mathbf{I}_{n_r-1}(\alpha_{01} + \alpha_{02}n_r)$. Note that the decrease in the number of observations by one in each group is merely a reduction in the number of degrees of freedom, since the information of all n_r observations in each group is still implied in the data. Further note the simplicity of Eq. (8). Interestingly, Lee et al. (2010) do not write the transformed model in this simple form, introducing transformed versions of **A**, **B** and **W** instead (see their equations 3.3 and 3.4). With suitable redefinitions we may thus write the model for the entire transformed sample as

$$\mathbf{B}^*\left[\mathbf{A}^*\mathbf{Y}^* - \mathbf{X}^{**}\boldsymbol{\beta}^{**}_0\right] = \boldsymbol{\varepsilon}^* \tag{9}$$

in which $\mathbf{B}^*$ and $\mathbf{A}^*$ are defined in terms of a transformed weight matrix, $\mathbf{W}^*$ say.

However, since

$$\mathbf{A}^* = \left(\mathbf{I} - \rho_0\mathbf{W}^*\right), \tag{10}$$

$\mathbf{W}^*$ matches Eq. (8) only if it has diagonal blocks of the form

$$\mathbf{W}^*_r = \frac{-1}{n_r-1}\mathbf{I}_{n_r-1} \tag{11}$$

and zeros everywhere else, giving an object that is much easier to interpret. From Eq. (11) it immediately follows that $Tr\{\mathbf{W}_r^*\} = -1$ and that all its eigenvalues are $\frac{-1}{n_r-1}$. This implies that the eigenvalues of $\mathbf{W}^*$ are $\bar{r}$ sets of $\frac{-1}{n_r-1}$ each with multiplicity $(n_r - 1)$. Furthermore, except for the eigenvalues of $\mathbf{W}$ that are identical to those of $\mathbf{W}^*$, it follows that $\mathbf{W}$ has $\bar{r}$ additional eigenvalues of 1, one for each group r.

Using the results of the **F**-transformation, we now demonstrate that in our setting a model with GFE and spatially lagged exogenous variables, **WX**, encounters near multicollinearity. Consider the first expression in Eq. (1)

$$\mathbf{Y}_r = \rho_0 \mathbf{W}_r \mathbf{Y}_r + \mathbf{1}_{n_r}\delta_{r0} + \mathbf{X}_r\boldsymbol{\beta}_0 + \mathbf{W}_r\mathbf{X}_r\gamma_0 + \mathbf{U}_r \quad \text{with}$$
$$\mathbf{W}_r = \frac{1}{n_r - 1}\left(\mathbf{1}_{n_r}\mathbf{1}'_{n_r} - \mathbf{I}_{n_r}\right).$$

In this model the inclusion of all the group intercept terms would give the same coefficients on everything else as we obtain by first subtracting all the group means from $\mathbf{Y}_r$, $\mathbf{X}_r$ and $\mathbf{WX}_r$ by multiplication by $\mathbf{J}_{n_r} = [\mathbf{I}_{n_r} - n_r^{-1}\mathbf{1}_{n_r}\mathbf{1}'_{n_r}]$. Consequently, after transformation by group de-meaning we obtain a set of columns each with blocks of entries of the form $\left(\mathbf{I}_{n_r} - \frac{1}{n_r}\mathbf{1}_{n_r}\mathbf{1}'_{n_r}\right)\mathbf{X}_r$ and similarly a second set with blocks of the form $\left(\mathbf{I}_{n_r} - \frac{1}{n_r}\mathbf{1}_{n_r}\mathbf{1}'_{n_r}\right)\mathbf{W}_r\mathbf{X}_r$. However, since

$$\begin{aligned}\left(\mathbf{I}_{n_r} - \frac{1}{n_r}\mathbf{1}_{n_r}\mathbf{1}'_{n_r}\right)\mathbf{W}_r &= \left(\mathbf{I}_{n_r} - \frac{1}{n_r}\mathbf{1}_{n_r}\mathbf{1}'_{n_r}\right)\frac{1}{n_r - 1}\left(\mathbf{1}_{n_r}\mathbf{1}'_{n_r} - \mathbf{I}_{n_r}\right) \\ &= \frac{-1}{n_r - 1}\left(\mathbf{I}_{n_r} - \frac{1}{n_r}\mathbf{1}_{n_r}\mathbf{1}'_{n_r}\right) + \frac{1}{n_r - 1}\left(\mathbf{I}_{n_r} - \frac{1}{n_r}\mathbf{1}_{n_r}\mathbf{1}'_{n_r}\right)\mathbf{1}_{n_r}\mathbf{1}'_{n_r} \\ &= \frac{-1}{n_r - 1}\left(\mathbf{I}_{n_r} - \frac{1}{n_r}\mathbf{1}_{n_r}\mathbf{1}'_{n_r}\right)\end{aligned} \tag{12}$$

the second set of transformed variables obtained by transforming $\mathbf{W}_r\mathbf{X}_r$ are only different from the first set obtained by transforming $\mathbf{X}_r$ by virtue of the leading $\frac{-1}{n_r-1}$ terms This implies that they would be perfectly collinear if all the groups were the same size. However, also if group sizes differ, they are most likely to be near collinear. In Section 5 we show that the degree of multicollinearity in our empirical analysis is indeed rather high; we find values up to 0.99. In other words, while the parameters of the GFE-GNS model might be formally identified under the conditions summarised above, the case of near multicollinearity will create statistical problems in that the parameter estimates are imprecise.

2.3. Direct and Indirect Effects in the Case without GFE

In our application $\mathbf{Q}_r = \mathbf{W}_r$, thus the reduced form of the model (1) with $\bar{r}$ groups is

$$\mathbf{Y} = \left(\mathbf{I}_N - \rho_0\mathbf{W}\right)^{-1}\left\{\mathbf{1}_N\delta_0 + \mathbf{X}\boldsymbol{\beta}_0 + \mathbf{W}\mathbf{X}\boldsymbol{\gamma}_0 + \mathbf{U}\right\}.$$

We obtain the direct and indirect (spillover) effects from the above equation building on the assumption that $\mathbf{X}$ is independent of $\mathbf{U}$ and therefore causally predetermined with respect to $\mathbf{Y}$. Following LeSage and Pace (2009), the direct effect is calculated as the average diagonal element of the matrix $\left(I_N - \rho_0\mathbf{W}\right)^{-1}\{\mathbf{I}_N\boldsymbol{\beta}_0 + \mathbf{W}\boldsymbol{\gamma}_0\}$, and the indirect effect as the average row or column sum of the off-diagonal elements of that matrix.

Because of the group structure, the matrix $\left(\mathbf{I}_N - \rho_0\mathbf{W}\right)^{-1}$ is block-diagonal, composed of $\bar{r}$ blocks, the rth having dimension n_r, the number of individuals in the rth group. In addition, the inverse of each block is known to be

$$\left(\mathbf{I}_{n_r} - \rho_0\mathbf{W}_r\right)^{-1} = \left(\frac{n_r - 1}{n_r - 1 + \rho_0}\right)\left[\mathbf{I}_{n_r} + \left(\frac{\rho_0}{(n_r - 1)(1 - \rho_0)}\right)\mathbf{1}_{n_r}\mathbf{1}_{n_r}'\right]. \quad (13)$$

As a result, the direct and indirect effects are associated with each of the blocks (i.e. each group has potentially different effects). For group r, the direct effect has two components, being the sum of a typical diagonal element of $\left(\mathbf{I}_{n_r} - \rho_0\mathbf{W}_r\right)^{-1}$ scaled by $\boldsymbol{\beta}_0$ and a typical diagonal element of $\left(\mathbf{I}_{n_r} - \rho_0\mathbf{W}_r\right)^{-1}\mathbf{W}_r$ scaled by $\boldsymbol{\gamma}_0$. Similarly, the indirect effects have two components, one obtained by summing the off-diagonal entries of a typical column of $\left(\mathbf{I}_{n_r} - \rho_0\mathbf{W}_r\right)^{-1}$ scaled by $\boldsymbol{\beta}_0$ and the other by summing the off-diagonal entries of a typical column of $(\mathbf{I}_{n_r} - \rho_0 \mathbf{W}_r)^{-1}\mathbf{W}_r$ scaled by γ_0.

By inspection a typical diagonal entry of $(\mathbf{I}_{n_r} - \rho_0 \mathbf{W}_r)^{-1}$ is

$$\left(\frac{n_r - 1}{n_r - 1 + \rho_0}\right)\left[1 + \frac{\rho_0}{(n_r - 1)(1 - \rho_0)}\right] = \frac{n_r - 1 - \rho_0(n_r - 2)}{(n_r - 1 + \rho_0)(1 - \rho_0)} \equiv \mathrm{DE}_{\beta_0}(r) \tag{14}$$

denoting the direct effect associated with $\boldsymbol{\beta}_0$ in group r. Similarly, the typical off-diagonal entry, summed over a column, is

$$\left(\frac{n_r - 1}{n_r - 1 + \rho_0}\right)\frac{\rho_0(n_r - 1)}{(n_r - 1)(1 - \rho_0)} = \frac{(n_r - 1)\rho_0}{(n_r - 1 + \rho_0)(1 - \rho_0)} \equiv \mathrm{IE}_{\beta_0}(r). \tag{15}$$

representing the indirect effect associated with $\boldsymbol{\beta}_0$.

By writing $\boldsymbol{\Gamma}_r = \mathbf{1}_{n_r}\mathbf{1}'_{n_r}$, we have $\mathbf{W}_r = (n_r - 1)^{-1}(\boldsymbol{\Gamma}_r - \mathbf{I}_{n_r})$ and $\boldsymbol{\Gamma}_r^2 = n_r\boldsymbol{\Gamma}_r$, as a result of which

$$\begin{aligned}
[\mathbf{I}_{n_r} - \rho_0 \mathbf{W}_r]^{-1}\mathbf{W}_r &= \left(\frac{n_r - 1}{n_r - 1 + \rho_0}\right)\left[\mathbf{I}_{n_r} + \left(\frac{\rho_0}{(n_r - 1)(1 - \rho_0)}\right)\boldsymbol{\Gamma}_r\right]\mathbf{W}_r \\
&= \left(\frac{1}{n_r - 1 + \rho_0}\right)\left[\mathbf{I}_{n_r} + \left(\frac{\rho_0}{(n_r - 1)(1 - \rho_0)}\right)\boldsymbol{\Gamma}_r\right](\boldsymbol{\Gamma}_r - \mathbf{I}_{n_r}) \\
&= \left(\frac{1}{n_r - 1 + \rho_0}\right)\left[(1 - \rho_0)^{-1}\boldsymbol{\Gamma}_r - \mathbf{I}_{n_r}\right].
\end{aligned} \tag{16}$$

By inspection, the typical diagonal element of this matrix takes the form

$$\left(\frac{1}{n_r - 1 + \rho_0}\right)\left[(1 - \rho_0)^{-1} - 1\right] = \frac{\rho_0}{(n_r - 1 + \rho_0)(1 - \rho_0)} \equiv \mathrm{DE}_{\gamma_0}(r), \tag{17}$$

which is the direct effect associated with γ_0. Similarly, the off-diagonal element, summed over a column

$$\left(\frac{1}{n_r - 1 + \rho_0}\right)(1 - \rho_0)^{-1}(n_r - 1) = \frac{n_r - 1}{(n_r - 1 + \rho_0)(1 - \rho_0)} \equiv \mathrm{IE}_{\gamma_0}(r) \quad (18)$$

gives the indirect effect associated with γ_0. To obtain the direct and indirect effects over the whole sample, one should calculate the average over the $\bar{r}$-different groups.

3. ESTIMATION ROUTINES

To maximise the likelihood function (2) of the different general nesting models numerically, we developed routines building on previous work of LeSage (1999). LeSage provides a Matlab routine called "SAC" at his web site[2] that can be used to maximise the log-likelihood function of the homoskedastic general nesting model. Even if this routine was originally developed for estimating a SAC model, that is a model with a spatially lagged-dependent variable and a spatially autocorrelated error term, by computing the spatially lagged exogenous variables **WX** in advance and by specifying the argument **X** of this routine as [**X WX**], it is also possible to obtain parameter estimates of the full model with homoskedastic errors. Since individual groups within our group interaction matrix **W** are relatively small and each group has its own set of characteristic roots, we also replaced the approximate calculation of $\log|\mathbf{I} - \rho_0 \mathbf{W}| + \log|\mathbf{I} - \lambda_0 \mathbf{W}|$ (see LeSage & Pace, 2009, Ch. 4) by the exact calculation $\sum_i \log(1 - \rho_0 \omega_i) + \sum_i \log(1 - \lambda_0 \omega_i)$, where ω_i $(i = 1, \ldots, n)$ denote the characteristic roots of the matrix **W** given below (11). Consequently, the calculation of the log determinants of the matrices **A** and **B** in the (concentrated) log-likelihood functions (2) and (4) produces more accurate results.[3] Finally, we also adapted this routine for heteroskedastic model specifications and for models with GFE.

Since the coefficient vector $\boldsymbol{\beta}_0^*$ can be solved from the first-order conditions (Anselin, 1988, equations 6.21–6.24), the log-likelihood function only needs to be maximised for the parameters ρ_0, λ_0 and $\boldsymbol{\alpha}_0$. An incidental advantage of the concentrated likelihood is reduced computation time. The standard errors and t-values of the parameter estimates are calculated from the asymptotic variance-covariance matrix following Anselin (1988, equations 6.25–6.34). The standard errors and t-values of the direct and indirect effects estimates are more difficult to determine, even though the analytical expressions of the direct and indirect effects are known (see Eqs. (14)–(18)). They depend on $\boldsymbol{\beta}_0$, $\boldsymbol{\gamma}_0$ and ρ_0 in a rather complicated way. To draw inferences regarding the statistical significance of the direct and indirect effects, we follow the suggestion of LeSage and Pace (2009, p. 39) and simulate the distribution of the direct and indirect effects using the variance-covariance matrix implied by the maximum likelihood estimates. If the full parameter vector $\boldsymbol{\theta}$ is drawn D times from $N(\hat{\boldsymbol{\theta}}, \text{AsyVar}(\hat{\boldsymbol{\theta}}))$, the standard deviation of the estimated (in)direct effects is approximated by the standard deviation of the mean value of Eqs. (14)–(18) over these D draws. We test the significance of our original ML (in)direct effects estimates using the corresponding simulated standard deviation.

4. EMPIRICAL ILLUSTRATION

For our empirical analysis, we draw on a database that covers all researchers specializing in economics, business and finance employed at universities in German speaking countries.[4] For our purposes, we extracted from this database all scientists beyond PhD level along with their journal publications released over the 1999–2008 period. To allow time for the youngest scholars' publications to appear, we included only those who graduated earlier than 2007. We excluded emeritus professors and academic staff involved only in administrative or teaching duties. Using these criteria, our data set contains 2,580 researchers employed by 83 universities covering nearly the whole "space" of university research in economics, finance and business across the German speaking region.[5]

For each individual i in the data set, we measure the dependent variable, research productivity, as the researcher's average annual research productivity:

$$\text{Prod}_i = \frac{1}{y_i} \sum_{p_i=1}^{P_i} \frac{w_{p_i}}{a_{p_i}}. \tag{19}$$

This is the quality weighted sum of all journal articles of i, (P_i), published over the decade 1999–2008. Each article is divided by the corresponding number of coauthors a_{p_i}. The y_i is either the number of years since graduation or 10 if the graduation year goes back to more than 10 years. The weights w_{p_i} express the quality index of the journal in which the article was published.

For Eq. (19), we adopted the weighting scheme developed originally by the German business newspaper, Handelsblatt, which publishes individual and department rankings in economics and business administration across the German speaking countries. Handelsblatt uses distinct weighting schemes for economists and for researchers in finance and business administration. The scheme for economics is based on the so called CL-weights of EconLit journals by Combes and Linnemer (2003). Handelsblatt considers about 1,200 journals, which are divided into seven quality levels, ranging from 1 down to 0.05. The weighting scheme for finance and business administration includes only 761 journals and the journal quality is based on two sources: (i) the weighting scheme compiled by the German Academic Association for Business Administration,[6] and (ii) the SSCI[7] impact factor. The two informations are then combined to assign each journal into one of the above 7 quality levels (Krapf, 2011). Both schemes include international and German journals. Even though the weights of German journals tend to be small, they might be of some relevance for the career of German economists. Since our data set combines economists, finance and business researchers, our final individual productivity is a simple average of productivities (19) based on the two weighting schemes. To normalise for the skewed distribution of productivity – few researchers produce many articles and many publish few or none – our dependent variable is then $\log(\text{Prod}_i + 1)$.

Our study uses the GNS model to estimate group effects. In this study, groups are represented by universities. Each researcher is considered to be a member of the university he or she was affiliated to at the end of 2009. Each individual's entire publication stock (1999–2008) is assigned via Eq. (19) to that particular university, even if the affiliation might have changed during that period. Combes and Linnemer (2003) label this productivity measure a "stock" measure and defend its use from the perspective of human capital currently embedded in a given university. The use of the stock measure also means that our GNS model reflects a steady-state equilibrium in distribution of human capital across groups.

The Lee et al. (2010) identification condition (cf Section 2) that groups should be of different sizes is readily fulfilled by the data. The department sizes of the 83 universities range from 10 to 160 with mean 31 and standard deviation of 23.

4.1. Determinants of Research Productivity

Economic theory describes the reward system in science as a collegiate reputation-based system and as such it functions well in satisfying efficiency in increasing the stock of reliable knowledge (Dasgupta & David, 1994).

Since reputation in science is strongly priority based, researchers race to be the first in publishing advances within their research fields. The best placed of this publication race are rewarded with top academic positions. The top positions allow these individuals to continue performing better than individuals employed at lower ranked institutions. The research output is thus marked by the advantage acquired in the early stage of somebody's career which cumulates over the life cycle. The concept of cumulative advantage is a basic feature of theoretical models of academic competition (e.g. Carayol, 2008). The monetary reward in science consists of two components: a fixed salary and a bonus based on individual contributions to science. The non-monetary reward consists of the reward from puzzle solving and from recognition. In addition, research productivity is fed by individual inputs stemming from human capital formation, including age, cohort, and gender effects. Other individual inputs are time, cognitive abilities, knowledge base, extent of collaboration, and access to resources (Stephan, 2010). The theories of human capital formation predict an inverse U-shape relationship between age and research productivity. Although gender has been found to affect research productivity, its impact seems to have decreased more recently (Xie & Shauman, 2003).

The empirical literature explains research productivity, either at the individual or at the aggregated level, building on the specificities of the scientific reward system and on individual and institutional characteristics. In line with the human capital theories, Levin and Stephan (1991) and Rauber and Ursprung (2008) found positive age and cohort effects, and Maske, Durden, and Gaynor (2003) significant gender differences. Collaboration also pays as demonstrated by a recent study of Bosquet and Combes (2013). Elhorst and Zigova (2014) showed that neighbouring economics departments compete in producing research output by identifying a robust negative spatial lag coefficient on average department productivity. Other studies found positive scale effects (e.g. Bonacorsi & Daraio, 2005) and positive spillover effects stemming from good university location (Kim, Morse, & Zingales, 2009).

In our empirical model, we include career age, gender, level of collaboration, and type of academic position as possible productivity determinants at the individual level. Career age is measured by the number of years since PhD graduation. As the impact of age may be non-linear, we include both log of career age and log of career age squared. Gender effects are captured by a female dummy, while dummies for post-doc and junior professors control for productivity differences relative to full professors. Collaboration activity is measured by the share of externally coauthored papers to all papers, where an external coauthor is somebody from outside the affiliated university. The institutional variables are department size and publishing "culture" of the department. Like career age, department size enters the model as log and log squared to allow for potential and non-linear scale effects. The share of department members who did not publish any articles in a journal with non-zero quality weight over the relevant decade, represents the publication "culture" of the department. Following other studies focusing on German speaking countries (Elhorst & Zigova, 2014; Fabel, Hein, & Hofmeister, 2008), we use country dummies for Swiss and Austrian departments to compare their productivity with their German counterpart.

Alternatively, we may hold out Swiss and Austrian departments and use these samples for post-fitting evaluation. However, to identify the model with heteroskedastic shocks, we require variation in department size. Since we have a relatively small number of universities (83) in the sample, taking a truly random sample of departments would risk weakening identification. Table 1 shows the size distribution of the departments in the sample. Another problem is that the size of departments will turn out to be both a significant determinant of research productivity and of the extent of heteroskedasticity. By holding out observations, these findings may get lost due to insufficient variation. We therefore propose to conduct the analysis with a pooled sample and suitable dummy variables to capture the sample split, followed by statistical tests on the significance of these dummies. The dummies for Swiss and Austrian departments will be used for this purpose.

Table 1. Size Distribution across the Universities.

Size	Frequency
10–19	22
20–29	32
30–39	12
40–49	4
50–59	6
60–99	5
100	1
160	1

New strands of empirical literature focus on measuring peer effects in academia using a natural experiment setting. Azoulay, Zivin, and Wang (2010) measure productivity losses of collaborators of star scientists after an unexpected death. They estimate an up to 8% decrease in research productivity of American life scientists. On the contrary, Waldinger (2011), finds no evidence of peer effects applying in historical 1925–1938 productivity data of German scientists, who were colleagues of expelled Jewish faculty. One of the explanations Waldinger suggests is that scientists were much more specialised in the past, hence a loss of a peer might not affect individual productivities. A recent study by Borjas and Doran (2014) finds productivity losses of Soviet mathematicians exposed to vast emigration in the 1990s of their colleagues to the United States or to western Europe. Whereas the emigration of average collaborators appeared to have no effect on the research output of a mathematician, the emigration of just 10% of high-quality coauthors implied roughly a 8% percent decline. Our study adds another piece to the so far rather mixed evidence on peer effects in academia using the GNS model applied to non-experimental data.

4.2. GNS and Modelling Research Productivity Interactions

The concept of cumulative advantage in science (Carayol, 2008) leads to weaker overall significance of models explaining research productivity, because observed individual and institutional variables cannot fully explain why research productivity among scientists is so skewed (Stephan, 2010). The terms **WY**, **WX** and/or **WU** in the GNS model, or in models nested within it, can add more explanatory power because they bear additional information on colleagues' average productivity, the determinants of their productivity and common unobserved characteristics. In our setting, **X** consists of variables that vary at the individual and at the university level. Since the group interaction matrix **W** is block diagonal and the institutional variables do not vary over the department members working at the same university, pre-multiplying the institutional variables with the group interaction matrix would lead to an identical set of variables. For this reason, we multiply **W** only with individual-level variables. The condition that the matrix $\mathbf{X}^{*\prime}\mathbf{B}'\boldsymbol{\Omega}^{-1}\mathbf{B}\mathbf{X}^{*}$ should have full rank will also not be satisfied if GFE are added, that is, one dummy for every group of researchers working at the same university. Due to perfect multicollinearity, such fixed effects would absorb the effects of the institutional variables. This means that institutional variables need to be fully removed from the regression equation if GFE are added.

Applying Elhorst's (2010) terminology to our setting, a significant endogenous effect (ρ_0) would mean that the productivity of an individual researcher depends on the productivity of department colleagues. Significant exogenous effects (γ_0) signal that somebody's productivity is influenced by observed characteristics of these colleagues, while correlated effects (λ_0) signal that individual productivity varies with unobserved characteristics common to all colleagues from one department. By estimating these parameters, we could conclude on the existence, type, and extent of these localised peer effects. But as Waldinger (2011) points out, sorting of individuals complicates the estimation of peer effects, as highly productive scientists often choose to co-locate. Sorting may therefore introduce a positive correlation of scientists' productivities within universities not caused by pure peer effects. Since the spatial parameters ρ_0, λ_0 and γ_0 may be contaminated by sorting, because individuals "settle" in equilibrium at the best achievable university given their observed output, we need to be careful in interpreting the interaction parameters. By considering direct and indirect (spillover) effects (Section 2.3), especially regarding the publishing culture of a department, and different model specifications nested within GNS, we will nonetheless be able to draw conclusions regarding the kind of peer effects that drive research productivity within departments, as well as whether sorting matters. The overall effect of the publishing culture potentially consists of a direct effect and a spillover effect. The direct effect of this variable to research productivity reflects sorting; staff members self-select into departments with peers of similar quality and departments appoint new staff of similar productivity. The spillover effect of this variable measures the extent to which individual productivity is affected by that of its peers, including the impact of newly appointed colleagues. Since models in which $\rho_0 \neq 0$ cover this spillover effect and models with $\rho_0 = 0$ do not (see Eq. (15)), and these models can be tested against each other, we can draw conclusions regarding the existence of this peer effect in addition to sorting.

5. ESTIMATION RESULTS

Table 2 reports our estimation results. We consider eight different model specifications, from the simplest OLS to the most complex GNS specification. The GNS model includes all three types of interaction effects, while the other models nested within it lack one or more of these effects which explains the empty entries in Table 2. Fig. 1 shows the restrictions (next to the arrows) that need to be imposed on the parameters of the GNS model to obtain these simpler models. This figure is taken from Halleck Vega and Elhorst (2015) and adjusted to the mathematical notation used in this paper. In addition, the SLX and the SEM models have been switched.

The weight matrix is specified as a block-diagonal matrix given by $\mathbf{W}_r = \frac{1}{n_r - 1}\left[\mathbf{1}_{n_r}\mathbf{1}'_{n_r} - \mathbf{I}_{n_r}\right]$, where n_r is the number of researchers in the rth department ($r = 1, \ldots, 83$). In other words, we are using a row-normalised spatial weights matrix whose elements have a value of one if researchers are in the same department, and zero otherwise.

5.1. *Model with GFE*

We first focus on GFE. According to Lee et al. (2010), the GFE-GNS model can be estimated using two log-likelihood functions defined in equations (4.1) or (4.2) of their paper. The first is based on transformed variables and the transformed spatial weights matrix $\mathbf{W}^*$. Since all eigenvalues of the transformed $\mathbf{W}^*$ are $\frac{-1}{n_r - 1}$ for $r = 1, \ldots, \bar{r}$ (see Section 2.2), the upper bound of the interval on which the SAR or spatial autocorrelation coefficients are defined is $1/\left(\frac{-1}{n_{\max} - 1}\right)$, where $n_{\max} = \max(n_r) = 160$ is the size of the largest group in the sample (see Table 1). Since this upper bound is clearly greater than one, $1/|-1/(160-1)|$, we obtained parameter estimates exceeding 1 for the SAR, SEM, SDM and SDEM model specifications; the largest estimate appeared to be 9.127.

The second log-likelihood is based on the original observations, adjusted for the reduction in the number of degrees of freedom. This approach keeps the upper bound of the interval on which the SAR or spatial autocorrelation coefficients are defined at 1. Unfortunately, this helped only partly, because in this case we obtained unrealistic parameter estimates close to 1. For example, for the GNS model, we estimated $\rho_0 = 0.910$ with t-value 0.59 and $\lambda_0 = 0.955$ with t-value 1.25. The explanation for these unrealistic findings is the presence of near multicollinearity between the $\mathbf{X}$ variables and their spatially lagged values, $\mathbf{WX}$, caused by the inclusion of GFE. To further investigate this, we calculated the correlation coefficient for the six individual-specific variables (recall that the institutional variables are absorbed by the GFE), which ranged from 0.9866 for the square of the

Table 2. Explaining Log Research Productivity using Different Model Specifications.

Determinants	OLS	SAR	SEM	SLX	SDM	SDEM	SAC	GNS
intercept	0.006	0.011	−0.005	0.344*	0.236	0.326	−0.007	0.262
	(0.08)	*(0.16)*	*(−0.05)*	*(1.81)*	*(1.24)*	*(1.16)*	*(0.07)*	*(0.64)*
Austria	0.004	0.009	0.004	−0.003	−0.002	−0.002	0.004	−0.002
	(0.50)	*(1.28)*	*(0.40)*	*(−0.25)*	*(−0.16)*	*(−0.13)*	*(0.32)*	*(−0.13)*
Switzerland	0.018**	0.013*	0.018*	0.014*	0.010	0.015	0.018	0.011
	(2.43)	*(1.74)*	*(1.68)*	*(1.75)*	*(1.25)*	*(1.34)*	*(1.45)*	*(0.64)*
log size	0.087**	0.063*	0.089*	0.060*	0.043	0.063	0.092	0.049
	(2.70)	*(1.96)*	*(1.90)*	*(1.79)*	*(1.28)*	*(1.37)*	*(1.61)*	*(0.64)*
$\log^2$ size	−0.009**	−0.006	−0.009	−0.006	−0.005	−0.007	−0.009	−0.005
	(−1.99)	*(−1.43)*	*(−1.44)*	*(−1.40)*	*(−1.01)*	*(−1.10)*	*(−1.26)*	*(−0.60)*
no top publishers	−0.183**	−0.110*	−0.184**	−0.183**	−0.126**	−0.178**	−0.188*	−0.140
	(−11.26)	*(−5.58)*	*(−7.11)*	*(−8.61)*	*(−5.43)*	*(−5.60)*	*(−2.29)*	*(−0.73)*
log career age	0.001	0.005	0.008	0.004	0.007	0.004	0.008	0.006
	(0.03)	*(0.21)*	*(0.33)*	*(0.15)*	*(0.27)*	*(0.15)*	*(0.34)*	*(0.22)*
$\log^2$ career age	−0.010*	−0.011*	−0.011**	−0.010*	0.011**	−0.010*	0.011**	−0.011*
	(−2.06)	*(−2.26)*	*(−2.39)*	*(−2.19)*	*(−2.34)*	*(−2.17)*	*(−2.42)*	*(−2.08)*
post-doc	0.075**	0.077**	0.078**	0.077**	0.078**	0.077**	0.079**	0.078**
	(−12.66)	*(−13.02)*	*(−13.17)*	*(−13.03)*	*(−13.28)*	*(−12.98)*	*(−13.26)*	*(−11.56)*
junior professor	0.051**	0.052**	0.053**	0.053**	0.054**	0.053**	0.053**	0.054**
	(−7.57)	*(−7.86)*	*(−8.06)*	*(−7.97)*	*(−8.10)*	*(−8.09)*	*(−7.98)*	*(−7.87)*
female	0.027**	0.027**	0.027**	0.027**	0.027**	0.027**	0.027**	0.027**
	(−5.04)	*(−5.08)*	*(−5.16)*	*(−5.06)*	*(−5.11)*	*(−5.09)*	*(−5.14)*	*(−5.09)*
collaboration	0.045**	0.044**	0.043**	0.043**	0.043**	0.043**	0.043**	0.043**
	(8.38)	*(8.30)*	*(8.02)*	*(8.03)*	*(8.04)*	*(7.95)*	*(8.14)*	*(7.84)*

$W \cdot Y$		0.323**			0.303**		−0.017	0.226
		(6.55)			*(5.65)*		*(−0.05)*	*(0.22)*
$W \cdot$log career age				−0.278*	−0.199	−0.276		−0.222
				(−2.05)	*(−1.46)*	*(−1.37)*		*(−0.70)*
$W \cdot \log^2$ career age				0.057*	0.044*	0.057		0.048
				(2.25)	*(1.73)*	*(1.52)*		*(0.86)*
$W \cdot$ post-doc				0.092**	0.087**	0.086*		0.087**
				(3.37)	*(3.20)*	*(2.13)*		*(2.79)*
$W \cdot$ junior prof.				0.037	0.042	0.036		0.040
				(1.14)	*(1.30)*	*(0.74)*		*(0.96)*
$W \cdot$ female				0.008	0.014	0.009		0.013
				(0.28)	*(0.51)*	*(0.22)*		*(0.36)*
$W \cdot$ collaboration				0.026	0.008	0.035		0.015
				(0.96)	*(0.30)*	*(0.88)*		*(0.18)*
$W \cdot U$			0.350**			0.300**	0.363	0.102
			(6.99)			*(5.57)*	*(1.63)*	*(0.08)*
intercept (*Het.*)	0.650**	0.646**	0.644**	0.646**	0.641**	0.640**	0.656**	0.661**
	(14.65)	*(14.81)*	*(14.95)*	*(14.71)*	*(14.79)*	*(14.90)*	*(14.71)*	*(11.67)*
size (*Het.*)/100	0.698**	0.666**	0.663**	0.684**	0.664**	0.666**	0.634**	0.620**
	(6.86)	*(6.70)*	*(9.19)*	*(6.81)*	*(6.72)*	*(9.26)*	*(6.47)*	*(8.41)*
Log Lik. (*Het.*)	2340.8	2357.4	2361.3	2353.7	2367.3	2367.0	2361.4	2367.3
Log Lik. (*Hom.*)	2331.9	2349.0	2352.8	2345.1	2358.8	2358.5	2352.8	2359.0
p-val LR-test Het/Hom	0.0001	0.0002	0.0002	0.0002	0.0002	0.0002	0.0002	0.0002

t-values in parentheses.
**significant at 5%.
*significant at 10%.

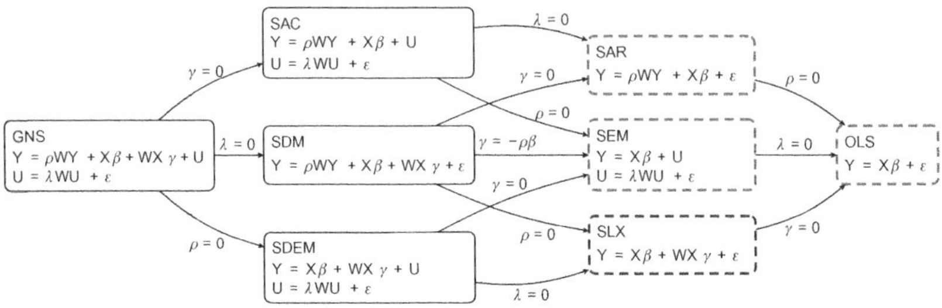

Fig. 1. The Relationships between Different Spatial Dependence Models for Cross-sectional Data. Subscripts 0 Are Left aside for Simplicity. *Source*: Adapted from Halleck Vega and Elhorst (2015).

career age variable up to 0.9961 for the dummy of junior professors. We mathematically predicted these high correlation coefficients in Eq. (12). It should be stressed that this result hinges strongly on the group interaction matrix. If a different spatial weights matrix would be adopted, these GFE may retrieve their significance again.

One may also leave the interaction effects aside and just control for the GFE instead. The coefficient estimates of this model are comparable to those of the OLS model reported in the first column of Table 2: 0.002 for log career age, −0.013 for $\log^2$ career age, −0.083 for post-docs, −0.055 for junior professors, −0.028 for females, and 0.044 for collaboration. We will see shortly that these coefficient estimates are close to the direct effects derived from a broad range of spatial econometric models. One disadvantage of this model however is that it cannot provide information about potential spillover effects. Another drawback is that it does not provide information about the institutional variables, since they are absorbed by the GFE.

In view of these outcomes, we endorse and follow Corrado and Fingleton's (2012) recommendation that it is better to retain the institutional variables than to introduce dummy variables that combine their effects with those of any omitted variables. Therefore, Table 2 contains estimates of the eight models without group fixed effects.

5.2. Heteroskedasticity and Model Reduction

The second round of testing concerns heteroskedasticity and model reduction. In interpreting the evidence in Table 2, we consider the various LRs that are constructed as approximately Chi-square distributed with the usual degrees of freedom under the relevant null hypothesis.[8] We specified group heteroskedasticity as $\sigma_r^2 = \alpha_1 + \alpha_2 n_r$, where n_r is the size of the economics department measured by the number of people. The test for reduction to homoskedasticity thus means testing the hypothesis that $\alpha_2 = 0$, and therefore has one degree of freedom. The most general model, the HGNS, reduces to the GNS, under homoskedasticity. The likelihood ratio (LR) test statistic is equal to 2(2367.3 − 2359.0) = 16.6 which is highly significant if treated as χ_1^2 under the null. This keeps the HGNS as the maintained model.

Next, we test for the HGNS model reductions to (i) the heteroskedastic SDM ($\lambda_0 = 0$) (1 d.f.) for which LR = 2(2367.3 − 2367.3) = 0 to within rounding error, or to (ii) the heteroskedastic SDEM ($\rho_0 = 0$) (1 d.f.) for which LR = 2(2367.3 − 2367.0) = 0.6, or to (iii) the heteroskedastic SAC ($\gamma_0 = \mathbf{0}$) (6 d.f.) for which LR = 2(2367.3 − 2361.4) = 11.8. Neither model reduction (i) or (ii) is rejected, while (iii) is rejected at 10% significance level.

Further simplification of the heteroskedastic SDM to the homoskedastic SDM is rejected by the likelihood ratio of LR = 2(2367.3 − 2358.8) = 17.0 (1 d.f.). Similarly, the reduction in the heteroskedastic SDM to the heteroskedastic SLX ($\rho_0 = \lambda_0 = 0$) (2 d.f.) gives LR = 2(2367.3 − 2353.7) = 27.2 and is clearly rejected. Reduction of the heteroskedastic SDEM to the homoskedastic SDEM is equally rejected by the likelihood ratio of LR = 2(2367.0 − 2358.5) = 17.0 (1 d.f.). Finally, the reduction in the heteroskedastic SDEM to the heteroskedastic SLX is also rejected. No further model reductions need to be tested, because already the simpler models nested by either the SDM or SDEM are rejected by the data. This strongly suggests that either the heteroskedastic SDM or SDEM could serve as the maintained model. Given that heteroskedastic specifications outperform the homoskedastic ones for the three non-rejected models, Table 2 contains estimates of the eight models with group heteroskedastic disturbances.

5.3. Direct and Indirect Effects

We now turn our attention to an interpretation and comparison of the results for the heteroskedastic GNS, SDM and SDEM models.[9] We consider the estimates of the direct and indirect (spillover) effects of the different explanatory variables to see whether they can be used as an alternative means to select the best model from the three non-rejected models. Table 3 reports the estimates of the direct effects of the explanatory variables of the

Table 3. Direct Effects on Research Productivity of Individual Researchers.

Determinants	OLS	SAR	SEM	SLX	SDM	SDEM	SAC	GNS
Austria	0.004	0.010	0.004	−0.003	−0.003	−0.002	0.004	−0.002
	(0.50)	*(1.28)*	*(0.40)*	*(−0.25)*	*(−0.20)*	*(−0.13)*	*(0.33)*	*(−0.04)*
Switzerland	0.018**	0.012*	0.018*	0.014*	0.010	0.015	0.018	0.011
	(2.43)	*(1.74)*	*(1.68)*	*(1.75)*	*(1.23)*	*(1.34)*	*(1.41)*	*(0.17)*
log size	0.087**	0.081*	0.089*	0.060*	0.059	0.063	0.092*	0.049
	(2.70)	*(1.94)*	*(1.90)*	*(1.79)*	*(1.32)*	*(1.37)*	*(1.72)*	*(0.62)*
$\log^2$ size	−0.009*	−0.009	−0.009	−0.006	−0.007	−0.007	−0.009	−0.005
	(−1.99)	*(−1.42)*	*(−1.44)*	*(−1.40)*	*(−1.04)*	*(−1.10)*	*(−1.35)*	*(−0.10)*
no top publishers	0.183**	0.113**	0.184**	0.183**	0.127**	0.178**	−0.188*	−0.140
	(−11.26)	*(−5.41)*	*(−7.11)*	*(−8.61)*	*(−5.31)*	*(−5.60)*	*(−2.26)*	*(−0.78)*
log career age	0.001	0.006	0.008	0.004	0.003	0.004	0.008	0.003
	(0.03)	*(0.16)*	*(0.33)*	*(0.15)*	*(0.13)*	*(0.15)*	*(0.32)*	*(0.09)*
$\log^2$ career age	−0.010*	−0.011*	0.011**	−0.010*	−0.010*	−0.010*	−0.011*	−0.010
	(−2.06)	*(−2.17)*	*(−2.39)*	*(−2.19)*	*(−2.12)*	*(−2.17)*	*(−2.24)*	*(−0.87)*
post-doc	0.075**	0.080**	0.078**	0.077**	0.079**	0.077**	0.079**	−0.077
	(−12.66)	*(−12.70)*	*(−13.17)*	*(−13.03)*	*(−13.48)*	*(−12.98)*	*(−5.12)*	*(−0.70)*
junior professor	0.051**	0.053**	0.053**	0.053**	0.054**	0.053**	0.053**	−0.054
	(−7.57)	*(−7.70)*	*(−8.06)*	*(−7.97)*	*(−8.05)*	*(−8.09)*	*(−4.38)*	*(−0.70)*
female	0.027**	0.028**	0.027**	0.027**	0.028**	0.027**	0.027**	−0.027
	(−5.04)	*(−5.10)*	*(−5.16)*	*(−5.06)*	*(−5.00)*	*(−5.09)*	*(−3.80)*	*(−0.34)*
collaboration	0.045**	0.046**	0.043**	0.043**	0.045**	0.043**	0.043**	0.043
	(8.38)	*(8.42)*	*(8.02)*	*(8.03)*	*(8.41)*	*(7.95)*	*(4.07)*	*(0.60)*

t-values in parentheses.
**significant at 5%.
*significant at 10%.

different models. A direct effect represents the impact of a change in one **X** variable of the average researcher on the productivity of the average researcher, measured by the mean of $\text{DE}_{\beta_0}(r) + \text{DE}_{\gamma_0}(r)$ in Eqs. (14) and (17) over all r.

The general pattern that emerges from Table 3 is the following. The differences between the direct effects and the coefficient estimates reported in Table 2 are generally very small. In the rejected OLS, SEM and SLX and non-rejected SDEM models, they are exactly the same by definition; in the rejected SAR and SAC models and the non-rejected SDM and GNS models, they may be different due to the feedback from the endogenous interaction effects ($\rho\mathbf{WY}$). Empirically, however, these feedback effects appear to be very small.

In the three non-rejected models, the differences between the direct effects are in most cases also very small. But, the GNS model clearly suffers from inefficiency as all of its estimates are insignificant, even if the size of the direct effect is in most cases of the same magnitude as in the SDM and the SDEM. For instance, the coefficients of the variable "No top publishers" (varies at the university level) are similar for the GNS and SDM models, but in the GNS model the effect is insignificant. Similarly, the coefficient of the dummy for "Junior professor" (varies at the individual level) is around −0.054 in all three models, but it is only significant in the SDM and SDEM. Another notable exception is the "$\log^2$(career age)" which has a significant and sizeable direct effect estimate of less than −1.0 in the SDM and SDEM, but a negligible and insignificant direct effect estimate of about −0.01 in the GNS. From these inspections, it is clear that the results for the SDM and SDEM models are more consistent with each other rather than with the GNS model that nests them.

The importance of basing inferences on the estimates from the non-rejected GNS, SDM, SDEM models can be clearly seen in the case of the "Switzerland" and the "log size" effects. An analyst using the results from OLS, SAR, SEM or SLX, that is, models that cover at most one type of interaction effects, would conclude that researchers in Switzerland are more productive than in Austria and Germany, and so the researchers employed by larger departments, while analysts adopting the SDM, SDEM or GNS model would not. Since only the SDM, SDEM and the GNS models are not rejected by the data, the former group of analysts in this case would be basing their calculations, and hence their contrary conclusions, on a rejected model. Furthermore, they might erroneously conclude that holding out Swiss and Austrian departments or departments of certain size classes would lead to different outcomes when carrying out post-fitting evaluations.

The levels of the *t*-values reported for the direct effects of variables that vary at the individual level (Table 3) are almost the same in all models, except for the SAC and the GNS models. In the SAC model it halves in most cases, while in the GNS model, it always drops (in absolute value) below 1. The explanation for this is that the significance level of the endogenous peer effect coefficient (ρ_0) of the **WY** variable in the SAC and the GNS models falls considerably, presumably because this variable competes in these two models for significance with the interaction coefficient (λ_0) of the disturbance **WU**. Additionally, for the GNS model, we observe that also the *t*-values of the explanatory variables that vary at the university level (see Table 2) decrease so much that all these variables become insignificant and therefore also the respective direct effects reported in Table 3. To some extent this also applies to the spatially lagged values of the explanatory variables in the GNS model.

Table 4 reports the spillover effects of the explanatory variables of the different models. A spillover effect represents the impact of a change in one **X** variable of the average researcher on the productivity of other researchers working at the same university. It is measured by the mean of $IE_{\beta_0}(r) + IE_{\gamma_0}(r)$ in Eqs. (15) and (18) over all r. In contrast to the direct effects, the differences between the estimated spillover effects in the different models are very large. Nevertheless, we can observe some general patterns. The rejected OLS, SAR, SEM and SAC models produce no or contradictory spillover effects compared to the SDM, SDEM and GNS models. For example, whereas the spillover effect of post-docs in the SDM and SDEM models is positive and significant, it is zero by construction in the OLS and SEM models, negative in the SAC model, and negative and "significant" in the SAR model. The negative but insignificant effect in the SAC model can be explained by the fact that this model closely resembles the SEM model; as in the SAC the autoregressive coefficient of **WY** is so small that spillover effects cannot occur in this model. The negative and significant effect in the SAR model can be explained by the fact that in this model the ratio between the spillover effect and the direct effect is the same for each explanatory variable (Elhorst, 2010). Consequently, this model is too rigid to model spillover effects adequately, and is, of course, rejected by the data.

The spillover effects identified by the rejected SLX and the non-rejected SDM, SDEM and GNS models are of the same order of magnitude, at

Table 4. Spillover Effects of Individual Research Productivity on Research Colleagues at the Same University.

Determinants	OLS	SAR	SEM	SLX	SDM	SDEM	SAC	GNS
Austria		0.005			−0.001		−0.008	−0.001
		(1.21)			*(−0.19)*		*(−0.06)*	*(−0.04)*
Switzerland		0.006*			0.004		0.002	0.003
		(1.65)			*(1.14)*		*(0.04)*	*(0.03)*
log size		0.038*			0.025		0.002	0.014
		(1.77)			*(1.23)*		*(0.02)*	*(0.02)*
$\log^2$ size		−0.004			−0.004		−0.000	−0.002
		(−1.33)			*(−0.98)*		*(−0.04)*	*(−0.01)*
no top publishers		0.053**			0.054**		0.011	−0.040
		(−5.08)			*(−3.98)*		*(0.14)*	*(−0.04)*
log career age		0.003		−0.278*	−0.344	−0.276	0.003	−0.282
		(0.15)		*(−2.05)*	*(−1.30)*	*(−1.37)*	*(0.04)*	*(−0.09)*
$\log^2$ career age		−0.005*		0.057*	0.069	0.057	−0.003	0.058
		(−1.95)		*(2.25)*	*(1.45)*	*(1.52)*	*(−0.06)*	*(0.05)*
post-doc		−0.037**		0.092**	0.086*	0.086*	−0.021	0.089
		(−4.20)		*(3.37)*	*(2.32)*	*(2.13)*	*(−0.07)*	*(0.02)*
junior professor		−0.025**		0.037	0.023	0.036	−0.015	0.035
		(−3.83)		*(1.14)*	*(0.82)*	*(0.74)*	*(−0.06)*	*(0.01)*
female		−0.013**		0.008	0.016	0.009	0.008	0.001
		(−3.45)		*(0.28)*	*(0.22)*	*(0.22)*	*(−0.07)*	*(0.02)*
collaboration		0.021**		0.026	0.032	0.035	0.013	0.032
		(4.00)		*(0.96)*	*(0.76)*	*(0.88)*	*(0.06)*	*(0.03)*

t-values in parentheses.
**significant at 5%.
*significant at 10%.

least for the variables that vary at the individual level. By construction there are no spillover effects for the variables that vary at the university level for the SLX and SDEM models. The *t*-values in the SLX model are however clearly too high, because this model ignores interaction effects either among the dependent variable or the error terms The *t*-values of the spillover effects of the SDM and the SDEM models are of the same order of magnitude, while they are insignificant in the GNS model. For example, according to the SDM, SDEM and GNS models, the spillover effect of post-docs ranges from 0.086 to 0.089, and is therefore rather stable, whereas the t-values in the first two models are 2.32 and 2.13, respectively, and in the last model only 0.02. As recently pointed out by Gibbons and Overman (2012), the explanation for this finding is that interaction effects among the dependent variable and interaction effects among the error terms are only weakly identified. Considering them both, as in the GNS model, highlights this problem; it leads to a model that is overparameterised, which reduces the significance levels of all variables. This finding is worrying since the interpretation of the two types of interaction effects is completely different. In our case, a model with endogenous interaction effects posits that the research productivity of a researcher depends on the research productivity of other researchers working at the same university, and vice versa. By contrast, a model with interaction effects among the error terms assumes that the research productivity of a researcher depends on unobserved characteristics that affect all researchers working at the same university.

Although the SDM and SDEM specifications produce spillover effects that are of the same order of magnitude and significance for the variables measured at the individual level, the results reported in Tables 3 and 4 indicate that this does not hold for the variable "No top publishers" that varies only across universities and measures the publication culture of a university. According to the SDEM specification, a unit change in the proportion of colleagues who do not publish in top journals appears to have a negative total/direct effect on a productivity of 0.178; the SDM specification produces an almost similar negative total effect of 0.181, but according to this model it can be split up into a negative direct effect of 0.127 on individual researchers (Table 3) and a negative spillover effect of 0.054 on other researchers within the same university (Table 4).

Although the total effects of the explanatory variables, the sum of the direct effects and the corresponding spillover effects, and their significance levels have been calculated, they are not reported to save space. Generally, we find that if the direct effect is insignificant, the total effect is also insignificant. The total effect of a particular variable is also insignicant if its direct effect and its spillover effect have opposite signs. Finally, if the direct effect is significant and the spillover effect has the same sign, then the total effect is also (weakly) significant. This holds for "no top publishers" and "collaboration", indicating that researchers working on papers with external coauthors and in departments with a strong publishing culture tend to be more productive.

5.4. Choice between the SDM and SDEM

Ideally the GNS model should serve as a means of selection between the SDM and SDEM models, but given the demonstrated weak identification of this model a Bayesian perspective on whether either the SDM or the SDEM specification generated the data is more appropriate. We apply a novel Bayesian approach here taken from LeSage (2014). By addressing the marginal likelihood of both specifications, and thereby integrating out all parameters of the model, we calculate the Bayesian posterior model probabilities of the SDM and SDEM specifications, conditional on the sample data. With the two tested models, we have $p(\text{SDM}|\mathbf{Y}, \mathbf{X}^*, \mathbf{W}) + p(\text{SDEM}|\mathbf{Y}, \mathbf{X}^*, \mathbf{W}) = 1$. If the probability of one model is greater than that of the other, we conclude that it describes the data better, because the comparison is based on the same set of explanatory variables, that is, both model specifications include **X** and spatially lagged **X** (denoted by **WX**) variables, and the comparison is independent of any specific parameter values as they have been integrated out.

The main strength of this Bayesian approach is that it compares the performance of one model against another model, in this case SDM against SDEM, on their entire parameter space. The popular LR, Wald and/or Lagrange multiplier statistics only compare the performance of one model against another model based on specific parameter estimates within the parameter space. Inferences drawn on the log marginal likelihood function values for the SDM and SDEM model are further justified because they have the same set of explanatory variables, **X** and **WX**, and are based on the same uniform prior for ρ_0 and λ_0. This prior takes the form $p(\rho_0) = p(\lambda_0) = 1/D$, where $D = 1/\omega_{\max} - 1/\omega_{\min}$ and $\omega_{\max}$ and $\omega_{\min}$ represent respectively the largest and the smallest (negative) eigenvalue of the spatial weights matrix **W**. This prior requires no subjective information on the part of the practitioner as it relies on the parameter space $(1/\omega_{\min}, 1/\omega_{\max})$ on which ρ_0 and λ_0 are defined, where $\omega_{\max} = 1$ if **W** is row-normalised. Full details regarding the choice of model can be found in LeSage (2014).

The Bayesian posterior model probabilities based on this approach are found to be in the proportion of 0.0124 for the SDM specification and 0.9876 for the SDEM specification, indicating that it is almost 80 times more likely that the interaction effect that has been found in addition to exogenous interaction characteristics (**WX**) is due to unobserved characteristics common to all colleagues within a department (**WU**) rather than that peers affect the productivity of colleagues (**WY**). Consequently, we may conclude that only one variable produces significant spillover effects within a department: the presence of post-docs (see Table 4). Post-docs appear to publish less than junior professors, who in turn publish less than senior staff members, but they do have a positive effect on their environment; a post-doc within a department has a positive spillover effect of 0.086 on the research productivity of his or her colleagues. Since the SDEM specification is more likely than the SDM specification, a unit change in the proportion of colleagues who do not publish in top journals may be said not to produce a spillover effect, rejecting peer effects and reflecting the importance of sorting. Suppose that due to department policy changes more researchers become active in publishing, as a result of which the proportion of colleagues who do not publish within the department decreases. This would cause a shock to the equilibrium situation and lead to a reshuffling of researchers. Not only will more productive researchers join the department, due to the absence of peer effects they will probably also replace inactive or unproductive colleagues since the latter are not able to benefit from this productivity impulse. This prediction follows from rejecting peer effects (SDM specification) and is in line with recent studies of Waldinger (2011) and Borjas and Doran (2014) using a natural experiment setting, who also found no or only small localised peer effects.

6. CONCLUSIONS

This paper is among the first to study the theoretical model of group interactions suggested by Lee et al. (2010) in an empirical setting, throwing more light on its feasibility, empirical relevance, and its empirical implications. Based on this study, the current unpopularity of the GNS model with a full set of interaction effects among the dependent variable, the exogenous variables, and among the disturbances, can be explained by following two reasons, of which especially the second has not yet been empirically documented in the literature.

The first reason is that general conditions under which the parameters of the GNS model are identified have only recently been given, by Lee et al. (2010) for a specific form of spatial weights, namely a group interaction matrix. Unfortunately, this matrix is not very popular in applied spatial econometric research. The second reason is that the GNS model can be overparameterised which leads to weak identification of the interaction effects among the dependent variable and among the error terms. Considering them both, as in the GNS model, has the effect that the significance levels of all variables go down, and hence the GNS model provides no additional information over the nested SDM and SDEM specifications. This implies that the potential advantage of the GNS model that either of the SDM or SDEM could be rejected against does not hold from an empirical perspective.

This paper also goes a step further than the GNS model with all types of interaction effects set out in Lee et al. (2010). Firstly, we show that spatial econometric models with limited numbers of spatial interaction effects lead to incorrect inferences. This justifies the path to more general models in empirical modelling. The spillover effects produced by the SAR, SEM, SLX and SAC models, often the main focus of the analysis, are demonstrably false. A much better performance is obtained when adopting the SDM or the SDEM model.

Secondly, whereas Lee et al. (2010) advocate the extension of the GNS model with group fixed effects, we provide evidence, both mathematically and empirically, that this extension has hardly any empirical relevance due to near multicollinearity. By contrast, we find a strong evidence in favour of heteroskedasticity; the heteroskedastic models outperform their homoskedastic counterparts, signalling that spatial econometricians should devote more attention to accounting for heteroskedasticity. Although Anselin (1988) advocated the incorporation of heteroskedastic disturbances in spatial econometric models over twenty-five years ago, only a few empirical studies have appeared since then that followed his call. By making our routines downloadable for free, we hope to stimulate more such studies.

Inability to decide between the SDM and SDEM specifications based on the GNS estimates, implies that more information is needed to discriminate between the two types of interaction effects described by these models. By taking a Bayesian approach (LeSage, 2014), we were able to show that the SDEM specification is more appropriate. This specification predicts a small positive and significant spillover effect from the presence of post-docs but no spillover effects from non-publishing faculty. These results are in line with experimental studies on peer effects in academia, finding no effects (Waldinger, 2011) or no effects for average collaborators (Borjas & Doran, 2014).

NOTES

1. Elhorst (2010) labels this model the Kelejian-Prucha model after their article in 1998 since they are the first to set out an estimation strategy for this model, also when the spatial weights matrix used to specify the spatial lag and the spatial error is the same. Over time, Harry Kelejian and Ingmar Prucha themselves alternately use the terms SARAR or Cliff-Ord-type spatial model.
2. www.spatial-econometrics.com
3. We also improved two programming errors in the calculation of the variance-covariance matrix of the parameter estimates. The adapted SAC routine will be made available at http://www.regroningen.nl/elhorst/software.shtml or can be supplied on request.
4. The database is under the auspices of the German Economic Association: www.socialpolitik.org. It is known across the German speaking region as the research monitoring database: www.forschungsmonitoring.org
5. We dropped 14 universities with small economics and/or finance and business departments, losing only about 90 individuals.
6. http://vhbonline.org
7. Social Sciences Citation Index.
8. The quality of this approximation obviously deserves some attention, but as will be apparent from the details, the conclusions would not be likely to change much if a more accurate reference distribution was available.
9. As an alternative to the LR tests for homoskedasticity, one may also estimate the homoskedastic model and then carry out the Breusch-Pagan test for heteroskedasticity. The outcomes of this LM-test range from 3.46 in the SAR model to 4.26 in the SEM model with one degree of freedom. The evidence in favour of heteroskedasticity from this perspective is slightly weaker than from the perspective of the more powerful LR-test.

REFERENCES

Anselin, L. (1988). Spatial econometrics: Methods and models. Dordrecht: Kluwer Academic Publishers.

Anselin, L., & Bera, A. K. (1998). Spatial dependence in linear regression models with an introduction to spatial econometrics. In A. Ullah & D. E. A. Giles (Eds.). *Handbook of applied economic statistics* (pp. 237–289). New York, NY: Marcel Dekker.

Azoulay, P., Zivin, J. S. G., & Wang, J. (2010). Superstar extinction. *The Quarterly Journal of Economics*, *125*, 549–589.

Bonacorsi, A., & Daraio, C. (2005). Exploring size and agglomeration effects on public research productivity. *Scientometrics*, *63*, 87–120.

Borjas, G. J., & Doran, K. B. (2014). Which peers matter? The relative impacts of collaborators, colleagues, and competitors. *Review of Economics and Statistics*, *97*, 1104–1117.

Bosquet, C., & Combes, P.-P. (2013). Are academics who publish more also more cited? Individual determinants of publication and citation records. *Scientometrics*, *97*, 831–857.

Bramoullé, Y., Djebbari, H., & Fortin, B. (2009). Identification of peer effects through social networks. *Journal of Econometrics*, *150*, 41–55.

Carayol, N. (2008). An economic theory of academic competition: dynamic incentives and endogenous cumulative advantages. In M. Albert, S. Voigt, & D. Schmidtchen (Eds.). *Scientific competition. Conferences on new political economy* (Vol. 25, pp. 179–203). Tübingen: Mohr Siebeck.

Combes, P.-P., & Linnemer, L. (2003). Where are the economists who publish? Publication concentration and rankings in Europe based on cumulative publications. *Journal of the European Economic Association*, *1*, 1250–1308.

Corrado, L., & Fingleton, B. (2012). Where is the economics in spatial econometrics? *Journal of Regional Science*, *52*, 210–239.

Dasgupta, P., & David, P. A. (1994). Toward a new economics of science. *Research Policy*, *23*, 487–521.

Elhorst, J. P. (2010). Applied spatial econometrics: Raising the bar. *Spatial Economic Analysis*, *5*, 9–28.

Elhorst, J. P., & Zigova, K. (2014). Competition in research activity among economic departments: Evidence by negative spatial autocorrelation. *Geographical Analysis*, *46*, 104–125.

Fabel, O., Hein, M., & Hofmeister, R. (2008). Research productivity in business economics: An investigation of Austrian, German and Swiss Universities. *German Economic Review*, *9*, 506–531.

Gibbons, S., & Overman, H. G. (2012). Mostly pointless spatial econometrics. *Journal of Regional Science*, *52*, 172–191.

Halleck Vega, S., & Elhorst, J. P. (2015). The SLX model. *Journal of Regional Science*, *55*, 339–363.

Kelejian, H. H., & Prucha, I. R. (1998). A generalized spatial two-stage least squares procedure for estimating a spatial autoregressive model with autoregressive disturbances. *Journal of Real Estate Finance and Economics*, *17*, 99–121.

Kim, E. H., Morse, A., & Zingales, L. (2009). Are elite universities losing their competitive edge? *Journal of Financial Economics*, *93*, 353–381.

Krapf, M. (2011). Research evaluation and journal quality weights: Much ado about nothing. *Zeitschrift für Betriebswirtschaft*, *81*, 5–27.

Lee, L. F. (2007). Identification and estimation of econometric models with group interactions, contextual factors and fixed effects. *Journal of Econometrics*, *140*, 333–374.

Lee, L. F., Liu, X., & Lin, X. (2010). Specification and estimation of social interaction models with network structures. *The Econometrics Journal*, *13*, 145–176.

LeSage, J. P. (1999). *Spatial econometrics*, University of Toledo, Toledo, OH, USA. Available at www.spatial-econometrics.com/html/sbook.pdf.

LeSage, J. P. (2014). Spatial econometric panel data model specification: A Bayesian approach. *Spatial Statistics*, *9*, 122–145.

LeSage, J. P., & Pace, R. K. (2009). *Introduction to spatial econometrics*. Boca Raton, FL: CRC Press\Taylor & Francis Group.

Levin, S. G., & Stephan, P. E. (1991). Research productivity over the life cycle: Evidence for academic scientists. *The American Economic Review*, *81*, 114–132.

Manski, C. (1993). Identification of endogenous social effects: The reflection problem. *Review of Economic Studies*, *60*, 531–542.

Maske, K. L., Durden, G. C., & Gaynor, P. E. (2003). Determinants of scholarly productivity among male and female economists. *Economic Inquiry*, *41*, 555–564.

Rauber, M., & Ursprung, H. W. (2008). Life cycle and cohort productivity in economic research: The case of Germany. *German Economic Review*, *9*, 431–456.

Stephan, P. E. (2010). The economics of science. In B. H. Hall & N. Rosenberg (Eds.). *Handbook of the economics of innovation* (Vol. 1, pp. 217–273). Amsterdam: North Holland.

Waldinger, F. (2011). Peer effects in science: Evidence from the dismissal of scientists in Nazi Germany. *Review of Economic Studies*, *20*, 1–24.

Xie, Y., & Shauman, K. A. (2003). *Women in science. Career processes and outcomes.* Cambridge, MA: Harvard University Press.

HOW TO MEASURE SPILLOVER EFFECTS OF PUBLIC CAPITAL STOCK: A SPATIAL AUTOREGRESSIVE STOCHASTIC FRONTIER MODEL

Jaepil Han[a], Deockhyun Ryu[b] and Robin Sickles[c]

[a]*Korea Development Institute, Sejong, South Korea*
[b]*School of Economics, Chung-Ang University, Seoul, South Korea*
[c]*Department of Economics, Rice University, Houston, TX, USA*

ABSTRACT

This paper aims to investigate spillover effects of public capital stock in a production function model that accounts for spatial dependencies. In many settings, ignoring spatial dependency yields inefficient, biased and inconsistent estimates in cross country panels. Although there are a number of studies aiming to estimate the output elasticity of public capital stock, many of those fail to reach a consensus on refining the elasticity estimates. We argue that accounting for spillover effects of the public capital stock on the production efficiency and incorporating spatial dependences are crucial. For this purpose, we employ a spatial

Spatial Econometrics: Qualitative and Limited Dependent Variables
Advances in Econometrics, Volume 37, 259–294

ISSN: 0731-9053/doi:10.1108/S0731-905320160000037017

autoregressive stochastic frontier model based on a number of specifications of the spatial dependency structure. Using the data of 21 OECD countries from 1960 to 2001, we estimate a spatial autoregressive stochastic frontier model and derive the mean indirect marginal effects of public capital stock, which are interpreted as spillover effects. We found that spillover effects can be an important factor explaining variations in technical inefficiency across countries as well as in explaining the discrepancies among various levels of output elasticity of public capital stock in traditional production function approaches.

Keywords: Public capital; spillover effect; stochastic frontier model; spatial panel model; time-varying spatial weights

JEL classifications: C23; D24; O47

1. INTRODUCTION

Public capital includes many types of goods which are used to produce final goods and services for consumers. The infrastructures such as highways, streets, roads, and public educational buildings take the largest components of public capital and also electric, gas, and water supply facilities, administration, police, military service, hospital facilities, and many other forms of goods and services are included in public capital. In the United States, the real government gross fixed capital formation is between 3% and 4% of real GDP and about 20% of the real gross fixed capital formation in the private sector. Based on the estimates of Kamps (2006), the public capital stock is sizable, taking about 55% of real GDP and more than 20% of private capital stock on average of the 22 OECD countries during the sample periods: 1960–2001. This implies that ignoring public capital can be problematic when analyzing productivity and efficiency. Delorme, Thompson, and Warren (1999) also argue that public infrastructure reduces the technical inefficiency of private-sector production.

The economic impact of public investment has been received great attention in numerous studies for the last few decades. Many studies have tried to estimate the output elasticity of public capital and there has been a debate on the effects of public capital on output. The output elasticities of public capital estimated by various models and samples range from 0.1 to 0.4. Specifically, the earlier studies such as Aschauer (1989) or Munnell (1990) report relatively large elasticities, while they are considered implausibly high by subsequent studies such as Tatom (1991) or Holtz-Eakin (1994). Recently, Bom and Ligthart (2014) estimate an average output elasticity of public capital to be around 0.15 using meta-analysis with 68 studies for the 1983–2008 period. Even though the magnitudes of the effects of public capital stock are far from consensus, there is little doubt on the positive sign and statistical significance (Pereira & Andraz, 2013).

There has been several explanations for the disagreement on the magnitude of the effects of public capital. Major explanations are related to econometric issues. Tatom (1991) points out the significant influence of the relative price of energy on productivity, the omitted time trend, and possibility of spurious regressions as main shortcomings of the previous studies. Moreover, in general, ignorance of cross-sectional dependency results in inefficient and biased estimates and invalid inference when it actually exists. Another explanation is the possible existence of spillover effects and the different levels of samples of studies. Pereira and Andraz (2013) pointed that the large effects of public investment observed at the aggregate level cannot be replicated at the regional level. They also mentioned that the spillover effects captured by aggregate level studies can give a clue for this paradox. They insist that the significant spillover effects are observed in some empirical studies and this can explain some of the divergences found between regional and aggregate studies.

However, the issue of the possible existence of spillovers of public capital has received relatively little attention and also. Holtz-Eakin and Schwartz (1995) examine the degree of geographical spillovers in productivity with state highway investment but no evidence of important regional spillovers is found. Pereira and Roca-Sagales (2003) investigate the regional effects of public investment and the spillovers in Spain using vector autoregressive (VAR) models. Recently, spatial econometric methods are extensively used in regional science studies to assess spatial spillovers.

Spatial econometrics consists of econometric techniques dealing with interactions of economic units in space. For a cross-sectional model, the spatial autoregressive model by Cliff and Ord (1973) has received the most attention. The technique is extended to panel data models. Anselin, Gallo, and Jayet (2008) provide a panel regression model with error components and spatial autoregressive disturbances. Kapoor, Kelejian, and Prucha (2007) propose a method of moments estimation. Lee and Yu (2010c) investigate the quasi-maximum likelihood estimation of spatial panel models under the fixed effects specification. We form exogenous spatial weights matrices that capture the interactions between individuals. The interactions can be of geographical or economic characteristics. The spatial weights matrices tend to be time invariant because mostly spatial weights are based on geographical concepts such as border sharing characteristics or centroid distances, which are not change over time. However, we can also consider the economic/socioeconomic distances or demographic characteristics as sources of cross-sectional dependence. As Lee and Yu (2012) point out, when spatial weights matrix is constructed from those characteristics in a panel or dynamic setting, the characteristics might change over time.

Spatial dependency and the heterogeneity of the spatial dependence structure influence on the productivity or efficiency of the economic units. The standard stochastic frontier models do not take spatial interactions into account. Pavlyuk (2012) estimates the efficiency in the presence of spatial dependency and presents a general specification of the spatial stochastic frontier model. Glass, Kenjegalieva, and Sickles (2013) develop a spatial autoregressive frontier model with time-varying efficiency. They shed lights on the possible interpretations of spillover of returns to scale (Table 1).

In this paper, we mainly concern how to estimate the effects of public capital stock on output separating out the direct and indirect effects. The direct effects include the feedback effects which pass through neighboring regions and back to the region itself. The indirect effects are interpreted as spillover effects. We consider the possible existence of spatial dependence by incorporating the spatially correlated terms with a variety of spatial dependence structures. Also, we measure the technical efficiencies of countries. We expect to improve the estimation of the technical efficiency by adding public capital as a factor input and controlling the possible cross-sectional dependence. To this end, we investigate the quasi-maximum likelihood (QML) estimation of Spatial Autoregressive Stochastic Frontier Model. Finally, we apply the model to a dataset from 21 OECD countries under the settings of both time-invariant and time-varying spatial weights matrices. We found significant and sizable output elasticity of public capital, and significant spillover effects, and also we estimated the relative technical efficiency scores of each models.

The paper continues with the following structure. Section 2 presents a spatial autoregressive stochastic frontier (SARSF) model we are interested in. We also discuss on the direct, indirect, and total output elasticities of factor inputs and connect the interpretation to the spillover effects. In Section 3, we apply the SARSF model to a dataset of 21 OECD countries with the applications of 10 spatial weights matrices. In particular, we allow spatial weights matrix vary over time. We discuss the properties of the coefficient estimates, output elasticities, and spillover effects. Efficiency score results are discussed as well. In Section 3.1, we conclude this paper.

Table 1. Various Studies on Output Elasticity of Public Capital Stock and Spillover Effect.

Author (Year)	Data	Public Capital Measure	Model Specification	Conclusions
Aschauer (1989)	U.S.; T.S. 1949–1985	Public capital stock; core infrastructures	C-D; log	Positive effects of public capital on output. Elasticity of output with respect to total public capital is 0.39. The elasticity of output with respect to core infrastructure is 0.24.
Bom and Ligthart (2014)	OECD countries; P.D: 1983–2008	Infrastructure and public capital stock	Meta-analysis with 68 studies	Short-run output elasticity of public capital at central government level is 0.083 and long-run 0.122. Average output elasticity of public capital stock amounts to 0.106.
Holtz-Eakin (1994)	U.S.; 48 states and 9 regions; P.D. 1969–1986	Revised public capital stock from Munnell (1993)	C-D; fixed and random state effects; time effects; IV estimation.	Insignificant effects of public capital on output. Elasticity is −0.022.
Holtz-Eakin and Schwartz (1995)	U.S.; 48 states; P.D. 1971–1986	Infrastructure capital and public capital stock	C-D; Δlog	Infrastructure has negligible effects on output.
Munnell (1990)	7 OECD countries; P.D. 1963–1988	Public investment	C-D; log	Positive effects of public capital on output. Elasticity of output with respect to total public capital is 0.31 and Elasticity of output with respect to core infrastructures is 0.49.
Pereira and Roca-Sagales (2003)	Spain; 17 regions; T.S. 1970–1995	Transports and communications	VAR; Δlog	Spillovers represent 50% of the total effects
Tatom (1991)	U.S.; T.S. 1949–1989	Public capital stock	C-D; Δlog	Insignificant effects of public capital on output. Elasticity is 0.04.

Source: from Pereira and Andraz (2013), Rearranged.

2. SPATIAL AUTOREGRESSIVE STOCHASTIC FRONTIER MODEL

We begin with a non-spatial production function. The production function is of the form:

$$y_{it} = \beta_0 + X_{it}\beta + \varepsilon_{it}, \quad i = 1, \ldots, N, \; t = 1, \ldots, T, \tag{1}$$

where i indexes cross-section of economic units and t indexes time periods. y_{it} represents logged output of the ith unit at time t, whereas X_{it} is a $(1 \times K)$ logged input vector of the ith unit at time t. β_0 is a constant, β is the $(K \times 1)$ parameter vector to be estimated, and ε_{it} is an *i.i.d.* disturbance term with zero mean and variance σ_ε^2.

In general, we can introduce spatial interactions via three routes: Endogenous interaction effects, which are explaining dependence among dependent variables, Exogenous interaction effects, which are explaining dependence between y_i and X_j, and Interaction effects among the error terms. A full model with all types of spatial interaction effects can be written as follows:

$$\begin{aligned} y_{it} &= \rho \sum_{j=1}^{N} w_{ij} y_{jt} + \beta_0 + X_{it}\beta + \sum_{j=1}^{N} w_{ij} X_{jt}\theta + \varepsilon_{it}, \\ \varepsilon_{it} &= \lambda \sum_{j=1}^{N} w_{ij} \varepsilon_{jt} + u_{it}. \end{aligned} \tag{2}$$

The model in matrix notation is given in:

$$\begin{aligned} Y &= \rho(I_T \otimes W)Y + \beta_0 \iota_{NT} + X\beta + (I_T \otimes W)X\theta + \varepsilon, \\ \varepsilon &= \lambda(I_T \otimes W)\varepsilon + u, \end{aligned} \tag{3}$$

where W is an exogenous $(N \times N)$ spatial weights matrix with non-negative elements, $(I_T \otimes W)Y$, $(I_T \otimes W)X$, and $(I_T \otimes W)\varepsilon$ represent the endogenous interaction effects, exogeneous interaction effects, and interaction effects among the disturbance term, respectively.[1]

Among the spatial interactions, we are specifically interested in the endogenous interaction effects.[2] Hence, we impose the restrictions of $\theta = 0$ and $\lambda = 0$. The model in Eq. (2) reduces to

$$y_{it} = \rho \sum_{j=1}^{N} w_{ij} y_{jt} + \beta_0 + X_{it}\beta + \varepsilon_{it}. \tag{4}$$

The model is called Spatial Autoregressive Model; hereafter SAR. This is the Cliff-Ord-type production function, suggested by Cliff and Ord (1981).

Typically, productivity is measured by Solow residual of a production function such as Eq. (1). However, with a symmetric assumption on the distribution of ε_{it}, we esitmate the average practice production function, which do not provide maximum output for given amounts of inputs utilized if some economic units are inefficient. Stochastic frontier analyses typically decompose the error term into a productivity component and a statistical noise term to incorporate the possible inefficiency of economic units. By assuming that the productivity component follows a non-negative distribution, we are able to estimate the best practice production function rather than the average practice production function. Therefore, the stochastic frontier specification associated to Eq. (4) can be obtained by assuming the disturbance term ε_{it} is a composed error with a non-negative random variable u_i, which represents the technical inefficiency, and a systematic random noise v_{it}.

We assume u_i to be time-invariant without any further assumptions on the distributional form following Schmidt and Sickles (1984), and v_{it} is *i.i.d.* with zero mean and variance σ_v^2. The model of interest is given:

$$y_{it} = \rho \sum_{j=1}^{N} w_{ij,t} y_{jt} + \beta_0 + X_{it}\beta - u_i + v_{it}. \tag{5}$$

Note that we allow the spatial weights, $w_{ij,t}$, to vary over time. Since we are unable to identify the constant term, β_0, and the productivity term, u_i, we define $\alpha_i \equiv \beta_0 - u_i$. Then Eq. (5) becomes

$$y_{it} = \rho \sum_{j=1}^{N} w_{ij,t} y_{jt} + \alpha_i + X_{it}\beta + v_{it}. \tag{6}$$

A relative inefficiency (or efficiency) measure accounts for the output of each unit to the output that could be produced by a fully efficient unit. Because the most efficient unit has the largest α_i, the relative inefficiency measure can be derived by defining it as the distance between $\max(\hat{\alpha}_i)$ and α_i as follows:[3]

$$u_i^* \equiv \max(\hat{\alpha}_i) - \hat{\alpha}_i. \tag{7}$$

The stacked form of Eq. (6) is

$$Y_t = \rho W_t Y_t + X_t \beta + \boldsymbol{\alpha} + V_t, \quad t = 1, \ldots, T, \tag{8}$$

where $Y_t = (y_{1t}, y_{2t}, \ldots, y_{Nt})'$ and $V_t = (v_{1t}, v_{2t}, \ldots, v_{Nt})'$ are $(N \times 1)$ column vectors, and v_{it}'s are *i.i.d.* across i and t with zero mean and variance σ^2. The X_t is an $(N \times K)$ matrix of non-stochastic regressors, and $\boldsymbol{\alpha}$ is an $(N \times 1)$ column vector of individual effects. The spatial weights matrix W_t is a non-stochastic and row-normalized, and time-varying $(N \times N)$ matrix. Let us call the model in Eq. (8) a Spatial Autoregressive Stochastic Frontier Model (hereafter SARSF).

The spatial weights matrix, W_t, is taken to be exogenous and captures cross-section dependence among observations. The spatial weights matrix is mostly specified to be time invariant because it is usually based on the characteristics that are rarely changing over time such as geographical distance or a border sharing feature. However, spatial relationship can be defined by a variety of concepts and it is also possible that relationship to change over time. We may need to define a distance by economic, socio-economic, or demographic characteristics when geographic relationship cannot be used because the dataset we are interested in is collected from an aggregate economy or an agglomeration. We incorporate the time-varying characteristics of the spatial weights matrix in this paper, so we add time-subscript t in Eq. (8) as follows:

$$Y_t = \rho W_t Y_t + X_t \beta + \boldsymbol{\alpha} + V_t. \tag{9}$$

The reduced form of Eq. (9) is

$$Y_t = (I_N - \rho W_t)^{-1}(X_t \beta + \boldsymbol{\alpha} + V_t). \tag{10}$$

The marginal direct and indirect effects are derived separately in spatial models, while the coefficient estimates of non-spatial models are only interpreted as the direct marginal effects of factor inputs on output. Specifically, the marginal effects of Eq. (10) simply have a matrix form of $(I_N - \rho W_t)^{-1}\beta_k$. In the matrix, the diagonal elements represent the direct marginal effects of each explanatory variable, and the row (or column) sum of off-diagonal elements are the indirect marginal effects. Moreover, by approximating $(I_N - \rho W_t)^{-1}$, the marginal effects of input k can be written as

$$(I_N - \rho W_t)^{-1}\beta_k = \left(I_N + \rho W_t + \rho^2 W_t^2 + \rho^3 W_t^3 + \cdots\right)\beta_k. \tag{11}$$

The first two terms of Eq. (11), $I_N\beta_k$ and $\rho W_t\beta_k$, represent a direct effect of a change in X_k and an indirect effect of a change in X_k, respectively. The rest terms represent higher order direct and indirect effects, which include the feedback effects of other units.[4]

To test whether spatial spillovers exist or not, the estimated indirect effects should be used, not the estimate of ρ. This is because the indirect effects are derived from the multiplication of $(I_N - \rho W_t)^{-1}$ and β_k, and the variation in the indirect effects depends on the variation of all coefficient estimates. In other words, even though each coefficients are estimated to be significant, this does not mean that the mean indirect effect is significant, and vice versa. LeSage and Pace (2009) suggest simulating the distribution of the direct and indirect effects. The simulation procedure is basically in two steps: (1) computing the mean value over D draws of direct/indirect effects for the approximation of the overall effects and (2) obtaining t-statistics by dividing the sample mean by the corresponding standard deviation.

Spatial models can be estimated by maximum likelihood, QML, instrumental variables, generalized method of moments, or by Bayesian Markov Chain Monte Carlo methods. One advantage of QML is that it does not rely on the assumption of normality of the disturbances. For the standard panel data model with fixed effects, one can estimate jointly the common parameters of interest and fixed effects by the maximum likelihood estimation. However, it is well known that the MLE of the variance is inconsistent when T is finite. Similar consequences are found for the spatial panel data model with fixed effects. To avoid the incidental parameter problem, we can use a data transformation, which is a demeaning procedure of each variables. Lee and Yu (2010c) provide asymptotic properties of QML estimators for spatial dynamic panel data with both time and individual fixed effects.

Elhorst (2014) summarizes how to estimate spatial autoregressive model with fixed effects when spatial weight matrix is time invariant. In this paper, we use QML estimation for spatial autoregressive model with fixed effects when spatial weight matrix is time variant. The reader interested in the estimation and asymptotic property can refer to Appendix A.

3. AN EMPIRICAL APPLICATION

In this section, we apply the SARSF model to a dataset from 21 Countries[5] in the Organisation for Economic Co-operation and Development (OECD) for the period of 1960–2001. We construct 10 spatial weights matrices based on geographic and economic distance concepts as described in Section 3.1. We use contiguity and distance decaying weighting schemes for geographic weights, and a distance decaying scheme for economic distance weights. For economic distance weights, we allow weights to vary over time since the underlying economic variables defining economic distance are time dependent.

3.1. Specifications of the Spatial Weights Matrices

Prior to the estimation, we need to specify the spatial dependence structure between observations. The approaches to construct the spatial weight matrices often used in practice are roughly categorized into two groups: contiguity and distance decaying. We utilize both schemes following the tradition. For the geographical relations, we used the border sharing feature and the centroid distance between capital cities of each countries. The bilateral trade volume measured by the sum of bilateral exports and bilateral imports is used for economic distance. The spatial weights matrices are:

- **Contiguity:** W_{G1}
  For $\forall i \neq j$,

$$w_{ij} = \begin{cases} 1 & \text{if countries } i \text{ and } j \text{ share a border;} \\ 0 & \text{otherwise.} \end{cases}$$

- **Geographical Distance:** W_{G2}
  For $\forall i \neq j$,

$$w_{ij} = bd_{ij}^{-\gamma},$$

where bd_{ij} denotes the bilateral distance between capital cities of countries i and j, and γ is any positive exponent.[6]

- **Average Bilateral Trade:** W_E^A

$$w_{ij} = \frac{1}{T}\sum_{t=1}^{T}\left(ex_{ij,t} + im_{ij,t}\right),$$

where $ex_{ij,t}$ and $im_{ij,t}$ represent the bilateral exports and imports volume between country i and j at time t, respectively.

- **Yearly Bilateral Trade:** W_E^t

$$w_{ij,t} = ex_{ij,t} + im_{ij,t}.$$

W_{G1} is the most typical weights concept. In many cases, the boundaries shared between spatial units play an important role in terms of spatial influence. Moreover, the contiguity approach lessens burden of calculation making the weights matrix sparser than one from other specifications. On the other hands, the distance weights such as W_{G2}, W_E^A, and W_E^t have the advantages in that they provide more affluent information. However, all the elements of the weights matrices tend to be non-zero, so if the number of cross-sectional units gets larger, the numerical calculation can be burdensome. Hence, we generate distance weights with thresholds for the purpose of robustness check.[7] We order the centroid distances and pick the k closest (or biggest trade volume) units. In this paper, we used $k=5$ and $k=10$. It should be noted that the weights matrices are row-normalized to satisfy the regularity conditions for the asymptotic analysis listed in Appendix A.

3.2. Data Description

The variables needed for the estimation of the production function typically include real GDP as output, and labor participation and private capital stock as factor inputs. We obtained the variables from Penn World Table Version 7.1 (Heston, Summers, & Aten, 2012). Specifically, we extracted PPP converted GDP per capita (*rgdpl*), PPP converted GDP per worker (*rgdpl2wok*), population (*pop*) and investment share of *rgdpl* (*ki*) and calculated real GDP, y, and labor participation, l, as $y = rgdpl \times pop$ and $l = (rgdpl \times pop)/rgdpl2wok$, respectively. For the estimation of private capital stock, *Kp*, we use the perpetual inventory method after obtaining real aggregate investment, which is $rgdpl \times ki \times pop/100$. In using the perpetual inventory method, we assume that the real capital stock in 1960 is depreciated real aggregate investment in 1959 and the fixed depreciation rate of 6% for all countries for all periods.

Major challenge of empirical study on public capital productivity is finding public capital data. Kamps (2006) provides the public capital stock estimates of 22 OECD countries from 1960 to 2001. However, the estimates are based on the 2002 version of the OECD Analytical Database, so the estimates are not compatible with the up-to-date Penn World Table dataset, and also the estimates are in national currencies, which is not suitable for international comparison.[8] Fortunately, Kamps (2006) provide *the ratio between public capital stock to real GDP*. Hence, we could recover the public capital stock using the ratio and the real GDP from PWT 7.1 assuming the ratio is stable over time. The summary statistics of the key variables are shown in Table 2.

To construct the spatial weight matrices, we need the contiguity relations, geographical distances, and economic distances. The contiguity relations are examined using the queen criterion. We need to be careful in the construction of the contiguity relationship, because we handle only a subset of the entire world and some of the countries are supposed to be geographically located far from others. If we consider an island country as isolated, we may end up with a misspecified model because the country is also adjacent to other countries' marine boundaries. Although we do not consider marine boundaries strictly, but we do have two supplementary assumptions for choosing neighbors: (1) Norway, Denmark, Netherlands, Belgium, France, and United Kingdom are neighbors because they share North Sea. (2) Japan, Australia, and New Zealand are neighbors as they are located in the west part of Pacific Ocean. The bilateral geographical distances (both in miles and km) between capital cities are accessible from the website of

Table 2. Summary Statistics.

	Mean	St. Dev.	Min	Max
Real GDP (millions)	875.8	1598.5	3.9	11,265.5
Labor participation (thousands)	16,448.0	26,188.0	79.0	144,746
Private Capital (millions)	1941.3	3434.6	7.5	24,753.4
Public Capital (millions)	528.0	1004.8	2.1	5705.4

Professor Kristian Skrede Gleditsch in University of Essex.[9] For the economic distances, we obtained the bilateral trade data from NBER-UN Trade Data 1962–2000 (Feenstra, Lipsey, Deng, Ma, & Mo, 2005). The dataset is based on the reports by the importing country assuming that they are more accurate than the reports by the exporting countries. For a limitation, the dataset contains several data points that indicate a country imports from itself. This happens because some aggregate items of the statistics are created simply by adding up the subcategories. To keep the regularity assumption (Assumption A1), we ignored the "self-trade" data points and we set them zeros.

3.3. Empirical Findings

Table 3 reports the LM test statistics and the robust LM test statistics for a spatially lagged-dependent variable and a spatial error term and the associated p-values to determine which spatial terms are appropriate.[10] This is the so-called specific-to-general approach that tests the non-spatial model against the spatial lag and/or the spatial error model (Elhorst, 2014). The hypothesis of no spatially lagged-dependent variable is rejected at 1% significance in both classical LM tests and robust LM tests with all time-invariant spatial weights matrices. However, the test results on spatial error correlation are arguable; the hypothesis of no spatially autocorrelated error term cannot be rejected with all spatial weights matrices when using the classical LM tests, while the Elhorst's robust LM test rejects the nulls in all spatial weights except for the contiguity case.

Tables 4 and 5 show the estimation results when adopting a non-spatial panel fixed effects model and SARSF with selected spatial weights matrices. There are 11 estimated models depending on the spatial matrix specifications: (1) Non-spatial fixed effects, (2) Geographical contiguity, (3) Geographical distance without cut-off, (4) Average bilateral trade, and (5) Yearly bilateral trade, and the k-nearest sub-models with $k = 5, 10$ associated with the models (3)–(5). The first two columns of Table 4 are the results of non-spatial fixed effects model, which is a benchmark model. The coefficient estimates are significantly different from zero and have the expected signs. However, we found the spatial lag model is more appropriate from the results of LM tests, so the estimates are likely to be biased. The rest of the columns show the results from each spatial specifications.

Table 3. Lagrange Multiplier Tests for a Spatially Lagged-Dependent Variable and Spatial Error Correlation.

Spatial Weights	**Spatial Lag** ($H_0 : \rho = 0$)				**Spatial Error** ($H_0 : \lambda = 0$)			
	LM		Robust LM		LM		Robust LM	
Geo: Contiguity	36.17	(0.000)	36.75	(0.000)	0.07	(0.784)	0.65	(0.419)
Geo: Distance (no cut off)	2106.36	(0.000)	3184.42	(0.000)	0.36	(0.550)	1078.42	(0.000)
Geo: Distance (closest 5)	755.43	(0.000)	947.97	(0.000)	0.18	(0.667)	192.73	(0.000)
Geo: Distance (closest 10)	1730.85	(0.000)	2322.63	(0.000)	0.31	(0.575)	592.09	(0.000)
Average Trade (no cut off)	902.68	(0.000)	1128.23	(0.000)	0.14	(0.705)	225.69	(0.000)
Average Trade (biggest 5)	813.92	(0.000)	1116.02	(0.000)	0.10	(0.756)	302.19	(0.000)
Average Trade (biggest 10)	907.07	(0.000)	1174.70	(0.000)	0.12	(0.726)	267.76	(0.000)

Note: The numbers in parentheses are p-values.

Table 4. Estimation Results of a Non-Spatial Panel Fixed Effects Model and SARSF.

Determinants	(1)		(2)		(3)		(4)		(4)	
	Non-spatial FE		Geo: Contiguity		Geo: Distance		Average Trade		Yearly Trade	
Log(*L*)	0.489	(15.922)	0.663	(17.878)	0.327	(9.954)	0.300	(8.994)	0.197	(5.811)
Log(*Kp*)	0.240	(22.279)	0.294	(20.572)	0.175	(10.692)	0.177	(11.605)	0.167	(10.903)
Log(*Kg*)	0.302	(15.191)	0.352	(16.392)	0.236	(12.092)	0.241	(12.490)	0.253	(12.550)
$W \cdot \text{Log}(Y)$	–	–	−0.236	(−8.401)	0.284	(7.464)	0.276	(8.004)	0.337	(19.015)
$\hat{\sigma}_v^2$	0.008		0.010		0.008		0.008		0.008	
Log-likelihood	11.313		882.778		909.202		912.892		2,154.899	

Note: The numbers in parentheses are *t*-stats.

Table 5. Estimation Results of the k-Nearest Sub-Models.

Determinants	Geo: Distance				Average Trade				Yearly Trade			
	(3-1)		(3-2)		(4-1)		(4-2)		(5-1)		(5-2)	
	Closest 5		Closest 10		Biggest 5		Biggest 10		Biggest 5		Biggest 10	
Log(L)	0.341	(10.191)	0.330	(9.980)	0.288	(8.466)	0.301	(8.972)	0.233	(6.823)	0.190	(5.622)
Log(Kp)	0.193	(12.110)	0.183	(11.014)	0.186	(12.674)	0.179	(11.827)	0.194	(12.903)	0.163	(10.876)
Log (Kg)	0.261	(13.383)	0.243	(12.446)	0.244	(12.686)	0.243	(12.630)	0.262	(13.085)	0.254	(12.617)
$W \cdot$ Log(Y)	0.213	(6.001)	0.259	(6.688)	0.261	(7.979)	0.270	(7.955)	0.252	(7.664)	0.336	(10.106)
$\hat{\sigma}_v^2$	0.008		0.008		0.008		0.008		0.008		0.008	
Log-likelihood	894.227		903.506		908.300		911.369		2,158.198		2,157.316	

Note: The numbers in parentheses are t-stats.

The estimates of Model (2) are larger, while the coefficients of Model (3)–(5) are estimated smaller than the estimates of Model (1), respectively. In addition, the estimates of Model (3) and (4) are comparable, while the labor coefficient of Model (5) is estimated smaller than other specifications. The coefficient estimates of the spatial models should not be directly compared to the coefficients of the non-spatial model, because the coefficient estimates in the spatial models capture the direct marginal effects only. For appropriate comparisons, we need to obtain the mean direct effects, mean indirect effects, and total effects as we discussed in Section 2.

The spatial autoregressive parameter ρ is estimated similarly except for Model (2) and (5). Specifically, we find that the parameter estimate has a negative sign when we use the geographic contiguity spatial weights matrix. We expect that the true spatial dependence structure is reflected by the underlying distance concept for the spatial weights matrix. However, we may face a misspecification if we use a weak concept for the spatial relationship. Contiguity relation is not appropriate when we consider a geographically incomplete dataset. The OECD dataset contains a subset of countries from various continents. It also contains some countries that have less neighbors than others simply because they are located in other continents or in islands. This is problematic because two countries can be regarded as unrelated by the contiguity concept even if they are geographically or economically close, for example, Belgium and Switzerland. In other words, the contiguity concept considers what might be regarded as absolute relationship, while geographic and economic distance concepts allow us to consider relative relationships. For this reason, the spatial specification (1) based on contiguity concept captures the weak form of spatial dependency that may be exhibited in the OECD data, while the other spatial specifications can capture the global form of spatial dependency.

In Tables 6 and 7, we present the direct and indirect output elasticity estimates based on the coefficient estimates in Tables 4 and 5. The direct and indirect output elasticities are computed by averaging the diagonal elements and the row sums of the off-diagonal elements of $(I_N - \rho W_t)^{-1}\beta_k$, respectively, with 1,000 parameter combinations draws. The total output elasticities are the sum of direct and indirect output elasticities. Table 6 shows the results of the time-invariant spatial models. The total output elasticity estimates are roughly similar to the coefficient estimates of the non-spatial fixed effects model in Table 4. The direct output elasticity estimates are comparable to the coefficient estimates of

Table 6. Direct and Indirect Output Elasticity Estimates of the Time-Invariant Spatial Models.

Elasticities	Geo: Contiguity		Geo: Distance						Average Trade					
	(2)		(3)		(3-1)		(3-2)		(4)		(4-1)		(4-2)	
			No cut off		Closest 5		Closest 10		No cut off		Biggest 5		Biggest 10	
log(L)														
Total	0.537	(20.450)	0.459	(11.451)	0.447	(11.099)	0.433	(11.356)	0.416	(10.336)	0.413	(11.083)	0.387	(9.887)
Direct	0.679	(17.300)	0.331	(10.507)	0.333	(9.973)	0.343	(10.202)	0.304	(9.475)	0.305	(9.802)	0.290	(8.761)
Indirect	−0.143	(−6.912)	0.128	(5.814)	0.114	(5.502)	0.090	(5.510)	0.112	(6.421)	0.109	(6.710)	0.097	(6.796)
log(Kp)														
Total	0.238	(24.879)	0.242	(16.159)	0.247	(17.077)	0.246	(17.852)	0.244	(16.140)	0.244	(16.408)	0.251	(17.776)
Direct	0.301	(18.958)	0.175	(11.086)	0.184	(11.281)	0.195	(12.738)	0.178	(11.679)	0.180	(11.780)	0.188	(13.551)
Indirect	−0.063	(−6.869)	0.067	(7.436)	0.063	(6.900)	0.051	(6.460)	0.066	(8.370)	0.064	(8.308)	0.063	(8.043)
log(Kg)														
Total	0.285	(15.833)	0.332	(11.822)	0.328	(11.522)	0.332	(12.566)	0.333	(11.410)	0.333	(11.721)	0.330	(12.252)
Direct	0.360	(16.148)	0.239	(12.068)	0.244	(12.430)	0.262	(13.667)	0.243	(12.175)	0.245	(12.573)	0.247	(12.874)
Indirect	−0.075	(−7.610)	0.093	(5.474)	0.084	(4.944)	0.070	(4.877)	0.090	(5.801)	0.088	(5.720)	0.083	(5.995)

Note: The numbers in parentheses are t-stats.

the spatial models in Table 4. In fact, the direct output elasticity of Table 6 includes the first-order direct effect and the feedback effects from the higher order dependency.[11] By subtracting the coefficient estimates from the direct output elasticity estimates, we can calculate the feedback effects of each factor inputs. In Model (3), for example, the direct effects of factor inputs are 0.331, 0.175, and 0.239, the indirect effects are 0.128, 0.067, and 0.093, and the feedback effects are 0.004, 0.000, and 0.003 for labor, private capital, and public capital, respectively. The indirect part of the output elasticity explains roughly about 25–30% of the total output elasticities. The other columns of Table 6 show more or less similar results to the results from Model (3) except for Model (2). We conclude that the discrepancy of Model (2) is due to the weakness of the specification based on the contiguity concept as discussed above. In terms of scale economy, we have comparable results between the non-spatial model and time-invariant spatial models. Returns to scale are estimated as 1.031 for the non-spatial model (Model 1), 1.060, 1.033, 0.993 for each spatial Model (2)–(4).

Table 7 provides the direct and indirect effects estimates when we use the time-varying spatial weights matrix. We constructed the spatial weights matrix using the yearly bilateral trade volume hence we can compute the output elasticities over time. It is hard to observe the variations in the output elasticities across the period. This is because the proportionality of bilateral trade volume is quite stable even though each countries prefer different countries for their partners. The total output elasticities are estimated in ranges of 0.293–0.300 for labor, of 0.251–0.253 for private capital, of 0.380–0.384 for public capital. The indirect output elasticity explains about 33% of the total output elasticity, which is slightly larger than the indirect proportion from the time-invariant spatial models. We find that the total effects of labor are smaller than the results of the time-invariant weights specifications, while the total effects of private capital and public capital are greater than the corresponding total effects. Especially, the difference in the total output elasticity of labor are mainly due to the difference in the direct part, while the difference in the total output elasticity of private and public capital are due to the difference in the indirect part. Fig. 1 illustrates the variations of output elasticities over time. All series of output elasticities look very stable with some variation in labor. Although the point estimates of returns to scale are less than one, they are insignificantly different than 1.

Table 7. Direct and Indirect Output Elasticity Estimates of the Time-Varying Spatial Models.

Elastcities	1960	1961	1962	1963	1964	1965	1966	1967	1968	1969	1970	1971	1972	1973	1974	1975	1976	1977	1978	1979	1980
log(*L*)																					
Total	0.295	0.296	0.297	0.296	0.294	0.293	0.294	0.296	0.296	0.296	0.297	0.297	0.297	0.297	0.296	0.295	0.295	0.298	0.296	0.300	0.296
	(6.555)	(6.193)	(6.451)	(6.392)	(6.496)	(6.222)	(6.245)	(6.278)	(6.226)	(6.264)	(6.278)	(6.362)	(6.238)	(6.209)	(6.455)	(5.938)	(6.348)	(6.470)	(6.259)	(6.237)	(6.471)
Direct	0.198	0.199	0.200	0.199	0.198	0.197	0.197	0.199	0.199	0.199	0.200	0.200	0.200	0.200	0.200	0.199	0.198	0.201	0.199	0.202	0.199
	(6.034)	(5.742)	(5.967)	(5.969)	(5.980)	(5.778)	(5.815)	(5.791)	(5.753)	(5.773)	(5.850)	(5.899)	(5.711)	(5.752)	(5.914)	(5.527)	(5.832)	(6.057)	(5.768)	(5.840)	(6.013)
Indirect	0.097	0.096	0.097	0.097	0.096	0.095	0.097	0.097	0.097	0.096	0.097	0.097	0.097	0.097	0.096	0.096	0.097	0.097	0.097	0.098	0.096
	(5.815)	(5.584)	(5.717)	(5.722)	(5.847)	(5.518)	(5.672)	(5.684)	(5.528)	(5.620)	(5.522)	(5.758)	(5.706)	(5.690)	(5.768)	(5.478)	(5.737)	(5.683)	(5.791)	(5.551)	(5.785)
log(*Kp*)																					
Total	0.251	0.252	0.252	0.251	0.252	0.252	0.251	0.251	0.252	0.252	0.251	0.252	0.251	0.253	0.252	0.252	0.252	0.252	0.251	0.251	0.252
	(15.181)	(14.884)	(15.257)	(15.084)	(15.561)	(14.517)	(15.055)	(14.644)	(14.816)	(15.053)	(14.668)	(15.083)	(15.396)	(15.606)	(15.109)	(15.102)	(14.976)	(14.868)	(14.673)	(14.868)	(15.004)
Direct	0.169	0.170	0.170	0.169	0.169	0.170	0.169	0.169	0.170	0.170	0.169	0.169	0.169	0.170	0.170	0.170	0.169	0.170	0.169	0.169	0.170
	(11.131)	(11.018)	(11.429)	(11.248)	(11.712)	(10.64)	(11.179)	(10.746)	(10.67)	(11.373)	(10.737)	(11.323)	(11.435)	(11.418)	(11.144)	(11.058)	(11.074)	(11.001)	(11.218)	(11.139)	(11.245)
Indirect	0.083	0.082	0.082	0.082	0.082	0.082	0.083	0.082	0.083	0.082	0.082	0.082	0.082	0.082	0.082	0.082	0.083	0.082	0.082	0.082	0.082
	(9.329)	(9.446)	(9.201)	(9.842)	(9.309)	(9.378)	(9.724)	(9.579)	(9.408)	(8.932)	(9.203)	(9.549)	(9.054)	(9.807)	(9.107)	(9.753)	(9.414)	(9.790)	(9.339)	(9.682)	(9.596)
log(*Kg*)																					
Total	0.384	0.382	0.381	0.384	0.383	0.383	0.384	0.384	0.382	0.381	0.382	0.382	0.382	0.381	0.382	0.382	0.383	0.381	0.384	0.383	0.382
	(11.787)	(11.497)	(12.154)	(11.812)	(11.931)	(11.423)	(11.949)	(11.509)	(11.221)	(11.801)	(11.652)	(11.514)	(11.832)	(11.873)	(11.774)	(11.412)	(11.464)	(11.471)	(11.422)	(11.509)	(11.652)
Direct	0.257	0.257	0.256	0.257	0.257	0.257	0.257	0.257	0.256	0.257	0.257	0.257	0.257	0.256	0.257	0.257	0.257	0.256	0.257	0.257	0.257
	(12.692)	(12.390)	(12.786)	(12.940)	(12.492)	(12.471)	(13.073)	(12.897)	(12.539)	(12.255)	(12.582)	(12.338)	(12.532)	(12.848)	(12.594)	(12.731)	(12.632)	(12.542)	(12.222)	(12.451)	(12.577)
Indirect	0.127	0.125	0.125	0.126	0.126	0.125	0.127	0.127	0.126	0.125	0.126	0.125	0.125	0.125	0.125	0.125	0.127	0.125	0.126	0.126	0.125
	(6.499)	(6.452)	(6.654)	(6.622)	(6.756)	(6.323)	(6.646)	(6.285)	(6.111)	(6.580)	(6.394)	(6.513)	(6.526)	(6.664)	(6.398)	(6.306)	(6.376)	(6.461)	(6.528)	(6.527)	(6.598)

Effects	1981	1982	1983	1984	1985	1986	1987	1988	1989	1990	1991	1992	1993	1994	1995	1996	1997	1998	1999	2000	2001
log(*L*)																					
Total	0.294	0.295	0.297	0.296	0.295	0.293	0.295	0.298	0.299	0.295	0.295	0.295	0.295	0.296	0.295	0.296	0.294	0.295	0.295	0.297	0.296
	(6.386)	(6.317)	(6.376)	(6.360)	(6.224)	(6.472)	(6.164)	(6.478)	(6.115)	(6.158)	(6.479)	(6.470)	(6.142)	(6.165)	(6.355)	(6.408)	(6.410)	(6.337)	(6.481)	(6.322)	(6.410)
Direct	0.198	0.198	0.2	0.2	0.199	0.197	0.198	0.2	0.201	0.199	0.199	0.199	0.199	0.199	0.2	0.199	0.198	0.199	0.199	0.2	0.199
	(5.803)	(5.714)	(5.864)	(5.963)	(5.805)	(5.956)	(5.766)	(6.040)	(5.754)	(5.735)	(5.932)	(5.943)	(5.718)	(5.873)	(5.928)	(5.880)	(5.908)	(5.783)	(6.091)	(5.857)	(5.871)
Indirect	0.096	0.096	0.097	0.097	0.096	0.096	0.096	0.097	0.098	0.096	0.096	0.097	0.096	0.097	0.096	0.097	0.096	0.097	0.096	0.097	0.097
	(5.915)	(5.815)	(5.811)	(5.589)	(5.606)	(5.826)	(5.556)	(5.656)	(5.514)	(5.560)	(5.914)	(5.878)	(5.500)	(5.367)	(5.620)	(5.851)	(5.881)	(5.868)	(5.683)	(5.740)	(5.792)
log(*Kp*)																					
Total	0.252	0.251	0.252	0.251	0.251	0.253	0.252	0.251	0.252	0.252	0.252	0.251	0.252	0.251	0.252	0.251	0.252	0.252	0.253	0.252	0.251
	(14.717)	(14.362)	(15.569)	(14.502)	(14.733)	(15.154)	(15.524)	(14.243)	(15.111)	(15.245)	(15.228)	(14.276)	(15.007)	(14.830)	(14.327)	(15.511)	(15.510)	(15.263)	(16.037)	(15.238)	(15.229)
Direct	0.170	0.169	0.170	0.169	0.169	0.170	0.169	0.169	0.169	0.170	0.169	0.169	0.170	0.169	0.170	0.169	0.169	0.170	0.171	0.170	0.169
	(10.946)	(10.474)	(11.469)	(10.826)	(10.842)	(11.371)	(11.662)	(10.805)	(11.401)	(11.235)	(11.318)	(10.833)	(11.087)	(11.082)	(10.689)	(11.557)	(11.485)	(11.388)	(11.881)	(11.519)	(11.096)
Indirect	0.082	0.082	0.082	0.082	0.082	0.083	0.082	0.082	0.083	0.082	0.082	0.082	0.082	0.082	0.082	0.082	0.082	0.083	0.082	0.083	0.083
	(9.232)	(9.190)	(9.571)	(9.604)	(9.768)	(9.231)	(9.517)	(9.220)	(9.773)	(9.480)	(9.563)	(9.431)	(9.401)	(9.719)	(9.411)	(9.388)	(9.857)	(9.359)	(9.519)	(9.540)	(9.436)
log(*Kg*)																					
Total	0.382	0.383	0.382	0.383	0.384	0.382	0.383	0.383	0.382	0.382	0.383	0.384	0.382	0.383	0.382	0.383	0.383	0.382	0.380	0.381	0.384
	(11.232)	(10.906)	(11.626)	(11.345)	(11.707)	(12.151)	(12.119)	(11.017)	(11.961)	(11.686)	(11.795)	(11.346)	(11.785)	(11.549)	(10.981)	(12.115)	(12.006)	(11.627)	(12.510)	(11.937)	(11.675)
Direct	0.257	0.257	0.256	0.257	0.258	0.256	0.257	0.257	0.256	0.256	0.257	0.258	0.257	0.257	0.257	0.257	0.257	0.256	0.256	0.256	0.257
	(12.168)	(12.208)	(12.776)	(12.456)	(13.110)	(13.013)	(12.785)	(11.847)	(12.818)	(12.734)	(12.871)	(12.411)	(12.783)	(12.336)	(11.985)	(12.803)	(13.050)	(12.813)	(13.097)	(12.703)	(12.770)
Indirect	0.125	0.126	0.125	0.126	0.126	0.126	0.126	0.126	0.126	0.125	0.126	0.126	0.125	0.126	0.124	0.126	0.126	0.126	0.124	0.126	0.127
	(6.375)	(6.003)	(6.420)	(6.399)	(6.426)	(6.617)	(6.786)	(6.367)	(6.782)	(6.503)	(6.525)	(6.374)	(6.429)	(6.611)	(6.257)	(6.714)	(6.665)	(6.449)	(6.849)	(6.730)	(6.364)

Note: The numbers in parentheses are *t*-stats.

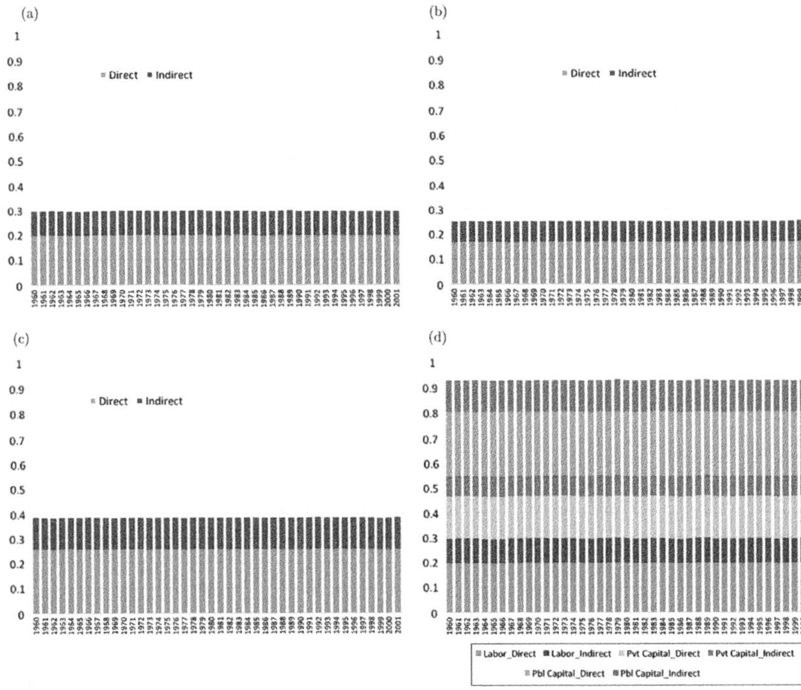

Fig. 1. Output Elasticity. Output Elasticity of (a) Labor; (b) Private Capital; (c) Public Capital; and (d) Factor Inputs.

3.4. *Inflow and Outflow Spillovers*

Regarding the spillover effects of public capital stock, examining the spillover effects of a particular country to other countries or the spillover effects from other countries to a specific country is crucial. We separated the total effects of public capital stock on output into the direct and indirect effects on average. However, the average indirect effects do not give the information about the spillover effects of each country to other countries or vice versa. In this section, we parse the marginal indirect effects by country. First of all, the marginal effects of spatial autoregressive model can be found as:

$$\frac{\partial Y_t}{\partial X_{k,t}} = (I_N - \rho W_t)^{-1}\beta_k. \tag{12}$$

Here $(I_N - \rho W_t)^{-1}$ is an $(N \times N)$ matrix, which makes β_k be no longer interpreted as marginal effects. Because of the pre-multiplication of $(I_N - \rho W_t)^{-1}$, the marginal effects $\frac{\partial Y_t}{\partial X_{k,t}}$ is also $(N \times N)$ matrix. The diagonal elements represent the direct effects of regressors. In other words, the effects of a unit increment of an input in a particular country on the production of the country. The off-diagonal elements can be interpreted as indirect effects. For instance, the *ij*th element $(i \neq j)$ represent the effect of a unit increment of an input in country i on the production of country j. Hence, the row-sum, $\sum_{i \neq j} \frac{\partial Y_i}{\partial X_{k,j}}$, can be interpreted as the spillover effects from other countries to a specific country when all other countries increase a unit in a factor input. On the other hands, the column-sum, $\sum_{j \neq i} \frac{\partial Y_i}{\partial X_{k,j}}$, can be interpreted as the total spillover effects of a particular country to the outputs of other countries. We obtain the measures using the Bayesian MCMC approach suggested by LeSage and Pace (2009) as discussed in Section 2.

Table 8 shows the spillover effects from all other countries to a specific country. We name the effects *Inflow spillover effects*. Interestingly, the spillover effects of increasing a unit of factor inputs in all other countries are almost similar across the countries. This implies that the sample of OECD countries get affected roughly same by a global shock. Table 9 shows the total spillover effects of a particular country to other countries. We name the effects *Outflow spillover effects*. The effects measure how much a country impact other countries. In this case, the spillover effects of increasing a unit of factor inputs in a particular country shows some variations across the countries. Specifically, the countries with large economies, such as United States, United Kingdom, and France, have larger impacts on other countries than smaller economies.

3.5. Efficiency Analysis

Let us turn our attention to the results of the efficiency analysis. With the estimation results, we obtained the efficiency scores and rankings of countries. Table 10 displays the relative efficiency scores estimates and the rankings. In the non-spatial fixed effects model, Iceland appears to be the most efficient country, while Japan is the least efficient country. However, we regard the estimation results as biased because we found the spatial lag model is more appropriate from the Lagrange Multiplier tests, hence the efficiency estimates are also biased. The other four models show relatively

Table 8. Inflow Spillover Effects (Row-Sum): $\sum_{i \neq j} \frac{\partial Y_i}{\partial X_{k,j}}$.

	Labor		Private Capital		Public Capital	
	Indirect effects	t-stat	Indirect effects	t-stat	Indirect effects	t-stat
Australia	0.113	6.725	0.067	8.315	0.091	5.694
Austria	0.113	6.704	0.067	8.277	0.092	5.675
Belgium	0.111	6.781	0.065	8.418	0.090	5.745
Canada	0.106	6.904	0.063	8.645	0.086	5.855
Denmark	0.113	6.714	0.067	8.297	0.092	5.685
Finland	0.113	6.705	0.067	8.280	0.092	5.676
France	0.109	6.833	0.065	8.514	0.089	5.792
Greece	0.114	6.692	0.067	8.256	0.092	5.665
Iceland	0.114	6.684	0.067	8.242	0.093	5.658
Ireland	0.113	6.710	0.067	8.288	0.092	5.681
Italy	0.111	6.785	0.066	8.425	0.090	5.748
Japan	0.109	6.844	0.064	8.535	0.088	5.802
Netherlands	0.111	6.777	0.066	8.410	0.090	5.741
New Zealand	0.113	6.699	0.067	8.269	0.092	5.671
Norway	0.113	6.715	0.067	8.298	0.092	5.686
Portugal	0.113	6.702	0.067	8.274	0.092	5.674
Spain	0.112	6.738	0.066	8.340	0.091	5.706
Sweden	0.112	6.740	0.066	8.344	0.091	5.708
Switzerland	0.113	6.722	0.067	8.311	0.092	5.692
United Kingdom	0.110	6.820	0.065	8.490	0.089	5.780
United States	0.101	7.103	0.060	9.027	0.082	6.039

low efficiency scores than the efficiency scores of non-spatial fixed effects model. Moreover, the efficiency scores change dramatically when we incorporate the spatial autoregressive term. Except for Model (2), which uses geographical contiguity as spatial weights, Model (3)–(5) are showing quite robust results. In these models, United States is the most efficient, while Iceland is the least efficient. From the change between the Model (1) and other models, we conclude that smaller economies get relatively less benefits from other countries, while larger economies get more benefits from other countries. The countries that have relatively low average GDP, such as Iceland, Ireland, and New Zealand, get lower ranks in efficiency, while

Table 9. Outflow Spillover Effects (Column-Sum): $\sum_{j \neq i} \frac{\partial Y_i}{\partial X_{k,j}}$.

	Labor		Private Capital		Public Capital	
	Indirect effects	*t*-stat	Indirect effects	*t*-stat	Indirect effects	*t*-stat
Australia	0.053	7.015	0.031	9.417	0.043	5.953
Austria	0.035	6.802	0.020	8.999	0.028	5.770
Belgium	0.130	6.596	0.076	8.611	0.104	5.596
Canada	0.108	5.735	0.064	7.111	0.087	4.886
Denmark	0.058	7.139	0.034	9.661	0.047	6.061
Finland	0.037	6.967	0.022	9.318	0.030	5.912
France	0.253	6.818	0.149	9.031	0.204	5.784
Greece	0.015	6.659	0.009	8.729	0.012	5.649
Iceland	0.003	6.962	0.002	9.308	0.002	5.907
Ireland	0.032	6.315	0.019	8.099	0.026	5.361
Italy	0.187	6.914	0.110	9.217	0.150	5.866
Japan	0.198	6.665	0.116	8.743	0.159	5.653
Netherlands	0.149	6.782	0.088	8.962	0.120	5.753
New Zealand	0.014	6.913	0.008	9.215	0.011	5.864
Norway	0.055	7.027	0.032	9.438	0.044	5.964
Portugal	0.028	6.885	0.016	9.160	0.022	5.841
Spain	0.090	6.842	0.053	9.077	0.072	5.804
Sweden	0.105	7.189	0.061	9.762	0.084	6.105
Switzerland	0.070	6.735	0.041	8.871	0.056	5.713
United Kingdom	0.303	7.056	0.178	9.495	0.244	5.988
United States	0.427	6.722	0.251	8.850	0.344	5.700

the countries that have relatively high average GDP, such as France, Italy, Japan, United Kingdom, and United States, get higher ranks in SARSF models.

From the results, one can observe some variations in efficiency ranking between non-spatial model and spatial models. As our spatial weights rely on the economic distance, specifically on the relative importance as trade partner, we roughly guess that the changes in efficiency ranking are caused by the (relative) size of trade or the size of the economy. Hence, we examined the relationship between the changes in efficiency scores and either GDP share (% of World GDP) or Trade-to-GDP share.[12] Assuming all spatial models deliver similar effects, we confine the analysis on the

Table 10. Estimation Results of Efficiency Scores.

Country	(1)		(2)		(3)		(4)		(5)	
	Non-spatial FE		Geo: Contiguity		Geo: Distance		Average Trade		Yearly Trade	
	Eff. Score (%)	Ranking	Eff. Score (%)	Ranking	Eff. Score (%)	Ranking	Eff. Score (%)	Ranking	Eff. Score (%)	Ranking
Australia	77.3	8	22.0	17	48.0	7	34.9	11	25.2	11
Austria	71.7	13	38.9	8	34.3	14	32.4	14	23.4	13
Belgium	86.8	4	51.0	3	39.0	12	39.3	9	28.4	9
Canada	87.3	3	66.9	2	45.7	8	32.8	13	23.9	12
Denmark	72.7	12	38.2	9	32.4	15	32.1	15	22.2	15
Finland	69.7	16	32.0	12	30.3	17	28.9	17	20.4	16
France	73.0	11	25.3	16	60.9	2	60.1	2	52.5	3
Greece	67.8	19	44.7	5	31.3	16	29.1	16	20.3	17
Iceland	100.0	1	100.0	1	17.2	21	15.5	21	7.7	21
Ireland	68.2	18	31.9	13	22.9	20	19.3	20	12.1	20
Italy	70.9	15	21.5	18	60.2	3	56.5	4	47.6	4
Japan	51.6	21	0.1	21	58.3	5	41.4	8	36.5	6
Netherlands	76.1	9	35.9	11	43.1	10	42.6	6	32.0	7
New Zealand	69.4	17	44.5	6	23.5	19	20.2	19	12.4	19
Norway	83.2	6	36.2	10	36.2	13	33.7	12	23.1	14
Portugal	66.8	20	39.4	7	28.1	18	28.1	18	19.9	18
Spain	76.1	10	28.2	15	53.7	6	48.7	5	37.4	5
Sweden	83.8	5	31.1	14	45.3	9	42.5	7	31.7	8
Switzerland	87.6	2	49.4	4	40.1	11	37.3	10	26.6	10
United Kindom	71.0	14	17.7	20	60.0	4	59.3	3	53.9	2
United States	78.3	7	19.6	19	100.0	1	100.0	1	100.0	1

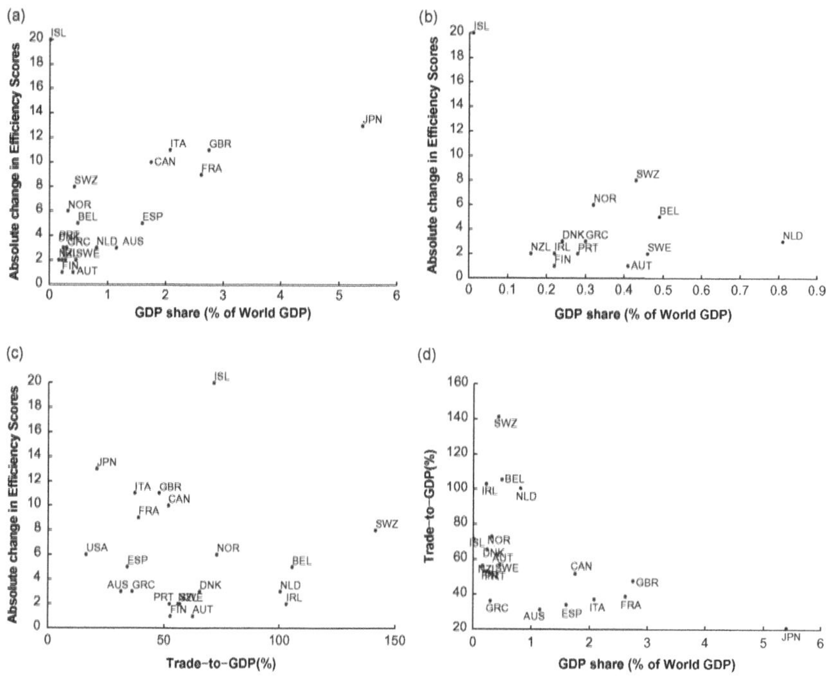

Fig. 2. Comparisons of Country Characteristics. (a) GDP Share versus Change in Efficiency Scores; (b) GDP Share versus Change in Efficiency Scores (Selected Countries); (c) Trade Openness versus Change in Efficiency Scores; and (d) GDP Share versus Trade Openness.

comparison of Model (1) and (4). Fig. 2 shows the relation between the absolute change in efficiency ranking and GDP share. We observe the positive correlation between the two indices. The correlation coefficient is 0.149. The relation is reasonable because we have checked the indirect effects tend to be larger if the size of economy is larger (Table 9). The non-spatial Fixed effects model cannot capture the indirect effects appropriately that the efficiency rankings might be inaccurate. Fig. 2 displays the same plots with GDP share < 1%. We still can see the positive correlation.[13] For the next, Fig. 2 illustrates the relation between the changes in efficiency scores and the trade openness. The trade openness is measured by Trade-to-GDP share. We observe a negative correlation. The correlation coefficient is −0.10. This is possible because the correlation coefficient between

GDP share and Trade-to-GDP is −0.45. In other words, the relative trades to GDPs of the countries that have relatively small economies tend to be large. Hence, for those countries the indirect effects are relatively small, which results in the negative relation between the changes in efficiency scores and trade openness.

For the distributional comparisons of the models, we plot the kernel densities of the efficiency scores in Fig. 3. We found the distribution from the non-spatial fixed effects model located slightly to the right side of the density plots of other four models. Finally, in Fig. 4 we compared the efficiency scores distributions when we include the public capital stock as a factor input with the distributions when we exclude the public capital stock. We observe the efficiency scores distributions are shifted to the right when we add public capital as a factor input except for the case of Model (2), which implies that the inclusion of public capital stock variable helps to explain some of variations in production.

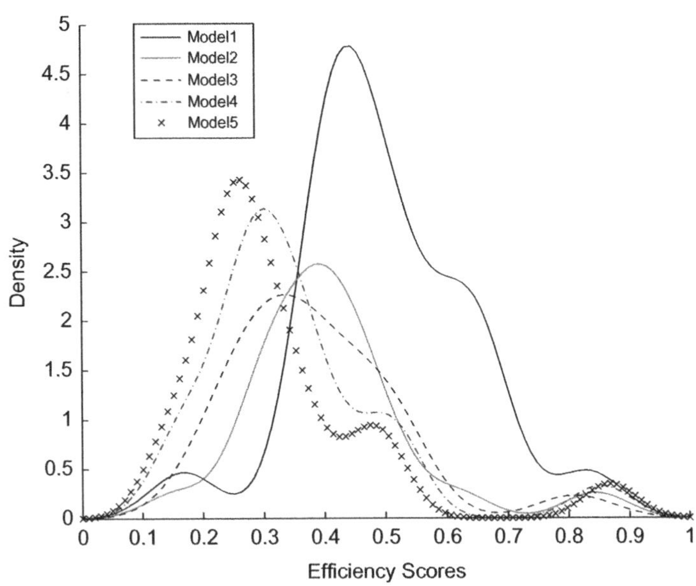

Fig. 3. Kernel Densities of Efficiency Scores.

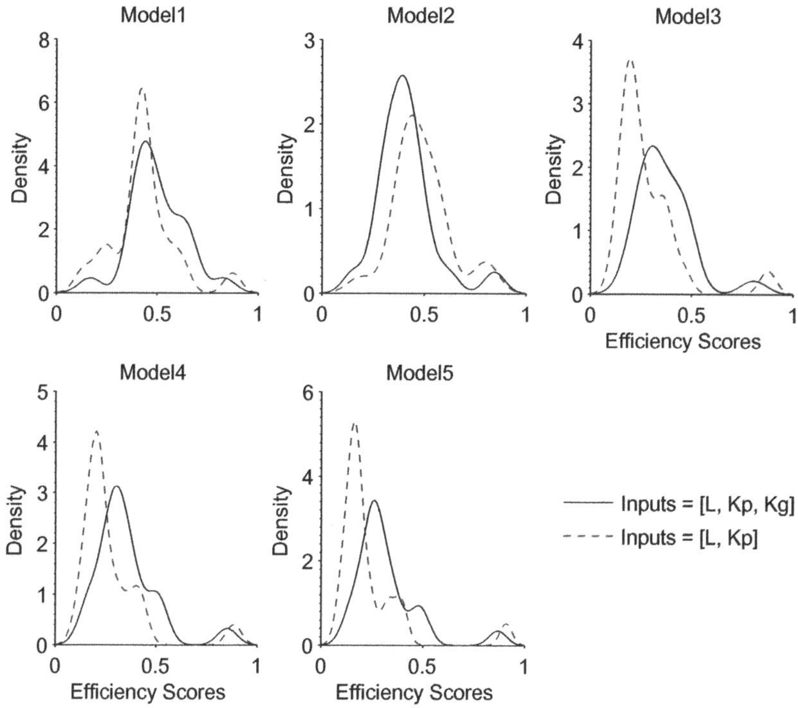

Fig. 4. Comparisons of Densities of Efficiency Scores.

4. CONCLUSIONS

In this paper, we investigate the spillover effects of public capital stock in a production frontier model that accounts for cross-sectional dependency among countries. We estimate the output elasticity of public capital stock as well as labor and private capital stock in a Cliff-Ord-type production frontier function. Especially, we separate out the direct and indirect effects of factor inputs and interpret the indirect effects as the spillovers. Moreover, the spatial autoregressive stochastic frontier model allows us to gain the relative efficiencies of countries as well. The spatial weights matrix is the essential characteristic of the approach and we exploit the geographical and economic interactions to construct our spatial weights matrices. Specifically, we allow for the spatial weights matrix to vary across time, which is reasonable for economic/socioeconomic spatial weights. In addition, we compare the estimation results based on a number of specifications of the spatial dependency structure and observe robustness of our model.

We estimate the output elasticities of factor inputs at international level by the empirical application to the data for 21 OECD countries from 1960 to 2001. We found relatively large total output elasticities of public capital stock and observe that the indirect effects comprise around 30% of the total elasticities, which supports the argument of Pereira and Andraz (2013). We obtained larger total output elasticity of public capital stock when we use the time-varying weights matrix. Finally, we measure the relative technical efficiencies of countries. Concerning the spatial dependency, SARSF model is expected to give the less biased relative efficiency estimates than the non-spatial counterpart, but more delicate comparison between efficiency estimates from different models should be analyzed by the future works. Compare to the analysis that utilizes only the traditional factor inputs, labor and private capital stock, inclusion of public capital stock results in shift of the efficiency score distribution to the right, which implies that some of production process is explained by public capital stock variable additionally.

NOTES

1. Elhorst (2014) named this equation as the general nesting spatial (GNS) model.

2. For model selection, Anselin et al. (2008) provide Lagrange Multiplier tests for a spatially lagged-dependent variable and for a spatial error term under panel data setting. Elhorst (2010) also suggested the robust counterparts of the LM tests. We provide the LM test results in Section 3. We can use likelihood ratio test to choose a model among nested models.

3. Since output is in logarithms, relative technical efficiency is defined as $\hat{r}_i \equiv \exp(-u_i^*)$.

4. We can report the averages of the direct and indirect effects for a single marginal effect measure as suggested by LeSage and Pace (2009). However, researchers may be interested in direct and indirect effects of each unit depending on the research purposes. In this paper, we examine which country has more impacts on other countries and also which country is more likely to be affected by other countries by looking at the estimated direct and indirect effects by country.

5. The 21 countries are Australia, Austria, Belgium, Canada, Denmark, Finland, France, Greece, Iceland, Ireland, Italy, Japan, Netherlands, New Zealand, Norway, Portugal, Spain, Sweden, Switzerland, United Kingdom, and United States. Germany is excluded because of a truncation in data at 1990.

6. We assume $\gamma = 1$ in this paper.

7. Spatial models have a major weakness in the exogeneity of the spatial weights matrix W. W needs to be specified prior to the estimation but the specification of W is not tested in most cases. For this reason, it is examined whether the empirical results are robust to the specifications of W by estimating the same model with different spatial weights matrices in empirical research. In this paper, we check the sensitivity of the results to the choice of W using the 10 specifications of W.

8. It is challenging to find appropriate price indexes and PPP exchange rates for all countries for the periods.

9. http://privatewww.essex.ac.uk/~ksg/

10. The reviewer suggested that we estimate the Spatial Durbin Model (SDM) and pointed out possible overestimation problems when time period fixed effects are ignored. As this is an empirical study such modeling choices are of course interesting but are only possible given the data and the empirical study we have pursued. First, all SDM results return negative marginal products. Although the SDM of course allows flexibility in the ratios of the direct and indirect effects, the flexibility is at the cost of results that are meaningless economically. Moreover, the results changed substantially when we consider time-period fixed effects instead of spatial fixed effects. In particular, the total impacts of labor and public capital decreased while the impact of private capital increased. The results for the indirect effects mirror this pattern. Regarding proportionality of indirect effects, the indirect effects take about 16% out of total effects for the geographic weighting matrices and averaged about 1.5% for the economic weighting matrices. The results when we include both spatial and time-period fixed effects are quite unreasonable. The data do not appear capable of supporting such an empirical specification. Results are available from the authors on request.

11. The feedback effects are the effects, which pass through neighbors and back to the country itself. A feedback effect is computed as the average of the diagonal elements of $(\rho W_t + \rho^2 W_t^2 + \rho^3 W_t^3 + \cdots)\beta_k$.

12. The data sources of GDP share and Trade-to-GDP are https://www.quandl.com/collections/economics/gdp-as-share-of-world-gdp-at-ppp-by-country and World Bank (http://data.worldbank.org/indicator/NE.TRD.GNFS.ZS), respectively.

13. For Iceland, we guess that the spatial effects might be reflected excessively because the size of economy is too small relative to other observations in the sample. One needs to be careful for interpretation on this sample.

14. The bias-corrected $\hat{\sigma}^2_{v,BC}$ proposed by Lee and Yu (2010a) to avoid possible bias caused by the demeaning procedure can be obtained as $\hat{\sigma}^2_{v,BC} = \frac{T}{T-1}\hat{\sigma}^2_v$.

15. This is a modification of the asymptotic variance matrix provided by Elhorst and Freret (2009).

ACKNOWLEDGMENT

The authors would like to thank Ziyang (Bob) Chen for his valuable research assistance.

REFERENCES

Anselin, L. (1988). *Spatial econometrics: Methods and models*. Springer Netherlands.

Anselin, L., Gallo, J., & Jayet, H. (2008). Spatial panel econometrics. In L. Matyas & P. Sevestre (Eds.). *The econometrics of panel data* (Vol. 46, pp. 625–660). Advanced Studies in Theoretical and Applied Econometrics. Springer Berlin Heidelberg.

Aschauer, D. A. (1989). Is public expenditure productive? *Journal of Monetary Economics*, *23*, 177–200.

Aschauer, D. A. (1990). Infrastructure and the economy. *Journal of Contemporary Water Research and Education*, *81*(1), 18–21.

Bom, P. R., & Ligthart, J. E. (2014). What have we learned from three decades of research on the productivity of public capital? *Journal of Economic Surveys*, *28*(5), 889–916.

Cliff, A., & Ord, J. (1973). *Spatial autocorrelation*. London: Pion.

Cliff, A., & Ord, J. (1981). *Spatial processes, models and applications*. London: Pion.

Delorme, C. D., Thompson, H. G., & Warren, R. S. (1999). Public infrastructure and private productivity: A stochastic-frontier approach. *Journal of Macroeconomics*, *21*, 563–576.

Elhorst, J. P. (2010). Spatial panel data models. In M. Fischer & A. Getis (Eds.). *Handbook of applied spatial analysis* (pp. 377–407). Springer Berlin.

Elhorst, J. P. (2014). *Spatial econometrics: From cross-sectional data to spatial panels*. Springer-Verlag Berlin Heidelberg.

Elhorst, J. P., & Freret, S. (2009). Evidence of political yardstick competition in france using a two-regime spatial durbin model with fixed effects. *Journal of Regional Science*, *49*(5), 931–951.

Feenstra, R. C., Lipsey, R. E., Deng, H., Ma, A. C., & Mo, H. (2005, January). *World trade flows: 1962-2000*. Working Paper No. 11040, National Bureau of Economic Research.

Glass, A. J., Kenjegalieva, K., & Sickles, R. (2013). *A spatial autoregressive production Frontier model for panel data: With an application to European countries*.

Heston, A., Summers, R., & Aten, B. (2012, July). *Penn World Table Version 7.1*. Center for International Comparisons of Production, Income and Prices at the University of Pennsylvania.

Holtz-Eakin, D. (1994). Public-sector capital and the productivity puzzle. *The Review of Economics and Statistics*, *76*, 12–21.

Holtz-Eakin, D., & Schwartz, A. E. (1995). Spatial productivity spillovers from public infrastructure: Evidence from state highways. *International Tax and Public Finance*, *2*(3), 459–468.

Kamps, C. (2006). *New estimates of government net capital stocks for 22 OECD countries, 1960-2001*. IMF Staff Papers No. 53, pp. 120–150.

Kapoor, M., Kelejian, H. H., & Prucha, I. R. (2007). Panel data models with spatially correlated error components. *Journal of Econometrics*, *140*, 97–130.

Lee, L., & Yu, J. (2010a). Estimation of spatial autoregressive panel data models with fixed effects. *Journal of Econometrics*, *154*, 165–185.

Lee, L., & Yu, J. (2010b). Estimation of spatial panels. *Foundations and Trends in Econometrics*, *4*, 1–164.

Lee, L., & Yu, J. (2010c). A spatial dynamic panel data model with both time and individual fixed effects. *Economic Theory*, *26*, 564–597.

Lee, L. F., & Yu, J. (2012). QML estimation of spatial dynamic panel data models with time varying spatial weights matrices. *Spatial Economic Analysis*, *7*(1).

LeSage, J., & Pace, R. K. (2009). *Introduction to spatial econometrics*. Boca Raton, FL: Chapman & Hall/CRC.

Munnell, A. H. (1990). Why has productivity declined? Productivity and public investment. *New England Economic Review*, Jan/Feb, 3–22.

Munnell, A. H. (1993). *An assessment of trends and economic impacts of infrastructure investment, infrastructure policies for the 1990s*. Paris: OECD.

Pavlyuk, D. (2012). Maximum likelihood estimator for spatial stochastic frontier models. In *12th International conference "reliability and statistics in transportation and communication"*, Riga, Latvia, pp. 11–19.

Pereira, A. M., & Andraz, J. M. (2013). On the economic effects of public infrastructure investment: A survey of the international evidence. *Journal of Economic Development*, *38*(4), 1–34.

Pereira, A. M., & Roca-Sagales, O. (2003). Spillover effects of public capital formation: Evidence from the Spanish regions. *Journal of Urban Economics*, *53*, 238–256.

Schmidt, P., & Sickles, R. C. (1984). Production frontiers and panel data. *Journal of Business and Economic Statistics*, *2*(4), 367–374.

Tatom, J. A. (1991). Public capital and private sector performance. *Federal Reserve Bank of St. Louis Review*, *73*, 3–15.

Wang, Y. C. (2014). Evidence of public capital spillovers and endogenous growth in Taiwan. *Economic Modelling*, *39*, 314–321.

APPENDIX ML ESTIMATION OF SPATIAL AUTOREGRESSIVE MODEL WITH TIME-VARYING SPATIALWEIGHTS MATRICES

Let $\theta = (\beta, \rho, \sigma_v^2)'$. The log-likelihood function of the Model (9) is

$$\text{Log}L_{N,T}(\theta, \boldsymbol{\alpha}) = -\frac{NT}{2}\ln\left(2\pi\sigma_v^2\right) + \sum_{t=1}^{T}\ln|I_N - \rho W_t| - \frac{1}{2\sigma_v^2}\sum_{t=1}^{T}V_t'(\theta)V_t(\theta), \tag{A.1}$$

where $V_t(\theta) = (I_N - \rho W_t)Y_t - X_t\beta - \boldsymbol{\alpha}$. We can get the analytic solution to α_i by solving the first-order conditions of Eq. (A.1) with respect to α_i as follows:

$$\alpha_i = \frac{1}{T}\sum_{t=1}^{T}\left(y_{it} - \rho\sum_{j=1}^{N}w_{ij}^t y_{jt} - X_{it}\beta\right), \quad i = 1, \ldots, N. \tag{A.2}$$

By substituting Eq. (A.2) into Eq. (A.1), we concentrate out $\boldsymbol{\alpha}$ in Eq. (A.1) and get the concentrated log-likelihood function as follows:

$$\text{Log}L_{N,T}(\theta) = -\frac{NT}{2}\ln\left(2\pi\sigma_v^2\right) + \sum_{t=1}^{T}\ln|I_N - \rho W_t| - \frac{1}{2\sigma_v^2}\sum_{t=1}^{T}\tilde{V}_t'(\theta)\tilde{V}_t(\theta), \tag{A.3}$$

where $\tilde{V}_t(\theta) = \tilde{Y}_t - \rho\widetilde{W_tY_t} - \tilde{X}_t\beta$, $\tilde{Y}_t = Y_t - \frac{1}{T}\sum_{t=1}^{T}Y_t$, $\widetilde{W_tY_t} = W_tY_t - \frac{1}{T}\sum_{t=1}^{T}W_tY_t$, and $\tilde{X}_t = X_t - \frac{1}{T}\sum_{t=1}^{T}X_t$. As one can see, the concentrated log-likelihood function (A.3) is same as the log-likelihood function from Eq. (9) after demeaning variables. We can write the transformed model after demeaning as follows:

$$\tilde{Y}_t = \rho\widetilde{W_tY_t} + \tilde{X}_t\beta + \tilde{V}_t. \tag{A.4}$$

Assuming we know the true value of $\rho = \rho^*$, the ordinary least-squares estimates of β and σ_v^2 of Eq. (A.4) can be found analytically as follows:[14]

$$\hat{\beta} = \left(\tilde{X}'\tilde{X}\right)^{-1}\tilde{X}'\left[\tilde{Y} - \rho^*\widetilde{WY}\right], \tag{A.5}$$

$$\hat{\sigma}_v^2 = \frac{1}{NT}\left(\tilde{Y} - \rho\widetilde{WY} - \tilde{X}\hat{\beta}\right)'\left(\tilde{Y} - \rho\widetilde{WY} - \tilde{X}\hat{\beta}\right). \tag{A.6}$$

Substituting Eqs. (A.5) and (A.6) into the likelihood (A.3) gives a concentrated likelihood function depending on a single unknown parameter ρ:

$$\text{Log}L_{N,T}(\rho) = C - \frac{NT}{2}\left(\tilde{Y} - \rho\widetilde{WY} - \tilde{X}\hat{\beta}\right)'\left(\tilde{Y} - \rho\widetilde{WY} - \tilde{X}\hat{\beta}\right) + \sum_{t=1}^{T}\ln|I_N - \rho W_t|, \tag{A.7}$$

where C is a constant term which is not relying on ρ. Finally, by maximizing Eq. (A.7), we can obtain a solution to ρ. Even though a closed-form solution of ρ does not exist, the numerical solution is unique because the concentrated log-likelihood (A.7) is a concave function in ρ. Once we have an ML estimator of ρ, we can compute the estimates of β and σ_v^2 by replacing it in Eqs. (A.5) and (A.6).

For the asymptotic properties of the QML estimators, we need the following regularity assumptions for the spatial weight matrix, W_t.

Assumption A1 W_t's are row-normalized non-stochastic spatial weights matrices with zero diagonals for all t.

Assumption A2 $I_N - \rho W_t$ is invertible for all t and for all $\rho \in \Lambda$, where the parameter space Λ is compact and ρ_0 is in the interior of Λ.

Assumption A3 W_t's are uniformly bounded in both row and column sums in absolute value, uniformly in t. Also, $(I_N - \rho W_t)^{-1}$'s are uniformly bounded, uniformly in $\rho \in \Lambda$ and t.

The asymptotic variance matrix of the parameters[15] is derived as

$$\text{Asy.Var}\left(\beta,\rho,\sigma_v^2\right) = \begin{bmatrix} \frac{1}{\sigma^2}\tilde{X}'\tilde{X} & - & - \\ \frac{1}{\sigma^2}\tilde{X}'W^{*'}\tilde{X}\beta & \sum_{t=1}^{T} tr\left(W_t^* W_t^* + W_t^{*'} W_t^*\right) + \frac{1}{\sigma^2}\beta'\tilde{X}'W^{*'}W^*\tilde{X}\beta & - \\ 0 & \frac{1}{\sigma^2}\sum_{t=1}^{T} tr\left(W_t^*\right) & \frac{NT}{2\sigma^4} \end{bmatrix}^{-1}, \tag{A.8}$$

where $W_t^* = W_t(I_N - \rho W_t)^{-1}$.

PART V
CONTINUOUS DEPENDENT VARIABLES – BAYESIAN

LOCAL MARGINAL ANALYSIS OF SPATIAL DATA: A GAUSSIAN PROCESS REGRESSION APPROACH WITH BAYESIAN MODEL AND KERNEL AVERAGING

Jacob Dearmon[a] and Tony E. Smith[b]

[a]*Meinders School of Business, Oklahoma City University, Oklahoma, OK, USA*
[b]*Department of Electrical and Systems Engineering, University of Pennsylvania, Philadelphia, PA, USA*

ABSTRACT

Statistical methods of spatial analysis are often successful at either prediction or explanation, but not necessarily both. In a recent paper, Dearmon and Smith (2016) showed that by combining Gaussian Process Regression (GPR) with Bayesian Model Averaging (BMA), a modeling framework could be developed in which both needs are addressed. In particular, the smoothness properties of GPR together with the robustness of BMA allow local spatial analyses of individual variable effects that yield remarkably stable results. However, this GPR-BMA approach is not without its

Spatial Econometrics: Qualitative and Limited Dependent Variables
Advances in Econometrics, Volume 37, 297–342

ISSN: 0731-9053/doi:10.1108/S0731-905320160000037018

limitations. In particular, the standard (isotropic) covariance kernel of GPR treats all explanatory variables in a symmetric way that limits the analysis of their individual effects. Here we extend this approach by introducing a mixture of kernels (both isotropic and anisotropic) which allow different length scales for each variable. To do so in a computationally efficient manner, we also explore a number of Bayes-factor approximations that avoid the need for costly reversible-jump Monte Carlo methods.

To demonstrate the effectiveness of this Variable Length Scale *(VLS) model in terms of both predictions and local marginal analyses, we employ selected simulations to compare VLS with Geographically Weighted Regression (GWR), which is currently the most popular method for such spatial modeling. In addition, we employ the classical Boston Housing data to compare VLS not only with GWR but also with other well-known spatial regression models that have been applied to this same data. Our main results are to show that VLS not only compares favorably with spatial regression at the aggregate level but is also far more accurate than GWR at the local level.*

Keywords: Gaussian process regression; bayesian model averaging; local spatial analysis

JEL classifications: C11; C14; C21

1. INTRODUCTION

Gaussian Process Regression (GPR) with Bayesian Model Averaging (BMA) is a powerful analytical method for modeling spatial data in contexts where little is known about either functional forms or relevant variables. In a previous paper, Dearmon and Smith (2016) [DS] compared the GPR-BMA method to a range of alternative approaches using both actual and simulated spatial data sets. This method was shown to outperform other approaches with respect to the identification of relevant predictor variables. In addition, the differentiability of GPR-BMA predictors was shown to allow local marginal estimates of individual variable effects to be calculated explicitly. While other methods can be used to study such effects, most notably Geographically Weighted Regression (GWR), it is shown below that the smooth nature of GPR-BMA predictors yields more stable estimates of these effects. Thus, the main objective of the current paper is to extend model averaging to include kernel averaging and to demonstrate its usefulness for local marginal analysis in terms of selected simulations and empirical applications. Here we focus on the well-known Boston Housing data, and show that GPR-BMA allows this data to be analyzed at a new level of spatial detail.

To do so, we start by observing that the standard isotropic version of GPR-BMA applied in [DS] is somewhat limited in terms of local marginal analysis. In particular, this model treats all variables symmetrically in terms of their influence on covariance. Thus a secondary objective of this paper is to relax this isotropy assumption in a manner that allows individual marginal influences of variables to be identified more directly (when warranted by the data). The simplest anisotropic extension of this model is to introduce separate directional length-scale effects for each variable (Section 5.1 in Rasmussen & Williams, 2006 [RW]). But there are several well-known difficulties with this extension. From a computational viewpoint, Monte Carlo estimation with individual length scales requires costly reversible-jump methods (Green, 1995). Moreover, for cases involving many candidate variables, the simpler isotropic model with its common length scale for all variables is not only more efficient in terms of model selection but often produces superior results. These observations suggest that the standard Bayesian method for resolving model uncertainty, namely model averaging, be extended to allow for kernel uncertainty as well. To do so, we broaden the definition of candidate models to include isotropic versus anisotropic specifications of covariance kernels. To distinguish this extended version from (isotropic) GPR-BMA, we designate the present model as the *Variable Length Scale* (VLS) model. By applying VLS to both simulated and empirical data, this extended version of BMA is shown to yield more robust results than either specification by itself.

A third objective of this paper is to increase the efficiency of BMA simulations in the VLS model by exploring methods for approximating Bayes factors. Such approximations not only avoid the need for costly reversible-jump methods in anisotropic cases, but more generally, require only single posterior estimates for each model considered. The best known method utilizes the Bayes Information Criterion (BIC) based on maximum likelihood estimates of parameters. A recent scaled-prior version of this BIC approximation (SPB), proposed by Bollen, Ray, Zavisca, and Harden (2012), reweights this approximation to allow a fuller range of complex models to be considered. Our final approach involves a more direct application of the Laplace method underlying all these approximations, and utilizes maximum a posteriori (MAP) estimates of posterior mode values of parameters rather than maximum likelihood estimates. These three approaches are compared in terms of selected simulations. Our preliminary findings here suggest that while BIC is the most efficient procedure for large sample sizes, SPB and MAP appear to be more effective in identifying true models.

To develop these results, we begin in the next section with a brief overview of GPR and BMA. This is followed in Section 3 with a development of the VLS model. In Section 4, this model is compared with GWR in terms of two selected simulation models that exhibit isotropic and anisotropic structures, respectively. Finally, this VLS model is applied to the classic Boston Housing data in Section 5.

2. GAUSSIAN PROCESSES

We start with a spatial process characterized by some *response variable*, y_l, at each spatial location, l, together with a set of possible *explanatory variables*, $x_l = (x_{l1}, x_{l2}, ..., x_{lk})$ (which are implicitly taken to include spatial identifiers of location, l, such as latitude and longitude). Our fundamental assumption is that stochastic variations in y_l over space are governed by a *zero-mean stationary Gaussian process*, which in essence implies that the joint realization of responses, $y = (y_l : l = 1, ..., n)$, at any finite set of n locations with associated explanatory variables, $X = (x_l : l = 1, ..., n)$ is *multinormally* distributed as

$$y \sim N[0_n, c(X, X)]. \tag{1}$$

The underlying covariance matrix,

$$c(X, X) = \begin{bmatrix} c(x_1, x_1) & \cdots & c(x_1, x_n) \\ \vdots & \ddots & \vdots \\ c(x_n, x_1) & \cdots & c(x_n, x_n) \end{bmatrix} \tag{2}$$

is assumed to be generated by a *kernel function*, $c(x_l, x_h) = \text{cov}(y_l, y_h)$, depending only on the attribute profiles of response variates. Spatial stationarity implies a constant mean over space, which for convenience is typically set equal to zero.[1] In essence, such processes are thus driven almost entirely by their covariance structure. In the standard *isotropic* version of this model, the covariance kernel is given by the *squared exponential function*,

$$c_{\text{iso}}(x_l, x_h) = v \exp\left[-\frac{1}{2\tau^2}||x_l - x_h||^2\right] = v \exp\left[-\frac{1}{2\tau^2}\sum_{i=1}^{k}(x_{li} - x_{hi})^2\right], \tag{3}$$

which essentially hypothesizes that the covariance between responses decreases as the (Euclidean) distance between their x-attribute profiles increases. In particular, this implies that such covariances are *spherically symmetric* in all x variables. As for the parameters of this model, note first that if $x_l = x_h$ then the exponential term collapses to unity, so that parameter v is seen to be the common variance of all responses, that is, $\text{var}(y_l) = c(x_l, x_l) = v$. The parameter, τ, is of central importance for this kernel function, and will be discussed further below.

For our present purposes, the appropriate *anisotropic* extension of this model is given by

$$c_{\text{aniso}}(x_l, x_h) = v \exp\left[-\sum_{i=1}^{k} \frac{1}{2\tau_i^2}(x_{li} - x_{hi})^2\right], \tag{4}$$

where v has the same interpretation, and where each positive weight, $\tau_i > 0$, is designated as the *length scale* for variable x_i. In these terms, the isotropic model above is characterized by a common length scale, τ, for all explanatory variables. While length scales are often interpreted as "fluctuation rates" (where shorter length scales imply more rapid variation [RW, p. 4]), the important point to stress is that variables with larger length scales must necessarily have less influence on covariance. Here it should also be stressed that such interpretations are only meaningful when variables are *standardized* to eliminate differences in measurement units. This standardization assumption will thus be implicit in all analysis to follow.

2.1. Gaussian Process Regression

Within this Gaussian process framework, the central task has traditionally been to use a given set of data observations, $\tilde{y} = (\tilde{y}_1, \ldots, \tilde{y}_n), \tilde{X} = (\tilde{x}_1, \ldots, \tilde{x}_n)$, to predict unobserved responses, y_l, at locations l with attributes, x_l. To do so, one additional distinction is typically made between observed and unobserved realizations of the process, namely that the observed data are also subject to observation errors. In particular, it is assumed that at each datum location, l,

$$\tilde{y}_l = y_l + \varepsilon_l, \quad \varepsilon_l \sim N(0, \sigma^2),\ l = 1, \ldots, n, \tag{5}$$

where y_l is the process response at l and where the *observation error*, ε_l, is assumed to be independent of y_l and all other observations. Thus the joint distribution of observations, $\tilde{y}$, is taken to be

$$\tilde{y} \sim N\left[0_n, c\left(\tilde{X}, \tilde{X}\right) + \sigma^2 I_n\right]. \tag{6}$$

In these terms, the fundamental relation between observed and unobserved responses for prediction purposes is then given (as in expression (2.21) of [RW]) by

$$\begin{pmatrix} y_l \\ \tilde{y} \end{pmatrix} \sim N\left[\begin{pmatrix} 0 \\ 0_n \end{pmatrix}, \begin{pmatrix} c(x_l, x_l) & c\left(x_l, \tilde{X}\right) \\ c\left(\tilde{X}, x_l\right) & c\left(\tilde{X}, \tilde{X}\right) + \sigma^2 I_n \end{pmatrix}\right]. \tag{7}$$

As is well known, the conditional distribution of y_l given $\tilde{y}$ must then be of the form,

$$y_l | x_l, \tilde{y}, \tilde{X} \sim N\left[E\left(y_l | x_l, \tilde{y}, \tilde{X}\right), \mathrm{var}\left(y_l | x_l, \tilde{y}, \tilde{X}\right)\right], \tag{8}$$

where

$$E\left(y_l | x_l, \tilde{y}, \tilde{X}\right) = c\left(x_l, \tilde{X}\right)\left[c\left(\tilde{X}, \tilde{X}\right) + \sigma^2 I_n\right]^{-1} \tilde{y} \tag{9}$$

and

$$\mathrm{var}\left(y_l | x_l, \tilde{y}, \tilde{X}\right) = c(x_l, x_l) - c\left(x_l, \tilde{X}\right)\left[c\left(\tilde{X}, \tilde{X}\right) + \sigma^2 I_n\right]^{-1} c\left(\tilde{X}, x_l\right). \tag{10}$$

In particular, the conditional expectation in Eq. (9) provides the desired mean prediction of y_l, which forms the corner stone of *GPR*. More generally, the same derivation applies to vectors of unobserved responses, $y = (y_l : l = 1, \ldots, m)$. For our later purposes, it is also important to note from Eq. (9) that measurement-error variance, σ^2, acts formally as a "smoothing" parameter for mean predictions. In particular, if σ^2 is too close to zero, then Eq. (9) tends to over-fit the sample data.[2] Similarly, very large values σ^2 tend to dominate the covariance structure in Eq. (6), effectively over-smoothing all mean predictions in Eq. (9). This is of particular importance when one considers the local marginal effects of such predictions, to which we now turn.

2.2. Local Marginal Effects Analysis

To develop the local marginal effects of individual variables based on Eq. (9), observe first that if we employ the following simplifying notation:

$$K(\tilde{X},\tilde{X}) = c(\tilde{X},\tilde{X}) + \sigma^2 I_n \tag{11}$$

and expand Eq. (9) as follows:

$$E(y_l|x_l,\tilde{y},\tilde{X}) = c(x_l,\tilde{X})K(\tilde{X},\tilde{X})^{-1}\tilde{y} = [c(x_l,\tilde{x}_h) : h = 1,\ldots,n]K(\tilde{X},\tilde{X})^{-1}\tilde{y}, \tag{12}$$

then the *marginal effect* of each explanatory variable, x_i, at location l is given by the partial derivative,

$$\mathrm{ME}_{il} = \frac{\partial}{\partial x_{li}}E(y_l|x_l,\tilde{y},\tilde{X}) = \left[\frac{\partial}{\partial x_{li}}c(x_l,\tilde{x}_h) : h = 1,\ldots,n\right]K(\tilde{X},\tilde{X})^{-1}\tilde{y}. \tag{13}$$

For the *anisotropic* kernel, c_{aniso}, in Eq. (4), we see in particular that

$$\begin{aligned}\frac{\partial}{\partial x_{li}}c_{\text{aniso}}(x_l,\tilde{x}_h) &= v\frac{\partial}{\partial x_{li}}\exp\left[-\sum_{j=1}^{k}\frac{1}{2\tau_j^2}(x_{lj}-\tilde{x}_{hj})^2\right] \\ &= v\exp\left[-\sum_{j=1}^{k}\frac{1}{2\tau_j^2}(x_{lj}-\tilde{x}_{hj})^2\right]\frac{1}{\tau_i^2}(\tilde{x}_{hi}-x_{li}) \\ &= \frac{1}{\tau_i^2}(\tilde{x}_{hi}-x_{li})c_{\text{aniso}}(x_l,\tilde{x}_h)\end{aligned} \tag{14}$$

and similarly, for the isotropic kernel, c_{iso}, in Eq. (3), that

$$\frac{\partial}{\partial x_{li}}c_{\text{iso}}(x_l,\tilde{x}_h) = \frac{1}{\tau^2}(\tilde{x}_{hi}-x_{li})c_{\text{iso}}(x_l,\tilde{x}_h). \tag{15}$$

These expressions will thus allow marginal effects of all variables to be calculated in closed form. Here it should be emphasized that since all variables are assumed to be standardized, the specific magnitudes of such effects are of less importance for our purposes than their signs,[3] as discussed further in the Section 4.1.

3. BMA AND VARIABLE SELECTION

While the above framework implicitly treats all k explanatory variables, $x_l = (x_{l1}, \ldots, x_{lk})$, as being relevant for predicting y_l, it should be clear that a fundamental part of any such analysis is to determine which variables are "most relevant." The approach adopted in [DS] (following Chen & Wang, 2010) was to treat each subset of these variables as a potential model and to allow the observed data to reveal which of these models is most relevant. More precisely, this amounts to treating the above Gaussian process as a Bayesian prior model of responses, and then deriving the posterior probabilities of each potential model given these observations. Here, we extend this approach by allowing for uncertainty about the covariance kernel of each model as well as the variables included. To formalize these ideas, we now characterize each *model*, M, as an ordered pair

$$M = (c_M, V_M), \tag{16}$$

where c_M is a possible *covariance kernel type* for M, and where $V_M \subseteq \{1, \ldots, k\}$ denotes set of *explanatory variables* in model M. While many covariance kernel types are possible for Gaussian processes (as elaborated, e.g., in Chapter 4 of [RW]), we focus only on the *isotropic* and *anisotropic* kernels in Eqs. (3) and (4), so that $c_M \in \{\text{iso}, \text{aniso}\}$. If the number of explanatory variables, $s_M = |V_M|$, is designated as the *size* of model M, the *kernel parameters*, θ_M, of this model are seen from Eqs. (3) and (4) to be specified as follows:

$$\theta_M = \begin{cases} \left(v, \tau, \sigma^2\right), & c_M = \text{iso} \\ \left(v, \tau_1, \ldots, \tau_{s_M}, \sigma^2\right), & c_M = \text{aniso} \end{cases}. \tag{17}$$

At this point, it should be noted that since c_{iso} appears to be simply the special case of c_{aniso} in which all length-scale parameters are the same, one may ask why the above distinction is useful. Here the key observation to be made is that even when $\tau_1 = \cdots = \tau_{s_M}$ in θ_{aniso}, the dimension of this parameter space is still $2 + s_M$ whereas the dimension of θ_{iso} is always 3, regardless of model size, s_M. As will be seen below, this implies that in cases where the data suggest that all length scales are roughly the same, c_{iso} will provide a more powerful (and computationally efficient) model than c_{aniso}. This extended notion of models forms the central element of our present *VLS* model.

The task remaining is to develop the full Bayesian structure of this VLS model in a manner paralleling [DS]. Here we start with the joint probability, $p(\tilde{y}, M, \theta_M)$, of any observed data vector, $\tilde{y}$, together with a parameterized model (M, θ_M). Note also that the relevant explanatory-variable data, $\tilde{X}_M$, consist precisely of those columns of $\tilde{X}$ that correspond to variables in V_M. For notational simplicity, we shall take $\tilde{X}_M$ to be implicit in every model specification. With these conventions, we now consider the probability decomposition,[4]

$$p(\tilde{y}, M, \theta_M) = p(\tilde{y}|M, \theta_M)p(\theta_M|M)p(M). \tag{18}$$

The conditional likelihood, $p(\tilde{y}|M, \theta_M)$, on the right-hand side is precisely the Gaussian-process prior developed above. The conditional prior on parameters, $p(\theta_M|M)$, and the model prior, $p(M)$, both remain to be specified. Following standard conventions, we treat all candidate models as equally likely apriori, so that relevant distinctions between models can be attributed entirely to the observed data. Our discussion of parameter priors is deferred to the next section.

3.1. Bayes-Factor Approximations

In contrast to [DS], we no longer focus on the conditional distribution, $p(\theta_M|\tilde{y}, M)$, obtainable from Eq. (18). Rather we now integrate out θ_M and focus directly on the joint distribution,

$$p(\tilde{y}, M) = \int_{\theta_M} p(\tilde{y}, M, \theta_M)\mathrm{d}\theta_M = p(M)\int_{\theta_M} p(\tilde{y}|M, \theta_M)p(\theta_M|M)\mathrm{d}\theta_M, \tag{19}$$

which in turn implies that

$$p(\tilde{y}|M) = \frac{p(\tilde{y}, M)}{p(M)} = \int_{\theta_M} p(\tilde{y}|M, \theta_M)p(\theta_M|M)\mathrm{d}\theta_M. \tag{20}$$

By evaluating these integrals, the desired relative posterior model probabilities for any models M_1 and M_2, based on data, $\tilde{y}$, can then be obtained (under our hypothesis that $p(M_1) = p(M_2)$) from the simple identity

$$\frac{p(M_1|\tilde{y})}{p(M_2|\tilde{y})} = \frac{p(M_1,\tilde{y})}{p(M_2,\tilde{y})} = \frac{p(\tilde{y}|M_1)}{p(\tilde{y}|M_2)} = \frac{\int_{\theta_{M_1}} p(\tilde{y}|M_1,\theta_{M_1})p(\theta_{M_1}|M_1)\mathrm{d}\theta_{M_1}}{\int_{\theta_{M_2}} p(\tilde{y}|M_2,\theta_{M_2})p(\theta_{M_2}|M_2)\mathrm{d}\theta_{M_2}}. \tag{21}$$

These relative posterior model probabilities are thus determined entirely by the ratios, $p(\tilde{y}|M_1)/p(\tilde{y}|M_2)$, designated as the *Bayes factors* for model pairs (M_1, M_2). However, exact evaluation of the integrals in these Bayes factors is seldom possible. Here there are several approaches. By employing appropriate conjugate priors, one can in some cases obtain tractable integral forms, as for example in Fernandez, Ley, and Steel (2001). But the most common approach is to apply Laplace's method to obtain approximations of these integrals, as developed for example in Raftery (1995) and more recently in Bollen et al. (2012) [BRZH]. In particular, a range of such approximations are summarized in [BRZH]. Here we compare three of these approximations in our simulation analyses below.

The most general approximation of Eq. (20), which is essentially a direct result of Laplace's method, is given in natural log terms as follows. If the number of distinct parameters in each model M is denoted by q_M (so that $q_M = 3$ for $c_M = c_{\text{iso}}$ and $q_M = s_M + 2$ for $c_M = c_{\text{aniso}}$), then,[5]

$$\ln p(\tilde{y}|M) \approx \ln p(\tilde{y}|M,\hat{\theta}_M) + \ln p(\hat{\theta}_M|M) + \frac{q_M}{2}\ln(2\pi) - \frac{1}{2}\ln\det[-H(\hat{\theta}_M)], \tag{22}$$

where $\hat{\theta}_M$ is an estimate of the *posterior parameter mode* obtained by maximizing the first two terms on the right-hand side (given data $(\tilde{y}, \tilde{X})$), that is,

$$\hat{\theta}_M = \arg\max_{\theta_M}[\ln p(\tilde{y}|M,\theta_M) + \ln p(\theta_M|M)] \tag{23}$$

and where $\det[-H(\hat{\theta}_M)]$ is the determinant of the (negative definite) Hessian matrix

$$H(\theta_M) = \frac{\partial^2}{\partial\theta_M \partial\theta_M'}[\ln p(\tilde{y}|M,\theta_M) + \ln p(\theta_M|M)] \tag{24}$$

evaluated at the maximum, $\hat{\theta}_M$. In terms of Eq. (23), it is natural to refer to approximation (22) as the *MAP* approximation.

Note finally that this MAP approximation requires the specification of a prior distribution, $p(\theta_M|M)$, for θ_M. Here we start by observing that all parameters in the present framework are positive. So in the context of Gaussian processes, it is most natural to assume that the logs of all parameters have normal priors as well. As in Chen and Wang (2010), we assume that parameters are independent apriori with very "diffuse" marginals, where in particular it is assumed for $c_M = c_{\text{aniso}}$ that

$$p(\theta_M|M) = p(v)\,p\left(\sigma^2\right)\prod_{i=1}^{s_M} p(\tau_i), \tag{25}$$

with log normal marginal distributions derivable from[6]

$$\begin{aligned} &\ln v \sim N(-3,9), \\ &\ln \tau_i \sim N(-3,9), \quad i = 1,\ldots,s_M\,. \\ &\ln \sigma^2 \sim N(-3,9), \end{aligned} \tag{26}$$

The assumptions are the same for $c_M = c_{\text{iso}}$ with τ replacing τ_i in Eq. (26).

There is, however, a second approximation which involves no explicit priors at all, namely the well-known *Bayes information criterion* (BIC),[7]

$$\ln p(\tilde{y}|M) \approx \ln p\left(\tilde{y}|M,\hat{\theta}_M\right) - \frac{q_M}{2}\ln(n), \tag{27}$$

where the MAP estimator, $\hat{\theta}_M$, is now replaced by the *maximum likelihood estimator*,

$$\hat{\theta}_M = \arg\max\nolimits_{\theta_M} \ln p(\tilde{y}|M,\theta_M). \tag{28}$$

Roughly speaking, this approximation is obtained by keeping only the largest terms in the Taylor series expansion underlying Laplace's integral approximation.

However, the BIC approximation can also be obtained by assuming a specific type of multinormal prior distribution for parameters, known as the "unit information" prior. Since this approach to BIC forms the basis for our third and final approximation, we start by noting (as in Eq. (26)) that multinormal priors are only reasonable for the *logs* of our positive parameters. Hence, to develop this approach, it is necessary reparameterize our model in terms of log parameter values,

$$\ln\theta_M = \begin{cases} \left(\ln v, \ln\tau, \ln\sigma^2\right), & c_M = \text{iso} \\ \left(\ln v, \ln\tau_1,\ldots,\ln\tau_{s_M}, \ln\sigma^2\right), & c_M = \text{aniso}, \end{cases} \tag{29}$$

which amounts simply to replacing each parameter value, θ_i, in Eqs. (3) and (4) with the equivalent representation, $e^{\ln \theta_i}$. In these terms, the *unit information prior* for $\ln \theta_M$ is given by a multinormal distribution with any choice of prior mean, $\ln \theta_o$, and with covariance matrix,

$$\mathrm{cov}(\ln \theta_M | M) = \left[\frac{1}{n} I_o \left(\widehat{\ln \theta_M} \right) \right]^{-1} \tag{30}$$

based on *observed Fisher Information* evaluated at $\widehat{\ln \theta_M}$, that is, by

$$I_o \left(\widehat{\ln \theta_M} \right) = \frac{\partial^2}{\partial \ln \theta_M \, \partial \ln \theta_M'} [-\ln p(\tilde{y} | M, \ln \theta_M)]_{\ln \theta_M = \widehat{\ln \theta_M}}, \tag{31}$$

where $\widehat{\ln \theta_M}$ is obtained by replacing θ_M with $\ln \theta_M$ in the maximization problem (Eq. (28)). Here it is important to note that this reparametrization has no effect on the resulting value for BIC in Eq. (27). In particular, it follows from the invariance of maximum likelihood estimators that $p\left(\tilde{y} | M, \widehat{\ln \theta_M} \right) = p\left(\tilde{y} | M, \hat{\theta}_M \right)$, and moreover that

$$\widehat{\ln \theta_M} = \ln \hat{\theta}_M. \tag{32}$$

For our later purposes, it is also important to note that Eq. (31) can be calculated directly from the log-likelihood expression, $\ln p(\tilde{y} | M, \theta_M)$, in Eq. (28) without the need for explicit log transformations. In particular, it can be shown that if

$$I_o \left(\hat{\theta}_M \right) = \frac{\partial^2}{\partial \theta_M \, \partial \theta_M'} [-\ln p(\tilde{y} | M, \theta_M)]_{\theta_M = \hat{\theta}_M} \tag{33}$$

denotes the corresponding observed Fisher information matrix for the original log-likelihood, $\ln p(\tilde{y} | M, \theta_M)$, then each cell, $I_o(\widehat{\ln \theta_M})_{ij}$, of the matrix in Eq. (31), can be calculated entirely in terms of $\theta_M = (\theta_{Mi} : 1 = 1, \ldots, s_M)$ as follows:

$$I_o \left(\widehat{\ln \theta_M} \right)_{ij} = \hat{\theta}_{Mi} \hat{\theta}_{Mj} I_o \left(\hat{\theta}_M \right)_{ij}. \tag{34}$$

With these preliminaries, our final approximation is motivated in [BRZH] by the observation that in many parametric settings (such as regression) the second "penalty" term in BIC tends to heavily favor models with fewer parameters (usually involving fewer explanatory variables).[8] These authors proposed a rescaling of this prior covariance which places more weight on the likelihoods of individual models (which are higher for more complex models). In particular, if we now let

$$g\left(\widehat{\ln\theta}_M\right) = \left(\widehat{\ln\theta}_M - \ln\theta_o\right)' I_o\left(\widehat{\ln\theta}_M\right)\left(\widehat{\ln\theta}_M - \ln\theta_o\right), \tag{35}$$

then this rescaling yield the following *scaled-prior BIC* (SPB) approximation of $\ln p(\tilde{y}|M)$:

$$\ln p(\tilde{y}|M) = \begin{cases} \ln p\left(\tilde{y}|M, \widehat{\ln\theta}_M\right) - \frac{q_M}{2}\left(1 - \ln(q_M) + \ln g\left(\widehat{\ln\theta}_M\right)\right), & q_M < g\left(\widehat{\ln\theta}_M\right) \\ \ln p\left(\tilde{y}|M, \widehat{\ln\theta}_M\right) - \frac{1}{2} g\left(\widehat{\ln\theta}_M\right), & q_M \geq g\left(\widehat{\ln\theta}_M\right) \end{cases}. \tag{36}$$

To be consistent with our choice of priors in Eq. (26), we here set the prior mean vector, $\ln\theta_o$, in Eq. (30) equal to -3 for all analyses to follow.

3.2. Metropolis-Hastings MCMC

Given these three approximations, MAP, BIC, and SPB, one could in principle simply calculate values of $p(\tilde{y}|M)$ for all possible models, and take the highest of these to be the model of choice. But for even modest numbers of potential explanatory variables, the number of possible models (for even a single kernel) can be prohibitive. Moreover, while there are methods for reducing this number (such as the "Occam's window" procedure of Raftery and Madigan, 1994), our present objectives are somewhat different. Here we are primarily interested in (i) identifying those explanatory variables that are statistically most relevant for responses, y, and (ii) estimating the local marginal effects of these variables. With respect to objective (i) in particular, note that if a given variable was to appear in many models exhibiting high model probabilities in Eq. (21), then even though this variable may not be included in the most probable model, it might still be very relevant for predicting y. So our present approach is to simulate a stochastic search process over the model space which generates model frequencies that approximate model probabilities, and at the same time allows Bayesian averaging over those models visited. This not only provides a natural statistical measure of variable relevance but also yields more robust estimates of both the predicted responses and local marginal effects of these explanatory variables.

This procedure was developed in [DS] for models differing only in terms of included variables, that is, $M = V_M$. So our objective here is to extend this procedure to models including kernel uncertainty as well. As above, we again suppress explanatory variables $\tilde{X}_M$ in each model specification, and let $\hat{p}(\tilde{y}|M)$ denote the (exponentiated) approximations of the probabilities, $p(\tilde{y}|M)$, for either MAP, BIC, or SPB as in expressions Eqs. (22), (27), and (36). If we now denote the (finite) set of possible models by

$$\mathbb{M} = \{M = (c_M, V_M) : c_M \in \{\text{iso}, \text{aniso}\}, V_M \subseteq \{1, \ldots, k\}\}, \tag{37}$$

then the desired approximation of relative model probabilities for any $M_1, M_2 \in \mathbb{M}$ is given (as in Eq. (23)) by

$$\frac{\hat{p}(M_1|\tilde{y})}{\hat{p}(M_2|\tilde{y})} = \frac{\hat{p}(\tilde{y}|M_1)}{\hat{p}(\tilde{y}|M_2)}. \tag{38}$$

Here it should be noted (from exponentiation) that all probabilities, $\hat{p}(\tilde{y}|M)$, are necessarily positive, so that Eq. (38) is well defined. In this setting, we now employ the *Metropolis-Hastings* (M-H) method to construct a Markov Chain Monte Carlo (MCMC) process on $\mathbb{M}$ with unique steady-state distribution, $\{\hat{p}(M|\tilde{y}, \tilde{X}) : M \in \mathbb{M}\}$.

For any Markov process, π, on $\mathbb{M}$ with transition probabilities, $\{\pi(M_j|M_i) : M_i, M_j \in \mathbb{M}\}$, the standard sufficient condition for $\hat{p}(M|\tilde{y})$ to be the unique steady state of π is that these transition probabilities satisfy the following "detailed balance" condition,

$$\hat{p}(M_i|\tilde{y})\pi(M_i|M_j) = \hat{p}(M_j|\tilde{y})\pi(M_j|M_i), \tag{39}$$

for all distinct $M_i, M_j \in \mathbb{M}$. Moreover, from the positivity of model probabilities, condition (39) in turn requires the "symmetric positivity" condition that

$$\pi(M_i|M_j) > 0 \Leftrightarrow \pi(M_j|M_i) > 0, \quad M_i, M_j \in \mathbb{M}. \tag{40}$$

The M-H approach to satisfying this condition is to decompose these transition probabilities into a *proposal process*, pr, and an *acceptance process*, *a*, as follows,

$$\pi(M_j|M_i) = \mathrm{pr}(M_j|M_i)a(M_j;M_i). \tag{41}$$

In this context, if the proposal process, pr, is chosen to satisfy symmetric positivity, that is, if

$$\mathrm{pr}(M_i|M_j) > 0 \Leftrightarrow \mathrm{pr}(M_j|M_i) > 0, \quad M_i, M_j \in \mathbb{M} \tag{42}$$

and if the acceptance process is defined in terms of pr by

$$a(M_j;M_i) = \min\left\{1, \frac{\hat{p}(M_j|\tilde{y})\,\mathrm{pr}(M_i|M_j)}{\hat{p}(M_i|\tilde{y})\,\mathrm{pr}(M_j|M_i)}\right\}, \tag{43}$$

then it is a simple matter to verify that the detailed balance condition (39) is automatically satisfied. So all that remains is to construct a proposal process satisfying Eq. (42).

If we employ the simplifying notation, $M_i = (c_i, V_i)$, then the desired proposal process, pr, takes the form,

$$\mathrm{pr}(M_j|M_i) = \mathrm{pr}(c_j, V_j|c_i, V_i), \quad M_i, M_j \in \mathbb{M}. \tag{44}$$

The key point to note here is that for any set of variables, $V_i \subset \{1, \ldots, k\}$, both kernel types $\{\mathrm{iso}, \mathrm{aniso}\}$ are equally well defined in terms of Eqs. (3) and (4), so that either can in principle be proposed in any situation. With this in mind, the proposal procedure used here consists of two steps that are designed to allow variable switching to occur more frequently than kernel switching. In the first step, variable switching is chosen with probability 0.9 and kernel switching otherwise. Since only two kernel types are used, kernel switches are completely determined. For variable switching, we again adopt the "birth-death" proposal process, pr_V, detailed in [DS]. As shown there, if the set, V_i, is equivalently defined by an indicator vector, δ_i, of dimension k with $\delta_i(h) = 1 \Leftrightarrow h \in V_i$, then the set of feasible proposal sets consists precisely of those sets, V_j, which differ from V_i by exactly one variable, that is, for which $\sum_{h=1}^{k} |\delta_j - \delta_i| = 1$. From this it follows that

$$\mathrm{pr}(c_j, V_j|c_i, V_i) > 0 \Leftrightarrow \left\{(c_j = c_i) \& \left(\sum_{h=1}^{k} |\delta_j - \delta_i| = 1\right)\right\} \text{ or } \{(V_j = V_i) \& (c_j \neq c_i)\}, \tag{45}$$

where the first bracket corresponds to *variable switching* and the second is *kernel switching*. But since all operations on the right-hand side are seen to be symmetric in indices i and j (where, e.g., $|\delta_i - \delta_j| = |\delta_j - \delta_i|$), it follows that the left-hand side must also be symmetric, and thus that symmetric positivity condition (42) must hold.

3.3. Model Probabilities and Variable Inclusion Probabilities

The above MCMC process is thus guaranteed to generate a sequence of visited models with frequencies converging to the posterior probabilities of these models. After an initial "burn in" sequence, the subsequent sequence of models, say

$$\mathcal{M} = \{M_s = (c_s, V_s) : s = 1, \ldots, N\} \tag{46}$$

can thus be treated as (approximate) samples from the steady-state distribution over models. If the indicator functions $\{\delta_M : M \in \mathbb{M}\}$ are defined for sequence, $\mathcal{M}$, by

$$\delta_M(s) = 1 \Leftrightarrow M_s = M, \quad s = 1, \ldots, N \tag{47}$$

and if we again employ the notational convention in Eq. (38) that $\hat{p}(M|\tilde{y})$ denotes the approximation of $p(M|\tilde{y})$ under either MAP, BIC, or SPB, then we may obtain natural relative-frequency estimates of these probabilities in terms of $\mathcal{M}$ as follows:

$$\hat{p}(M|\tilde{y}, \mathcal{M}) = \frac{1}{N}\sum_{s=1}^{N} \delta_M(s), \tag{48}$$

where, of course, $\hat{p}(M|\tilde{y}, \mathcal{M}) = 0$ unless model M appears at least once in $\mathcal{M}$. In turn, one can employ Eq. (48) to obtain estimates of kernel probabilities. In particular, if

$$\delta_{\text{iso}}(s) = 1 \Leftrightarrow c_s = \text{iso}, \quad s = 1, \ldots, N, \tag{49}$$

then the *isotropy* and *anisotropy* probabilities, $\hat{p}(\text{iso}|\tilde{y})$ and $\hat{p}(\text{aniso}|\tilde{y})$, can be estimated, respectively, by

$$\hat{p}(\text{iso}|\tilde{y}, \mathcal{M}) = \frac{1}{N}\sum_{s=1}^{N} \delta_{\text{iso}}(s) \tag{50}$$

and

$$\hat{p}(\text{aniso}|\tilde{y}, \mathcal{M}) = 1 - \hat{p}(\text{iso}|\tilde{y}, \mathcal{M}). \tag{51}$$

Of more importance for our present purposes are estimates of posterior *variable inclusion probabilities*, $\hat{p}(i|\tilde{y})$, for each variable, $i = 1, \ldots, k$, which can be obtained using variable indicators,

$$\delta_i(s) = 1 \Leftrightarrow i \in V_s, \tag{52}$$

as follows,

$$\hat{p}(i|\tilde{y}, \mathcal{M}) = \frac{1}{N}\sum_{s=1}^{N} \delta_i(s). \tag{53}$$

As in [DS], these inclusion probabilities provide a natural statistical measure of relevance for each variable, which (unlike p-values) is *larger* for more relevant variables.

3.4. BMA of Predictions and Marginal Effects

Finally, the model sequence, $\mathcal{M}$, can also be used to obtain more robust estimates of both predictions and marginal effects. By again employing the same "hat" notation for a representative approximation method, MAP, BIC, or SPB, we now let $\hat{\theta}_s$ denote the relevant parameter estimates of θ_{M_s} for each model M_s visited under that approximation method. So in particular, $\hat{\theta}_s$ denotes the posterior mode estimates in Eq. (23) under MAP, and denotes the maximum likelihood estimates in Eqs. (27) and (36), respectively, under BIC and SPB (where for notational simplicity we take $\hat{\theta}_s$ to represent the log value, $\widehat{\ln \theta_s}$ in SPB).

If the corresponding predictions at each location l are denoted by

$$\hat{E}\left(y_l|x_l, \tilde{y}, \tilde{X}, M_s, \hat{\theta}_s\right) = c_{M_s}(x_l, \tilde{X}_{M_s})K(\tilde{X}_{M_s}, \tilde{X}_{M_s})^{-1}\tilde{y}, \tag{54}$$

then the resulting *BMA prediction* based on model sequence, $\mathcal{M}$, is given by

$$\hat{E}(y_l|x_l,\tilde{y},\tilde{X}) = \frac{1}{N}\sum_{s=1}^{N}\hat{E}\left(y_l|x_l,\tilde{y},\tilde{X},M_s,\hat{\theta}_s\right). \tag{55}$$

Similarly, if the corresponding marginal effect of each variable, x_i, $i = 1,...,k$, at location l is defined (as in [DS]) by

$$\widehat{\text{ME}}_{il}^{s} = \begin{cases} \frac{\partial}{\partial x_i}\hat{E}\left(y_l|x_l,\tilde{y},\tilde{X},M_s,\hat{\theta}_s\right), & i\in V_{M_s} \\ 0, & i\notin V_{M_s}, \end{cases} \tag{56}$$

then the resulting *BMA marginal effect* based on model sequence, $\mathcal{M}$, is given by

$$\widehat{\text{ME}}_{il} = \frac{1}{N}\sum_{s=1}^{N}\widehat{\text{ME}}_{il}^{s}. \tag{57}$$

As mentioned in the Introduction, these BMA marginal effects will form the main focus of our subsequent analysis. So it is of particular importance to develop some measure of "posterior credibility" for at least the directions (signs) of these effects. But the posterior distributions of both mean responses and their partial derivatives are only obtainable in terms of the posterior distributions of the parameters, θ_M, defining these values. Moreover, unlike the two-stage MCMC procedure in [DS] which generates samples of θ_M from this posterior distribution, all parameters here have been integrated out in Eqs. (19) and (20). So there is no direct sampling mechanism for approximating posterior distributions of marginal effects.

But in a manner similar to our asymptotic approximations of posterior model probabilities (using MAP, BIC, or SPB), it is possible to obtain asymptotic approximations of the posterior distribution of θ_M, and to sample marginal effects based on this distribution. Here our initial approach was to follow the general recommendations in Gelman et al. (2013, Section 13.3) by applying a multinormal approximation to the log posterior, $\ln\theta_M$. However, experimentations with such approximations revealed that local marginal effects are particularly sensitive to measurement-error variance, σ^2 (as mentioned at the end of Section 2.1). In particular, variations in such effects for any given model, M, tend to be magnified by only small deviations from the maximum likelihood estimate, $\hat{\sigma}_M^2$. So for purposes of the present analysis, we choose to treat $\hat{\sigma}_M^2$ as the optimal value of this smoothing parameter, and consider only variations in the *kernel parameters*, $\theta_M^c = \theta_M - \{\sigma^2\}$. In this setting, both the posterior mean and mode of $\ln \theta_M^c$ are identical under asymptotic normality, and are thus asymptotically approximated by $\widehat{\ln \theta_M^c} = \ln \hat{\theta}_M^c$. Similarly (following Gelman et al., 2013) posterior covariances for unimodal distributions are generally well approximated by the inverse of *observed Fisher Information* (i.e., by the local curvature of the log-likelihood around the mode). This yields a posterior approximation of the form,

$$\ln \theta_M^c \underset{\text{approx}}{\sim} N\left[\ln \hat{\theta}_M^c, \operatorname{cov}\left(\ln \hat{\theta}_M^c\right)\right], \tag{58}$$

where $\ln \hat{\theta}_M^c$ is simply the sub-vector of $\ln \hat{\theta}_M = (\ln \hat{\theta}_M^c, \ln \hat{\sigma}_M^2)$ in Eq. (32), and where $\operatorname{cov}(\ln \hat{\theta}_M^c)$ is the corresponding sub-matrix of the inverse, $I_o(\ln \hat{\theta}_M)^{-1}$, of the observed Fisher Information in Eq. (34) (given $\hat{\sigma}_M^2$).

By drawing samples, $\ln \theta_M^c$, from these multinormal distributions and transforming back to the model parameters, $\theta_M = \left(\theta_M^c, \hat{\sigma}_M^2\right)$ with $\theta_M^c = \exp\left(\ln \theta_M^c\right)$, we can construct corresponding samples from the posterior distributions of both mean predictions (54) and marginal effects (56) for each visited model, M. For marginal effects in particular, if we now write $M \in \mathcal{M}$ whenever model M appears in sequence $\mathcal{M}$, and if we draw, say, $S_M = 1{,}000$ samples from Eq. (58) and transform to parameter samples $\left(\theta_M^s : s = 1, \ldots, S_M\right)$, then in terms of Eq. (56), we can construct corresponding marginal-effect samples

$$\mathrm{ME}_{ilM}^s = \begin{cases} \dfrac{\partial}{\partial x_i} E\left(y_l | x_l, \tilde{y}, \tilde{X}, M, \theta_M^s\right), & i \in V_M \\ 0, & i \notin V_M. \end{cases} \tag{59}$$

Similarly, we can employ Eq. (54) to construct prediction samples, and can in principle then construct standard credibility intervals based on these sample frequencies. But here our main interest focuses on marginal effects, where such credible intervals are somewhat more difficult to interpret directly (in view of the standardization of explanatory variables mentioned at the end of Section 2). Thus to evaluate these effects, we begin by observing that standardizations have no influence on the *signs* of such effects. Moreover, since the overall relevance of individual variables has already been gauged in terms of variable inclusion probabilities (VIPs), it is the signs (directions) of their local effects on mean responses that are of most interest. With this in mind, our main objective is to construct a measure of the "sign credibility" of estimated marginal effects.

While many approaches are in principle possible here, the most sensible (to us) is simply to estimate the posterior probability of such signs. In particular, if in terms of Eq. (59) we now let $p_M(\mathrm{ME}_{ilM})$ denote the posterior probability distribution of marginal effects, ME_{il}, in model M, and let S^+_{ilM} (resp., S^-_{ilM}) denote the number of positive (resp., negative) values of samples, ME^s_{ilM}, in Eq. (59) then the natural posterior estimates of these signs are given by

$$\hat{p}_M(\mathrm{ME}_{ilM} > 0) = \frac{S^+_{ilM}}{S_M} \tag{60}$$

and

$$\hat{p}_M(\mathrm{ME}_{ilM} < 0) = \frac{S^-_{ilM}}{S_M}, \tag{61}$$

that is, by the fractions of sampled marginal effects that are positive (or negative). Finally, by using the estimated model probabilities in Eq. (48), we can then obtain the following overall (BMA) estimates of *posterior sign probabilities*:

$$\hat{p}(\mathrm{ME}_{il} > 0) = \sum_{M \in \mathcal{M}} \hat{p}_M(\mathrm{ME}_{ilM} > 0)\, \hat{p}(M|\tilde{y}, \mathcal{M}) \tag{62}$$

and

$$\hat{p}(\mathrm{ME}_{il} < 0) = \sum_{M \in \mathcal{M}} \hat{p}_M(\mathrm{ME}_{ilM} < 0)\, \hat{p}(M|\tilde{y}, \mathcal{M}). \tag{63}$$

While it is evident that this procedure for determining "sign credibility" involves a number of assumptions, our simulations below show that it does indeed provide reasonable results. In particular, the estimated signs of marginal effects for relevant variables turn out to have sign probabilities exceeding 0.95 in most cases where these effects are not too close to zero.

3.5. Simulation Analyses

In this section, we develop two simulation models that are specifically designed to test the ability of the VLS model to detect differences between spatial isotropic and anisotropic processes.

The general form of these simulated processes is as follows:

$$y_l = \phi(x_{l1}, x_{l2}) + \varepsilon_l, \quad \varepsilon_l \underset{iid}{\sim} N(0, 0.25), \tag{64}$$

where the use of only two explanatory variables in the mean-value function, ϕ, allows results to be mapped and analyzed visually as well as numerically. In addition, these mean-value functions are chosen to be continuously differentiable to allow local marginal analyses to be tested against actual partial derivatives at each location. As in [DS], the random spatial errors, ε_l, are thus chosen to be sufficiently small [$\text{var}(\varepsilon_l) = 0.25$] to ensure that these functional specifications always dominate residual noise.[9]

Within this framework, our *isotropic* simulation model is chosen to have the following mean-value function,

$$\phi_{\text{iso}}(x_{l1}, x_{l2}) = 2\sin(2x_{l1}) + 2\sin(2x_{l2}), \tag{65}$$

which is clearly symmetric in x_{l1} and x_{l2}. So there should be no discernible difference between the length scales of these two variables as identified by VLS. In addition, the local marginal effects of both x_1 and x_2 are identical, and are given by

$$\frac{\partial}{\partial x_i}\phi_{\text{iso}}(x_{l1}, x_{l2}) = 4\cos(2x_{li}) \quad i = 1, 2. \tag{66}$$

The *anisotropic* simulation model has the more complex form

$$\phi_{\text{aniso}}(x_{l1}, x_{l2}) = 2\sin(2x_{l1}) + \sin\left(\frac{1}{2}x_{l2}\right) + \sin(4x_{l1})\sin(x_{l2}) \tag{67}$$

involving an interaction term. Note also from the first term that values of x_1 are more influential than x_2. In particular, the local marginal effects of each variable are now given by

$$\frac{\partial}{\partial x_{l1}}\phi_{\text{aniso}}(x_{l1}, x_{l2}) = 4\cos(2x_{l1}) + 4\cos(4x_{l1})\sin(x_{l2}) \tag{68}$$

$$\frac{\partial}{\partial x_{l2}}\phi_{\text{aniso}}(x_{l1}, x_{l2}) = \frac{1}{2}\cos\left(\frac{1}{2}x_{l2}\right) + \sin(4x_{l1})\cos(x_{l2}) \tag{69}$$

In our simulation analyses below, it is important to compare VLS with the alternative kernel-based family of Locally Weighted Regression (LWR) models that are specifically designed to estimate local marginal effects. As mentioned in the Introduction, we focus here on GWR, which is by far the most commonly used method for spatial applications.

3.6. Geographically Weighted Regression

Since this method is available in many software packages, we simply use the "off the shelf" version that is currently available in ArcMap. Moreover, since there is an extensive literature on this technique (most notably, the monograph by Fotheringham, Brunsdon and Charlton, 2002), we sketch only those aspects needed for our present comparison.[10] In terms of the observed data $(\tilde{y}, \tilde{X})$ given above, this approach directly estimates both predictions and local marginal effects at each location, l, by means of a weighted regression scheme of the form,

$$\min_{\beta_l} \sum_{j=1}^{n} \left(\tilde{y}_j - \tilde{x}_j'\beta_l\right)^2 w_l(j), \tag{70}$$

where the *spatial kernel* weights, $w_l(j)$, emphasize those locations, j, closest to location, l. To facilitate the present comparison with VLS, the spatial kernel is chosen to have the *squared exponential* form,

$$w_l(j) = \exp\left(-d_{lj}^2/b^2\right), \tag{71}$$

which is seen to parallel our present use of the squared exponential covariance kernel in Eqs. (3) and (4) (and which is also the default choice in ArcMap). However, it is important to emphasize that while "distances" in the covariance kernels of VLS involve *all* explanatory variables, distances, d_{ij}, in Eq. (71) involve only the spatial coordinates of locations i and j. Finally, the parameter $b > 0$ is usually designated as the *bandwidth* of the kernel and plays a role somewhat analogous to length scales (restricted to spatial coordinates). The choice of an appropriate bandwidth is typically carried out by standard "leave-one-out" cross-validation techniques.[11]

Given this basic GWR model, the desired beta coefficients, $\beta_l = (\beta_{l1}, \ldots, \beta_{lk})'$, are estimated by ordinary least squares to obtain the closed-form solution:

$$\hat{\beta}_l = \left(\tilde{X}' W_l \tilde{X}\right)^{-1} \tilde{X}' W_l \tilde{y}, \tag{72}$$

where W_l is a diagonal matrix with components, $w_l(j), j = 1, \ldots, n$. With these estimates, the *mean response prediction*, $E\left(y_l | x_l, \tilde{y}, \tilde{X}\right)$, at location l is simply the standard regression prediction,[12]

$$\hat{E}\left(y_l | x_l, \tilde{y}, \tilde{X}\right) = \tilde{X}\hat{\beta}_l = \sum_{j=1}^{n} \hat{\beta}_{lj} x_{lj}. \tag{73}$$

So the desired *local marginal effects* of variable, x_i, at location l are simply the estimated beta coefficients themselves, that is,

$$\frac{\partial}{\partial x_i} \hat{E}\left(y_l | x_l, \tilde{y}, \tilde{X}\right) = \frac{\partial}{\partial x_i} \sum_{j=1}^{n} \hat{\beta}_{lj} x_{lj} = \frac{\partial}{\partial x_i}\left(\hat{\beta}_{li} x_{li}\right) = \hat{\beta}_{li}. \tag{74}$$

In this setting, the "sign credibility" of such marginal effects is now replaced by p-values for local "pseudo t-tests" of these betas.[13] In doing so, however, it should be emphasized that such tests are well known to be unstable in the presence of either small samples ($n < 150$) or multicollinearity, where the usual convention (as for example in ArcMap) is to require that the condition number (ratio of maximum and minimum eigenvalues) of the positive semidefinite matrix $\tilde{X}' W_l \tilde{X}$ not exceed 30. But since $n = 150$ in the simulations used for comparisons below, and since almost all condition numbers turn out to be well less than 30,[14] the present simulations appear to provide a reasonably fair comparison with GWR.

4. SIMULATION RESULTS

For all simulations conducted, the range of values chosen for the explanatory variables in Eqs. (65) and (67) was $-2 \leq x_i \leq 2, i = 1,2$. A series of 12 sample sizes were chosen, ranging from $n = 40$ to $n = 150$ in increments of 10. For each sample size, a set of 20 simulations were conducted in which n values of x_1 and x_2 were randomly drawn from the interval [−2,2]. Values of y were then simulated from models (65) and (67). For testing purposes, three irrelevant variables (x_3, x_4, x_5) were also drawn randomly from [−2,2], and both VLS and GWR were then applied to each of these data sets $\{(y_i, x_{1i}, x_{2i}, x_{3i}, x_{4i}, x_{5i}) : i = 1, \ldots, n\}$. However, our initial investigations showed that GWR was so sensitive to the presence of irrelevant variables, that a reasonable comparison was only made possible by dropping the irrelevant variables from the GWR applications.[15] In contrast, such variables had almost no effect on VLS results. In fact the VIPs in Table 1 below show that for the post burn-in sample sequence, $\mathcal{M}$, in Eq. (46) above, these irrelevant variables were virtually eliminated by the Metropolis-Hastings procedure.

The same out-of-sample prediction set was used for each simulation, and consisted of a regular grid of points on the square $[-2, 2] \times [-2, 2]$, spaced at intervals of 0.1. This produced a set of $1,681 (= 41^2)$ prediction points which (as seen in Fig. 1) allowed the prediction surfaces to be interpolated and plotted in full detail. With these preliminary observations, we turn now to the results of these simulations.

4.1. Predictions and Variable Relevance

The prediction results for both Sim 1 (isotropy) and Sim 2 (anisotropy) can be seen most vividly by examining y predictions for typical simulation runs at sample size, $n = 150$, as shown in Fig. 1 (using the SPB approximation method).[16] Here plots of the true mean-value functions in Eqs. (65) and (67) are shown in the middle panels, (b) and (e), of Fig. 1, respectively. The corresponding prediction results for GWR are shown on the left [panels (a) and (d)], and those for VLS are shown on the right [panels (c) and (f)]. Here it is seen that both GWR and VLS are able to capture the overall surface pattern quite well, especially in the simpler isotropic case (which is symmetric in the two explanatory variables). However, it is also clear that VLS does a noticeably better job of capturing the finer details, especially for the more complex anisotropic case. This contrast will be even more dramatic in the marginal-effect results.

Table 1. Variable Inclusion Probabilities (VIP).

			SPB	BIC	MAP	SPB	BIC	MAP	SPB	BIC	MAP
Simulation 1	Relevant	X_1	1	1	1	1	1	1	1	1	1
		X_2	1	1	1	1	1	1	1	1	1
	Irrelevant	X_3	0.050	0.102	0.008	0.000	0.030	0.001	0.000	0.018	0.000
		X_4	0.050	0.102	0.008	0.000	0.034	0.002	0.000	0.015	0.000
		X_5	0.051	0.142	0.019	0.000	0.034	0.002	0.000	0.014	0.000
		n	50	50	50	100	100	100	150	150	150
Simulation 2	Relevant	X_1	1	1	1	1	1	1	1	1	1
		X_2	0.985	0.999	0.996	1	1	1	1	1	1
	Irrelevant	X_3	0.009	0.300	0.090	0.003	0.169	0.040	0.003	0.200	0.050
		X_4	0.063	0.367	0.176	0.002	0.161	0.044	0.006	0.197	0.050
		X_5	0.013	0.313	0.093	0.033	0.200	0.073	0.000	0.154	0.028
		n	50	50	50	100	100	100	150	150	150

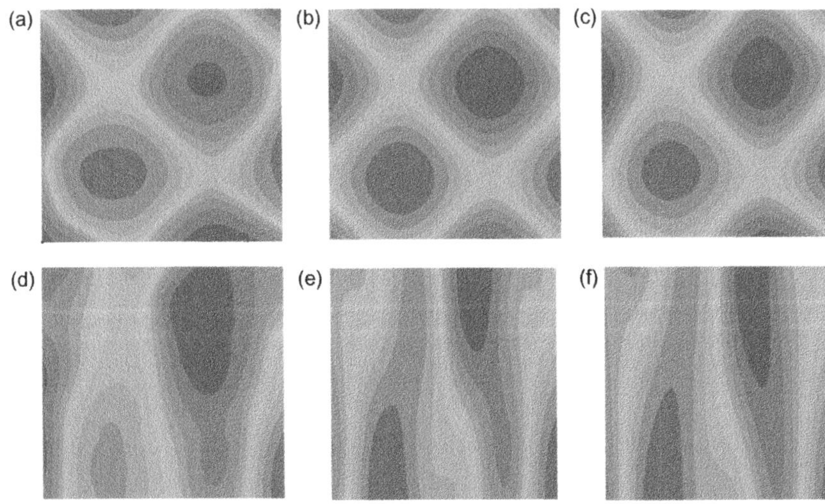

Fig. 1. Prediction Results for Simulations. (a) GWR predictions of Y for Sim 1, (b) True mean values of Y for Sim 1, (c) VLS predictions of Y for Sim 1, (d) GWR predictions of Y for Sim 2, (e) True mean values of Y for Sim 2, (f) VLS predictions of Y for Sim 2.

But for the present, we focus on certain more detailed aspects of VLS, and in particular, on the relative performance of the three Bayes-factor approximation methods (MAP, BIC, SPB). The first question of interest relates to how well these three methods predict the y response in Sim 1 and Sim 2. In Fig. 2, these results are summarized for each sample size in terms of Root Mean Squared Error (RMSE), where the results shown are averaged over the 20 simulations at each sample size. Here all three methods are seen to be roughly comparable and exhibit the same degree of improvement at larger sample sizes.[17]

Next we observe that VLS successfully identifies the isotropic and anisotropic nature of Sim 1 and Sim 2, respectively, but that again, both SPB and MAP do substantially better than BIC in identifying the isotropy in Sim 1 (Fig. 3).

In terms of length scales, VLS does equally well in distinguishing between the isotropic and anisotropic cases. As seen in Fig. 4 (using only SPB),[18] the estimated length scales of both explanatory variables, x_1 and x_2, are almost identical, as expected. In addition, the more influential nature of x_1 in Sim 2 is here reflected by a substantially shorter length scale than x_2 across all sample sizes. While length-scale results for the irrelevant variables

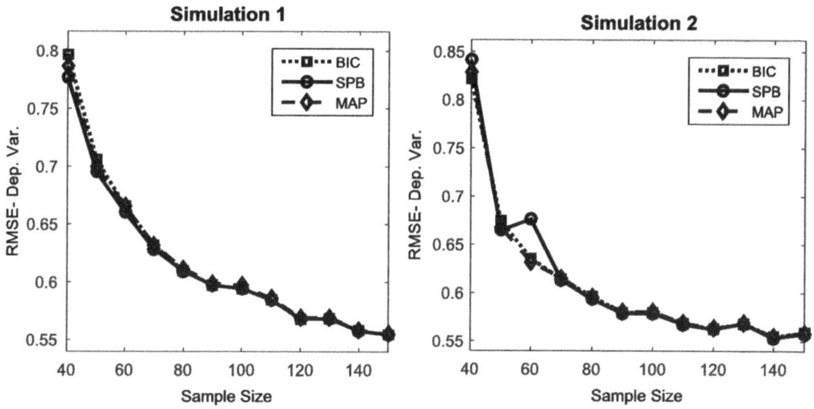

Fig. 2. Comparative Prediction Fits.

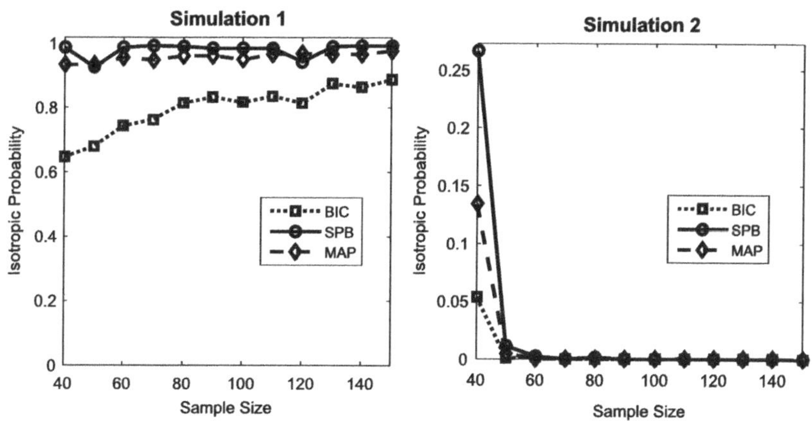

Fig. 3. Comparison of Model Probabilities.

are not shown, it suffices to say that for all irrelevant variables (x_3, x_4, x_5), length scales were much larger than those of x_2 in Fig. 4 for all sample sizes (and all models for which that variable was included).

But much sharper (and more easily interpretable) results for variable relevance are given in terms of VIPs, as shown in Table 1 (for three representative sample sizes). In particular, these results show that for both Sim 1 and Sim 2, the relevant variables (x_1, x_2) were present in virtually all models of the post burn-in sequences, $\mathcal{M}$. However, there are considerable differences between the three Bayes-Factor approximation method (MAP, BIC,

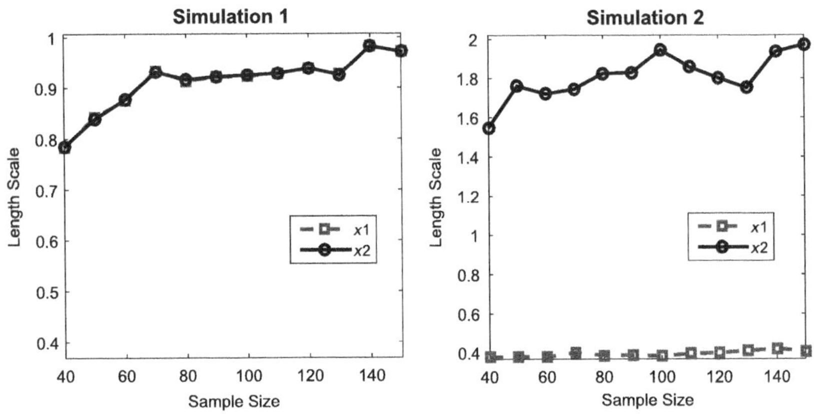

Fig. 4. Length Scale Comparisons.

SPB), with respect to the irrelevant variables, (x_3, x_4, x_5). In particular, BIC exhibits by far the worst performance in this respect, and certain irrelevant variables are included in more than 30% of the models in $\mathcal{M}$. Here it is clear that in almost all cases, SPB is doing the best in this regard (especially in the more complex anisotropic case where irrelevant variable inclusion is reduced to less than 1% at larger sample sizes).

Because we are only concerned with local marginal effects of the most relevant variables, we have adopted SPB as the default choice for the empirical analysis in Section 5. In addition, it is for this reason that the SPB approximation was used in constructing Fig. 1, together with Fig. 5.

4.2. Local Marginal Effects

Finally we turn to a consideration of the local marginal effects that form the central focus of the present paper. As a parallel to Fig. 1, we begin with a graphical comparison (Fig. 5) of both VLS and GWR marginal effects for Sim 2 with the true marginal effects of variables x_1 and x_2 in expressions (68) and (69), respectively.[19] Here we again focus on the same representative sample of size 150 (using SPB) in Fig. 1.

Notice first that the true marginal effects in this anisotropic model are substantially different between x_1 and x_2. In particular, it can be seen from the vertically elongated contours of ϕ_{aniso} in panel (e) of Fig. 1 that the

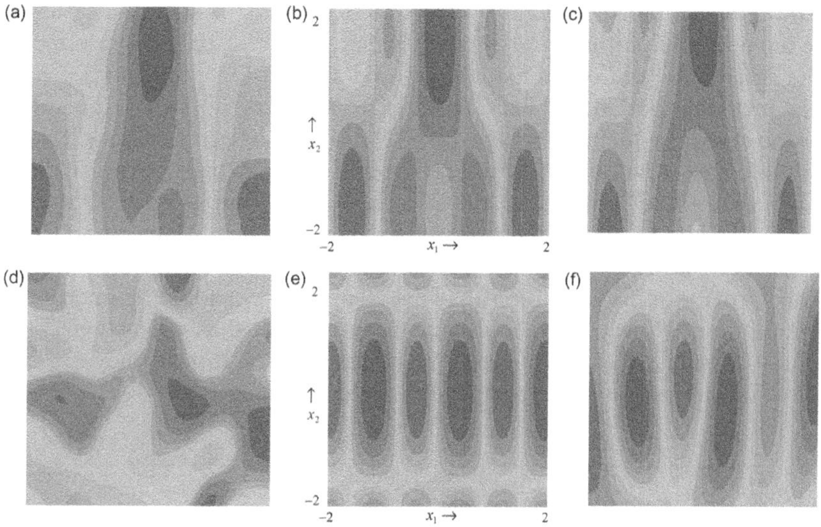

Fig. 5. Comparison of Marginal Effects. (a) GWR estimations of ME1 for Sim 2, (b) True values of ME1 for Sim 2, (c) VLS estimations of ME1 for Sim 2, (d) GWR estimations of ME2 for Sim 2, (e) True values of ME2 for Sim 2, (f) VLS estimations of ME2 for Sim 2.

marginal effect (ME2) of x_2 is relatively small, with more fluctuations around zero.[20]

For the most important variable, x_1, we see from panel (a) of Fig. 5 that GWR is still able to capture the overall qualitative nature of the true marginal effect pattern (ME1) in panel (b). But it is again clear that VLS in panel (c) is able to pick up the finer details of this pattern with much greater precision. However, the most dramatic differences between these two methods are seen when comparing their performance on variable, x_2. Here it is evident from panel (d) of Fig. 5 that GWR is simply not able to detect the more subtle (and rapid) variations of these marginal effects (ME2).[21] In marked contrast, the true pattern in panel (e) continues to be reflected in the VLS results of panel (f). So this example serves to underscore the differences in sensitivity between these two approaches. Note finally that even VLS is unable to detect the very intricate pattern variations near the upper boundary of panel (e), and like all interpolation methods, is limited by pattern "edge effects."

These results are also supported by the corresponding significance and credibility levels for estimates in each case. Turning first to GWR, rather than complicating these figures with exact contours of significance levels, we have simply plotted local t-values in Sim 2 against their corresponding beta values x_1 and x_2 in panels (a) and (b) of Fig. 6. Here we have also included horizontal lines to indicate the sets of significant values for the standard "default" range, $|t| \geq 2$.[22] Here it is seen that betas for the unstable case of x_2 are insignificant over a much broader range of beta values than for x_1. Even more telling is the fact (hard to gauge from the figure) that while 86.3% of the beta values for x_1 are significant, only 27.2% of the beta values for x_2 are significant. So these default levels of significance provide some indication that the results for x_2 should be interpreted with caution. However, it should also be noted that the extremely negative values of beta for x_2 are all very "significant," even though they are way below the actual minimum partial slope value of −0.5.

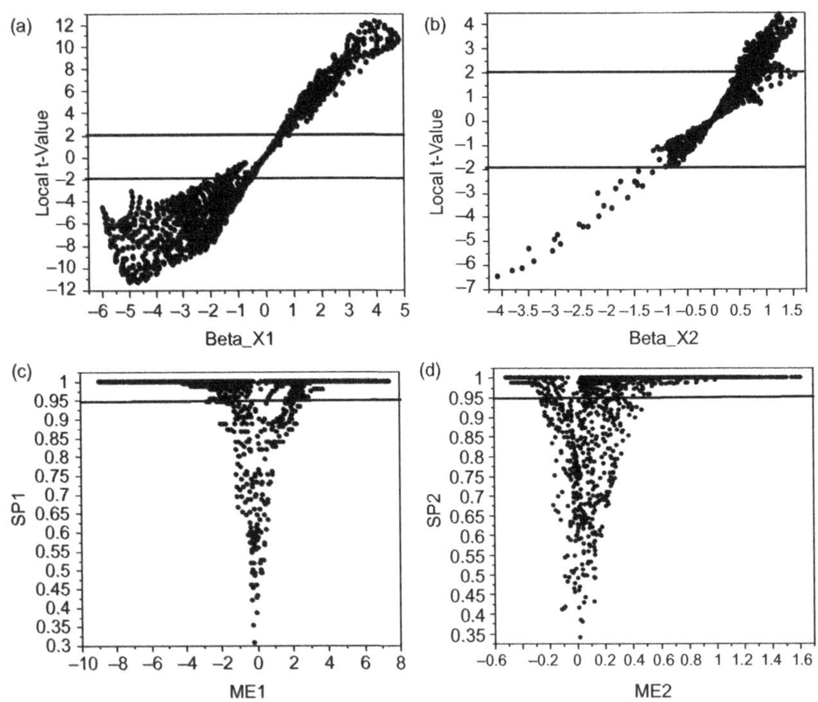

Fig. 6. GWR Significance versus VLS Credibility. (a) Local t-Values for $X1$ Beta, (b) Local t-Values for X2 Beta, (c) Sign Probabilities for ME1, (d) Sign Probabilities for ME2.

To compare these significance results with VLS, the sign probabilities of each marginal effect for variables x_1 and x_2 are plotted in panels (c) and (d) of Fig. 6. Here the dots above the horizontal lines at 0.95 identify values that are credible at the 95% level or above. Note that (as stated at the end of Section 3.4) the tapering of these scatter plots around zero shows that less credible marginal effects tend to be those with values closer to zero. However, what is more difficult to gauge from the figure is the overwhelming concentration of values at the upper end. In fact, the percentages of marginal-effect values with sign probabilities above 0.95 are 83.5% for x_1, and 72.2% for x_2. So with respect to x_2 in particular, these results are seen to be consistent with the qualitatively better fit in panel (f) than in panel (d) of Fig. 5.

Finally, as with prediction and variable relevance above, it remains to consider the relative marginal-effect performance of our three Bayes-factor approximation methods (MAP, BIC, SPB), as shown in Fig. 7. Here again it is clear that these estimates are roughly comparable across all methods.[23] This is especially true at larger samples sizes ($n \geq 80$), where all three methods again produced much sharper results.[24]

5. EMPIRICAL APPLICATION: BOSTON HOUSING

In this final section, we apply VLS to a standard spatial data set, namely the Boston housing data first studied by Harrison and Rubinfeld [HR] (1978). These authors employed multiple regression (OLS) to identify the effect of "demand for clean air" on median housing prices for each of the 506 census tracts in Boston (at the time of the 1970 census). But the first explicit attempt to analyze this data from a spatial perspective was that of Pace and Gilley (1997), who collected centroid data for these tracts and applied a spatial errors model with weight matrix based on centroid distances. More recently, Deng (2008) has analyzed this same data set using a spatial lag model in which the underlying weight matrix explicitly incorporates certain types of anisotropies based on this data. So one objective of our present analysis is to compare the variables found to be significant in these two spatially oriented studies with those found to be most relevant in terms of our present variable inclusion probabilities. However, our main objective is to explore this data set at a finer level of spatial detail by focusing on the local marginal effects of relevant explanatory variables.

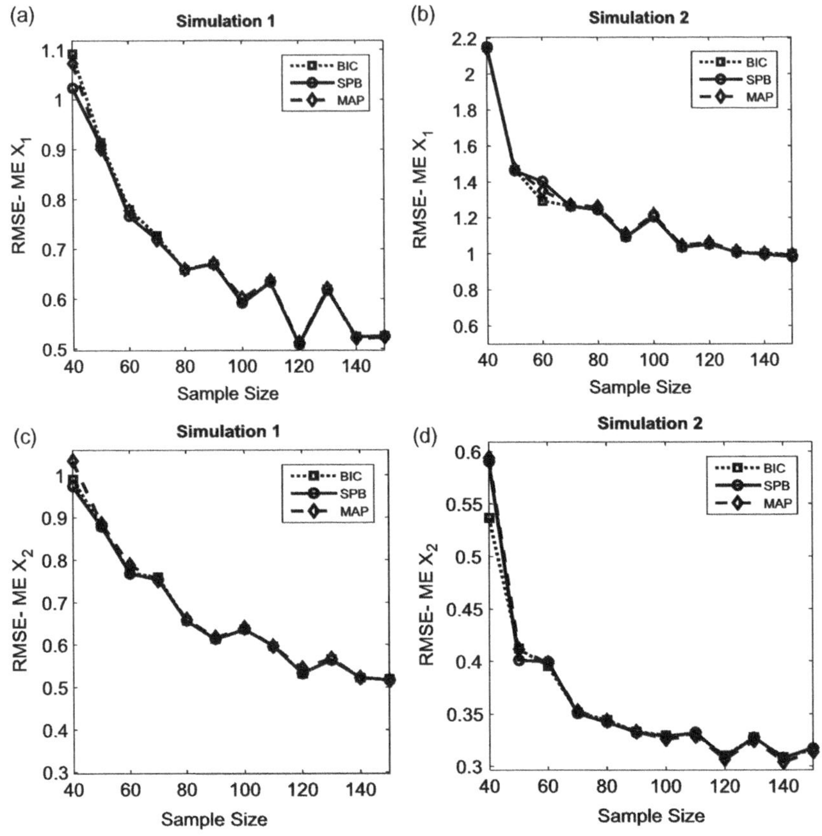

Fig. 7. Comparisons of Local Marginal Effects. (a) ME_X1 for SIM 1, (b) ME_X1 for SIM 2, (c) ME_X2 for SIM 1, (d) ME_X2 for SIM 2.

To do so, we begin by summarizing the original [HR] model, with the *median value* (MV) of housing in each tract as the dependent variable, and with *nitrogen-oxide* (NOX) representing the air-quality variable of interest. The additional 13 control variables include *particulate concentrations* (PART), *average number of rooms* (RM), *proportion of structures built before 1940* (AGE), *black population proportion* (B), *lower status population proportion* (LSTAT), *crime rate* (CRIM), *proportion of area zoned with large lots* (ZN), *proportion of nonretail business areas* (INDUS), *property tax rate* (TAX), *pupil-teacher ratio* (PTRATIO), *location contiguous to the Charles River* (CHAS), *weighted distances to the employment centers* (DIS), and an index of *accessibility to radial roads* (RAD). As with many regressions, a number of these variables were transformed for purposes of analysis.[25] Subsequently, Pace and Gilley (1997) added the spatial coordinates, *latitude* (LAT) and *longitude* (LON), together with a full quadratic specification of these two variables (i.e., LAT^2, LON^2, $\text{LAT} \times \text{LON}$) for their spatial analysis. In this light, one important additional feature of VLS is that such nonlinearities are implicitly captured by this flexible nonparametric model. So in the analysis to follow, the original variables (including LAT and LON) will be used for VLS analyses. The only variable that requires further comment is black proportion, B. If for convenience we now use BP to denote the *proportion (fraction) of tract population that is Black*, then the actual specification of explanatory variable, B, above is $B = (\text{BP} - 0.63)^2$. However, it was possible to recover the original variable, BP, from the 1970 census, and it is this variable that is used in our present analysis.

5.1. Global Predictions and Variable Relevance

Here we begin with global results including both mean predictions of median housing prices and identification of relevant variables. The relevant data on median housing prices for Boston census tracts is shown on the left panel in Fig. 8 (and is one of the first *spatial* representations of this classical

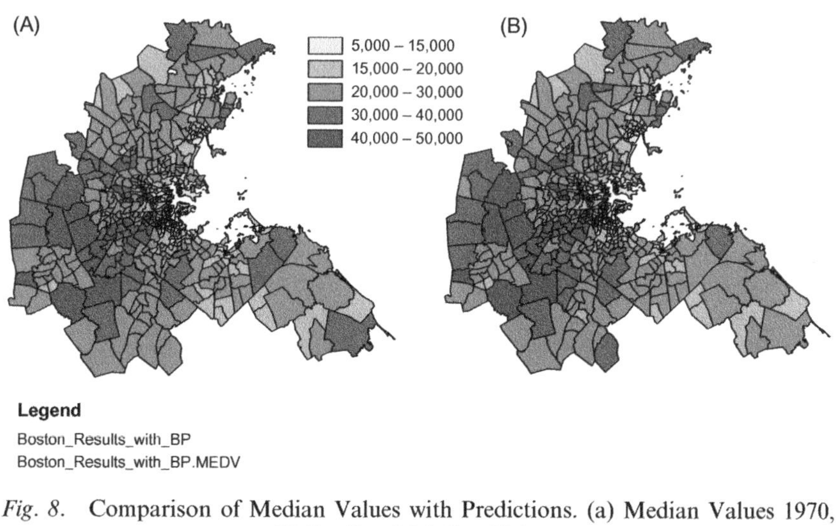

Fig. 8. Comparison of Median Values with Predictions. (a) Median Values 1970, (b) Predicted Median Values.

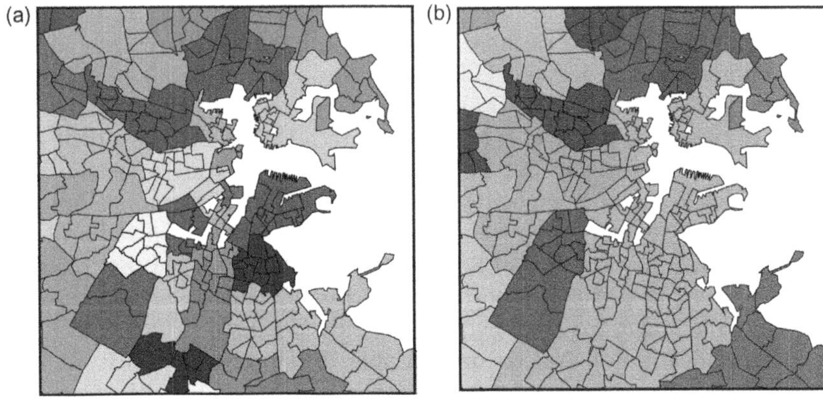

Fig. 9. Variables with Higher Aggregation Levels. (a) NOX Constancy, (b) RAD Constancy.

data set that has appeared).[26] The right panel shows the mean predictions generated by VLS using SPB,[27] which are almost indistinguishable from the original data (at this level of choropleth approximation). So even though these are necessarily *in-sample* predictions,[28] they do provide empirical support for the predictive accuracy of this method, as seen in the simulation studies.

But unlike the simulation examples above, it is more difficult to compare these prediction results with GWR. The main difficulty here relates to the nature of this Boston housing data itself, which in many cases is spatially far coarser that individual census-tract units. In particular, for the key explanatory variable, NOX, there are only 81 distinct values. Moreover, these are in contiguous patches (shown in Fig. 9(a) for the central Boston area) that constitute a higher level of aggregation than census tracts.[29]

The situation is even worse for variables like RAD, where each Town in the Boston area was assigned a unique value (as shown for the central Boston area in Fig. 9(b)). The local collinearities created by such variables make it very difficult to apply GWR to this data set.[30] So for purposes of comparison with VLS, we have employed a more robust version of GWR constructed by James LeSage,[31] which employs pseudo inversion to circumvent problems of singular (or almost singular) matrices. This allows approximate predictions to be constructed as in Eq. (72) and compared with those of VLS. The results of this comparison are shown for the central Boston area in Fig. 10 (which is the area of most interest for our

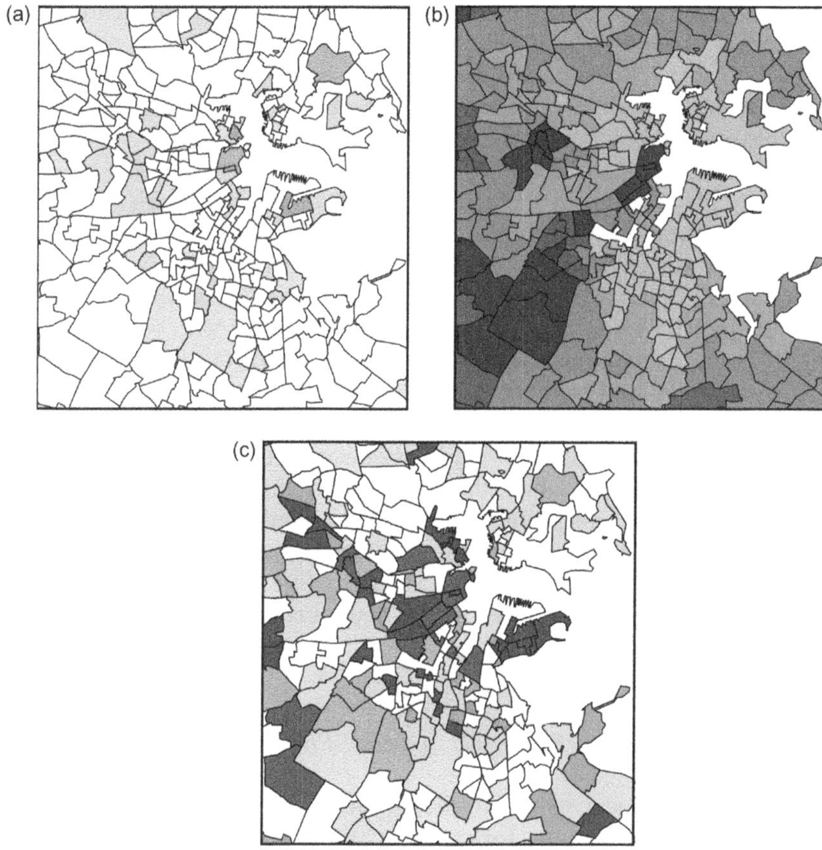

Fig. 10. Residual Comparison for Central Boston. (a) VLS Residuals, (b) True Median Values, (c) GWR Residuals.

subsequent analysis). In particular, prediction residuals for VLS (using SPB) and GWR are shown for each tract in panels (a) and (c),[32] respectively, with true MVs in panel (b).[33] This local comparison is sufficient to indicate that even with robust pseudo-inversion techniques, the predictions obtained by GWR are far less reliable. Moreover, even for those explanatory variables exhibiting distinct values for each tract, the beta estimates obtained by pseudo inversion are generally not interpretable. So in the local analysis of marginal effects below, we will focus only on VLS.

Given these general prediction results, we turn next to the identification of relevant variables. Recall that for VLS, such identification is in terms of VIPs. In Table 2, we compare these VIPs in panel (b) (using both SPB and MAP) with the spatial regression estimates and significance levels for each variable obtained by both Pace-Gilley and Deng in panel (a). As mentioned in the introduction to Section 5, none of the transformations of variables (in note 25) were used in VLS. So the variable labels in panels (a) and (b) differ in this respect. For convenience, these variables are ordered in terms of their VIP values (for SPB) from highest to lowest. As shown by the horizontal lines in the tables, there is close agreement between variables significant at the 0.05 level in panel (a) and variables with VIP ≥ 0.95 in panel (b). The only exceptions here are RAD and PTRATIO (the latter for SPB only), with VIPs well below 0.95. Like RAD in Fig. 9(b), PTRATIO is also constant in each town, so that both represent categorical variables that are spatially step functions. So while VLS is clearly more robust than GWR with respect to such variables, they can in some cases conflict with the continuity assumption underlying VLS (and in particular its GPR component). Finally, to compare the directions of influence for each variable, we have also included the average values of Marginal Effects (Avg. ME) across all 506 census tracts.[34] Here there is essentially complete agreement in signs between the two panels.

5.2. Local Marginal Effects

With respect to local marginal effects, we begin by observing that such effects are far more tenuous for variables at higher levels of spatial aggregation than census tracts. In particular, the NOX variable of most interest to [HR] falls into this category. So rather than attempt to reaggregate such data at the level of "NOX zones," we focus here on several variables that are well defined at the census-tract level. The two variables we have chosen to examine are Black Proportions (BP) and AGE.

5.2.1. Local Analysis of BP Effects

As mentioned above, this variable is of particular interest because it was originally specified as a quadratic expression $(BP - 0.63)^2$. As stated by [HR], this was done in order to capture not only the general negative effect of BP on median housing values but also its slight positive effect in areas with very high concentrations of Black population. One may ask why a quadratic term in BP was not used in their regression. The answer seems to

Table 2. Variable Relevance Comparisons.

(a) Spatial Regression Results

Variable	Deng		Pace and Gilley	
	β	t	β	t
CRIM	−0.007	6.513	−0.007	−6.830
RM2	0.009	8.613	0.009	8.390
AGE	0.000	−0.478	−0.002	−3.320
ln DIS	−0.032	−0.203	−0.187	−2.630
TAX	−0.001	−4.364	0.000	−3.510
B	0.000	3.765	0.001	5.990
ln LSTAT	−0.017	−10.063	−0.246	−11.350
NOX2	−0.221	−2.469	−0.369	−2.370
LON			−262.610	−1.380
PTRATIO	−0.014	−3.379	−0.017	−3.090
ln RAD	0.011	5.183	0.073	3.720
INDUS	−0.003	−1.510	−0.001	−0.350
ZN	0.000	2.344	0.001	1.810
LAT			555.950	1.990
CHAS	−0.018	−0.686	−0.012	−0.450
ρ	0.513		0.800	

(b) VIP Results for VLS

Variable	SPB Estimates		MAP Estimates	
	VIP	Avg. ME	VIP	Avg. ME
CRIM	**1.000**	−0.053	**1.000**	−0.056
RM	**1.000**	4.917	**1.000**	4.915
AGE	**1.000**	−0.074	**1.000**	−0.075
DIS	**1.000**	−1.168	**1.000**	−1.136
TAX	**1.000**	−0.016	**1.000**	−0.015
BP	**1.000**	−0.036	**1.000**	−0.029
LSTAT	**1.000**	−0.352	**1.000**	−0.347
NOX	**1.000**	−2.972	**1.000**	−2.477
LON	**0.995**	−8.722	**0.998**	−8.084
PTRATIO	0.796	−0.258	**0.987**	−0.304
RAD	0.270	0.029	0.570	0.061
INDUS	0.164	−0.013	0.225	−0.011
ZN	0.003	0.000	0.171	0.000
LAT	0.000	0.000	0.352	0.848
CHAS	0.000	0.000	0.000	0.000
ISO. PROB.	0.000		0.000	

Notes: The bold values denote those variable inclusion probabilities that are above 0.985.

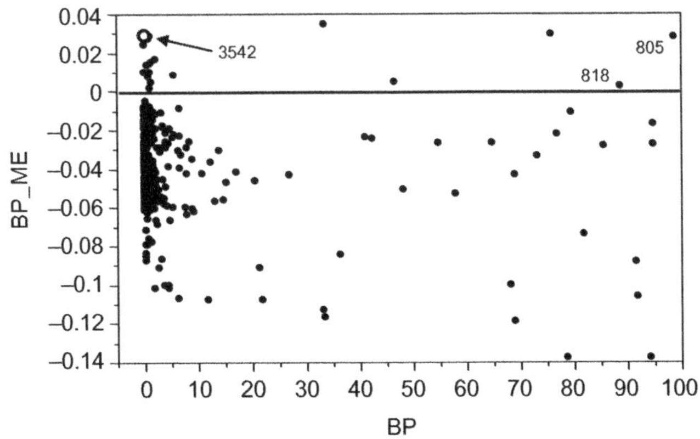

Fig. 11. Marginal Effects of BP.

be that (even with standard zero centering of the quadratic term) this nonlinear effect is not significant. Only by prespecifying an appropriately calibrated form can such a small effect be picked up. So in the present setting, it is of interest to ask whether such slight nonlinear effect can be identified by the marginal effects of BP estimated in VLS. To do so, we have plotted in Fig. 11 all BP values (in percent terms) against their marginal-effect values, ME_BP, obtained from an application of VLS.[35]

Here we have included only those ME values that are credible at the 95% level (eliminating mostly values close to zero). While the vast majority of these credible BP marginal effects are negative, there are a couple of tracts with very high BP and positive ME_BP. These two tracts (805 and 818) are in South Boston where Blacks are most heavily concentrated, and are thus fully consistent with the hypothesis of [HR]. So this small effect does indeed seem to be picked up by VLS. But much more interesting is the cluster of positive marginal effects in the upper left-hand corner of Fig. 11. This represents the opposite extreme where Black proportions are among the lowest – a phenomenon that seems to have been missed by [HR]. To gain further insight, we focus on one of these tracts (3542), as shown by the small circle in Fig. 11. This tract, which is just west of Harvard Square in Cambridge (as shown on the left in Fig. 12) has the highest 1970 median housing prices in this data set, and has a Black proportion of less than 2%. The dark shade of this tract shown on the right in Fig. 12 reflects its high positive ME_BP value (where the middle shade denotes lower positive ME_BP values, and the lightest shade denotes tracts with negative ME_BP values).[36] As for the socio-economic profile of this tract, more than half of all adults (25 and older) were college

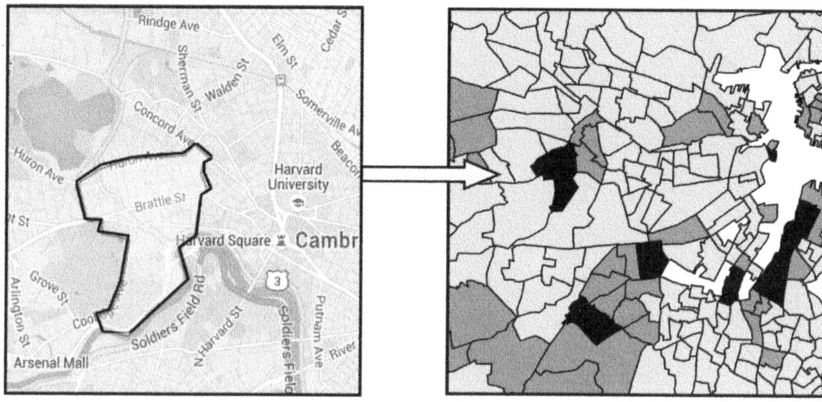

Fig. 12. Tract 3542 near Harvard Square.

graduates in 1970. This, together with its proximity to Harvard, suggest that most heads of households were upper-middle-income professionals. If so, then the positive marginal effect of BP found here might well reflect a very different population dynamic than in South Boston.[37] In any case, this example serves to illustrate how VLS can identify local variations in the spatial fabric that allow deeper levels of analysis.

5.2.2. Local Analysis of AGE Effects

An even more dramatic example is provided by the AGE variable (as measured by the proportion of housing units built before 1940). Here again we focus only on the central area of Boston, where some of the oldest residential areas can be found. As seen in Fig. 13(b) (where the qualitative value scale of Fig. 12 is again used here), most of the marginal effects for AGE are negative (lightest shade), indicating that that higher proportions of older homes tend to detract from median value. However, aside from the middle-shade area around MIT (with positive values so close to zero that none exceed 80% credibility),[38] there is seen to one striking exception right in the heart of Boston's South End district. This single dark-shade tract (709), with 80% Black population and all houses built before 1940, appears to be something of an anomaly – with a positive marginal AGE effect in the top 3% of all census tracts. However, further investigation reveals that this area contains the single "largest urban Victorian neighborhood in the country."[39] Moreover, the South End Historical Society was created in 1966 precisely to preserve this area, as shown by the larger bounded area in Fig. 13(a) (later designated as the Boston Landmark District). Tract

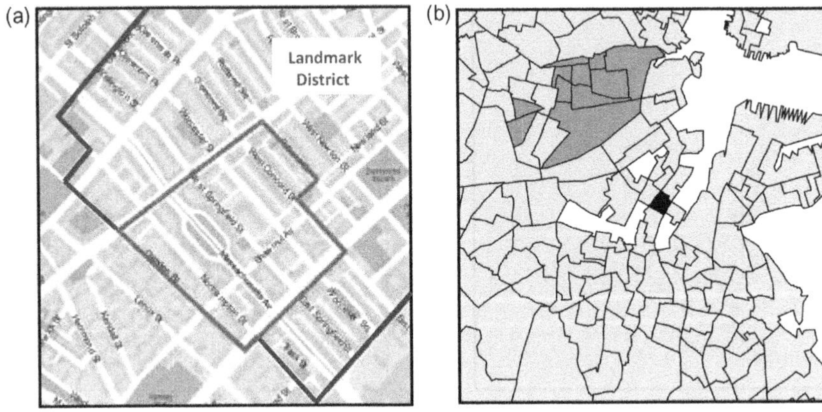

Fig. 13. Census Track 709. (a) Landmark District, (b) Age Marginal Effects.

709 is seen to lie entirely inside this area, as shown by the smaller bounded area in Fig. 13(a). Such preservation efforts led in turn to an influx of middle income families seeking to purchase and restore these houses – which may very well have been reflected in the 1970 census. So it would appear that these VLS estimates of local marginal AGE effects again reveal meaningful spatial variations that are by no means apparent from more conventional methods of analysis.

6. CONCLUDING REMARKS

In this paper, we have extended the basic GPR-BMA framework in [DS] to include alternative kernel choices for candidate models, as well as Bayes-factor approximations to expedite the process of stochastic model search in this extended framework. In particular, the inclusion of anisotropic kernels with individual length scales for candidate variables allows sharper identification of their local marginal effects. By employing selected simulations, this VLS model was shown to yield predicted responses and local marginal effects that are far more accurate than the currently prevailing method for doing so, namely GWR. In terms of Bayes-factor approximations (BIC, SPB, MAP) for VLS, it was found that both SPB and MAP tended generally to outperform BIC. However, this difference was noticeably reduced for larger samples sizes. This together with its relative computational simplicity suggest that BIC may well turn out to be the better choice for larger sample sizes.

In addition, both VLS and GWR were applied to the classical Boston Housing data, where VLS was shown to yield far more reliable (in-sample) prediction. In addition, VLS was shown to yield VIP results (together with average marginal-effect estimates) that are qualitatively very comparable to results obtained by previous spatial regression analyses of this data. In terms of local marginal analyses, where spatial regression methods cannot be applied, the lumpy nature of the Boston data also precluded any meaningful estimation by GWR. So the more robust nature of VLS is made fully evident by this application. In particular, several specific examples were developed to show that VLS allows deeper levels of local analysis than is possible by these other methods.

However, a number of research directions remain to be explored. Chief among these is the pragmatic issue of scalability. Even with Bayes-factor approximations, the VLS model continues to be computationally very costly (orders of magnitude more costly than either spatial regression or GWR). One approach here is to reduce the number of prior candidate models for VLS, using methods such as the "Occam's window" procedure of Madigan and Raftery (1994). More promising, perhaps, are the numerous data-reduction techniques currently used for reducing the costs of large matrix calculations. These range from simple random subsampling of the data to more complex methods of identifying "best representative subsamples," such as the recent "variational Bayes" approaches of Hensman, Fusi, and Lawrence (2013) and Gal, van der Wilk, and Rasmussen (2014).

Aside from computational efficiency, we are also exploring extensions of VLS that would broaden the application domain of this model. One direct extension would be to increase the range of covariance kernels considered. More generally, such extensions might include relaxations of spatial stationarity in terms of "multiple kernels" with possible interactions similar to Lloyd, Duvenaud, Grosse, Tenenbaum, and Ghahramani (2014).

NOTES

1. More generally the process can be viewed as deviations about some pre-specified mean, as discussed, for example, in Seeger (2004).
2. As is well known, GPR becomes an *exact* interpolator at data points when $\sigma^2 = 0$. This can be seen by evaluating Eq. (9) at all data points $(\tilde{y}, \tilde{X})$ and observing that $E(y|\tilde{X}, \tilde{y}, \tilde{X}) = c(\tilde{X}, \tilde{X})\left[c(\tilde{X}, \tilde{X}) + 0\right]^{-1}\tilde{y} = \tilde{y}$.

3. It is often argued that standardizing allows the *relative* sizes of such effects to be more comparable (in a manner similar to the beta coefficients of standardized regression). But such interpretations have been criticized on many grounds (as summarized, e.g., in Gelman & Pardoe, 2007), so that we choose to focus only on *directions* of change.

4. Following standard practice, we take p to represent both mass functions (such as for M) and density functions (such as for $\tilde{y}$).

5. While degrees of approximation, "≈", are here left unspecified, this general integral approximation is the sharpest, and is of order $O(n^{-1})$.

6. An alternative specification of priors for the kernel parameters in Eqs. (3) and (4) is the gamma distribution (as discussed, e.g., in Neal, 1997). However, the log normal specifications in Eq. (26) are not only more convenient for our present purposes, they are also qualitatively similar to a gamma (in the present case, with shape and scale parameters of roughly 0.17 and 24, respectively).

7. This form is taken from expression (9) in [BRZH]. As they point out, the usual expression for BIC multiplies this by -2.

8. While this appears to be less true in the present nonparametric setting, the variation of BIC proposed by [BRZH] continues to perform better than BIC in our simulation studies below.

9. The spatial errors in the simulations of [DS] were also chosen to be spatially autocorrelated. But this additional refinement turned out to make no discernible difference in the results, and has now been dropped.

10. Here it should be noted that GWR appears to have been introduced independently by both Brunsdon, Fotheringham, and Charlton (1996) and McMillen (1996). So while our present approach (using ArcMap software) is based on the former approach (as summarized in their 2002 monograph above), the reader is also referred to the excellent papers by McMillen (2010, 2012) and McMillen and Redfearn (2010).

11. See, for example, Brunsdon, Fotheringham, and Charlton (1996, Section 3.2).

12. See Harris, Fotheringham, Crespo, and Charlton (2010) for further elaboration on GWR predictions.

13. Most tests focus on the overall (average) relevance of explanatory variables in this context, such as the nonparametric test developed by McMillen and Redfearn (2010). However, since practitioners often tend to rely local pseudo t-tests for betas (as, e.g., in Mennis & Jordan, 2005; Matthews & Yang, 2012) which do appear in other software (such as GWR4 (https://geodacenter.asu.edu/gwr_software)), we choose this method for purposes of comparison. (See note 22 below for further discussion.)

14. Only one of the 1,681 local predictive regressions has a condition number above 30 (and this with value 30.92).

15. Such problems with GWR are well known, and the ArcMap documentation recommends that preliminary OLS regressions be done in an attempt to identify and remove irrelevant variables.

16. We use Vanhatalo et al.'s (2013) GPstuff package to conduct GPR runs and D'Errico's (2014) adaptive robust numerical differentiation for Hessian evaluation.

17. The only exception here is the one outlier case at sample size $n = 60$ in Sim 2, where SPB is performing noticeably worse than both MAP and BIC. Here it appears that larger numbers of simulations would be warranted.

18. Here both BIC and MAP yield almost identical results to SPB.

19. Recall that the (essentially one-dimensional) marginal effects for the separable symmetric model in Sim 1 are far less interesting from a spatial viewpoint, and will be considered only in terms of relative fit (for VLS).

20. The shapes of these ME2 contours can best be understood by visually verifying that the contour-tangency points on any vertical line in the ϕ_{aniso} plot [panel (e) in Fig. 4] correspond precisely to the ME2 = 0 contour, which is the second lowest (coolest) contour in panel (e) of Fig. 4.

21. Examinations of different sample patterns for this case produce the same qualitative results for GWR, and in addition, exhibit rather extreme variations from sample to sample.

22. Such default levels of significance are no doubt inflated, and should in principle be corrected by estimating "effective degrees of freedom" (as is typically done for tests of average beta values in GWR; Leung, 2000). So in the present setting such levels are best viewed as simply a benchmark for comparison with VLS.

23. For purposes of RMSE comparisons with Eqs. (66), (68), and (69), marginal effects of (dimensionless) standardized variates have been rescaled (multiplied by their sample standard deviations) to approximate their original dimensions.

24. Note that the effects of the single outlier case for $n = 60$ in Sim 2 of Fig. 2 are reflected by the corresponding marginal results of panel (b) in Fig. 7. But here, MAP seems to have been slightly affected as well as SPB.

25. The variables MV, LSTAT, DIS, and RAD were transformed to natural logs. In addition, NOX was transformed to NOX^2, and B was transformed as discussed in the text.

26. The present shapefile of 1970 Boston census tracts was extracted from the digital boundary files of the National Historical Geographic Information System (NHGIS). A similar shapefile was developed by Roger Bivand, and is now available as part of the *spdep* package in R.

27. Results for MAP are very similar here and are not shown.

28. Note that *out-of-sample* predictions are of limited use in studies of this type, where the given 506 census tracks form contiguous spatial units. However, for studies involving geocoded point data (such as individual housing sales), it is clear that out-of-sample predictions would be far more appropriate.

29. As discussed in Bivand (2015), this NOX data is based on measurements in 122 meteorological (TASSIM) zones that were in turn "copied out" to more aggregate collections of census tracts.

30. In ArcMap, for example, the condition-number restrictions mentioned in Section 4.1 above only allow GWR to be run with small subsets of the Boston variables.

31. The GWR program, ***gwr.m***, is part of his Matlab *Econometrics Toolbox* (Version 7, 2012).

32. The common residual scale for VLS and GWR is in median-value units with *white* = ±2, and with increments of 2 units on either side.

33. In this enlarged map it can also be seen that a number of census tracts are missing (including downtown Boston itself). As noted by Bivand (2015), this is in part due to missing data or to small number of housing units in these tracts.

34. Note that the zero values for LAT and CHAS reflect the fact that neither of these variables were included in any model of sequence *M*.

35. As stated above, all VLS applications in this section use the SPB approximation of Bayes Factors.

36. While the print version of this figure is in grey scale, the online color version more accurately depicts the dramatic variations among these localized marginal effects. In the color version, positive ME_BP values are shown in varying shades of red, and negative values in varying shades of blue. The same is true for Fig. 13(b). Many of the figures found in this article are available in color online at http://www.emeraldinsight.com/doi/full/10.1108/S0731-905320160000037018.

37. By way of contrast, fewer than 40% of all adults in tracts 805 or 818 were even high school graduates.

38. Aside from this MIT area, all other marginal effects in Fig. 13(b) are credible at the 95% level.

39. See, for example, "A Short History of Boston's South End" by Arlene Vadum (available online at http://www.south-end-boston.com/History).

ACKNOWLEDGMENTS

The authors are grateful to Kelley Pace, James LeSage, Chandra Bhat, and an anonymous referee for their constructive comments on an earlier version of this paper.

REFERENCES

Bivand, R. (2015). *Revisiting the Boston data set (Harrison and Rubinfeld, 1978): A case study in the challenges of system articulation*. Working Paper SAM 30 (ISSN: 0804-6824), Department of Economics, Norwegian School of Economics, Helleveien 30, N-5045 Bergen, Norway.

Bollen, K. A., Ray, S., Zavisca, J., & Harden, J. J. (2012). A comparison of Bayes factor approximation methods including two new methods. *Sociological Methods & Research*, *41*(2), 294–324.

Brunsdon, C., Fotheringham, A. S., & Charlton, M. E. (1996). Geographically weighted regression: A method for exploring spatial non-stationarity. *Geographical Analysis*, *28*, 281–298.

Chen, T., & Wang, B. (2010). Bayesian variable selection for Gaussian process regression: Application to chemometric calibration of spectrometers. *Neurocomputing*, *73*, 2718–2726.

D'Errico, J. (2014). *Adaptive robust numerical differentiation – File exchange – MATLAB central*. Retrieved from http://www.mathworks.com/matlabcentral/fileexchange/13490-adaptive-robust-numerical-differentiation. Accessed on January 16, 2015.

Dearmon, J., & Smith, T. E. (2016). Gaussian process regression and Bayesian model averaging: An alternative approach to modeling spatial phenomena. *Geographical Analysis, 42*, 82–111.

Deng, M. (2008). An anisotropic model for spatial processes. *Geographical Analysis, 40*(1), 26–51.

Fernandez, C., Ley, E., & Steel, M. F. J. (2001). Benchmark priors for Bayesian model averaging. *Journal of Econometrics, 100*, 381–427.

Fotheringham, A. S., Brunsdon, C., & Charlton, M. E. (2002). *Geographically weighted regression – The analysis of spatially varying relationships*. New York, NY: Wiley.

Gal, Y., van der Wilk, M., & Rasmussen, C. (2014). Distributed variational inference in sparse Gaussian process regression and latent variable models. *Advances in Neural Information Processing Systems, Paper* 1660, Montreal, Canada.

Gelman, A., & Pardoe, I. (2007). Average predictive comparisons for models with nonlinearity, interactions, and variance components. *Sociological Methodology, 37*, 23–51.

Gelman, A., Carlin, J. B., Stern, H. S., Dunson, D., Vehtari, A., & Rubin, D. B. (2013). *Bayesian data analysis* (3rd ed.). Boca Raton, FL: Chapman & Hall/CRC.

Green, P. J. (1995). Reversible jump Markov chain Monte Carlo computation and Bayesian model determination. *Biometrika, 82*, 711–732.

Harris, P., Fotheringham, A. S., Crespo, R., & Charlton, M. (2010). The use of geographically weighted regression for spatial prediction: An evaluation of models using simulated data sets. *Mathematical Geosciences, 42*, 657–680.

Harrison, D., & Rubinfeld, D. L. (1978). Hedonic housing prices and the demand for clean air. *Journal of Environmental Economics and Management, 5*, 81–102.

Hensman, J., Fusi, N., & Lawrence, N. D. (2013). Gaussian processes for big data. *arXiv preprint arXiv*: 1309.6835.

Leung, Y. (2000). Statistical tests for spatial nonstationarity based on the geographically weighted regression model. *Environment and Planning A, 32*, 9–32.

Lloyd, J. R., Duvenaud, D., Grosse, R., Tenenbaum, J. B., & Ghahramani, Z. (2014). Automatic construction and natural-language description of nonparametric regression models. *arXiv preprint arXiv*: 1402-4304.

Madigan, D., & Raftery, A. E. (1994). Model selection and accounting for model uncertainty in graphical models using occam's window. *Journal of the American Statistical Association, 89*, 1535–1546.

Matthews, S. A., & Yang, T. (2012). Mapping the results of local statistics: Using geographically weighted regression. *Demographic Research, 26*, 151–166.

McMillen, D. (2010). Issues in spatial data analysis. *Journal of Regional Science, 50*, 119–141.

McMillen, D. (2012). Perspectives on spatial econometrics: Linear smoothing with structured models. *Journal of Regional Science, 52*, 192–209.

McMillen, D., & Redfearn, C. (2010). Estimation and hypothesis testing for nonparametric hedonic house price functions. *Journal of Regional Science, 50*, 712–733.

McMillen, D. P. (1996). One hundred fifty years of land values in Chicago: A nonparametric approach. *Journal of Urban Economics, 40*, 100–124.

Mennis, J. L., & Jordan, L. M. (2005). The distribution of environmental equity: Exploring spatial nonstationarity in multivariate models of air toxic releases. *Annals, Association of American Geographers, 95*, 249–268.

Neal, R. M. (1997). Monte Carlo implementation of Gaussian process models for Bayesian regression and classification. *arXiv preprint physics/9701026*.

Pace, R. K., & Gilley, O. W. (1997). Using the spatial configuration of data to improve estimation. *The Journal of Real Estate Finance and Economics*, *14*, 333–340.

Raftery, A. E. (1995). Bayesian model selection in social research. *Sociological Methodology*, *25*, 111–163.

Rasmussen, C., & Williams, C. (2006). *Gaussian process for machine learning*. Cambridge, MA: MIT Press.

Seeger, M. (2004). Gaussian processes for machine learning. *International Journal of Neural Systems*, *14*, 69–106.

Vanhatalo, J., Riihimäki, J., Hartikainen, J., Jylänki, P., Tolvanen, V., & Vehtari, A. (2013). GPstuff: Bayesian modeling with Gaussian processes. *The Journal of Machine Learning Research*, *14*(1), 1175–1179.

CITY AND INDUSTRY NETWORK IMPACTS ON INNOVATION BY CHINESE MANUFACTURING FIRMS: A HIERARCHICAL SPATIAL-INTERINDUSTRY MODEL

Yuxue Sheng[a] and James P. LeSage[b]

[a]*China-ASEAN Research Institute, Guangxi University, Nanning, China*
[b]*Department of Finance & Economics, Texas State University, San Marcos, TX, USA*

ABSTRACT

We are interested in modeling the impact of spatial and interindustry dependence on firm-level innovation of Chinese firms The existence of network ties between cities imply that changes taking place in one city could influence innovation by firms in nearby cities (local spatial spillovers), or set in motion a series of spatial diffusion and feedback impacts across multiple cities (global spatial spillovers). We use the term local *spatial spillovers to reflect a scenario where only immediately neighboring cities are impacted, whereas the term* global *spatial spillovers represent a situation where impacts fall on neighboring cities, as*

Spatial Econometrics: Qualitative and Limited Dependent Variables
Advances in Econometrics, Volume 37, 343–386

ISSN: 0731-9053/doi:10.1108/S0731-905320160000037019

well as higher order neighbors (neighbors to the neighboring cities, neighbors to the neighbors of the neighbors, and so on). Global spatial spillovers also involve feedback impacts from neighboring cities, and imply the existence of a wider diffusion of impacts over space (higher order neighbors).

Similarly, the existence of national interindustry input-output ties implies that changes occurring in one industry could influence innovation by firms operating in directly related industries (local interindustry spillovers), or set in motion a series of in interindustry diffusion and feedback impacts across multiple industries (global interindustry spillovers).

Typical linear models of firm-level innovation based on knowledge production functions would rely on city- and industry-specific fixed effects to allow for differences in the level of innovation by firms located in different cities and operating in different industries. This approach however ignores the fact that, spatial dependence between cities and interindustry dependence arising from input-output relationships, may imply interaction, not simply heterogeneity across cities and industries.

We construct a Bayesian hierarchical model that allows for both city- and industry-level interaction *(global spillovers) and subsumes other innovation scenarios such as: (1)* heterogeneity *that implies level differences (fixed effects) and (2)* contextual effects *that imply* local spillovers *as special cases.*

Keywords: Bayesian; random effects; cross-sectional dependence

JEL classifications: C21; R12; R15

1. INTRODUCTION

Although innovation occurs at the firm level, firms operate in a regional and industry context. Empirical research on innovation has relied heavily on the knowledge production function (KPF) proposed by Griliches (1979) and modified by Jaffe (1989). A typical KPF is specified as a (log) linear relationship between innovation as the dependent variable and various inputs such as R&D expenditures and personnel as independent variables. One strand in the literature is to carry out firm-level examinations using innovation survey data such as Community Innovation Survey (CIS), Global Entrepreneurship Monitor (GEM), or China's National Bureau of Statistics

Census of Manufacturing (Baldwin, Beckstead, Mark Brown, & Rigby, 2008; Battisti & Stoneman, 2010; Dong & Yuan, 2014; Kampik & Dachs, 2011; Mairesse & Mohnen, 2005; Nathan & Lee, 2013; Zhang, He, & Sun, 2014; Zhang, Liu, & Zheng, 2007). A critique of firm-level empirical models is that when data are drawn from a population with a geographical (or industry) grouped structure (e.g., city or industry), this adds a common element to otherwise independent errors, thereby inducing correlated within-group errors (Corrado & Fingleton, 2012; Elhorst, 2014). Typical linear models of firm-level innovation based on KPFs rely on region- and industry-specific fixed effects to allow for differences in the level of innovation by firms operating in different regions and industries.

Other empirical use of the KPF has relied on regional aggregation of innovation inputs and outputs for firms operating in a single industry (Audretsch, Dohse, & Niebuhr, 2010; Audretsch & Feldman, 1996; Crescenzi, Rodriguez-Pose, & Storper, 2007, 2012; Feldman, 1994). Critiques of this approach are that aggregation of firm-level input and outputs for regions may destroy the functional form of the KPF from microeconomics, and aggregation may obscure firm-level behavior that underlies innovation. Here, the focus has been on the role of knowledge spillovers arising from the regional context in which firms operate, or regions viewed as linked networks through which knowledge diffuses over time (Audretsch et al., 2010; Cheng & Li, 2012; LeSage & Sheng, 2014; Van der Panne, 2004).

This empirical study of firm-level innovation relies on sample data consisting of over 11,600 Chinese manufacturing firms operating in 270 cities and 89 industries. We construct a Bayesian hierarchical model specification that allows for three different innovation scenarios. One scenario which we label *heterogeneity* is a simple extension of the fixed effects specification emphasizing level differences between cities and industries. Fixed effects in a spatial context are typically interpreted as heterogeneity arising from geographical differences, for example, location on major transport routes, superior climate amenities, ocean ports, etc., which might lead to persistently different levels of innovation over time. Similarly, industry-level fixed effects are viewed as reflecting persistent differences in industry-level production methods, engineering technology, returns to scale, etc.

A second scenario that we label *contextual effects* arises when a city or industry may benefit or be harmed by local spatial or industry spillovers from (first-order) neighboring cities or (first-order) input-output-related industries.[1]

There are numerous possible motivations for spatial dependence between cities when considering innovation by firms. One is that nearby cities may share the same knowledge infrastructure. Universities and research institutes typically locate in major cities to exploit scale economies, but the influence of these institutions on the stock of knowledge is not limited by city borders. For example, Liu and Tang (2010) using Chinese data found that significant knowledge spillovers extended to third-order neighbors.[2] Another motivation for spatial spillovers would be intercity movement of firms and resources such as human and venture capital used in the knowledge production process. Duranton and Puga (2001) argue that cities may be complementarity, with new firms starting in cities that are highly diversified in production that foster new ideas. Firms later migrate to nearby cities specialized in production as they mature in order to take advantage of localization economies. Examples of localization economies are: sharing of resources inputs, knowledge spillovers, advertising firms, firms supplying intermediate inputs that require face-to-face contact, or specialized labor pools. Finally, positive spatial dependence between cities could arise if cities emulate neighboring governments' development strategies and policies adopted to foster innovation. This could be particularly important in the case of China where city governments have a great deal of influence over economic development.

The motivation for positive interindustry dependence arises from input-output relationships where a firm operating in industry i uses inputs to its production process from a set of related industries j. Interindustry linkages imply that firms operating in a downstream industry could acquire R&D embodied in capital and intermediate goods it uses. This reasoning is compatible with the notion of knowledge externalities that play a central role in new theories of economic growth. Smith (2004) argues that indicators of R&D intensity need to be adjusted using input-output tables to take into account *acquired technology*, and shows that this produces important changes in the relationship between direct R&D and measured knowledge.

Feedback effects are the hallmark of the third scenario that we label *spatial interaction effects*. Feedback or self-reinforcing effects are associated with *global spatial spillovers* which arise when impacts diffuse to neighboring cities, then to neighbors of the neighboring cities, and on to other cities in the network of cities. By definition, a city is a neighbor to its neighbor, which implies that spatial spillovers traversing beyond immediate neighbors will produce a feedback effect. A similar argument applies to interindustry interaction effects, and traditional input-output models feature this type of feedback as well as *global interindustry spillovers*.

Our focus is on the nature and role of city- and industry-level characteristics on firm-level innovation processes. Do characteristics of city i (industry i) impact only innovation by firms in city i (industry i) (as in the fixed effects scenario)? Or, do characteristics of city/industry i also impact innovation of firms located in nearby/related cities/industries j (the contextual effects scenario), or do city/industry i characteristics imply a network of cities/industries where innovation taking place in city/industry i sets in motion feedback and diffusion impacts across the network of cities/industries. These would take the form of additional innovation by firms in neighboring cities/industries j that in turn feeds back to produce more innovation by firms in city/industry i, as well as a diffusion process where impacts fall on firms that neighbor cities/industries j (say cities/industries k), as well as more distant cities/industries that neighbor cities/industries k (a global spatial/interindustry spillovers scenario).

The hierarchical model we set forth relies on a general spatial simultaneous dependence structure that collapses to a contextual effects specification in the absence of spatial interaction, and further collapses to an extended spatial fixed effects specification in the absence of contextual spatial effects. Another level in the hierarchical model uses a general interindustry structure based on a simultaneous dependence specification that similarly collapses to a contextual effects specification in the absence of interindustry interaction, and further collapses to an extended interindustry fixed effects specification in the absence of contextual interindustry effects.

The firm-level model consists of a conventional KPF, with (logged) value of new products used to proxy innovation, and R&D expenditures, firm age, size, ownership type, exports, etc., as explanatory variables that model variation in firm-level innovation. Our focus is on latent unobservable effects vectors that replace conventional city-specific and industry-specific fixed effects in our hierarchical model. We impose a simultaneous Durbin model dependence specification as a Bayesian prior on the city- and industry-level latent effects parameters that are estimated. The interaction effects structure is parameterized such that fixed effects or contextual effects scenarios described above are subsumed as special cases of the more general interaction effects scenario. Estimates for parameters of this structure can be used to draw inferences regarding which of the innovation scenarios is most consistent with our sample data for Chinese manufacturing firms.

The next section describes the hierarchical spatial-interindustry model, and the following section outlines interpretation of the model estimates. Estimation procedures that are detailed in an appendix are discussed in Section 4. A simulated data example of our estimation methodology is provided in Section 5 to demonstrate that the model can produce accurate estimates and inferences regarding latent unobservable spatial and industry effects. Section 6 discusses the empirical implementation of the model for our sample of Chinese firms, with empirical results and discussion in Section 7.

2. A FIRM-CITY-INDUSTRY HIERARCHICAL MODEL

There is a great deal of literature that focuses on modeling what we have labeled unobserved latent effects.[3] In the case of spatial modeling, one approach is to introduce a latent vector of unobservable city effects treated as parameters to be estimated (Lacombe & McIntyre, 2014; LeSage & Fischer, 2007; Smith & LeSage, 2004), while others place a hierarchical structure on city-level variances (Baltagi, Fingleton, & Pirotte, 2014; Corrado & Fingleton, 2012; Parent & LeSage, 2008), or rely on a combination of these two approaches (Parent & LeSage, 2012). We extend this literature by including latent effects for interindustry interaction into the spatial model.

Our approach reflects an extension of Smith and LeSage (2004), who introduce a latent vector of unobservable city effects treated as parameters to be estimated. Assume there are n firms located in m cities, and r industries. Innovation output for firm i located in city j, industry k, Y_{ijk} can be written in a KPF form, with X_{ijk} representing a (1 ×k)-vector of inputs and θ_j the (scalar) unobservable city-level effect, γ_k the (scalar) unobservable industry-level effect as in Eq. (1).

$$Y_{ijk} = X_{ijk}\beta + \theta_j + \gamma_k + e_{ijk}. \tag{1}$$

We could assume that unobservable city-level effect of region j depends upon a vector of city characteristics C_j, an associated vector of parameters δ, with a normally distributed constant variance disturbance vector $u_j, j = 1, \ldots, m$. Taking a similar approach for the unobservable industry-level effect for industry k using Z_k as industry characteristics with associated vector ϕ, we have Eq. (2) and Eq. (3).

$$\theta_j = C_j\delta + u_j, \tag{2}$$

$$\gamma_k = Z_k\phi + v_k. \tag{3}$$

This reflects a simple extension of the fixed effects scenario, where level differences are modeled as a function of city and industry characteristics (C, Z). This hierarchical model specification could be implemented using matrix notation such that all firms in the same city share the same effect, as do firms in the same industry.

$$y = X\beta + \Delta_c\theta + \Delta_z\gamma + \varepsilon, \tag{4}$$

$$\theta = C\delta + u, \tag{5}$$

$$\begin{aligned} &\gamma = Z\phi + v, \\ &\varepsilon \sim N\left(0, \sigma_\varepsilon^2 I_n\right), \\ &u \sim N\left(0, \sigma_u^2 I_m\right), \\ &v \sim N\left(0, \sigma_v^2 I_r\right), \\ var(\Delta_c\theta + \Delta_z\gamma + \varepsilon) &= \sigma_\varepsilon^2 I_N + \sigma_u^2 \Delta_c \Delta_c' + \sigma_v^2 \Delta_z \Delta_z', \end{aligned} \tag{6}$$

where y is an $n \times 1$ vector of firms' (log transformed) innovation output, X is an $N \times k$ matrix of innovation inputs (log transformed), with β the associated parameters. The $m \times 1$ vector θ represent city-level effects, and the $n \times m$ matrix Δ_c assigns the appropriate city effect to each firm depending on its city location. Specifically, Δ_{ij} equals one if firm i is located in city j. Similarly, the $r \times 1$ vector γ denotes industry-level effects, with the $n \times r$ matrix Δ_z used to assign industry effects to firms depending on their industry grouping.

As in most regional applications of hierarchical models, we assume the disturbance terms (ε, u, v) are *i.i.d.*, homoscedastic and exhibit zero covariance. This specification represents a simple extension of the fixed effects specification, where the effects levels θ, γ for different cities/industries are modeled as a function of city/industry characteristics in the matrices C, Z.

An extension of this specification shown in Eqs. (8) and (9) allows characteristics of neighboring cities/industries (W_cC, W_zZ) to play a role in determining the unobserved effects for cities/industries, where the same assumptions regarding the disturbance terms ε and u, v are made. The $m \times m$ matrix W_c is a (row-normalized) spatial weight matrix that creates a linear combination of neighboring city characteristics (W_cC), and the $r \times r$ matrix W_z is a row-normalized input-output USE matrix (with main diagonal elements set to zero). This produces a combination of input-output-related industries characteristics (W_zZ)

$$y = X\beta + \Delta_c\theta + \Delta_z\gamma + \varepsilon, \tag{7}$$

$$\theta = \begin{pmatrix} CW_cC \end{pmatrix}\begin{pmatrix} \delta_c \\ \delta_w \end{pmatrix} + u, \tag{8}$$

$$\gamma = \begin{pmatrix} ZW_zZ \end{pmatrix}\begin{pmatrix} \phi_z \\ \phi_w \end{pmatrix} + v. \tag{9}$$

This specification subsumes that in Eq. (4) as a special case when the parameter vector associated with the spatial lag of city characteristics, $\delta_w = 0$. A similar statement applies to the case where $\phi_w = 0$, which produces the specification in Eq. (6).

A further elaboration is to allow for spatial interaction in the city-level effects vector using a spatial autoregressive process to govern formation of the effects vector θ, as shown in Eq. (11). Interindustry interaction for industry-level effects can also rely on a simultaneous interindustry input-output dependence specification, shown in Eq. (12).

In Eq. (11), W_c is an $m \times m$ (row-normalized) spatial weight matrix (with zeros on the main diagonal) reflecting spatial connectivity of the cities, so that $W_c\theta$ introduces a spatial lag reflecting a spatial autoregressive process assigned to govern the city-level effects. The scalar parameter ρ reflects the strength of spatial dependence in the city-specific effects θ, with the range of this parameter governed by minimum and maximum eigenvalues of the matrix W_c (see LeSage & Pace, 2009).

$$y = X\beta + \Delta_c\theta + \Delta_z\gamma + \varepsilon, \tag{10}$$

$$\theta = \rho W_c\theta + \begin{pmatrix} C & W_cC \end{pmatrix}\begin{pmatrix} \delta_c \\ \delta_w \end{pmatrix} + u, \tag{11}$$

$$\gamma = \tau W_z \gamma + \left(Z W_z Z \right) \begin{pmatrix} \phi_z \\ \phi_w \end{pmatrix} + v,$$

$$\theta = A^{-1} \left(C W_c C \right) \begin{pmatrix} \delta_c \\ \delta_w \end{pmatrix} + u,$$

$$\gamma = B^{-1} \left(Z W_z Z \right) \begin{pmatrix} \phi_z \\ \phi_w \end{pmatrix} + v,$$

$$A = I_m - \rho W_c,$$

$$B = I_r - \tau W_z,$$

$$\mathrm{var}\left(\Delta_c A^{-1} u + \Delta_z B^{-1} v + \varepsilon \right) = E\left(\sigma_u^2 \Delta_c (A'A)^{-1} \Delta_c' + \sigma_v^2 \Delta_z (B'B)^{-1} \Delta_z' + \sigma_\varepsilon^2 I_n \right). \tag{12}$$

A similar specification based on the input-output USE matrix W_z (row-normalized with main diagonal elements set to zero) was used in Eq. (12) to specify simultaneous interindustry dependence, allowing for global inter-industry interaction. The scalar parameter τ reflects the strength of interindustry dependence.

It should be noted that Smith and LeSage (2004) introduce a spatial autoregressive structure for (city-level) effects similar to Eq. (11), where δ_c and δ_w are set to zero. Lacombe and McIntyre (2014) use a specification similar to Eq. (11), with the parameters δ_w set to zero that they label spatially autocorrelated hierarchical model. Since the specification in Eq. (11) reflects what is known as a spatial Durbin model, we could label our model a hierarchical spatial-interindustry Durbin model (HSIDM).

3. INTERPRETING THE CITY- AND INDUSTRY-LEVEL EFFECTS ESTIMATES

Turning to model interpretation, the coefficient vector β for the explanatory variable matrix X is interpreted in a manner similar to the standard regression model. If we rely on the log-log form typically used for the KPF, the parameters β reflect elasticity responses of innovation to changes in firm-level characteristics that proxy inputs to the KPF.

A straightforward approach to interpretation of the simpler (non-spatial) model in Eqs. (4) and (5) would be that we have a linear model with grouped observations. Variation in city- and industry-specific effects are explained by own-city and own-industry characteristics (C, Z). This type of specification extends the fixed effects approach by introducing a linear relationship along with additional sample data (C, Z) in an attempt to produce a parsimonious summary representation of the fixed effects. The $m \times 1$ and $r \times 1$ vectors of fixed effects parameters are reduced to the number of parameters in δ and ϕ. Of course, this raises the problem of determining appropriate explanatory variables C, Z that produce a reasonable linear summary of the fixed effects parameters.

For the case of the local spatial/interindustry models, in Eqs. (7)–(9), and global spatial/interindustry models, in Eqs. (10)–(12), we follow Smith and LeSage (2004), who take an unobserved components view of the model. In their case, they postulate that unobserved (spatial) dependencies between firms located in different cities are captured by dependencies between the city-level effects parameters θ. In their choice theoretic/probit model, they posit that unobserved utility-differences common to firms in a given city i may be similar to those for firms in neighboring cities. This motivates imposing a spatial autoregressive structure as a Bayesian prior on the city-level effects parameters. This results in a special case of our model from Eq. (11), where δ_c and δ_w take values of zero, while ρ is different from zero. The same argument applies to unobserved interindustry dependencies. Input-output-related industries should exhibit effects parameters that take on similar values due to the simultaneous dependence structure imposed as a prior for these.

Our approach generalizes this to allow a role for city- and industry-specific characteristics in determining the magnitude of the city- and industry-level effects parameters, θ, γ, which we view as reflecting latent unobservables that arise after conditioning on the standard firm-level KPF relation. Since empirical KPF models are often used to explain variation in firm-level innovation behavior, these models may well exhibit spatial and interindustry interaction effects due to the varying spatial location and industry in which firms in the sample operate.

For our more general model (10) with spatial effects specification (11), consider how changes in city characteristics C would impact firm-level innovation y. Applying the chain rule to changes in the kth city characteristic in the matrix C, (which we denote C^k) we have:

$$\begin{aligned}\partial y/\partial C^{k'} &= \frac{\partial y}{\partial \theta}\frac{\partial \theta}{\partial C^{k'}} \\ &= \Delta_c(I_m - \rho W_c)^{-1}\left(I_m\delta_c^k + W_c\delta_w^k\right) \\ &= \Delta_c\left(I_m + \rho W_c + \rho^2 W_c^2 + \cdots\right)\left(I_m\delta_c^k + W_c\delta_w^k\right).\end{aligned} \tag{13}$$

Recall that Δ_c is an $n \times m$ matrix, so in Eq. (13) we have two $m \times m$ matrices pre-multiplied by Δ_c. The main diagonal elements of the matrix product $(I_m - \rho W_c)^{-1}(I_m\delta_c^k + W_c\delta_w^k)$ show how own-city changes in the kth characteristic impact own-city effects on innovation. Pre-multiplication by the matrix Δ_c would simply assign these own-partial derivatives to all firms in the same city. Specifically, we are referring to how the jth element of the vector θ responds to a change in the kth characteristic of the jth city, $(\partial\theta_j/\partial C_j^k)$, as the own-partial derivative. The i,j off-diagonal element of the matrix product $(I_m - \rho W_c)^{-1}(I_m\delta_c^k + W_c\delta_w^k)$ shows how changes in the kth characteristic of city j impact innovation in another city i, that is, $(\partial\theta_i/\partial C_j^k)$.

The conventional spatial weight matrix W_c has zeros on the main diagonal and non-zero elements in position i,j if cities i and j are neighbors, zeros otherwise. If we define the matrix W_c based on the nearest s neighboring cities, the matrix W_c^2 contains non-zero elements in rows and columns that reflect cities that are neighbors to the nearest s neighboring cities. Similarly, the matrix W_c^3 has non-zero elements for neighbors to the neighbors to the nearest s cities. An important point is that the matrix W^2 has non-zero elements on the main diagonal reflecting the fact that a city is a nearest neighbor to its nearest neighbor. This results in the own-partial derivatives reflecting feedback effects associated with changes in city i characteristics that influence neighboring city innovation, plus feedback to produce an impact on city i innovation.

Rather than calculate the entire $m \times m$ matrix of own- and cross-partial derivatives, we follow LeSage and Pace (2009) and calculate scalar summary measures of these derivatives. An average of the main diagonal elements is used as a scalar estimate of the own-partial derivative, which they label a direct effect, while an average of the cumulated off-diagonal elements from each row is used as a scalar summary estimate of the cross-partial derivatives, which they call an indirect effect.

Some discussion of the spirit in which the model operates to capture spatial interaction between cities using a spatial autoregressive process as a

Bayesian prior for the city-level effects parameters is in order. Our sample of cross-sectional observations on firms located in cities is viewed as reflecting a steady-state equilibrium that has arisen over time. Characteristics of individual cities such as: specialization and diversity in production and research and development and a host of other factors play a role in creating the long-run steady-state equilibrium reflected by our cross-sectional sample data. Changes in characteristics of individual cities will set in motion changes that lead to a new comparative static steady-state equilibrium, and the model partial derivatives are interpreted as reflecting the magnitude of these changes needed to arrive at a new equilibrium state. Over time, cities develop relationships with other cities in a host of ways. Movement of workers, graduates from universities, supply chain relationships in production and retailing, transportation routes, etc. All of these play a role in developing the strength of networking relationships that exist between cities. As with most spatial networks, it seems likely that nearby nodes exert a stronger influence on outcomes than distant nodes, and the spatial autoregressive process embodies this notion in terms like $\rho W_c, \rho^2 W_c^2, \ldots$ that assign declining influence to higher order neighboring cities. The non-linear declining influence assigned to more distant nodes in the network arises from the fact that the scalar parameter $\rho < 1$, so higher powers of W_c carry less weight. This might be viewed as a crude but statistically manageable approach to allowing for the possibility that cities exist as a network that allows for innovation feedback and diffusion across the network of cities in response to changes in characteristics of individual nodes in the network. Quantitative differences regarding our inferences about the role played by city-level characteristics in the innovation process in this type of scenario represent one focus of our model and empirical application.

An important focus of inference in our model is the parameter ρ. To see this, consider the case when this scalar parameter estimate is not significantly different from zero. In this case, the partial derivatives in Eq. (13) simplify to:

$$\begin{aligned} \partial y / \partial C^{k'} &= \frac{\partial y}{\partial \theta} \frac{\partial \theta}{\partial C^{k'}} \\ &= \Delta_c \left(I_m \delta_c^k + W_c \delta_w^k \right). \end{aligned} \tag{14}$$

The set of partial derivative estimates in Eq. (14) suggest city-level effects consistent with a contextual effects scenario, since changes in the kth characteristic of C in a neighboring city j will have a non-zero impact on innovation in city i. This impact arises since the i,j th element of W_c is non-zero when city j is a neighbor to city i. Note that averaging over diagonal and off-diagonal elements is not needed to produce scalar summary estimates in this case. Because the matrix W_c has row-sums of unity, we can simply interpret δ_c^k as the scalar summary direct effect estimate and δ_w^k as the scalar summary indirect (or spatial spillover) effect estimate. An important distinction between contextual effects and interaction effects is the lack of feedback effects. This distinction is what led LeSage and Pace (2014) to label this type of spatial spillover a local spillover effect, and the spatial interaction spillover a global spillover. Local spillovers impact only immediate neighbors with no feedback, and do not set in motion a process of diffusion of impacts across the network of cities as in the case of global spillovers.

Turning to interpretation of the interindustry effects parameters specification in Eq. (12), the model allows us to consider how changes in industry characteristics Z would impact firm-level innovation y. Applying the chain rule to changes in the kth industry characteristic in the matrix Z (which we denote Z^k), we have:

$$\begin{aligned} \partial y/\partial Z^{k'} &= \frac{\partial y}{\partial \gamma}\frac{\partial \gamma}{\partial Z^{k'}} \\ &= \Delta_z(I_r - \tau W_z)^{-1}\left(I_m\phi_c^k + W_z\phi_w^k\right) \\ &= \Delta_z\left(I_r + \tau W_z + \tau^2 W_z^2 + \cdots\right)\left(I_r\phi_z^k + W_z\phi_w^k\right). \end{aligned} \tag{15}$$

The row-normalized interindustry input-output use matrix (with zero diagonal elements) acts in a manner similar to the spatial weight matrix, with the ith row elements used to form a linear combination of effects parameters from related industries, those whose inputs are used in the ith industry production process. Higher order powers such as W_z^2 reflect second-order-related industries, those that supply inputs to the industries that directly supply inputs to industry i. Diagonal elements of W_z^2 are non-zero, reflecting the fact that industry i is one of the related industries that supply inputs to those that supply inputs to itself, allowing for feedback effects.[4] Unlike the input-output model, the scalar dependence parameter τ is constrained to be less than one, which results in higher order powers (reflecting more remotely related industry links) receiving declining weight/influence on changes that take place in the interindustry effects estimates as a result of changes in industry characteristics Z.

As in the case of the spatial effects, situations where $\tau = 0$ lead to industry-level contextual effects and local interindustry spillovers (those where only industries that directly supply inputs have an impact).

Estimates from the model might lead us to conclude that no spatial/interindustry spillovers exist. For example, suppose that ρ, τ equal zero and the parameters δ_w, ϕ_w associated with the spatial/interindustry lags of the C, Z variables are not (significantly) different from zero. In this case, the impact of changes in the kth characteristic of C, Z in city-industry i,j will take the form:

$$\begin{aligned}\partial y/\partial C^{k'} &= \frac{\partial y}{\partial \theta}\frac{\partial \theta}{\partial C^{k'}} \\ &= \Delta_c\left(\frac{\partial \theta}{\partial C^{k'}}\right) \\ &= \Delta_c\left(I_m \delta_c^k\right),\end{aligned} \tag{16}$$

$$\begin{aligned}\partial y/\partial Z^{k'} &= \frac{\partial y}{\partial \gamma}\frac{\partial \gamma}{\partial Z^{k'}} \\ &= \Delta_z\left(\frac{\partial \gamma}{\partial Z^{k'}}\right) \\ &= \Delta_z\left(I_m \phi_z^k\right).\end{aligned} \tag{17}$$

The partial derivative estimates from this scenario shown in Eqs. (16) and (17) lead to a situation where changes in city/industry i,j characteristics impact innovation outcomes only for firms within city i or industry j. Using the terminology of LeSage and Pace (2009), we have only direct effects, since indirect (spillover) effects are zero. This type of outcome reflects a slight extension of the conventional fixed effects used in models for firms/industries grouped by geographic location and industry type.

4. BAYESIAN ESTIMATION

Since we treat the simultaneous Durbin specification for city- and industry-effects as a Bayesian prior structure placed on the latent city- and industry-level effects, we will use Bayesian Markov Chain Monte Carlo methods to estimate the parameters of our HSIDM model. As Smith and LeSage (2004) argued, this Bayesian approach is more robust with respect to small sample sizes, and allows detailed analysis of parameter distributions obtained by simulating from the posterior distribution of all model parameters. We rely on the Bayesian organizing principle of: 'Likelihood function – Prior distributions – Posterior distributions'.

For the hierarchical model (10), the likelihood function takes the form in Eq. (18) where we define $\delta=(\delta_c\delta_w)', \phi=(\phi_z\phi_w)', C=(CW_cC), Z=(Z\ W_zZ)$:[5]

$$p(y|\beta,\theta,\gamma,\sigma_\varepsilon^2,\rho,\tau,\delta,\phi,\sigma_u^2,\sigma_v^2) = p(y|\beta,\theta,\gamma,\sigma_\varepsilon^2)p(\theta|\rho,\delta,\sigma_u^2)p(\gamma|\tau,\phi,\sigma_v^2), \quad (18)$$

where we assume the disturbances of the city- and industry-specific effects structures (u, v) are independent of each other[6]. From Eqs. (11) and (12), when $A = (I_m - \rho W_c), B = (I_r - \tau W_z)$ are nonsingular, the conditional densities of θ, γ given $(\rho, \delta, \sigma_u^2)$ and (τ, ϕ, σ_v^2) take the form:

$$\theta|(\rho,\delta,\sigma_u^2) \sim N\left(A^{-1}C\delta, \sigma_u^2(A'A)^{-1}\right), \quad (19)$$

$$\gamma|(\tau,\phi,\sigma_v^2) \sim N\left(B^{-1}Z\phi, \sigma_v^2(B'B)^{-1}\right). \quad (20)$$

Following Smith and LeSage (2004) as well as LeSage and Pace (2009, Chapter 5), we assign priors for the individual parameters of the model as follows:

$$\pi(\beta,\rho,\tau,\delta,\phi,\sigma_\varepsilon^2,\sigma_u^2,\sigma_v^2) = \pi(\beta)\pi(\rho)\pi(\tau)\pi(\delta)\pi(\phi)\pi(\sigma_\varepsilon^2)\pi(\sigma_u^2)\pi(\sigma_v^2), \quad (21)$$

$$\pi(\beta) \sim N_h\left(\underline{\beta}, \underline{V_\beta}\right), \quad (22)$$

$$\pi(\sigma_\varepsilon^2) \sim \mathrm{IG}(a_1, b_1), \quad (23)$$

$$\pi(\delta) \sim N_p\left(\underline{\delta}, \underline{V_\delta}\right), \quad \pi(\phi) \sim N_q\left(\underline{\phi}, \underline{V_\phi}\right), \tag{24}$$

$$\pi\left(\sigma_u^2\right) \sim \mathrm{IG}(a_2, b_2), \quad \pi\left(\sigma_v^2\right) \sim \mathrm{IG}(a_3, b_3), \tag{25}$$

$$\pi(\rho) \sim U\left(\lambda_{\min}^{-1}, \lambda_{\max}^{-1}\right), \quad \pi(\tau) \sim U\left(\psi_{\min}^{-1}, \psi_{\max}^{-1}\right). \tag{26}$$

We use normal prior distributions for β, δ, ϕ, as shown in Eqs. (22) and (24), where h, p, and q denote the number of explanatory variables in the matrices X and C, Z respectively. $N_h(\mu, \Sigma)$ represents a h-variate normal distribution with mean μ and variance-covariance matrix Σ. We wish to specify relatively uninformative prior distributions for the parameter vectors β and δ, ϕ that allow the sample data to play a major role in determining values for the estimates, since these parameters represent one focus of inference. Uninformative priors are centered on zero with a large standard deviation: $\underline{\beta} = \underline{\delta} = \underline{\phi} = 0$, $\underline{V_\beta} = sI_h$, $\underline{V_\delta} = sI_p$, $\underline{V_\phi} = sI_q$ $s = 10^{10}$.

Gelman (2006) discusses many prior distributions for variance parameters in hierarchical models. We assign an uninformative inverse-gamma (IG) prior for the parameters σ_ε^2 and σ_u^2, σ_v^2 by setting $a_1 = b_1 = a_2 = b_2 = a_3 = b_3 = 0$. According to Gelman (2006), it is reasonable to assume a uniform prior distribution on σ_ε^2 and σ_u^2, σ_v^2 when the number of regions m and industries r is large.

For ρ, τ, we rely on a uniform distribution over the interval defined for this parameter by minimum and maximum eigenvalues (λ) of the spatial weights W_c and eigenvalues (ψ) of the interindustry weights W_z. Since we rely on row-standardized weight matrices, $\lambda_{\max} = 1, \psi_{\max} = 1$, leading to: $U(\lambda_{\min}^{-1}, 1), U(\psi_{\min}^{-1}, 1)$.

The posterior distribution is proportional to the likelihood times the independent priors (where we use $\cdot$ to indicate the set of parameters: $\theta, \gamma, \rho, \tau, \delta, \phi, \sigma_\varepsilon^2, \sigma_u^2, \sigma_v^2$, in Eqs. (27) and (28)).

$$p(\beta, \cdot\,|y) \propto \left(\sigma_\varepsilon^2\right)^{-n/2} \exp\left\{ -\frac{1}{2\sigma_\varepsilon^2}(y - X\beta - \Delta_c\theta - \Delta_z\gamma)'(y - X\beta - \Delta_c\theta - \Delta_z\phi) \right\}$$

$$\times\, |A| \left(\sigma_u^2\right)^{-m/2} \exp\left\{ -\frac{1}{2\sigma_u^2}(A\theta - C\delta)'(A\theta - C\delta) \right\}$$

$$
\begin{aligned}
&\times |B|\left(\sigma_v^2\right)^{-r/2}\exp\left\{-\frac{1}{2\sigma_v^2}(B\gamma - Z\phi)'(B\gamma - Z\phi)\right\}\\
&\times |\underline{V_\beta}|^{-\frac{1}{2}}\exp\left\{-\frac{1}{2}\left(\beta-\underline{\beta}\right)'\underline{V_\beta}^{-1}\left(\beta-\underline{\beta}\right)\right\}\times\left(\sigma_\varepsilon^2\right)^{-(a_1+1)}\exp\left\{-\frac{b_1}{\sigma_\varepsilon^2}\right\}\\
&\times|\underline{V_\delta}|^{-\frac{1}{2}}\exp\left\{-\frac{1}{2}(\delta-\underline{\delta})'\underline{V_\delta}^{-1}(\delta-\underline{\delta})\right\}\times\left(\sigma_u^2\right)^{-(a_2+1)}\exp\left\{-\frac{b_2}{\sigma_u^2}\right\}\\
&\times|\underline{V_\phi}|^{-\frac{1}{2}}\exp\left\{-\frac{1}{2}\left(\phi-\underline{\phi}\right)'\underline{V_\phi}^{-1}\left(\phi-\underline{\phi}\right)\right\}\times\left(\sigma_v^2\right)^{-(a_3+1)}\exp\left\{-\frac{b_3}{\sigma_v^2}\right\}\\
&\times U\left(\lambda_{\min}^{-1},1\right)\times U\left(\psi_{\min}^{-1},1\right)
\end{aligned}
\tag{27}
$$

Given the uninformative and uniform priors, we have some simplification producing:

$$
\begin{aligned}
p(\beta,\cdot|y)\propto&\left(\sigma_\varepsilon^2\right)^{-n/2}\exp\left\{-\frac{1}{2\sigma_\varepsilon^2}(y-X\beta-\Delta_c\theta-\Delta_z\gamma)'(y-X\beta-\Delta_c\theta-\Delta_z\gamma)\right\}\\
&\times|A|\left(\sigma_u^2\right)^{-m/2}\exp\left\{-\frac{1}{2\sigma_u^2}(A\theta-C\delta)'(A\theta-C\delta)\right\}\\
&\times|B|\left(\sigma_v^2\right)^{-r/2}\exp\left\{-\frac{1}{2\sigma_v^2}(B\gamma-Z\phi)'(B\gamma-Z\phi)\right\}\\
&\times\left(\sigma_\varepsilon^2\right)^{-1}\times\left(\sigma_u^2\right)^{-1}\times\left(\sigma_v^2\right)^{-1}\times U\left(\lambda_{\min}^{-1},1\right)\times U\left(\psi_{\min}^{-1},1\right)
\end{aligned}
\tag{28}
$$

Markov chain Monte Carlo estimation involves sampling from the complete sequence of conditional distributions for the parameters $(\beta,\theta,\gamma,\rho,\tau,\delta,\phi,\sigma_\varepsilon^2,\sigma_u^2,\sigma_v^2)$ of our model. The conditional distributions for each of these parameters are described in the appendix, as well as details provided regarding use of a Metropolis within Gibbs procedure (Koop, 2003) to produce estimates.

5. A SIMULATED EXAMPLE ILLUSTRATING THE MODEL AND ESTIMATION

A vector y was generated using the model from Eq. (10), with parameters set as indicated in Table 1. The number of firm-level observations used was 11,639, the same sample size as used in the empirical application described in the next section. These firms were distributed over 270 cities and 89 industry groups in an identical fashion to the firm-level observations used in our examination of firm-level Chinese innovation discussed in Section 6. Spatial and interindustry weight matrices used were similar to those used in our empirical application. The spatial weight matrix W_c

Table 1. Parameters and Estimates for Simulated Example.

Parameter	True Value	Estimated Posterior Mean	Estimated Posterior Std	Parameter	True Value	Estimated Posterior Mean	Estimated Posterior Std
β_1	1	0.9986	0.0095	δ_1	0.5	0.5345	0.0508
β_2	−1	−1.0116	0.0094	δ_2	0.5	0.5509	0.0545
β_3	1	1.0223	0.0094	δ_3	−0.5	−0.4258	0.0532
β_4	1	1.0113	0.0094	δ_4	0.5	0.4763	0.0518
β_5	−1	−1.0068	0.0096	δ_5	−0.25	−0.1695	0.0509
β_6	1	1.0019	0.0095	δ_6	0.25	0.4318	0.0599
β_7	0.5	0.4992	0.0094	δ_7	−0.25	−0.3945	0.0574
β_8	0.5	0.5023	0.0095	δ_8	−0.25	−0.1329	0.0497
σ_ε^2	1	1.0191	0.0589	ρ	0.5	0.5109	0.0701
ϕ_1	0.5	0.3859	0.0923	σ_u^2	0.5	0.5325	0.0589
ϕ_2	0.5	0.2608	0.0886				
ϕ_3	−0.5	−0.4485	0.0917				
ϕ_4	−0.5	−0.5583	0.0916				
ϕ_5	−0.25	−0.1152	0.1056				
ϕ_6	0.25	0.1553	0.1235				
ϕ_7	0.25	0.2604	0.1025				
ϕ_8	−0.25	−0.2763	0.1142				
τ	0.4	0.3231	0.1151				
σ_v^2	0.5	0.6347	0.1112				

was constructed based on the six nearest (Euclidean distance) cities, equally weighted, normalized to have row sums of unity and zeros on the diagonal.

The interindustry weight matrix W_z consisted of the six industries providing the most inputs to each industry (excluding the industry itself), determined by the six largest off-diagonal elements from each row of the input-output USE matrix. After selecting the six most input-related industries, the diagonal was set to zero and the six elements were normalized to sum to one. This means that related industries receive weights based on their relative importance in the set of six largest input supplying industries. Attempts to use the full input-output USE matrix produced less accurate estimates, suggesting that small non-zero elements in this matrix introduced interindustry linkages that were problematical. Limiting the structure of the matrix W_z to the largest six (off-diagonal) elements transforms the matrix to a form taken by commonly used spatial weight matrices. Since the prior structure placed on interindustry relationships mimics the prior spatial structure, this might be a requirement for successful implementation of the model proposed here.

Table 1 presents posterior mean estimates and standard deviations for the model parameters from a single run of 20,000 draws with 10,000 draws excluded for start-up of the MCMC sampler. This took around 300 seconds on a laptop computer. The table shows high levels of precision in the estimates for the firm level of the hierarchical model where $n = 11,639$, less precise estimates for the city level of the hierarchy where $m = 270$ and the least precise estimates for the industry level where $r = 89$. This is a typical result for hierarchical models. In general, the estimates presented in the table suggest no problems with our code for implementing the model.

Fig. 1 shows scatterplots of the actual versus estimated city- and industry-effects parameters, which appear quite accurate.

The most important estimates are those for the partial derivative impact of changes in city- and industry-specific characteristics on the outcome variable y discussed in Section 3. These are shown in Table 2 alongside the true magnitudes.

As in the case of the parameters associated with the city and industry levels of the hierarchical model, the marginal effects estimates for the city level where we have more observations appear more accurate than those for the industry level where fewer observations are available.

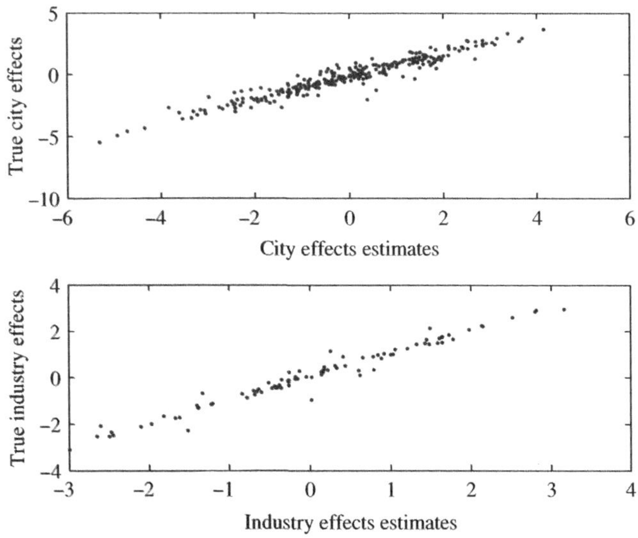

Fig. 1. Actual versus Estimated Effects (θ, γ).

6. AN EMPIRICAL EXAMINATION OF INNOVATION BY FIRMS LOCATED IN CHINESE CITIES

We use data on 11,639 Chinese manufacturing firms located in 270 cities and operating in 89 different industry categories to implement our model. The cross section of firms used in this study is from the Chinese National Bureau of Statistics (NBS) Census of Manufacturing for the year 2007. The annual survey conducted by NBS contains only large and medium-sized manufacturing enterprises (LMEs) defined as those with sales in excess of five million RMB. The survey has detailed information on 336,790 firms that account for nearly 95% of all industrial output, and the survey contains information from financial statements as well as information on: starting year of the firms, an industry code (four-digit code based on Industrial Classification of National Economy, GB/T4754-2002) for main products of the firm and location information.[7]

The location information was based on a definition of cities from NBS of China, specifically, the first four-digit administrative code of 2007.[8] Unlike cities in the United States or Europe that are separated by rural areas, the definition used here reflects a series of contiguous districts under

Table 2. Actual versus Estimated Marginal Direct, Indirect, and Total Effects Estimates.

City Level Variables	True	Mean	Std	Industry Level Variables	True	Mean	Std
Direct effect				Direct effect			
C_1	0.5000	0.5458	0.0535	Z_1	0.4989	0.3863	0.0933
C_2	0.5488	0.6248	0.0573	Z_2	0.5100	0.2650	0.0895
C_3	−0.5488	−0.4890	0.0550	Z_3	−0.4989	−0.4467	0.0924
C_4	0.5000	0.4884	0.0544	Z_4	−0.5100	−0.5668	0.0932
Indirect effect				Indirect effect			
C_1	0	0.2131	0.1409	Z_1	−0.0822	0.0216	0.1816
C_2	0.9512	1.4168	0.2605	Z_2	0.7400	0.3587	0.1968
C_3	−0.9512	−1.2136	0.2145	Z_3	0.0822	0.1665	0.1603
C_4	0	0.2282	0.1427	Z_4	−0.7400	−0.7013	0.2727
Total effect				Total effect			
C_1	0.5000	0.7589	0.1700	Z_1	0.4167	0.4079	0.2343
C_2	1.5000	2.0416	0.2857	Z_2	1.2500	0.6237	0.2354
C_3	−1.5000	−1.7026	0.2375	Z_3	−0.4167	−0.2801	0.2053
C_4	0.5000	0.7166	0.1712	Z_4	−1.2500	−1.2681	0.3054

the governance of a central city. This seems more similar to US counties, or European NUTS two or three level regions. Some prior research by Yang, Lin, and Li (2013) and Yoshihiro and Kiyoyasu (2013) used this census information to explore the relationship between firm-level productivity and agglomeration economies in China. After cleaning the survey data to delete observations with unreasonable values (e.g., negative or zero values for the sales, capital and employment information), we obtained a sample of 11,639 firms that had positive new product output.

6.1. KPF Variables

There are several indicators that could be used to represent firm-level innovation: patent applications or patents granted to the firm, or firms' new product output or R&D inputs used by firms Due to data availability, we use (logged) new product output to represent firm-level innovation (our dependent variable vector y), following work of others (Van der Panne, 2004; Boschma & Weterings, 2005; Xu, Li, & Zhang 2011; Nathan & Lee, 2013).

We follow conventional KPF practice and rely on a host of firm-level characteristics as proxies for inputs to the innovation production process. Past literature has relied on: firm characteristics such as R&D input, firm age and size, export status, industry, organizational status, and so on (Johansson & Lööf, 2008). We use firm characteristics enumerated below.

We follow the KPF literature and include (logged) firm-level expenditures on R&D as an input to knowledge production. Firm size, measured by the (logged) value of the firm's assets. The literature points out that firm size influences both the capability and incentive of firms for innovation. For example (An, Shi, & Ludovico, 2006), note that large firms may have a more sustained and reliable stream of new product output.

Firm-level (logged) exports, measured by the value of exports produced was also included because China has been the largest exporting country since 2009. Exports can impact firm-level innovation in two ways. First, a firm may need to innovate to meet higher standards in foreign markets. However, Chinese firms tend to produce at the low end of the global value chain, which may have an adverse impact on firm-level innovation (Zhang et al., 2007).

Logged firm age (in years) was also included because we might expect a negative impact on innovation for older firms Finally, a dummy variable for the type of ownership was constructed. Ownership dummies were relative to *state-owned* with the four other types of ownership being: *Collective*, *Private*, *Foreign*, or owned by *Hong Kong, Macao, Taiwan.*

Use of the log transformation applied to y and X-variables (with the exception of the ownership-type dummies) allows us to interpret estimates for the KPF explanatory variables as elasticity responses of innovation to changes in firm-level R&D, age, size, and exports.

6.2. City-Level Characteristics

The regional innovation literature emphasizes the positive role played by agglomeration economies, arising from things like labor market pooling, input sharing, knowledge spillovers, as well as more recent literature pointing to home market effects, urban consumption opportunities, and rent-seeking (Rosenthal & Strange, 2004). On the other hand, agglomeration could also have negative impacts due to increased production cost, and local intellectual "lock-in" effects that make it difficult for firms to keep pace with the latest techniques, and reduce competitiveness (Audretsch, 1998). There is also a debate in the literature regarding which kind of agglomeration, Marshall-Arrow-Romer (MAR) or Jacobs externalities, is the most beneficial for economic growth or innovation (Beaudry & Schiffauerova, 2009; Feldman & Audretsch, 1999). Chinese empirical research also reflects these divided views (Bo, 2007; Peng & Jiang, 2011; Sheng, Liu, & Ding, 2013). There are also shifting views regarding the way in which cities specialize (by industry sector or by function as argued by Duranton & Puga, 2005).

Feldman and Audretsch (1999), Paci and Usai (1999), and Greunz (2003) distinguish two kinds of agglomerations (MAR and Jacobs) for two kinds of firm functions (R&D versus production). According to Beaudry and Schiffauerova (2005), the location quotient is the most common MAR externalities indicator utilized, while the inverse Hirschman-Herfindahl index is the most common indicator of Jacobs externalities. Following Duranton and Puga (2000), we use these two indicators to construct four variables that measure city levels of production and R&D agglomeration that could impact innovation of firms located in the cities.

$$\mathrm{LQ}_j = \mathrm{Max}\left(\mathrm{LQ}_{jk}\right), \quad \mathrm{LQ}_{jk} = \frac{S_{jk}}{S_k}, \tag{29}$$

$$\mathrm{HHI}_j = \frac{1}{\left(\sum_k S_{jk}^2\right)}, \tag{30}$$

where S_{jk} is the share of industry k output/R&D by all firms in city j, S_k is the share of all firms output/R&D in industry k in the country. Our measure $\mathrm{LQ} \geqslant 0$, and a high LQ value for a city reflects that the city is highly specialized in a particular industry. For the HHI measure, $1 \leqslant \mathrm{HHI} \leqslant r$, where r ranges over industries in the firm data set. So if a city has only one industry, HHI is 1, whereas a city that has $r = 89$ industries with equal shares would result in HHI = 89, reflecting a high level of diversity.[9]

To construct these indices, output/R&D information for all 336,790 Chinese firms in the manufacturing census/survey, not simply that of the sub-sample of 11,639 firms that had positive new product output.

Summary statistics for these four variables are presented in Table 3, for both the log transformed and untransformed LQ and HHI measures. From the table, we see that HHI for production activity has a larger mean and variance than HHI for R&D activity. This indicates that production activity is more diversified across cities than R&D activity. The spatial distribution of innovation (new product output measured by value) is uneven, with

Table 3. Summary Statistics for City-Level Variables.

	Mean	Median	Std	Min	Max
(Log) Production LQ (C_1)	2.856	2.806	0.668	1.415	5.456
(Log) Production HHI (C_2)	2.319	2.417	0.693	0.232	3.545
(Log) R&D LQ (C_3)	3.918	3.726	1.128	1.561	8.871
(Log) R&D HHI (C_4)	1.325	1.307	0.710	0.005	3.223
Production LQ	22.529	16.552	22.448	4.117	234.305
Production HHI	12.500	11.216	7.310	1.262	34.667
R&D LQ	123.288	41.541	456.602	4.767	7122.820
R&D HHI	4.857	3.695	3.834	1.005	25.127

over 50% of the new product value produced in 14 large Chinese cities. A Gini coefficient indicated that the spatial distribution of new product output is more clustered than output of existing products, with a coefficient of 0.82 for new product output versus 0.67 for existing product output. This motivated use of firm assets as an explanatory variable to control for the size of firms, so variation in our dependent variable reflects more than simply the spatial distribution of new product output in large Chinese cities.

The log transformation was applied to these four variables to produce a more symmetric distribution, and they were studentized (put in deviation from means form with a variance of unity) for use in the model.

6.3. *Industry-Level Characteristics*

Much of the innovation literature focuses on variation in the level of technology used by firms, typically measured by the industry sector in which firms operate. For example, Gao and Wang (2012) use a technology classification scheme that separates firms into high, middle, and low technology industries.

Our approach allows for industry-specific latent effects that will be estimated. The prior structure placed on these effects parameters is similar in nature to the spatial structure used as a prior for city-specific effects, allowing for interindustry local or global spillovers/interaction.

Similar to the debate over which type of agglomeration is more beneficial for innovation in the regional economics literature, there is also a concern about what kind of market structure is helpful in promoting firm-level innovation. This debate goes back to early work of Schumpeter, where it is argued that a lack of competition tends to retard technological advance. However, many empirical studies have found more innovation in industries with higher levels of concentration. According to an industry life-cycle view, a Schumpeter Market I pattern of innovative activities may turn into a Schumpeter Market II, when large firms with monopolistic power come to the forefront of the innovation process (Malerba, 2004).

As in the case of our city-level LQ and HHI indicators, we construct four variables that measure industry levels of production and R&D specialization and diversity that could impact innovation of firms operating in the various industries.

$$\mathrm{LQ}_k = \mathrm{Max}\left(\mathrm{LQ}_{jk}\right), \quad \mathrm{LQ}_{jk} = \frac{S_{jk}}{S_j}, \tag{31}$$

$$\mathrm{HHI}_k = \frac{1}{\left(\sum_j S_{jk}^2\right)}, \tag{32}$$

where S_{jk} is the share of city j output/R&D by all firms in industry k, S_j is the share of all firms in city j output/R&D in the country.

The city and industry LQ measures are symmetric, since a city with a high LQ indicates specialization in a particular industry, whereas an industry with a high LQ means it is highly specialized in a particular city. The HHI measure indicates that if an industry locates only in one city, then HHI is 1, pointing to a high level of industry concentration. In contrast, if an industry locates evenly in all $m = 270$ cities, then HHI is 270, so higher HHI values point to more diversity.

Changes in specialization or diversity of industry output/R&D could potentially impact firm-level innovation of firms operating in own- and other-related industries. For example, more specialization in industry i that exploits returns to scale could impact innovation of firms operating in industry i as well as firms in related industries j who use output from i as inputs to their production process. Increased R&D diversity in industry i could provide improved choices of inputs for firms operating in this industry, as well as benefit firms operating in related industries j.

As in the case of the city LQ, HHI measures, these indices were constructed using output/R&D information for all 336,790 Chinese firms in the manufacturing census/survey was used, not simply that of the sub-sample of 11,639 firms that had positive new product output.

Table 4. Summary Statistics for Industry-Level Variables.

	Mean	Median	Std	Min	Max
(Log) Production LQ (Z_1)	2.856	2.806	0.668	1.415	5.456
(Log) Production HHI (Z_2)	2.319	2.417	0.693	0.232	3.545
(Log) R&D LQ (Z_3)	3.918	3.726	1.128	1.561	8.871
(Log) R&D HHI (Z_4)	1.325	1.307	0.710	0.005	3.223
Production LQ	40.522	26.886	47.346	3.590	340.415
Production HHI	34.136	32.184	19.988	6.566	119.766
R&D LQ	266.863	88.270	782.131	5.807	7122.820
R&D HHI	10.485	9.881	6.210	1.568	33.800

Summary statistics for these four variables are presented in Table 4, for both the log transformed and untransformed LQ and HHI measures. As in the case of city-level measures of HHI, we see that production HHI has a larger mean and variance than that for R&D activities. This points to more spatially diversified production than R&D activities with respect to our industry measure. The log transformation was applied to these four variables to produce a more symmetric distribution, and they were studentized (put in deviation from means form with a variance of unity) prior to use in the model.

6.4. The Spatial and Industry Connectivity Structures W_c, W_z

A six-nearest city neighbors weight matrix W_c was used for our model, with row-sums normalized to unity. This choice was motivated by the fact that there are on average 5.9 neighbors for each city in China. As a way of examining sensitivity of model estimates to use of six neighbors, we constructed correlation matrices for the vectors of effects estimates θ, γ produced by models based on five, six, and seven spatial neighbors, with the number of related industries used to construct W_z fixed at six. These are presented in Table 5, where we see high correlations with all above 0.9376, and all but one above 0.9561. This suggests our estimates are not overly sensitive to variation in the number of neighboring cities employed.

As already discussed, the interindustry weight matrix W_z consisted of the six industries providing the most inputs to each industry (excluding the industry itself), determined by the six largest off-diagonal elements from

Table 5. Correlation Matrices for θ, γ Estimates Based on Varying Spatial Neighbors, W_z Fixed at Six-Related Industries.

	$\theta, W_c = 5$	$\theta, W_c = 6$	$\theta, W_c = 7$
$\theta, W_c = 5$	1.0000	0.9640	0.9756
$\theta, W_c = 6$	0.9640	1.0000	0.9561
$\theta, W_c = 7$	0.9756	0.9561	1.0000
	$\gamma, W_c = 5$	$\gamma, W_c = 6$	$\gamma, W_c = 7$
$\gamma, W_c = 5$	1.0000	0.9376	0.9821
$\gamma, W_c = 6$	0.9376	1.0000	0.9813
$\gamma, W_c = 7$	0.9821	0.9813	1.0000

each row of the input-output USE matrix, which is extracted from the 2007 Input-Output (IO) tables of China.

The 2007 IO tables of China represent the fifth national benchmark input-output table compiled by the NBS of China. According to Industrial Classification of National Economy (GB/T4754-2002), there are 135 sectors in the 2007 input-output tables. The firm database used here has firms belonging to 89 sectors, including 5 sectors for mining, 81 sectors for manufacture, and 3 sectors for production and distribution of electricity, gas, and water.[10]

After selecting the six most input-related industries, the diagonal was set to zero and the six elements were normalized to sum to one. A similar set of correlation matrices were constructed for variation in the number of related industries over five, six, and seven used to construct the matrix W_z, with the number of neighboring cities fixed at six. The correlation matrices for this experiment are shown in Table 6. Here, we see that using only five related industries would result in estimates for the effects vectors θ, γ, that are not highly correlated with those based on six or seven related industries. Nonetheless, the effects vectors are highly correlated for models based on six and seven related industries.

7. ESTIMATION RESULTS

The HSIDM model in Eq. (33) was estimated using 20,000 MCMC draws, with the first 10,000 omitted for burn-in. Estimates reported here were based on six neighboring cities and six related industries.

Table 6. Correlation Matrices for θ, γ Estimates Based on Varying Related Industries, W_c Fixed at Six Neighboring Cities.

	$\theta, W_z = 5$	$\theta, W_z = 6$	$\theta, W_z = 7$
$\theta, W_z = 5$	1.0000	0.6509	0.6423
$\theta, W_z = 6$	0.6509	1.0000	0.9997
$\theta, W_z = 7$	0.6423	0.9997	1.0000
	$\gamma, W_z = 5$	$\gamma, W_z = 6$	$\gamma, W_z = 7$
$\gamma, W_z = 5$	1.0000	0.7564	0.6961
$\gamma, W_z = 6$	0.7564	1.0000	0.9827
$\gamma, W_z = 7$	0.6961	0.9827	1.0000

$$\begin{aligned} y &= X\beta + \Delta_c\theta + \Delta_z\gamma + \varepsilon, \\ \theta &= \rho W_c\theta + C\delta_c + W_c C\delta_w + u, \\ \gamma &= \tau W_z\theta + Z\phi_c + W_z Z\phi_w + v. \end{aligned} \tag{33}$$

Table 7 presents posteriors means, standard deviations, and 95% credible intervals based on the 10,000 retained draws from the posterior distribution for each parameter. It should be noted that estimates for δ and ϕ in Table 7 are not directly interpretable as partial derivative impacts as in the case of linear model specifications. Table 8 reports own- and cross-partial derivatives for the C, Z-variables that make up the city- and industry-level structured effects part of the model, with discussion of these estimates in the next section.

The parameters β associated with firm-level X-characteristics can be interpreted as reflecting partial derivative impacts arising from changes in the proxies for KPF inputs.

Based on the 0.05 and 0.95 credible intervals, firm-level R&D expenditures, firm size and exports have a positive effect on innovation by firms Age has a negative effect. These results conform to theoretical expectations. It should be noted that the elasticity response of firm-level innovation (new product output) to size (0.6094) is much greater than the response to firm-level R&D expenditures (0.1924) and firm-level exports (0.0727).

The coefficients for the type of ownership dummies, which reflect deviation from state-owned enterprizes, indicated that collective and private ownership categories were significantly better in innovation than state-owned,

Table 7. Parameters Estimate Results.

Parameters/Variables	W_c, W_z Matrices Based on Six Nearest Neighbors/Industries					
	Mean	Median	St. dev.	Mean/Std	Lower 0.05	Upper 0.95
Firm-level parameters						
β_1/ R&D	0.1924	0.1923	0.0088	21.8614	0.1753	0.2099
β_2/ Age	−0.0590	−0.0590	0.0072	−8.1596	−0.0732	−0.0450
β_3/ Collective[a]	0.0179	0.0179	0.0075	2.3946	0.0032	0.0324
β_4/ Private[a]	0.0552	0.0550	0.0106	5.1855	0.0346	0.0759
β_5/ Hong Kong, Macao, Taiwan[a]	−0.0022	−0.0021	0.0081	−0.2677	−0.0184	0.0137
β_6/ Foreign[a]	0.0099	0.0099	0.0083	1.1968	−0.0064	0.0259
β_7/ Size	0.6094	0.6093	0.0107	56.9662	0.5886	0.6301
β_8/ Exports	0.0727	0.0727	0.0082	8.9048	0.0566	0.0884
σ_ε^2	0.4621	0.4609	0.0110	42.0090	0.4444	0.4866
City-level parameters						
δ_{c1}/ Production LQ	0.0093	0.0094	0.0356	0.2605	−0.0604	0.0784
δ_{c2}/ Production HHI	0.0410	0.0414	0.0365	1.1216	−0.0315	0.1113
δ_{c3}/ R&D LQ	−0.0928	−0.0930	0.0354	−2.6196	−0.1625	−0.0245
δ_{c4}/ R&D HHI	0.0122	0.0118	0.0329	0.3707	−0.0511	0.0769
δ_{w1}/ $W\times$ Production LQ	−0.0647	−0.0639	0.0815	−0.7948	−0.2249	0.0930
δ_{w2}/ $W\times$ Production HHI	0.1346	0.1360	0.0826	1.6295	−0.0293	0.2902
δ_{w3}/ $W\times$ R&D LQ	−0.0950	−0.0955	0.0910	−1.0449	−0.2725	0.0861
δ_{w4}/ $W\times$ R&D HHI	−0.1838	−0.1839	0.0691	−2.6618	−0.3191	−0.0470
ρ	0.7941	0.7983	0.0531	14.9642	0.6811	0.8889
σ_u^2	0.1280	0.1238	0.0317	4.0378	0.0791	0.2022
Industry-level parameters						
ϕ_{z1}/ Production LQ	−0.0001	−0.0001	0.0349	−0.0029	−0.0698	0.0690
ϕ_{z2}/ Production HHI	−0.0460	−0.0463	0.0272	−1.6882	−0.0977	0.0085
ϕ_{z3}/ R&D LQ	0.0327	0.0330	0.0384	0.8517	−0.0433	0.1083
ϕ_{z4}/ R&D HHI	−0.0220	−0.0223	0.0297	−0.7417	−0.0804	0.0366
ϕ_{w1}/ $W\times$ Production LQ	0.0835	0.0827	0.0625	1.3371	−0.0374	0.2084
ϕ_{w2}/ $W\times$ Production HHI	−0.0957	−0.0958	0.0466	−2.0550	−0.1893	−0.0061
ϕ_{w3}/ $W\times$ R&D LQ	−0.0653	−0.0643	0.0544	−1.1986	−0.1751	0.0378
ϕ_{w4}/ $W\times$ R&D HHI	0.0487	0.0491	0.0547	0.8913	−0.0570	0.1575
τ	0.7498	0.7539	0.0624	12.0245	0.6187	0.8610
σ_v^2	0.0421	0.0401	0.0126	3.3412	0.0231	0.0718

[a]Relative to state-owned.

Table 8. Direct, Indirect, Total Effects Estimates.

Variables	W_c, W_z Matrices Based on Six Nearest Neighbors/Industries					
	Mean	Median	St. dev.	Mean/Std	Lower 0.05	Upper 0.95
City-level effects						
Direct effects						
Production LQ	−0.0077	−0.0060	0.0493	−0.1556	−0.1085	0.0842
Production HHI	0.0861	0.0865	0.0482	1.7868	0.0091	0.1803
R&D LQ	−0.1393	−0.1388	0.0513	−2.7165	−0.2416	−0.0400
R&D HHI	−0.0361	−0.0354	0.0441	−0.8176	−0.1244	0.0481
Indirect effect						
Production LQ	−0.3034	−0.2549	0.4686	−0.6475	−1.3565	0.4900
Production HHI	0.7938	0.7668	0.4468	1.7768	0.0114	1.7546
R&D LQ	−0.8184	−0.7761	0.5182	−1.5793	−1.9872	0.0956
R&D HHI	−0.8519	−0.7993	0.4240	−2.0095	−1.8333	−0.1655
Total effect						
Production LQ	−0.3111	−0.2605	0.5038	−0.6174	−1.4419	0.5423
Production HHI	0.8800	0.8548	0.4783	1.8396	0.0106	1.9054
R&D LQ	−0.9577	−0.9151	0.5558	−1.7231	−2.1984	0.0381
R&D HHI	−0.8880	−0.8351	0.4535	−1.9580	−1.9225	−0.1434
Industry-level effects						
Direct effects						
Production LQ	0.0059	0.0057	0.0382	0.1542	−0.0693	0.0819
Production HHI	−0.0555	−0.0555	0.0300	−1.8504	−0.1142	−0.0036
R&D LQ	0.0299	0.0302	0.0413	0.7233	−0.0520	0.1112
R&D HHI	−0.0197	−0.0199	0.0326	−0.6047	−0.08364	0.0449
Indirect effect						
Production LQ	0.3362	0.3214	0.2878	1.1685	−0.1959	0.9502
Production HHI	−0.5382	−0.5124	0.2413	−2.2302	−1.1014	−0.1353
R&D LQ	−0.1590	−0.1545	0.2565	−0.6198	−0.6755	0.3403
R&D HHI	0.1329	0.1238	0.2524	0.5266	−0.3532	0.6733
Total effect						
Production LQ	0.3421	0.3249	0.3060	1.1182	−0.2299	0.9872
Production HHI	−0.5937	−0.5687	0.2552	−2.3266	−1.1862	−0.1623
R&D LQ	−0.1291	−0.1247	0.2773	−0.4655	−0.6819	0.4161
R&D HHI	0.1132	0.1044	0.2672	0.4238	−0.4060	0.6795

while firms that were foreign-owned and owned by Hong Kong, Macao, Taiwan organizations were not.

Turning to estimates for parameters of the city level of the hierarchical model, the posterior mean for ρ was 0.7941 and different from zero based on the 0.05 and 0.95 credible intervals, pointing to positive spatial dependence in city-level effects. As discussed, this result is indicative of a global spillovers scenario consistent with an SDM specification rather than local spatial spillovers. This should be interpreted as indicating that changes in city j's specialization/diversity in production and R&D will have impacts on firm-level innovation output of firms in neighboring cities as well as firms operating in cities that are neighbors to the neighbors, and so on, and include reinforcing feedback impacts.

An area for future work would be developing Bayesian methods for comparing alternative specifications used to structure the latent unobservable effects in these models. Use of conventional Bayesian model comparison methods (see LeSage, 2014) is complicated by the need to integrate over the large number of effects parameters (as well as all other parameters) in these hierarchial models.

The parameters for the industry-level part of the model also point to significant interindustry interaction, indicated by the estimate for $\tau = 0.7498$, with lower and upper 0.05 and 0.95 credible intervals indicating positive and significant interindustry input-output dependence. This result is also indicative of a global spillovers scenario consistent with our simultaneous dependence specification rather than a local interindustry spillovers specification pointing to contextual effects. This should be interpreted as indicating that changes in industry k's specialization/diversity in production and R&D will have impacts on innovation output of firms operating in input-output-related industries as well as higher order interindustry linkages, and include reinforcing feedback impacts.

Given non-zero spatial and interindustrial interaction, we need to consider direct and indirect effects estimates to properly assess the impact of changing city-/industry-level characteristics on firm-level innovation output. We discuss the nature of these in the next section where estimates of the partial derivative impacts arising from changes in LQ and HHI variables are presented.

8. DIRECT, INDIRECT EFFECTS ESTIMATES FOR CITY- AND INDUSTRY-LEVEL INTERACTION

Estimates for the direct, indirect, and total effects arising from changes in city- and industry-level specialization and diversity in production and R&D

are presented in Table 8. From the results we see a positive and significant direct city-level effect associated with diversity in production (Production HHI), and a negative and significant direct city-level effect for specialization in R&D (R&D LQ).

The positive direct effect for city-level diversity in production (HHI) should be interpreted as indicating that more diversity in production in city *i* will have a positive impact on innovation activity by firms in city *i*. This is consistent with the model of Duranton and Puga (2001) that views cities as laboratories for innovation. For a new firm experimenting with alternative production processes, a city with more diversity in production provides opportunities for the firm to observe other firms working with diverse processes, and imitate these, or experiment more easily with multiple processes. They argue that firms move from cities with more diversity in production to more specialized cities as they mature, leading them conclude that firms view different cities as laboratories for different aspects of innovation.

The negative direct of city-level specialization (LQ) for R&D expenditures should be interpreted as indicating that more R&D specialization in a particular industry will lead to less innovation by firms in city *i*. This result might also be consistent with the model of Duranton and Puga (2001), since new firms experimenting with alternative prototype production processes might prefer less specialization in city-level R&D activities as well.

The positive indirect/spillover effects for production HHI mean that more diversity in city *i* will lead to positive innovation spillovers to firms in neighboring cities. This would be consistent with Duranton and Puga (2001) movement of firms from diverse cities to other cities that are more specialized as they mature.

Negative R&D HHI indirect/spillover effects indicate that more diversity in city *i* R&D activities will negatively impact innovation of firms in neighboring cities. This result would be consistent with findings by Autant-Bernard and LeSage (2011), who argue that interdisciplinary research does not produce spatial spillovers of the same magnitude and significance as more specialized research activities. They posit that industry-specific R&D results can be more easily disseminated through industry-specific conferences and organizations. In contrast, diverse R&D activities involving numerous actors from multiple disciplines makes it more difficult to transfer multidisciplinary research innovations to other locations.

These spatial spillovers are cumulated over neighboring cities, neighbors to the neighbors, and so on, which explains why the numerical magnitudes for indirect effects are greater than those of the direct effects. Total effects for changes in city-level specialization and diversity are the sum of the direct and indirect effects. Here, we see direct and indirect effects that have the same sign, reinforcing each other.

By way of summarizing these results, the estimates suggest a richer set of spatial interactions, reflecting more than merely heterogeneity across cities of the type that would be modeled by city-specific fixed effects. Changes in city i specialization or diversity can have non-zero impacts on other cities j. Further, the impacts fall on more than immediately neighboring cities, taking the form of diffusion over cities, suggesting a view of cities as representing a network of linkages.

Turning to the partial derivative impacts of industry-level characteristics, we see negative and significant direct interindustry spillover impacts on innovation arising from changes in production diversity (HHI). This means that a more equal distribution of industries over the city locations leads to lower innovation. This result is consistent with some empirical findings noted earlier (e.g., Malerba, 2004) that more innovation arises in industries with higher levels of concentration (less diversity), when large firms with monopolistic power come to the forefront of the innovation process.

Since the interindustry dependence parameter estimate (τ) was moderately large and significant, this points to latent interindustry global effects (γ) that exhibit interindustry dependence. This means that similarity in the magnitudes of the effects estimates exists for input-output-related industries. For example, a large positive (negative) value for γ_i implies a large positive (negative) value for γ_j, where j is the set of input-output-related industries. An implication of this is that the model suggests more than mere heterogeneity across industries that would be captured by use of traditional industry fixed effects.

Of all the 174 cities that have significant city-level effects, 163 of them have positive values while the remaining 11 cities are negative.[11]

Positive values of θ for a city i reflect latent unobservable factors consistent with higher levels of innovation for firms located in these cities (after conditioning on firm-specific characteristics captured by variables in the matrix X, and latent unobservable industry-specific factors modeled by the vector γ.

Fig. 2 presents estimates of the city-level effects vector (θ) on a map. Clustering of city-level effects by levels is consistent with the positive estimate for ρ. Of course, the city-level effects estimates include direct plus cumulative (indirect) spatial spillover impacts, since:

$$E(\theta) = (I_m - \hat{\rho} W_c)^{-1} \left(C\hat{\delta}_c + W_c C\hat{\delta}_w \right).$$

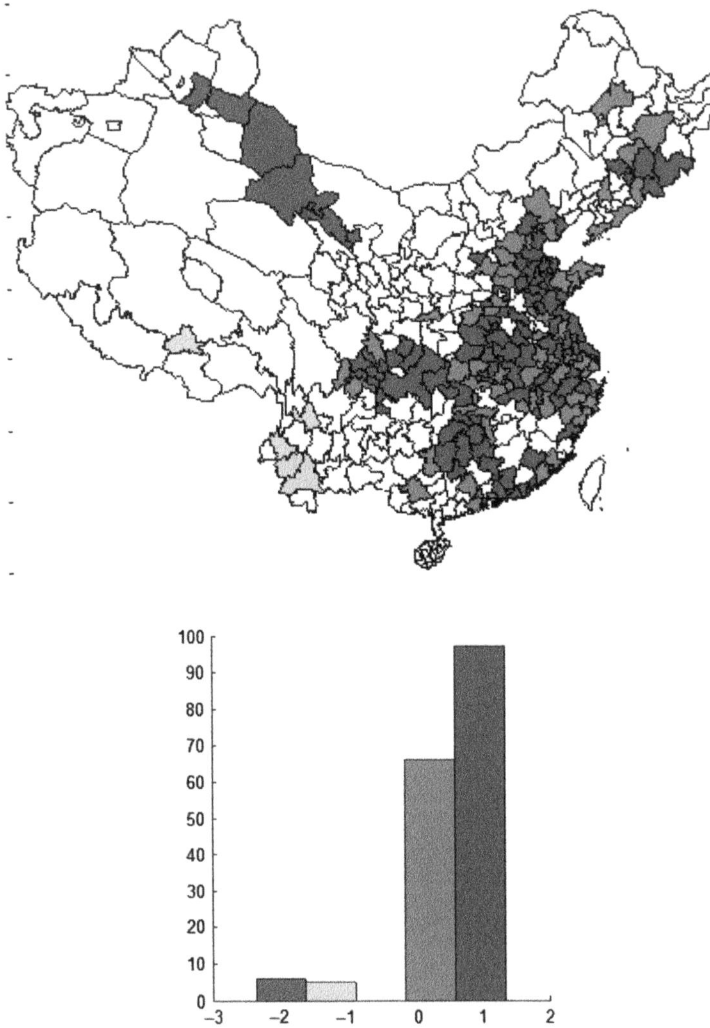

Fig. 2. Map of θ Effects.

This means that city-level effects estimates reflect a non-linear combination of positive and negative estimates $\hat{\delta}_c, \hat{\delta}_w$ associated with all four of our city-level characteristics measures C, as well as neighboring city characteristics W_cC. This complicates straightforward interpretation of these estimates.

A further complication is that city (and industry) effects are modeled as conditionally independent of firm-level characteristics.

On the map, cities with positive effects estimates are located in the eastern and middle part of China, regions generally considered to be leading in terms of development. Of note is the fact that the very largest cities (Beijing, Shanghai, and Shenzhen generally viewed as *growth poles* in China) have the largest amount of innovation (new product output) when cumulated over firms in these cities. Nonetheless, their city-level effects estimates are not among the largest in magnitude. The largest five positive effects are for cities: Zhumadian, Luohe, and Pingdingshan in Henan province; and Shanwei, Heyuan in Guangdong province, whose new product output cumulated over firms located in these cities account for much less measured innovation.

The map also shows negative values for the estimated effects vector θ. Nearly, all of the negative effects are in the northwestern and southwestern regions of China, generally considered less developed. For example, Lasa in Tibet, Lijiang and three other cities in Yunnan province. The most negative effects belong to three cities in Gansu province, one of which is Jiuquan, the closest major city to the Jiuquan Satellite Launch Center.

In terms of the industry effects estimates (γ), we found that of the 12 largest negative effects estimates 7 of these were in industries related to the manufacture of food or food processing. For example, manufacture of sugar, manufacture of grain mill products, manufacture of soft drinks and prepared tea manufacture of convenience foods, manufacture of condiments and fermented products, processing of other food products, and manufacture of other food products. This is of course indicative of clustering of effects for input-output-related industries.

Similarly, for the 12 most positive effects estimates, 6 involved industries related to iron mining and production. For example, steel smelting, non-ferrous smelting, and alloys manufacturing, mining of non-ferrous metal ores, ferro-alloys smelting, mining of iron ores, and iron smelting. Again, this reflects input-output-related clustering of the effects.

9. CONCLUSIONS

A Bayesian hierarchical model specification was set forth to explore the way in which city-level and industry-level interaction might impact firm-level innovation output. Focus was on distinguishing between: (1) a scenario where network ties between cities/industries arising from various types of interaction result in diffusion of innovation from one city/industry to only nearby cities/industries (local spillovers) and (2) a situation where network interaction sets in motion a series of network diffusion and feedback impacts on innovation output (global spillovers).

Typical linear models of firm-level innovation based on KPFs rely on city- and industry-level fixed effects, which allow for differences in the level of innovation by firms located in different cities or operating in different industries. In contrast to this approach that ignores possible network ties between nearby cities and input-output-related industries, our hierarchical model relies on a more elaborate specification for latent unobservable city-level effects as well as industry-level effects that may imply interaction (either local or global), not simply heterogeneity across cities and industries.

Empirical implementation of the model using a sample of over 11,600 Chinese manufacturing firms located in 270 cities and operating in 89 industries provided evidence in favor of a global spatial and interindustry spillovers scenario.

Avenues for future exploration are numerous. One avenue would be to compare the SDM specification used to structure the unobservable city-level effects with an SDEM (spatial Durbin error model) specification. The latter structure allows for local spatial spillovers in the presence of global shocks/disturbances that diffuse through the network of cities. This scenario would be consistent with the notion that spatially dependent shocks to innovation diffuse through the network of cities, while changes in city-level characteristics exhibit impacts on innovation taking place only in nearby (immediately neighboring) cities.

Another issue for exploration would be potential sample selection bias introduced by our use of only a sub-sample of firms having positive sales from new products.

NOTES

1. By analogy to first-order spatial neighbors, first-order input-output-related industries to industry i would be the set of industries j whose inputs are used in the production process of industry i.
2. In their case, third-order provinces.
3. Similar to organization effects in Raudenbush and Bryk (2002), regional effects in LeSage and Fischer (2007), spatially structured effects in Parent and LeSage (2008), individual effects in Koop (2003) and Jensen, Lacombe, and McIntyre (2012), or neighborhood effects.

4. This would be interpreted as second-round effects in input-output terminology.

5. We follow Smith and LeSage (2004) as well as Koop (2003) for much of this development.

6. Modeling these as exhibiting cross-equation covariance between the disturbances would have the advantage of potentially increasing precision of the effects estimates, but also the disadvantage of allowing for misspecification in one equation to impact effects estimate outcomes from the other equation. This is a typical issue that arises with seemingly unrelated regression specifications.

7. In order to use IO-table information, we matched GB/T4754-2002 industry codes to those used in the IO table, resulting in 89 industry sectors.

8. See: http://www.stats.gov.cn/tjsj/tjbz/xzqhdm/200802/t20080215_38311.html, Year 2007 version.

9. There are $r = 89$ different industry sectors and $m = 270$ cities in the sample of 11,639 firms that have positive new product output.

10. As noted earlier, we matched our firm industry codes to those used by the IO table, which align with International Standard Industrial Classification of All Economic Activities (ISIC, Rev.4) section B, C, D, E.

11. These were calculated using the mean and lower 0.05 and upper 0.95 intervals constructed from the set of 10,000 retained MCMC draws.

12. Smith and LeSage (2004) outline an inverse CDF method to produce draws for the ρ parameter that is more efficient than the standard random walk Metropolis-Hastings method.

ACKNOWLEDGMENT

The authors acknowledge the Grant support for Yuxue Sheng from the Chinese Ministry of Education, Project of Humanities and Social Sciences (Project No.16YJC790088).

REFERENCES

An, T., Shi, H., & Ludovico, A. (2006). An observation and empirical study of R&D behavior of Chinese manufacturing firms: Based on a survey of the manufacturing firms in Jiangsu Province. *Economic Research Journal*, *52*(2), 21–30.

Audretsch, B. (1998). Agglomeration and the location of innovative activity. *Oxford Review of Economic Policy*, *14*(2), 18–29.

Audretsch, D. B., & Feldman, M. P. (1996). R&D spillovers and the geography of innovation and production. *The American Economic Review*, *86*(3), 630–640.

Autant-Bernard, C., & LeSage, J. P. (2011). Quantifying knowledge spillovers using spatial econometric models. *Journal of Regional Science*, *51*(3), 471–496.

Baldwin, J. R., Beckstead, D., Mark Brown, W., & Rigby, D. L. (2008). Agglomeration and the geography of localization economies in Canada. *Regional Studies*, *42*(1), 117–132.

Baltagi, B. H., Fingleton, B., & Pirotte A. (2014). Spatial lag models with nested random effects: An instrumental variable procedure with an application to English house prices. *Journal of Urban Economics*, *80*, 76–86.

Battisti, G., & Stoneman, P. (2010). How innovative are UK firms? Evidence from the fourth UK community innovation survey on synergies between technological and organizational innovations. *British Journal of Management*, *21*(1), 187–206.

Beaudry, C., & Schiffauerova, A. (2009). Who's right, Marshall or Jacobs? The localization versus urbanization debate. *Research Policy*, *38*(2), 318–337.

Bo, W. (2007). Externalities and industrial economic growth – Evidences from Chinese Provincial panel data. *China Industrial Economy*, *24*(1), 37–44.

Boschma, R. A., & Weterings, A. B. R. (2005). The effect of regional differences on the performance of software firms in the Netherlands. *Journal of Economic Geography*, *5*(5), 567–588.

Cheng, S., & Li, H. (2012). New firm formation facing cultural and racial diversity. *Papers in Regional Science*, *91*(4), 759–774.

Crescenzi, R., Rodriguez-Pose, A., & Storper, M. (2007). The territorial dynamics of innovation: A Europe-United States comparative analysis. *Journal of Economic Geography*, *7*(6), 673–709.

Crescenzi, R., Rodriguez-Pose, A., & Storper, M. (2012). The territorial dynamics of innovation in China and India. *Journal of Economic Geography*, *12*(5), 1055–1085.

Dong, X., & Yuan, Y. (2014). Firm innovation, life cycle and agglomeration economies. *China Economic Quarterly*, *13*(02), 767–792.

Duranton, G., & Puga, D. (2000). Diversity and specialisation in cities: Why, where and when does it matter? *Urban studies*, *37*(3), 533–555.

Duranton, G., & Puga, D. (2001). Nursery cities: Urban diversity, process innovation, and the life cycle of products. *American Economic Review*, *91*(5), 1454–1477.

Duranton, G., & Puga, D. (2005). From sectoral to functional urban specialisation. *Journal of Urban Economics*, *57*(2), 343–370.

Elhorst, J. P. (2014). *Spatial econometrics: From cross-sectional data to spatial panels*. Heidelberg: Springer.

Feldman, M. P., & Audretsch, D. B. (1999). Innovation in cities: Science-based diversity, specialization and localized competition. *European Economic Review*, *43*(2), 409–429.

Feldman, M. P. (1994). *The geography of innovation*. Dordrecht, Boston: Kluwer.

Gao, H., & Wang, L. (2012). Analysis on the definition of the scope of the high middle low tech industry. *Science & Technology Progress and Policy*, *29*(13), 46–48.

Gelman, A. (2006). Prior distributions for variance parameters in hierarchical models (comment on article by Browne and Draper). *Bayesian Analysis*, *1*(3), 515–534.

Greunz, L. (2003). The impact of industrial specialisation and diversity on innovation. *Brussels Economic Review*, *46*(3), 11–36.

Hobday, M. (2005) Firm-level innovation models: Perspectives on research in developed and developing countries. *Technology Analysis & Strategic Management*, *17*(2), 121–146.

Jaffe, A. B. (1989). Real effects of academic research. *The American Economic Review*, *97*(5), 957–970.

Jensen, C. D., Lacombe D. J., & McIntyre, S. (2012). A Bayesian spatial individual effects probit model of the 2010 UK general election. SIRE Discussion Paper No. SIRE-DP-2012-20.

Johansson, B., & Lööf, H. (2008). Innovation activities explained by firm attributes and location. *Economics of Innovation New Technology*, *17*(6), 533–552.

Kampik, F., & Dachs, B. (2011). The innovative performance of German multinationals abroad: Evidence from the European community innovation survey. *Industrial and Corporate Change*, *20*(2), 661–681.

Koop, G. (2003). *Bayesian econometrics*. New York: Wiley.

Lacombe, D., & McIntyre, S. (2014). Bayesian estimation of the multilevel/hierarchical spatially autocorrelated random intercept model. Paper presented at the SRSA Annual Meeting, San Antonio, Texas.

LeSage, J. P. (2014). Spatial econometric panel data model specification: A Bayesian approach. *Spatial Statistics*, *9*, 122–145.

LeSage, J. P., & Pace, R. K. (2009). *Introduction to spatial econometrics*. Taylor-Francis/CRC press.

LeSage, J. P., & Pace, R. K. (2014). Interpreting spatial econometric models. In M. Fischer & P. Nijkamp (Eds.), *Handbook of regional science* (pp. 1535–1552). Berlin: Springer.

LeSage, J. P., & Sheng, Y. (2014). A spatial econometric panel data examination of endogenous versus exogenous interaction in Chinese province-level patenting. *Journal of Geographical Systems*, *16*(3), 233–262.

Liu, M., & Tang, H. (2010). Empirical study on effect of knowledge spillovers based on spatial Durbin model. *Science & Technology Progress and Policy*, *27*(18), 28–33.

Mairesse, J., & Mohnen, P. (2005). The importance of R&D for innovation: A reassessment using French survey data. *The Journal of Technology Transfer*, *30*(1–2), 183–197.

Malerba, F. (2004). Sectoral systems: How and why innovation differs across sectors. In J. Fagerberg, D. Mowery, & R. Nelson (Eds.). *Oxford handbook of innovation* (pp. 381–384). Oxford: Oxford University Press.

Nathan, M., & Lee, N. (2013). Cultural diversity, innovation, and entrepreneurship: Firm-level evidence from London. *Economic Geography*, *89*(4), 367–394.

Paci, R., & Usai, S. (1999). Externalities, knowledge spillovers and the spatial distribution of innovation. *GeoJournal*, *49*(4), 381–390.

Parent, O., & LeSage, J. P. (2008). Using the variance structure of the conditional autoregressive spatial specification to model knowledge spillovers. *Journal of Applied Econometrics*, *23*(2), 235–256.

Parent, O., & LeSage, J. P. (2012). Determinants of knowledge production and their effects on regional economic growth. *Journal of Regional Science*, *62*(2), 256–284.

Peng, X., & Jiang, C. (2011). Industrial agglomeration, technological spillovers and regional innovation: Evidences from China. *China Economic Quarterly*, *10*(3), 913–934.

Raudenbush, S. W., & Bryk, A. S. (2002). *Hierarchical linear models: Applications and data analysis methods*. Thousand Oaks: Sage.

Rosenthal, S. S., & Strange, W. C. (2004). Evidence on the nature and sources of agglomeration economies. *Handbook of regional and urban economics* (Vol. 4, pp. 2119–2171).

Sheng, Y., Liu, B., & Ding, M. (2013). Knowledge spillovers and enterprises' innovation based on the fragmentation of value chain. *Forum on Science and Technology in China*, *29*(11), 104–110.

Smith, K. (2004). Measuring innovation. In J. Fagerberg, D. Mowery, & R. Nelson (Eds.). *Oxford handbook of innovation* (pp. 155–158). Oxford: Oxford University Press.

Smith, T. E., & LeSage, J. P. (2004). A Bayesian probit model with spatial dependencies. *Advances in Econometrics*, *18*, 127–160.

Stuetzer, M., Obschonka, M., Brixy, U., & Sternberg, R. (2014) Regional characteristics, opportunity perception and entrepreneurial activities. *Small Business Economics*, *42*(2), 221–244.

Van der Panne, G. (2004) Agglomeration externalities: Marshall versus Jacobs. *Journal of Evolutionary Economics*, *14*(5), 593–604.

Xu, B., Li, X., & Zhang, X. (2011). Effects of regional innovative environment on enterprises innovation performance. *Science Research Management*, *32*(9), 147–156.

Yang, C., Lin, H., & Li, H. (2013). Influences of production and R&D agglomeration on productivity: Evidence from chinese electronics firms. *China Economic Review*, *27*, 162–178.

Yoshihiro, H., & Kiyoyasu, T. (2013). *Agglomeration and firm-level productivity: A Bayesian spatial approach*. IDE Discussion Paper No. 403.

Zhang, J., Liu, Z., & Zheng, J. (2007). Industrial chain positioning, divide, agglomeration and innovation: An empirical study based on questionnaire of manufacturing firms in Jiangsu Province. *China Industrial Economy*, *24*(7), 47–55.

Zhang, P., He, C., & Sun, Y. (2014). Agglomeration economies and firm R&D efforts: An analysis of China's electronics and telecommunications industries. *The Annals of Regional Science*, *53*(3), 671–701.

APPENDIX

We present conditional posterior distributions given the observed data for each parameter. We use $(\alpha|\cdot)$ to denote all parameters except α that we are interested in. From the posterior distribution in Eq. (28), the conditional posterior density of β is

$$
\begin{aligned}
p(\beta|\cdot) &\propto \exp\left\{-\frac{1}{2\sigma_\varepsilon^2}(y - X\beta - \Delta_c\theta - \Delta_z\gamma)'(y - X\beta - \Delta_c\theta - \Delta_z\gamma)\right\} \\
&\sim N_h\left(U_0^{-1}g_0, U_0^{-1}\right),
\end{aligned}
\tag{A.1}
$$

which implies a conditional posterior density for β proportional to a multinormal density with mean vector $U_0^{-1}g_0$, and covariance matrix, U_0^{-1}, where $U_0 = (\sigma_\varepsilon^2)^{-1}(X'X)$, $g_0 = (\sigma_\varepsilon^2)^{-1}X'(y - \Delta_c\theta - \Delta_z\gamma)$.

The conditional posterior for θ, γ, δ, and ϕ is similar to that for β. For θ,

$$
\begin{aligned}
p(\theta|\cdot) &\propto \exp\left\{-\frac{1}{2\sigma_\varepsilon^2}(y - \Delta_c\theta - \Delta_z\gamma)'(y - \Delta_c\theta - \Delta_z\gamma)\right\} \\
&\quad \times |A|\left(\sigma_u^2\right)^{-m/2}\exp\left\{-\frac{1}{2\sigma_u^2}(A\theta - C\delta)'(A\theta - C\delta)\right\} \\
&\sim N_h\left(U_1^{-1}g_1, U_1^{-1}\right),
\end{aligned}
\tag{A.2}
$$

so the conditional posterior density of θ is also proportional to the multinormal density shown in Eq. (A.2), where $U_1 = (\sigma_\varepsilon^2)^{-1}(\Delta_c'\Delta_c) + (\sigma_u^2)^{-1}(A'A)$, $g_1 = (\sigma_\varepsilon^2)^{-1}\Delta_c'(y - X\beta - \Delta_z\gamma) + (\sigma_u^2)^{-1}A^{-1}C\delta$.

For γ, we have

$$
\begin{aligned}
p(\gamma|\cdot) &\propto \exp\left\{-\frac{1}{2\sigma_\varepsilon^2}(y - \Delta_c\theta - \Delta_z\gamma)'(y - \Delta_c\theta - \Delta_z\gamma)\right\} \\
&\quad \times |B|\left(\sigma_v^2\right)^{-r/2}\exp\left\{-\frac{1}{2\sigma_v^2}(B\gamma - Z\phi)'(B\gamma - Z\phi)\right\} \\
&\sim N_h\left(U_2^{-1}g_2, U_2^{-1}\right),
\end{aligned}
\tag{A.3}
$$

where $U_2 = (\sigma_\varepsilon^2)^{-1}(\Delta_z'\Delta_z) + (\sigma_v^2)^{-1}(B'B)$, $g_2 = (\sigma_\varepsilon^2)^{-1}\Delta_z'(y - X\beta - \Delta_c\theta) + (\sigma_v^2)^{-1} B^{-1}Z\delta$.

Similarly, the conditional posterior density of δ is proportional to a multi-normal density as well, shown in Eq. (A.4).

$$\begin{aligned} p(\delta|\cdot) &\propto \exp\left\{ -\frac{1}{2\sigma_u^2}(A\theta - C\delta)'(A\theta - C\delta) \right\} \\ &\sim N_p\left(U_3^{-1}g_3, U_3^{-1}\right), \end{aligned} \tag{A.4}$$

where $U_3 = \left(\sigma_u^2\right)^{-1}(C'C)$, $g_3 = \left(\sigma_u^2\right)^{-1}C'(A\theta)$.

And for ϕ,

$$\begin{aligned} p(\phi|\cdot) &\propto \exp\left\{ -\frac{1}{2\sigma_v^2}(B\gamma - Z\phi)'(B\gamma - Z\phi) \right\} \\ &\sim N_p\left(U_4^{-1}g_4, U_4^{-1}\right), \end{aligned} \tag{A.5}$$

where $U_4 = \left(\sigma_v^2\right)^{-1}(Z'Z)$, $g_4 = (\sigma_v^2)^{-1}Z'(B\gamma)$.

The conditional posterior of disturbance variances $\sigma_\varepsilon^2, \sigma_u^2, \sigma_v^2$ is all inverse gamma distributions shown in Eqs. (A.6)–(A.8).

$$\begin{aligned} p\left(\sigma_\varepsilon^2|\cdot\right) \propto \left(\sigma_\varepsilon^2\right)^{-\frac{n}{2}-1} &\exp\left\{ -\frac{1}{2\sigma_\varepsilon^2}(y - X\beta - \Delta_c\theta - \Delta_z\gamma)'(y - X\beta - \Delta_c\theta - \Delta_z\gamma) \right\} \\ &\sim IG\left(\nu_1, \mu_1\right), \end{aligned} \tag{A.6}$$

$$\begin{aligned} p\left(\sigma_u^2|\cdot\right) &\propto \left(\sigma_u^2\right)^{-m/2-1}\exp\left\{ -\frac{1}{2\sigma_u^2}(A\theta - C\delta)'(A\theta - C\delta) \right\} \\ &\sim IG\left(\nu_2, \mu_2\right), \end{aligned} \tag{A.7}$$

$$\begin{aligned} p\left(\sigma_v^2|\cdot\right) &\propto \left(\sigma_v^2\right)^{-r/2-1}\exp\left\{ -\frac{1}{2\sigma_v^2}(B\gamma - Z\phi)'(B\gamma - Z\phi) \right\} \\ &\sim IG\left(\nu_3, \mu_3\right), \end{aligned} \tag{A.8}$$

where $\nu_1 = n/2, \mu_1 = (y - X\beta - \Delta_c\theta - \Delta_z\gamma)'(y - X\beta - \Delta_c\theta - \Delta_z\gamma)/2$, $\nu_2 = m/2$, $\mu_2 = (A\theta - C\delta)'(A\theta - C\delta)/2$, $\nu_3 = r/2, \mu_3 = (B\gamma - Z\phi)'(B\gamma - Z\phi)/2$.

The conditional posterior for ρ and τ shown in Eqs. (A.9) and (A.10) does not reflect any recognized distributional form (LeSage & Pace, 2009).

$$p(\rho|\cdot) \propto |A| \exp\left\{ -\frac{1}{2\sigma_u^2}(A\theta - C\delta)'(A\theta - C\delta) \right\} \times U\left(\lambda_{\min}^{-1}, 1\right), \tag{A.9}$$

$$p(\tau|\cdot) \propto |B| \exp\left\{ -\frac{1}{2\sigma_v^2}(B\gamma - Z\phi)'(B\gamma - Z\phi) \right\} \times U\left(\psi_{\min}^{-1}, 1\right). \tag{A.10}$$

We will rely on the Metropolis-Hastings (M-H) algorithm to draw samples from these two conditional distributions.[12]

Thus, we will combine M-H sampling for the parameter ρ and τ in our model and Gibbs sampling for the remaining parameters, that is sampling from normal distributions for β, θ, γ, δ, ϕ, and sampling from inverse gamma distributions for σ_ε^2, σ_u^2 and σ_v^2, to produce MCMC estimates for the HSIDM. This type of procedure is also called Metropolis within Gibbs sampling (Koop, 2003).

M-H sampling require a candidate value for $\rho(\tau)$, which we label $\rho^\star(\tau^\star)$, and the current value is $\rho^c(\tau^c)$. The acceptance probability is calculated using:

$$\mathrm{acc}\left(\rho^c, \rho^\star\right) = \min\left\{ 1, \frac{p(\rho^\star|\cdot)}{p(\rho^c|\cdot)} \right\}, \tag{A.11}$$

$$\text{or } \mathrm{acc}\left(\tau^c, \tau^\star\right) = \min\left\{ 1, \frac{p(\tau^\star|\cdot)}{p(\tau^c|\cdot)} \right\}. \tag{A.12}$$

We use the tuned random-work chain M-H algorithm described in LeSage and Pace (2009) to produce the candidate values for ρ and τ separately. The proposal distributions for ρ and τ in this algorithm are standard normal distributions along with tuning parameters *cc* and *dd* to avoid the situation where the samplers are stuck in a very low density part of the conditional distribution.

$$
\begin{aligned}
\rho^\star &= \rho^c + cc \cdot N(0,1), \\
c.c. &= cc/1.1, \quad \text{if } \mathrm{acc}_\rho < 40\%, \\
c.c. &= cc \times 1.1, \quad \text{if } \mathrm{acc}_\rho > 60\%,
\end{aligned} \tag{A.13}
$$

$$
\begin{aligned}
\tau^\star &= \tau^c + dd \cdot N(0,1), \\
dd &= dd/1.1, \quad \text{if } \mathrm{acc}_\tau < 40\%, \\
dd &= dd \times 1.1, \quad \text{if } \mathrm{acc}_\tau > 60\%.
\end{aligned} \tag{A.14}
$$

The goal is to achieve a situation where the tuning parameter settles to a fixed value resulting in an acceptance rate ($\mathrm{acc}_\rho, \mathrm{acc}_\tau$) between 40% and 60%.

Printed and bound by CPI Group (UK) Ltd, Croydon, CR0 4YY

15/09/2026

14962364-0005